Surviving Terror

Surviving Terror

Hope and Justice in a World of Violence

EDITED BY

Victoria Lee Erickson

AND

Michelle Lim Jones

A Division of Baker Book House Co
Grand Rapids, Michigan 49516

© 2002 by Victoria Lee Erickson and Michelle Lim Jones

Published by Brazos Press
a division of Baker Book House Company
P.O. Box 6287, Grand Rapids, MI 49516–6287

Printed in the United States of America

Library of Congress Cataloging-in-Publication Data

Surviving terror : hope and justice in a world of violence / edited by Victoria Erickson and Michelle Lim Jones
      p.   cm.
    Includes bibliographical references.
    ISBN 1-58743-028-2
    1. Violence—Religious aspects—Christianity. I. Erickson, Victoria Lee, 1955– II. Jones, Michelle Lim, 1957–
    BT736.15 S87 2002
    261.8—dc21
                                      2001056601

For current information about all releases from Brazos Press, visit our web site:
http://www.brazospress.com

Contents

Introduction   7

Part 1. History and Terror

1. Yearning for Freedom and Love in a Life of Terror   17
   David Kwang-sun Suh
2. Terror and Japan's Colonization of Korea 1910–1945   35
   Kosuke Koyama
3. The Terror of History and the Memory of Redemption:
   Engaging the Ambiguities of the Christian Past   43
   Dale T. Irvin
4. Troubled but Not Destroyed: A Reflection on Terror and
   Redemption in Contemporary Africa   56
   Akintunde E. Akinada
5. Dethroning Violence and Terror: An Undercurrent in the
   Hebrew Bible   66
   Jin Hee Han
6. Prophecy and Patriotism: A Tragic Dilemma from the Cross of
   Terror   87
   Luis N. Rivera-Pagán

Part 2. Politics and Sociology of Terror

7. The Terror in Ourselves   105
   Donald W. Shriver Jr.
8. Terror and Hope in the Minds of Russians   123
   Tony Carnes
9. Mapping Love and Terror: Walking the Terrain of *I AM Who Is
   Being-There*   140
   Victoria Lee Erickson
10. The Sexual Politics of Terror   159
    Katharine H. S. Moon

Part 3. Theological Leadership through Terror

11. Calling the Oppressors to Account for Four Centuries of Terror   175
    James H. Cone
12. Systemic Theology: Preliminary Principles   184
    Timothy Light
13. Faith and Redemption Revisited in the Japanese Context   206
    Hisashi Kajiwara
14. Korean Women's Christology: East Meets West   216
    Michelle Lim Jones

Part 4. The Gospel Is Life in the Age of Terror

15. Threat and Terror in the New Testament   235
    Robin Scroggs
16. Terror Next Door: A Homily on Extreme Fear in Our Midst   249
    Walter J. Burghardt, S.J.
17. The Tortured Christ   258
    Jürgen Moltmann
18. Terror and the Children of God: A Meditation on Fear and Ministry with Inner City Youth   267
    Harold Dean Trulear
19. God Hears Their Cries; God Dries Their Tears   273
    Jacqueline J. Lewis-Tillman
20. Self-Denial for Racists and Their Victims in Japan: A Homily   277
    Andrew Sung Park

Part 5. Reflections on Christian Understandings of Terror

21. Small Actions against Terror: Jewish Reflections on a Christian Witness   287
    Peter Ochs

Contributors   305
Notes   309

Introduction

This is a book with a purpose. The professional wisdom and life experience of the chapter authors led to an agreement in the year 2000 that this book was necessary for our future. It seemed to us that educated Americans were not responding to the everyday elements that make up terror and terrorist practices. Our urgency produced these chapters by Summer 2001. At the time of its completion, the book called us to give an account of the hope that is within us in a manner that is capable of addressing the violence and terror that have scourged our world. By September 11, 2001, the book became for the American authors a very personalized call from God to have hope in the midst of suffering following the destruction of the World Trade Center towers. Then, it became clear that all of the authors were suffering. Terrorism is a suffering the world bears. Terror is our common enemy. Yet, the very reason for the book was expressed on the front pages of newspapers. The front page of the September 12th *Star-Ledger* carried an eight-inch headline reading,

Terror
Beyond Belief
U. S. stunned by suicide attacks; death toll could reach thousands.

Terror is supposed to be something beyond our comprehension. However, the next sections of the *Star-Ledger* were titled, "Terror: The Impact" and "Terror: The Response." However unknown the source of terror is, we know that the way to live through it is to describe it and to respond to it. Headlines explained survivor stories of the experience as one in which they had *no air to breathe, no light to see, no time to think* (p. 4). In the middle of chaos, the *Star-Ledger* told us, local residents responded with "compassion and outrage" (p. 18). There were some who were pleased with the outcomes of terror. A Palestinian taxi driver was quoted as saying, "Palestinians have been crying and suffering and now it is the time for Americans to cry and suffer" (p. 23).

Thus this book is about the birth of responsibility, of looking out for the well-being of others, of answering the divine question, "How are your brothers and sisters in their community well-being?" In the middle of "reporting from Hell" the newspapers heroically kept up with our need to see the whole picture, to know what was happening to us. The *New York Times* September 12, 2001, cover page announced the "U.S. Attacked" and "Presidential vows for punishment." The message was clear: terror is an act of violence that needs quick response. The last page of the first section of the *Star-Ledger* told us that this "diabolical" act "will change us forever" (p. 32). The people know that the act and the response change us. In this case, it took less than twenty-four hours for us to know that we needed to start thinking about the terrorists. This is, after all, what they wanted us to do.

Emmanuel Lévinas called the change from thinking of the self alone to thinking of others a matter of "conversion."[1] The birth of language itself, Lévinas argued, is bound up with the birth of responsibility that comes with such a conversion. God spoke, and humanity answered. When our answer is a witness to the divine word, we become an obedient creation. Our obedience is never perfect, however, for we are called to announce the presence of *the evangel*, the Good News that lives in the midst of human failure. Telling the truth about such failures, what M. M. Bakhtin called "living with no alibis,"[2] is what the faithful call "good preaching."

The terror that we have sought to tell the truth about in these pages entails more than actual or threatened violence, although both are integral to its purposes. Keeping the level of stress and intimidation high, terror aims at inducing emotional reactions that will tear the fabric of social life apart.[3] It is a practice intended to destroy the humanity of its victims, and is thus a spiritual practice whose strength must be gathered from the common reservoir of spiritual authority otherwise known as the past.[4] Terrorism often makes recourse to the past, but it does so in order to "purge" the present of the opposition that the past offers against it. Whether it be in culture, politics, or religion, terror seeks to establish a new regime of truth in which a new person that it wishes to create can dwell. At the same time it must reject creativity outside of its narrowly approved framework and eliminate opposing viewpoints. For this reason reconstructing disappeared viewpoints, restoring diverse memories, and developing cross-cultural conversations become critical spiritual tasks.[5]

Our effort has been guided by more than a common desire to speak against the terrors of the age. The collection of essays that make up this book are a collegial honoring of a man whose life and work in the midst of terror kept open the possibility of speaking of God. David Kwang-sun Suh was born in northern Korea in 1931. He grew up under Japanese colonial rule and later witnessed the terror Japan unleashed against China and other parts of Asia. Following the end of Japanese occupation, he and his family experienced a new regime of terror in the form of North Korea's communist government.[6]

The 1960s brought David Suh to the United States as a student, and he experienced the civil rights movement in the streets of America firsthand. Upon returning to South Korea, he began working on behalf of the farmers and textile workers, and in opposition to the military dictatorship of Park Chung-hee. The insights that he and others gained from these endeavors eventually came to be expressed in the movement known as *minjung theology*. The personal consequence for David Suh was dismissal as dean of Ewha Women's University, and arrest and imprisonment in 1976. He eventually returned to Ewha after the fall of Park Chung-hee and served there as university chaplain until his retirement in 1995.

From this brief resume of his life, it is clear that David Suh has been all too familiar with the evil human beings have practiced against each other. Yet, unlike many, he was not a passive recipient nor silent observer. Shaped by a dynamic Christian faith, Suh's life has embodied an active witness against the terror he has lived through. Throughout his long career as teacher, dean, and university chaplain, he has sought to free humanity from the terror of events without taking flight from historical responsibility for the nature and consequences of these events. Like others in the movement of *minjung* theology, he often referred to the "messianic" dimensions of faith that called them to work on behalf of justice and peace in the world. The evil that produces terror must be addressed on multiple levels of personal and historical experience. Equally important to addressing the person responsible for terror (the oppressor) is the task of addressing the victim (the oppressed). These multiple levels of terror and fear need to be addressed by both pastoral practice and academic theorization. To this end he supported and strengthened a professional association for pastors and theologians who worked with the *minjung,* the poor and oppressed in history. Restored to his teaching post, he was later invited to serve as president of the World Alliance of YMCAs, which he did with distinction. A commissioned member of the World Council of Churches, his service was marked by passion and rationality. Throughout it all his colleagues have been humbled by his continued and vast resources of restraint and humor, informed by his pastoral practice and challenged by his theological reflections on the justice and liberation to which the gospel calls us.

The contributors to this book have kept David's life and commitments in view as they have sought to act in various ways throughout the world in the face of terror. Most of us have lived long enough to have gathered well-deserved critique for our imperfect, however faithful, responses to the demands of Christian living. Our lives have also brought us together in networks of pastors, theologians, social scientists, and laity who seek to bring our diverse resources to the table as we seek perfection, justice, and the peaceable kingdom. We are intentionally a diverse fellowship of Protestants and Catholics from Africa, Asia, Latin America, North America, and Europe. We embrace a variety of theological perspectives—radical, liberal, and conservative. Scholars and practitioners alike, we are all unapologetic for our commitments to a Christian witness.

The book itself is organized into five sections that follow an opening essay by David Suh himself. We invited him to begin the book with the story of his life, knowing of his commitments to autobiographical reflection in theology. By doing this we are also inviting readers to consider ethnographic and ethnomethodological[7] resources for addressing terror. Knowledge of the self in context is critical for all spiritual growth, especially for spiritual understanding and intervention against terror.[8]

With this life in view, the first section, *History and Terror,* seeks to examine the long historical memory of Christian engagement with terror. In this section we have included essays dealing with biblical texts as well. One assumption we make here is that the means of addressing terror are found in the biblical text and in the lives that are lived in response to the biblical text. Another is that history is continually making judgments aimed at diverting the convergence of emotions and actions that precipitate terror, even as it provides us with copious examples of the terror that we seek to oppose. The contributors in this section have examined a number of historical points at which human beings decided to act for or against terror in their age. They do so in order to increase our awareness and accountability for today.

The second section, on the *Politics and Sociology of Terror,* examines the sociopolitical and ethical dynamics of the decision-making practices of victims and perpetrators acting in the moment of terror. The section also seeks to document the role that emotions play in healing the long-term consequences of terror. Engaging and deconstructing terror is one of the many tasks society expects religion to perform well through its social institutions and agencies. Although all social institutions must participate in diverting terror, religion may well be the primary resource for the ongoing work of corralling the raw sensations that ripple through society and attaching to them appropriate emotional structures that seek stability, peace, harmony, and love. There are places where we find that religion teaches its institutions how to embrace fear and pain so that the violence they produce explodes "inside of religion" and not "in society." When religion loses its handle on terror and its ability to dismantle violence, society is the tragic victim. No sociability is possible in a terrorist state.

It is appropriate then to ask what goes wrong in religion when we see it manufacturing the enemy, violence, and even terror. But we need equally to ask what must we do to change things so that the religious live rightly. In the third section of the book, *Theological Leadership through Terror,* we return to the theme that opened this introduction. The contributors in this section have taken upon themselves the task of calling oppressors to account for their behavior. But they also have a word of hope for the oppressed, for the terrorized, whose lives cry out for redemption. Such a word can only come in the form of proclamation, or preaching. For this reason, in the fourth section, *The Gospel Is Life in the Age of Terror,* we have included sermons in the book, demonstrating an integrated approach that takes seriously the pastoral and prophetic dimensions alike of our historical praxis.

For reasons that are both pastoral and prophetic, we have invited Peter Ochs to provide a concluding response to these diverse essays and sermons. An observant member of the household of Israel, Peter is familiar with the theological questions and pastoral concerns that have shaped this book. Mindful that we can only be holy to the extent that we live beyond our own circle of experience, we have given Peter the task of concluding the essays in this volume, looking for the truth that is contained in them.

Truth-telling is always extremely difficult to do. If we were to do it more often, humans would have better models to help each other do it better. Yet this book is more than a stumbling toward the light. It is a recognition that we learn as we answer God's most basic questions about our neighbor. The practice of learning to be a Christian witness has historically been linked with confession. Confession in its affirmative sense meant to witness to one's faith in Christ, but the same term was used to describe the critical practice of naming one's own sins. Confession is a mode of truth-telling that calls us to account not only for the hope, peace, and joy that is within but also for the violence, pain, and fear that surround us. We have placed no buffer around the stories of suffering that are scattered throughout these pages. It is our hope that the reader will find here an honest response to the gritty realities of terror, a response that can only be called one of faith. The gritty realities of September 11, 2001, will stay with us forever. So too must the truth-telling that exposes our failures to respond to the needs of our enemies.

The contributors to this volume also recognize that it takes time to return analytically to terror. For this reason, we are glad that the book was finished before September 11. The emotions that terror controls and suppresses are the same that must now be tapped into as the well from which we draw the ability to reengage the subject. This is difficult work that must be accomplished by the very people who are the victims of terror. Victims know what terror is, but they also know (or need to know) that if they do not (re)turn in an act of conversion, they are themselves potential terrorizers. Having in their possession knowledge of how to create terror, they can also diffuse it. Hence, a world that knows terror calls out daily for Americans to take their hands; they want Americans to join them in a common search for the perpetrators. They promise to help us hold them accountable for their actions. At the same time, they remind us that they will hold us accountable for our actions. The world warns us that we and the entire world will suffer if we act out on our anger.

Eventually for many of us it will be the next generation that will have to find the emotional resources to pick up the task of analysis on behalf of loved ones who suffered. One reason we hold ourselves back from engaging terror is that we know that terror seeks death. We have family obligations, rent to pay, and promises to keep that are all potentially jeopardized if we side with already marked victims of terror. We pray secretly for the terrorized and place an invisible sign of the cross on them, hoping that our pleas are enough for divine intervention and rescue. What the history of terror has taught us is that once we have unleashed terror, our death is inevitable; the only way to live is to stop it. One preventative measure is to tell the story. We are the terrorized; this is only one selection of our many stories.

In the case of this book, we have decided that waiting for children and grandchildren to do the hard work of reconstructing terror is a clever strategy crafted by terror itself to provide hiding places in which to wait and watch. Herein the reader will find the analysis of African colonization, slave trade, and American white racism to be both historical and ongoing. The same is true for Chinese and Japanese colonization and continued racial struggles with the nation and people of Korea. The terror of the race, gender, political, and economic machines are exegeted and fully engaged by theologians, sociologists, and political scientists, all of whom are ordained or lay leaders in their church denominations. This engagement, then, is strikingly real and honest. These qualities are nudged out of us by our tradition that calls for naked truth, an "I did it," a "no alibi" type of life. This kind of living is such difficult work that it is easier to think of doing something else.

The editors and the contributors of this volume wish to thank David Suh for lending us his life and witness against all forms of oppression as an opportunity to do the much needed work of documenting the terror of this century so that our grandchildren's world may have the resources it needs to protect them from needless terror. We presented the collection of essays to him on the occasion of his seventieth birthday. The dignity of the lives of David Kwang-sun Suh and Sunyong Suh calls forth the dignified engagement found in these pages. We also acknowledge Dr. William Lee and Dr. Hwa In Chang Lee who made this book possible. Their lives of dedication and purpose have made life possible for many people all over the world. Likewise, we wish to thank Charles Amjad Ali and Sister Carol Rittner for the light they have shed over our pathway.

These pastoral calls for strength, courage, and purposeful action are tempered by an awareness of our own capacity to participate in terror through silence, ridicule, unbelief, and an unwillingness to defend or rescue; or, more likely, by our own capacity to maintain an unforgiving heart. These are themselves elements of terror, and when aggregated become terror. We must face the terror we are all capable of producing in order to transform and overcome it. *Respondeo etsi mutabor.*

Part 1

History and Terror

Yearning for Freedom and Love in a Life of Terror

David Kwang-sun Suh

A Life of Terror without a Real Mother

My mother died when I was thirteen. She died of tuberculosis. She died in my grandmother's home in Korea. My father, who was at her deathbed, sent me a cablegram to Manchuria, the northeastern region of China where we lived during the Second World War. We had to move to Manchuria because my father decided to leave Korea to take care of a Korean church in Manchuria as a missionary. My father refused to pay respect to the Japanese Shinto shrine. He was beaten up by the Japanese police. In defiance, he resigned from his parish in Northern Korea. We all got on the train heading to north and to a rural Korean ghetto in the wasteland of Manchuria. After the fifth childbirth, my mother became weaker. All of us in the family were hungry. We had no white rice in our daily diet. If we had a bowl of millet soup mixed with few grains of beans and *kimchi* for our meals, we were lucky. My mother died of malnutrition and the fatigue of feeding the poor preacher's family.

I got on the train and crossed the Yalu River on the west coast of the Korean peninsula. After a red-eye train ride of about ten hours, I had to change trains in Pyongyang, now the North Korean capital, to travel for more than six hours to my mother's hometown near the central Yalu River. As I crossed the Yalu River on a train, the Japanese military police checked on my identification and interrogated me about my school and my business in Korea. They first thought that I was a Japanese middle school kid, but then they were disappointed to find out that I was only a Korean boy.

They had to question me again more thoroughly on why my Japanese was so good. They always interrogated my father whenever he had to cross the Yalu River border that separates Korea from Manchuria. For them, Christian preachers were the archenemies of the Japanese Empire. During the Second World War when they had to fight the Americans, the situation for my father became much worse. My father was treated as a spy for the Americans. He could not speak English at all, nor did he speak Japanese. But he hated the Japanese. I still cannot understand why he sent me to the Japanese middle school in the Manchurian town, except that he said that I should get the best possible education. According to him, the Japanese did much better in educating their youngsters in China than did the Koreans. He likened my studying at a Japanese school to the Hebrew boys studying in the Egyptian schools in the Old Testament days.

I did well in school. My mother was very happy about that. When I was admitted to that school, as the only one Korean student among the two hundred Japanese student body, my mother went to see my name on the board. On foot, she walked more than five miles back and forth. Short of breath, she said she could die any time, because I was now somebody with the Japanese. I was the first one in the Suh clans to enter into the Japanese public middle school. That was something to be proud of. She could not come to my school for the school picnic or other events, for she fell ill and had to go to her mother's home in northern Korea for rest.

I was terrified to see my mother's death. I began crying. I felt so lonely. I felt I lost everything. I felt that there was no meaning in life without her. I no longer had a person I really loved. To whom can I brag about my school grades? With whom can I talk about my jealous Japanese classmates who tease and harass me when they find out that I did better than they in the Japanese, history, and math exams? I felt I lost everything that was so important to me. I wept all the way through the funeral service. I wept all the way home from her grave in the far away mountain valleys. That was early February of 1944, when we heard about the glorious victories of the Emperor's Army against the beasts of Allied forces in the South and Southeast Asia. We did not believe what we heard about the Japanese victory in the Pacific. My mother would not survive to see the liberation of Korea from the Japanese rule. She would not see the Soviet soldiers marching in on the Korean peninsula. She would not hear about the division of Korea into the North and the South.

My father and I returned to Manchuria by train. My father was severely interrogated again by the Japanese military police as the train crossed the Yalu River. They harassed him because he could not speak Japanese, and I had to interpret for him. They released my father because, according to them, he had a smart son who spoke excellent Japanese. I was so humiliated. Oh, I hated them so. I began weeping again all the way home—a mixture of the loss of my mother and my motherland. Actually, I had no idea what it meant to be a Korean boy except that I spoke Korean at home and read the Bible in Korean and sang Korean hymns at church. But in public and at school I spoke Japanese, I carried a Japanese name, I studied with Japanese classmates, I despised the Chinese kids. I learned Japanese history but very little of Korean history and Korean literature. My father told me that I should not lose my Korean identity. Yes, I am a Korean. This meant that I was neither Japanese nor Chinese. This meant that I was harassed and sometimes beaten by my classmates because I was a Korean. This meant loneliness. This meant that I was scared of being a Korean in Manchuria, which is a colony of the Japanese Empire. I was a lonely, helpless foreigner, a stranger—a terrified and terrorized stranger. I was always intimidated, insecure, suspicious, and unsure of anything. Only my mother gave me self-confidence and self-esteem about being a Korean boy. Now she was gone. Gone was my mother, my country, my confidence, myself, and my soul. I wept.

As soon as I returned home with my three younger brothers and a sister, I insisted that my father marry another woman. I told him that I could not take care of my siblings and a father. I needed a mother—any mother will do, I thought. A mother will give me my self-esteem and self-identity as a Korean boy, a stranger in a strange land. But from day one when my new mother set her foot into our house, I found out that she was no mother like my mother, and no woman like my mother. I was a dutiful son to my new mother for the rest of my life. With tears I can say that she was good to me and to my siblings for the rest of her life with us. She lived with me fifty years more than my mother; she died when I was sixty-three years old. Bless her soul, deep in my heart I am sorry to say that she was never my real mother. I long for my mother. I grew up in terror as a lonely boy without a real mother.

My Father and a Religion of Terror

My father used to repeat his story of our ancestors. He was born in a family of five sons. His father, my grandfather, was a general in the royal army of the Yi Dynasty (1392–1910) when the Japanese invaded Korea in 1905; they disbanded the Old Korea's army in 1907. My grandfather organized the Korean soldiers to fight against the invading Japanese. He was a heroic fighter for national independence, killing so many powerful Japanese invaders with modern weapons. However, he was arrested, imprisoned, and he died in prison. When my grandmother heard the rumors of my grandfather's death, she decided to kill all the children and herself. She poisoned and killed all of my father's older siblings, but she spared my

19

father who was then only three years old. Finally she killed herself. She was a virtuous woman of the old Korea. She refused to survive her husband. She refused to live under the Japanese rule as a slave. It was better to die than to live in slavery.

My father was taken to Northern Korea near the Yalu River where my grandmother's distant sister lived. I had a suspicion that she was not exactly my grandaunt, but one of my grandfather's many concubines. My father did not have a chance to tell me the truth, and I had never asked him about it.

There, in the deep mountains, my father raised and attended goats. A "cowboy," he was raised among the animals in the open air close to the blue skies and against the harsh wintry winds. One sleepy afternoon in late spring, he met a woman who carried the Korean translated Bible and books to give out or sell to anyone who was interested. She approached an idle boy sitting on the ground next to the grazing goats. She managed to give a copy of the gospel to my father. He confessed to the woman that he could not read or write. The Bible woman came to visit him every week; she taught him how to read the Korean script until my father was able to read the Bible and ask questions about what he read. She took my father to the nearest town where a mission school was recently opened for boys. The name of the mission school was Young Shil, and the missionary teacher was Archibald Campbell from Philadelphia. I remember that I sat on his lap when he came to visit our home in northern Korea.

Dr. Campbell not only took my father into his school, but he practically raised him and sent to the seminary and later to Manchuria as a missionary to the Koreans there. My father was well educated as a Bible fundamentalist and as a Confucian Puritan moralist in the American mission school and in the Presbyterian seminary in Pyungyang. He believed in the literal truth of the Christian Bible. He saw no contradictions in the Bible, and he believed that every word in the Bible is the Word of God. Once I asked him about the authorship of the first five books of the Old Testament; he struck me across my face and lamented on his raising a devil in a preacher's house. I only mentioned that Moses was dying toward the end of Deuteronomy, and asked how he could write that book! My question was answered by a blow on my face. I was told that I should believe what I was told in Christian religion, and that I should not question or doubt. The terror of religion and the religion of terror has terrified me ever since this encounter with my father's biblical fundamentalism.

My father was a Confucian Puritan. He was a perfect patriarch. He followed the Confucian teaching of propriety to the letter. He was a hardworking man. His work ethic was both Confucian and Christian Puritan. No smoking and no drinking and no dancing and no Korean folk songs and no Korean card games. He was a legalistic and a moralistic Christian. He condemned all that belonged to the free lifestyle—premarital affairs, dating, divorce, let alone extramarital affairs of any circumstances. He believed in chastity, celibacy, and a pure and clean life, and he taught me to follow his "moral" way of life. He would never compromise his faith and the commandments. He did not believe in the freedom of thinking, the freedom of doubting, and the freedom of a "deviant" life. He was so strict on my life. He beat me every so often to discipline me, even though I have no clear memories of misbehavior. I always feared his whip with terror. He punished me in the name of Christian religion and Christian God whose love is expressed in his anger and judgment. To me, God was a God of anger and terror. I was to worship this God with fear and trembling. The image of God was an angry father with a whip in his hand, the one who watched me all the time. I was always terrified by my father's announcement that I was a sinner, an unforgivably condemned sinner. I had nothing to be proud of. I was a "good for nothing" in front of our Almighty God. Yes, I believed that I was nothing and nobody in the eyes of an all-perfect God.

My father was a Christian nationalist. I deeply respected him for this. When he refused to pay respect to the Japanese Shinto shrine, he was taken into the local police station for interrogation. I followed him to the station and stood outside of the police office. I overheard the question about who was higher, the Japanese emperor or the Christian God. My father's resounding voice declared that the Japanese emperor is no God, therefore he cannot compare the two. My father did not give up his answer until he was beaten by the Japanese police and had to be carried home in the stretcher. He never compromised his faith. He quit his ministry and left the church until he was called again to go to Manchuria as a missionary. He did not believe in personal freedom, but he believed in the freedom of the Korean people from the Japanese colonial rule. So he preached on Moses, Exodus, and the liberation of the Hebrew people. He was a national freedom preacher. For that he had to go to jail every so often. He was always terrorized by the Japanese police because he would not compromise his religion.

Korea was liberated from the Japanese colonialism at the defeat of the Japanese in the Pacific War with the Americans. I did not know what it meant to be liberated, even though my father was so excited about the Japanese defeat. I was happy that I could go home to northern Korea where my mother was buried. No sooner had we settled in the old hometown than we found out that the Red Army had marched into North Korea to start a pro-Communist government that would persecute Christians and their preachers on the grounds that they were anti-Communist American spies. We were terrified by the red banners all over the school buildings, streets, and major government buildings; they praised the glorious victory of the heroic Red Army under the leadership of Stalin. The terror of ideological warfare had begun. Many churchgoers were chased out of their

21

homes and lands, as they were accused of being oppressors and exploiters of the working class. Many Christian land owners had to flee the North to the South and start a new life.

My father once again preached the Exodus stories, only now against the communist empire that denied religious freedom. The North Korean police often harassed him for what he preached about freedom and about communism. At the wake of the Korean War in 1950, he was taken in by the North Korean secret police. When General MacArthur marched into Pyungyang in October of 1950, my father's church members and I began searching for the whereabouts of my father. We found his body on the bank of the Daedong River. His hands were tied behind his back and he was strung together with five other preachers. His body was intact, for the October river water was icy cold. There were Soviet-made machine gun wounds all over his body and face. We were able to identify him.

We had a simple funeral service and buried him in a graveyard behind the church where he served for some time. Then we left for the South with the withdrawing American troops from the North. Chinese soldiers invaded the North to rescue the defeated North Korean Army.

My father lived under the terror of Japanese military police. My father had to fight the terror of communist anti-Christian ideology, and he was murdered. Although he struggled for freedom and preached about freedom, he taught me the religion of terror and the terror of religion. His religion did not give me freedom—freedom of thinking, freedom of choice, and freedom to make mistakes.

The Terror of Colonialism

I was born in 1931 when the Japanese swallowed up Manchuria and established the puppet regime of Manchukuo. I entered the Japanese-run elementary school in the northern Korean village in 1937 when the Japanese army marched into the mainland China. Henceforth, I had to live through the terrors of the Japanese assimilation policy that attempted to make all Koreans Japanese. The Korean children in the elementary school were forced to learn how to read and write in Japanese and to speak in Japanese. When we were caught in speaking in Korean amongst ourselves, we were severely punished and often beaten up by the Japanese teachers who used to carry their long swords on their waist. In 1938, all Koreans were forced to change our names—from three Chinese character names of the Korean style to four Chinese character names of the Japanese style. My father postponed the change as late as possible. He couldn't resist any longer when the local police harassed him and threatened him and all of us in the family. I am embarrassed to reveal that I had this Japanese name:

Omoto Eiichi. My father tried to explain to me why he chose such odd names for me, but I remember I refused to listen. I just hated it.

I lost my name to the Japanese authorities through the terror of colonialism. I lost my language by the terror of colonialism. I lost my history by the terror of colonialism. I lost everything as a Korean and as a human being. By military power, the Japanese invaded the Land of the Morning Calm with the terror of colonialism. We lost our land, our rivers, and our mountains. We lost our seashores, we lost our gold mines, and we lost our rice paddies and deep green forests. What was more devastating was our loss of our names, our language, and our culture. We lost our minds. Our minds and souls were colonized. We were forced to think like the Japanese. We were forced to talk like the Japanese. We lost not only our national identity but also our human identity. We were slaves. We lost our self-esteem and human dignity. We were nobody and we were dispensable.

As the War in the Pacific became intensified, my older cousins and older friends and uncles were drafted by the Japanese army. They were sent to the front lines to fight the war for the Japanese emperor. They never came back. When we were exiled to Manchuria, my favorite elementary school teacher came to live with us. She ran away from Ewha College in Seoul because she would be drafted by the Japanese to become a "comfort woman," a "sex slave," for the Japanese army. Hundreds and thousands of young women were kidnapped by the Japanese and sent to the war zones to be gang-raped by the soldiers. I grew up in terror, the terror of colonialism.

The Terror of War

The Manchurian town we lived in during the war was a mining town in which the Japanese war industries were thriving. Our town became the bombing target of the American air force. We, the middle school boys, were drafted to work odd jobs in the war factories toward the end of the war. Most of the time, we were asked to clean up the debris created from the bombing. The American air force bombs were devastating. They destroyed the center of the industries. Every time a plane flew in and bombed the factories, I had an exhilarating sense of joy and victory, while my Japanese schoolmates were crying and cursing the American planes. The louder they cried and the angrier they became, the more I became happy and satisfied. It was a sheer sense of revenge. I was not terrified by the American bombers. I enjoyed the terror of revenge.

Toward the end of the war, the fateful month of August of 1945, we, the middle school boys, were drafted again, this time to dig the so-called antitank ditches. The ditches we were digging in the hillside outside of the

23

town were supposed to trap Soviet tanks. The Soviet army was advancing to Manchuria to destroy the Japanese army just about a week before the emperor of Japan surrendered to the Allied forces. The terror of colonialism was over. The terror of war was over then.

The terror of war was over, but peace was far away. The terror of colonialism was over, but the terror of national division was imposed. As the Koreans rejoiced at the end of the Japanese colonial rule, they learned of the division of the peninsula into the North and the South. The thirty-eighth parallel had become a permanent divide. As the Japanese army retreated and evacuated from the Korean peninsula, the Soviet army occupied the North and the American GIs the South. There were rumors of negotiations between the Soviet and U.S. authorities for a possible reunification. There were rumors about the political leaders of the North and South meeting for a general election under the supervision of the United Nations. There were also rumors about "trusteeship" whereby Korea would be put under a multinational governance. In 1948, three years after the division, the South established the Republic of Korea under the sponsorship of the United States, and the North formed the Democratic People's Republic of Korea under the sponsorship of the Soviet Union. The thirty-eighth parallel had become a political and ideological line that divided the nation and kept its people further apart.

When we left Manchuria and returned to our Korean hometown, my father did not expect that this division would devastate our family through our losing him to the communist terror. I attended a middle school that was run by the communist government and dominated by communist teachers. We learned English and Russian at school. Our textbooks were filled with communist ideology and propaganda. We were required to read the history of the Soviet Union and the theories of Karl Marx. We learned very little about Korean history and Korean literature, even little about the liberation of the nation from the Japanese colonialist power. I felt that we were colonized again by the Russians. Some of us teenage middle school kids tried to organize an anti-Communist student club. We were caught on the spot, interrogated, tortured, and punished by the school authorities. I was suspended from school for a month and stayed home, reading more American history and learning more English, with no teachers to supervise me. After I graduated from a communist high school, I was employed by a village bank as a clerk in a very remote area near the central Yalu River country of the North. My father had decided this was not the right thing to do for my future. In 1948, we moved to Pyongyang, the capital city of the North Korea. He was invited to a Presbyterian church to take care of the remnant of that church while he was looking for the chance to take refuge in the South. Because of my "class" and my father's position, I could not think of applying to any university in the North. I decided to attend the Presbyterian Theological Seminary in Pyungyang. It was a good decision. I was able to learn English from the Reverend Park Dae Sun, who later became president of Yonsei University in Seoul. In 1950, my father was taken away by the North Korean secret police and the Korean War broke out. My seminary education was short-lived. As most of the faculty was taken in by the North Korean police, the school was shut down by the North Korean authorities.

The Korean War broke out on June 25, 1950. It was a Sunday morning. The village loudspeaker blasted the news that the heroic North Korean Army had pushed down the invading South Korean soldiers at the thirty-eighth parallel, and my father was missing from the church. The people came to ask me to preach on that Sunday, in place of my father. I did preach, but I cannot remember what I said on that tragic Sunday. I was only nineteen.

I was of draft age for the North Korean Army. My second mother had to hide me in a little dirt hole below the parsonage office; she supplied meals three times a day. I could not read and write during the day because we could not bring light into that little dirt hole where I squatted all day long. At night I came out to sleep in my own bed until we heard the rumors that the police come around at night to round up the youngsters for the Army. We were bombed by the American planes day and night. When planes came and bombed, no police were around, so I was able to come out of that little dirt hole to breathe. When the bombing was severe and it was too dangerous stay in the house, I ran out into the field with the neighbors. The American air force planes followed the civilians to shoot them down. I saw so many people shot by the airplane machine guns; I saw them dying. The terror of war was there.

After two months of living in a hideout, I was told that there was a possibility of going down to the South as a volunteer teacher of any subject. I applied for it. Instead of appointment, I was taken into the draft camp at the interview session for the volunteers. At the draft station, I was sent for a physical examination. I was coughing a little due to my living in the small dirt hole for about two months. The doctor said in a hushed voice that I should not be drafted, and he failed me. I was not qualified to go to the army, because, according to his diagnosis, I had contracted bronchitis. Even to this day, I cannot understand why the doctor told me that I should not be drafted, and why he wrote a false diagnosis. I was sent home immediately from the draft center.

As I was leaving the ground, I met my younger brother who was on his way with the other draftees. I told him about what happened and why I was going home. He left leaving a word with me saying that I should not be drafted and that he was glad. That was the last time I saw him. I lost him in the terror of the Korean War.

25

Refugee Camps: The Terror of Survival

In late September, the United Nations's troops crossed the thirty-eighth parallel and took over the North Korean capital Pyongyang. The United Nations's police force mainly consisted of the South Korean soldiers and the Americans. When they marched into the city, the North Koreans all came out to welcome them waving South Korean flags and the complicated American flags with many stars and stripes. They did the same when the Soviet soldiers marched into Pyongyang some five years before—they waved Soviet flags with a sickle on red paper. We were liberated again.

Our liberation did not last long. The Chinese were coming to aid the North Korean troops and to push the American soldiers down to the South. We had to evacuate from Pyongyang. We had just enough time to find my father's body and to bury him on the hill. Then we got onto the retreating cargo trains. We couldn't carry much, and we didn't know what to carry. I put an English-Korean dictionary and an English-language Bible in the two pockets of my heavy coat. I had a few extra clothes in my knapsack. When we arrived at the train station, refugees were everywhere. As we were climbing up on the top of the train, I was separated from my family. I lost them, and they lost me. I was pushed up by the crowd of people, and perhaps my family was pulled down by the crowd. The train ride was short. I had to get off the train, so I began walking with the crowd. It was a great march of refugees. I cannot remember how long I had to walk. I just walked and walked along the railroad and along with the crowd even without knowing where I was heading. I was cold and hungry and lonely.

When I arrived in Seoul, the South Korean capital, I went straight to a church where most of the North Korean refugees met for information about the whereabouts of their families and friends. I posted on the church building my name and "I came down to Seoul." That was all I could write on a sheet of paper. Later I added, "Let us meet in Pusan." About six months later, with the help the church grapevine, my stepmother found me in the navy training school.

In Seoul, I registered in a church organization that took care of Christian refugees from North Korea. American missionaries were directing the organization. They took me to the refugee cargo train, one that carried so many refugees further South. The cargo train was quite clean and warm and comfortable. They gave us food. I tasted American hamburgers and potato chips for the first time on that refugee train. After a two-night train ride, we were practically dumped into a Quonset building. They rationed a sheet blanket. I slept in the corner of the cold room and was squeezed by the crowd of people inside. I cannot remember how I survived. I only remember that I was lonely; I had no one to talk to. I was hungry, but I didn't know how to get food. I remember clearly I went to church almost every evening and there I was able to get hold of a bowl of rice porridge. The church held a revival meeting or a prayer meeting. The church was always crowded with refugees from the North. The revival preacher was shouting at the top of his voice saying that we have sinned against God, that is why we were suffering from the war, therefore, we must repent our sins. I prayed and prayed with tears trying to repent of my sins. I was crying because I was hungry, cold, and lonely. I was crying because I couldn't understand why we were suffering and why we had to fight in the war and why I had to run away from home in the North. I was crying out of fear. I was weeping out of the terror of war.

I was wandering around the city of Pusan looking for my family in almost every church where the refugees camped, looking for something to do to earn money and looking for somebody to talk to. Finally, I ran into a poster on the church wall stating that the South Korean navy was recruiting for the communications regiment. Immediately I applied. So many South Korean high school graduates had applied. Even some university students applied, according to the rumors around the naval headquarters. Therefore, a boy like myself who came from the North would not get in. The competition was something like six-to-one. I did not want to be drafted into the army only to be sent to the front line to be shot. After a written examination on history, Korean language, and even an exam in English—like a college entrance examination—and after a two-hour interview (which was more like a police interrogation), I was admitted to the naval boot camp.

My navy life began with a beating. I was on time to sail out to the naval school from Pusan port. There were several others who came on time, but we were told that we were late. We were severely beaten up to the point that we were not able to walk or stand up. We crawled into the bottom of the ship and crawled out from the ship at the next port where we were trained to be the "heroic" navy. Our training was nothing but how to endure harsh beatings day and night, how to endure humiliation, and how to endure physical and mental harassment. We were told that we were no longer human beings; we were only navy men. We were supposed to lose our self-identity. We were only loyal navy men for the country. They were beating our self-esteem out of us. We became nobody—we were crushed, tired, hungry, and cold.

I gnashed my teeth to endure this terror of training and inhumane harassment. I accepted the terror in me, endured it, and did well. I finished the naval communication school as the top student. I was posted in the school to train the newcomers as instructors' assistants. My family found me after some six months of separation in the naval camp.

The Korean navy recruited the noncommissioned officers to the United States navy for a specialized weapons training program. In 1953, I was selected as the first one to study in the U.S. Naval School in Yorktown, Virginia. It was a long journey. The Northwest Airlines propeller airplane took some thirty-six hours from Seoul to San Francisco via Guam and Hawaii. I stayed overnight at the San Francisco Naval Base. Then I journeyed on a cross-continental train from San Francisco to Chicago, and then from Chicago to Yorktown. The trip took a week. I was trained in a mines school. I had never used my training when I returned to the Korean navy, but I had experienced American navy life. I learned a great deal about the American lifestyle—about just simply being a young American. I was befriended by fellow American trainees in spite of my incorrigible English.

The Terror of Language

One of my fellow trainees was from the state of Montana. He turned out to be my best friend in the crowd. One day he approached me with a serious face and asked me what I wanted to do in the future. While I was hesitating to answer, he said that I should come to study in an American college or university because, he said, I was not a navy type. After I returned to the Korean naval base, he contacted his hometown church to sponsor my college education in Rocky Mountain College in Billings, Montana. After six years of military service, I was honorably discharged from the Korean navy to come to the United States to enter a small denominational liberal arts college in the winter of 1956.

Speaking in a foreign language is a terrifying experience. I was terrorized by the Japanese teachers because my Japanese was not good enough for them. My Japanese classmates always ridiculed me and humiliated me when my Japanese did not come out like they would speak in their own language. They even harassed me because of my Japanese. While I lived in Manchuria, the neighborhood Chinese kids beat me because I could not speak Chinese even though I looked like a Chinese boy. Now I was thrown into the English-speaking world, where I had to learn to speak, read, and write in English. To this day I don't feel confident or comfortable about my English. I feel insecure about my communication skills in English. I am timid and shy in my public speeches. I have been terrorized by the forced use of a foreign language. Foreign languages, including English, are a terror. When speaking a foreign language is forced on you against your will, having to speak that foreign tongue is terrorizing.

Living in a foreign country is in itself a terrifying experience. To be a foreigner in a strange land among strange people is an experience of terror. You cannot communicate your thoughts and desires. You look different.

You eat differently, and you act differently. To be different is to be vulnerable to terror. People are suspicious of the different people. They often become violent against people who are different. Terror against the different is legitimate. Therefore, you are forced to conform to the norms of that foreign country and to be assimilated into that culture, if only for survival. This is a terror that every immigrant experiences in everyday life in a strange country.

Every time I open my mouth to speak in English, and every time I have to write in English, I have this fear that I am making mistakes in my expressions. I struggle to be correct in grammar. I make a tremendous effort to make myself clear and coherent. I try very hard to be eloquent, but I am never sure of my English. My English terrorizes me, for I am afraid of my English. The more I use English, the more I sense the terror of having to use English.

Terror of language is in the theological language as well. To me, the Christian God-talk was like a foreign language. The God-talk was imposed on me, and I had to learn the language of God-talk. It seemed that God-talk had a special grammar. I had to learn the correct language of God-talk. The correct language of God-talk was imposed on me as an orthodoxy. I was supposed to talk in the orthodox language of God-talk. I did learn it well under the supervision of my fundamentalist father. I answered correctly all the questions of the elders who examined my baptismal catechism. At the same time, I doubted my correct answers, and I thought otherwise. I had to fight against the terror of orthodoxy, against the terror of God-language in my philosophical training and in my theological studies. In my struggles against the terror of orthodoxy and against the religion of terror in the seminary and graduate theological studies, I was liberated as I discovered that there are many different ways of speaking about God, and there are many different ways to approach God. The so-called orthodox way of speaking about God is only one of many ways of talking about God. It should not terrorize anybody. Christian God-talk cannot be a terror. It should not terrorize the people of other faiths than Christianity. It is supposed to be the language of liberation—liberation from the terror of religious language.

The Reign of Terror

I returned to Korea in September of 1969 with a Ph.D. in religion from Vanderbilt University. I was installed as the chair of the Department of Christian Studies in the College of Liberal Arts and Sciences at Ewha Women's University in Seoul. It was unusual to appoint a junior professor to a top leadership position. I hesitated to accept the offer from the president. In spite of my hesitation, the faculty supported my appointment, which made my work easy. As I, my wife Sunyong Ham, who was on the administration of Ewha, and our newborn son, John Jungshil, were struggling in our reentry adjustment to the country, I pushed myself to work hard for the department's development and for the development of my new courses in theology and philosophy. I was also invited to join a university faculty team to reform the university systems and curricula. It was gratifying to be immersed in the work of the university and in theological education. I felt that I was doing exactly what I had wanted to do and what I had prepared to do as a teacher, a scholar, and as a committed Christian leader in the university affairs and theological education.

As I was being accepted in the university community, I was drawn into the Korean ecumenical Christian circles of theologians and church leaders. I joined the various commissions and committees in the National Council of Churches, the YMCA movement, the Student Christian Movement, and the various editorial boards of popular and professional theological journals and periodicals. I was also invited to write regular newspaper columns commenting on and critiquing the national political and cultural affairs.

The Korean political scene in the late 1960s and early 1970s was more than turbulent and critical. The military government of General Park Chung Hee, who took power in 1961, pushed hard to implement national economic development plans as national security measures. He agreed with the U.S. military to send Korean mercenary forces to Vietnam to fight the jungle war, and he pushed into being the constitutional amendment to extend his term of office for a third term. After his narrow victory over opposition presidential candidate Kim Dae Jung in 1971, President Park declared a martial law and passed the so-called Yushin Constitution, which would allow him to stay in power for life. Throughout the 1970s the Korean people lived under a series of emergency decrees and martial laws of the Park regime. Under the emergency decrees, there was no freedom of speech, no freedom of assembly, no academic freedom, and no freedom of mission activities. Korea was again under the reign of terror.

The university students were the first to respond to the reign of terror with demonstrations on campus and in the streets against the new constitutions, the emergency decrees, and military dictatorship. They shouted for democracy, academic freedom, and basic human rights. They spoke not only for political democracy, but also for human rights for the workers who had been exploited in the system of rapid economic development. There were mass arrests of activist students. The arrested students were imprisoned, tortured, maimed, and killed in torture.

The Christian leaders protested against the government's reign of terror, advocating for human rights and democracy, issuing statement after statement, and joining the street demonstrations. They were in jail with the demonstrating students. Soon the university faculty joined the march with the students. I joined them. I learned from my fellow classmates in the seminary that in the U.S., in the 1960s, Christian commitment included joining marches such as the civil rights movement on the side of Martin Luther King Jr., the free speech movement, and the anti-Vietnam War movement. Furthermore, the oppositionist political movement against the reign of terror is a tradition in the long stream of Korean students and scholars.

The military government forced itself onto the university campuses with its intelligence agencies, police, and special security officers for student protest movement surveillance. University faculty members were under suspicion and under surveillance. I was no exception. My office phone was tapped. Our home phone was also tapped. Almost every morning during the weekdays, a designated agent from the national security office came to visit me, asking me about my lecture schedule and off-campus activities. They came to visit me at home whenever they had detected that I had contacts with my international friends who came to visit me. Sometimes they came to bar me from leaving our house for a speaking engagement on another university campus or in church gatherings of any nature. I was virtually on twenty-four-hour house arrest at home and at school. For the 1970s, the government denied issuing my passport. I was exiled in my own home country. My colleagues who were in the same situation called it "inxile," since we had been detained at home.

This was the sociopolitical context in which *minjung* theology was born. It was, in a way, an indigenous Korean theology against the reign of terror. It is a political theology of liberation for *minjung*, the people who are politically oppressed, economically exploited, and socially and culturally marginalized and discriminated against. It is also a cultural theology of liberation for *minjung* to reclaim their tradition and religion and culture for advancing self-esteem and self-identity. The *minjung* theology movement developed out of the people's struggle for political democracy, human rights, and economic justice. It is a theological voice of the Korean people that grew out of the 1970s. I joined this theological movement. It is a theological movement of the street; it sprang out of political activities, writing statements, and attending political rallies and demonstrations. It did not grow out of the book-lined studies buried deep inside the halls of academia. It is not an individual theological enterprise that is established in publications and lecture halls, but a collective and team effort. *Minjung* theology is not only the property of theologians; it is of the people and by the people and for the people.

In October of 1979, President Park Chung Hee was assassinated by his own Korean CIA chief at one of his lavish dinner parties. We mistook it to be the fall of military dictatorship and the victory of the people's movement for democracy. Within a month, the military lost no time in grabbing back control of the government. The military suspended all political activities and put down all student demonstrations through harsh martial law. Another reign of terror had set in. However, throughout the whole spring semester of 1980, the people joined the students in the street demonstrations against another military takeover. The repressive measures were escalated, and massive arrests of intellectuals, journalists, leading university professors, religious leaders, and leading opposition political leaders were made. Some of them were tortured and sent to the military court for trial. The top opposition leader, Kim Dae Jung, was one of those who were sentenced to death in the fall of 1980.

As part of this military's so-called sweeping reform measure, I was taken in to the interrogation center of the military headquarters for criminal investigation. Right in the middle of a faculty meeting over which I was presiding as Dean of the College of Liberal Arts and Sciences, I was called out to be arrested by the military intelligence agents. No lawyers were called in. No phone calls to home. As I was settling in the torture chamber, I was picked up and taken to my home and office in the university campus for a house search, without a warrant. My wife was at home. Our bedroom was thoroughly searched without anyone knowing what they were looking for. It was a clear harassment aimed at terrorizing my wife. When they came into my office at the university, they went through my bookshelves, taking out all the books that had red covers. Apparently they were looking for communist or Marxist books. They went through my file cabinet and took out all the files that were labeled in English.

When they took me back to the torture chamber, which had floor bedding, an iron desk, and two chairs, the plainclothes policemen ordered me to start writing a "confession" of my crimes.

They asked me to write an autobiography about my family, beginning with my grandparents, parents, and my early schooling, my teachers, the books I read, the major field of my scholarly work, the classes I taught, my theology, and my politics—everything that had to do with my life and thinking. Day and night I wrote my precocious autobiography without interruption. The interrogator came into my room from time to time to check on my writing; sometimes very late at night they woke me and forced me to continue writing even beyond midnight. This was torture.

After I finished my draft of my "criminal confession," which took some two weeks, I had to wait for another week for the military tribunal to decide what to do with me—either to send me to military courtmartial, which meant dismissal from the university, or to just discharge me from the torture chamber. Finally, I was forced to write a resignation paper. The plainclothesmen threatened me, saying that if I didn't write a resignation paper as they forced it upon me, I would go through a military courtmartial, which would take some six months to a year. I had "chosen" to send my resignation paper to the president of the university. I walked out of that torture chamber in one piece. I packed up my things from my university office and left.

After one year of work at the Presbyterian Theological Seminary, I was ordained and called to Hyundai Presbyterian Church, a parish right in the middle of a huge apartment complex in a newly developing community in the south of Seoul. I enjoyed preaching, teaching, visiting, and caring for the church members. I was deeply involved in the parish ministry, trying out new ways of doing ministry as I learned in an American theological seminary and as I had taught in the university.

In the meantime, as a dismissed professor, with some two hundred of us, I struggled for our reinstatement and joined the people's movement for human rights and democracy in South Korea. The harsh military rule continued for the next ten years. We fought squarely against the reign of terror, and we won. All of the dismissed professors were reinstated in 1984. In 1987, the military government gave in to the people's desire to revise the constitution and to elect the president by the popular vote. Finally, in 1997, the die-hard opposition democracy leader, Kim Dae Jung, was elected as president. Recognized for his life-long struggle for human rights and political democracy, he won the Nobel Peace Prize in 2000. This signified the victory of the people in their struggle against the reign of terror.

The Terror of Death

I have encountered many deaths and the terrors of death. I had to face my mother's death when I was only thirteen years old. At nineteen, I had to embrace the bullet-riddled face of my father. During the Korean War of the 1950s, to escape machine gun shots and bombings, I found myself running between the dead bodies of civilians and soldiers in the open fields and in the deep mountains. I buried my dead comrades in combat. I took care of dying members of my congregation and officiated many funerals of close friends and of people from high and low. I have lived among the dead, and I have survived the terror of death.

Socrates said to his disciples in his prison cell as he was facing his death that death is the separation of the soul from the body, it is liberation of the soul from the body. Hence, it is good to die; it is a philosopher's job to practice death. This understanding of death has prevailed in Western and Christian thought for centuries. It is good to know that there is no terror of death, for death is release, freedom, and liberation from the corrupt and dispensable body.

Buddha, on the other hand, was raised by his parents secluded from the world that was filled with suffering and the terror of death. But soon after he encountered aging people, sickness, and death, he had to leave the comfort-

33

able royal court for the world. After some forty years of meditation, Buddha declared that life is nothing but suffering. He saw death as a rebirth to another life of suffering; death itself is no release from the recycling of life's suffering.

Jesus raised the dead to life. He died on the cross as a political criminal of the Roman Empire. It is the Christian faith that confesses that Jesus has risen from his death and that all the believers will live eternal life after death. Celebrating my seventieth birthday, I feel that I have lived too long. My grandfather died in prison in his thirties. My father was murdered by the North Korean secret police at the age of forty-five. My mother died in her thirties. I am grateful to God that I have survived the terrors of death in war and political persecutions. I give thanks to God for giving me good health and longevity, which are great blessings in the many Asian traditions.

Thinking about my own death, which I feel so close to even in my good health at the moment, I sense freedom, release, and liberation from my long life of suffering and terror. At the same time I sense a terror of death. I sense the terror not just because of possible long years of illness that would exhaust me and my family and friends, or because I would lose everything that I had in this world, but because I don't know what is next or whether there is the next after this life. This unknowability of the next after death is at the same time a terror and a liberation. A total amnesia of life would be a terror and liberation at the same time. Nonetheless, I feel more freedom than terror in my forthcoming death.

I have not written my will as of yet, in spite of my friends' advice to do so. I might be doing it soon. But I have very little to leave in this world over which my two sons will have to fight. I only leave my life, which has been filled with terror and suffering and struggle for freedom. I tried to live the life of my grandfather and of my father, who fought for freedom—my grandfather for the freedom of the country, my father for the freedom of Christian faith. I tried to live and work for freedom from war, freedom from political oppression, freedom from economic exploitation, and freedom from ideologies, dogmas, and social and cultural prejudices and straitjackets. I can say that I have lived my life in struggle against the terrors of life— terror of hunger, cold, loneliness, war, and death.

I lived the life of longing for love and care. The love of my mother made me strong in my struggles for freedom against the terrors of life. In yearning for love with friends, I received undeservingly abundant love. I passionately loved my life and my work. My *godding* (experiencing divine mystery in human relationships) of love empowered me to live a full life. Freedom to love and love for freedom encouraged me and made me commit to *godding* with human beings and with God. Love and freedom. Yearning for these two things helped me grow, fight, and survive the terror of life.

Terror and Japan's Colonization of Korea 1910–1945

Kosuke Koyama

Eliminating its rivals by military victories over China (1895) and Russia (1905), Japan took the first step to annexation by forcing Korea to sign the Protectorate Treaty on November 18, 1905. Formally, Japan annexed Korea on August 29, 1910.[1] In the treaty issued on that day we read:

> Article One: His Majesty the Emperor of Korea makes the complete and permanent cession to His Majesty the Emperor of Japan of all rights of sovereignty over the whole of Korea.

The annexation was achieved by military threat and large-scale bribery. Japan's colonial policy over Korea had been decided in a cabinet meeting that took place on July 6, 1909. This policy document stipulates the suspension "for the time being" of the application of the Japanese Constitution for the population of the annexed territory. The suggestion is that the annexation does not imply elimination of ethnic discrimination. It draws a line between true Japanese and "second-class Japanese" who are to be colonized.

According to the 1910 Imperial Decree (#354), the Japanese governor general of Korea was to be appointed directly by the emperor from the ranks of army general and navy admiral (Article 2).[2] The governor general was answerable only to the emperor and was charged with the responsibility of military activities in and around Korea (Article 3). Article 21 stipulates the permanent appointment of two military strategy officers in the office of the governor general. This article clearly expresses the intention of employing the *kempei* (military security force) style of rule over Korea.

The history of Japanese colonialism of Korea is outright oppressive and repulsive. Judicial, executive, and legislative powers were subordinated to the sole power of the governor general. All political associations, speeches, and presses were banned. School textbooks written by Koreans were confiscated. Koreans were forced to "worship" at the state Shinto shrines that the governor general built in Korea. The military governor generals had little understanding of the cultural and religious life of the people. At the same time, Japan was flooded with propaganda that "Koreans are happy to be a part of the glorious Japanese Empire," and that "annexation is Japan's 'civilizing mission' of Korea." The annexation forced Korea to revert the name of the country to *Choson* from *Taehan Cheguk* or the Empire of the Great Han, which the Koreans adopted in 1897 after they were freed from the power of China.

The Koreans resolutely rejected Japanese rule. According to Korean records, in 1908 a "Righteous Army" *(uibyong)* of 69,832 soldiers engaged in a total of 1,451 clashes against the Japanese military. Although poorly armed, the Righteous Army was not overpowered by the professional Japanese army until 1914. Stimulated by the 1917 Russian Revolution and the American President Wilson's idea of the right of self-determination of nations pronounced in 1918, a nationwide protest against Japanese rule took place on March 1, 1919. Yi Sang-jae and Pak Hui-do, directors of the YMCA, inspired a nonviolent approach. A Declaration of Independence was solemnly proclaimed at 2:00 P.M. on March 1 in Pagoda Park in Seoul. It begins with these words:

> We herewith proclaim the independence of Korea and the liberty of the Korean people. We tell it to the world in witness of the equality of all nations and we pass it on to our posterity as their inherent right. We make this proclamation, having back of us five thousand years of history and twenty millions of a united loyal people. We take this step to insure to our children, for all time to come, personal liberty in accord with the awakening of consciousness of this new era. This is the clear leading of God, the moving principle of the present age, the whole human race's just claim. It is something that cannot be stamped out, or stifled, or gagged, or suppressed by any means.

Japanese reaction to the uprising was swift and atrocious. Tokyo quickly increased the Japanese military presence by sending six battalions and four hundred *kempeis*. Between March and December, 26,443 people were arrested. The fact that the majority of those arrested were farmers suggests that the uprising was an anti-imperialism movement staged by farmers. According to the *Comparative Chronology of Protestantism in Asia, 1792–1945*, in the first six months of the uprising, 1,360,000 participated, 6,670 were killed and 14,600 were wounded.[3] Son Pyong-hui, the leader of *Chondogyo* (formerly *Tonghak,* "Eastern Learning") was prominently involved in this protest. A significant majority of those arrested were Christians.

On April 11 the Korean Provisional Government in Exile in Shanghai was established.

The infamous Je-am Incident took place on April 15. The Japanese army confined thirty people in the Je-am Christian Church, set fire to it, and killed them. A massacre of Christians took place in sixty-four villages of Suwon and Ansong districts. Korean Christians suffered greatly for their active participation in the March One Protest. General Yoshimichi Hasegawa, the second governor general, who resigned taking responsibility for the March One Protest, was succeeded by admiral Makoto Saito. Hasegawa, surprised by the strength of the Korean resistance, left a memo to Saito confiding to him that the suppression of free speech under his regime might have been too extreme.

The March One Protest earned freedom to publish *Choson Ilbo* (Korean Daily) and *Tong-a Ilbo* (Asian Daily), though within very strict limits. They survived to 1940. Saito superficially relaxed the *Kempei* rule, but, in turn, strengthened the police power. The basic policy of terror continued, though the Saito policy was called "culturally sensitive government" *(bunka seiji)* by the Japanese. Saito asked Tokyo for two more divisions of soldiers in order to control any Korean uprising. One of the aims of his administration was to transfer rice, more than half of the Korean harvest, to Japan to pacify the rice insurrection in Japan that took place in 1918.

The Japanese Security Law of 1925 was applied to Korea by Imperial Decree (#175) in May of that year. This law, which contains a clause authorizing capital punishment, tightened Japanese control over Koreans. It was in this year the *Chosen Jingu* (Shinto shrine) in Seoul was built. (Japan became belligerent in September of 1931 in Manchuria, and in January 1932 in Shanghai. In March of 1933, Japan seceded from the League of Nations when advised to pull her army out from Manchuria.) The March 1938 Education Ordinance for Koreans required Koreans to abandon their own language and to adopt Japanese. In February of 1940, Koreans were forced to renounce their Korean names and adopt Japanese names. In July of 1939, Tokyo, issuing the National Labor Mobilization Ordinance, authorized the mobilization of Koreans to work in military factories in Japan. Between 1939 and 1945, six million Koreans were mobilized for the Japanese war effort, of which one million draftees were shipped from Korea to Japan. The October 1943 National General Mobilization Act developed into the Student Volunteer Ordinance of January 1944. By the power of these laws, Koreans were drafted for military service. Exploitative Japanese colonialism of Korea climaxed in the war years, 1941–1945. Koreans, forced to work in military factories in Hiroshima, perished in the nuclear blast

37

over the city. The mobilization included sexual slavery of many thousands of "comfort women" for the Japanese army.

On the day Japan was defeated by the allied powers, August 15, 1945, Korea was emancipated when the Cairo Declaration of November 27, 1943, stated by the United States, Great Britain, and China, was fulfilled.

Japan terrorized Korea for thirty-five years. One can rationally reflect upon terror *after* the event, but the raw experience of terror itself defies language. On the Nazi terror, for example, one can read *Topography of Terror, Gestapo, SS and Reichssicherheitshauptam*,[4] but this reading does not give the reader the experience of terror that the real victims, the Jews and others, personally experienced. Terror strikes us as a direct threat to life. Even this is a second-hand description. The twentieth century has defiled itself with terrors of our own making: the Japanese *Kempei*, Nazi *gestapo*, Soviet Union's *KGB*, and East Germany's *Stasi*. Terror means "one terrorizes other." It is born and grows in history. It has a story.

My first memory of Korea was contained in a story of terror told to me by my grandfather. On September 1, 1923, Tokyo was violently shaken by an earthquake. A vicious rumor began to circulate in the disaster areas that resident Koreans, in a state of insurrection, had poisoned the drinking water and engaged in arson. Terror spread in the broad daylight on the second of September, and intensified until the fifth throughout greater Tokyo, Yokohama, and adjacent prefectures, as resident Koreans were indiscriminately murdered by emergency army units and bands of armed citizens. Chinese people and "socialists" were also targeted. The brutality with which these innocents were destroyed defies description. The Japanese authorities' estimate of six thousand Koreans murdered was rejected by historians as too small.

Thoughts of 1923 take me back to 1889. The 1889 Meiji Constitution of Japan describes, in quasi-religious language, the self-aggrandizing national uniqueness and superiority. Thus, the year 1889 marks the time of self-glorification of Japan in her recent history, though the idea of "the divine land" had been a political ideology for some centuries already. Born in 1929 in Tokyo, I was brought up in a culture saturated with the Japanese version of "manifest destiny." Japan, we were taught, is incomparably the most beautiful and righteous of nations! Every schoolchild learned to look down on Chinese and Koreans. The offense to history of this notion is evident when we remember that it was these people who gave Japan her basic cultural symbols and sense of social values. From where did this chosen people "complex," which bred so much violence, come? The Japanese military victory over "white" Russia in 1905 must have boosted Japan's self-confident "chosenness." Japan, in her own estimation, had become the undisputed leader of all "yellow" Asian nations. This self-confidence, however, was unstable since it oscillated between an inferiority complex towards the West and a superiority complex towards the Asian neighbors.

Shigeyoshi Murakami, scholar of Japanese religious and cultural history, in his *The Imperial Ritual (Tenno no Saiki,* 1977 pp 152f), writes that the Japan ese politicians in the era of the emperor Meiji (1868–1912) detected the secret of the strength of the Western powers to be residing in the religion of Christianity, which ascribes absolute authority to God. The possession of this point of the absolute, they argued, makes nations strong. Their suggestion was to accord the similar quality of absolute power to the person of the emperor. Thus, in my view, the political ideology of the imperial cult, formerly unknown in Japanese history, began. In all civilizations rulers use *the absolute* to authenticate their rule and bolster their power. *The absolute,* by definition untamable, is then tamed. It is this moment that generates violence. One may adore the absolute, "god," or "heaven." One must not equate oneself with *the absolute.* Japanese violence thus generated reached every corner of Asia and beyond. Within less than one hundred years the violence of equating the self with absolute authority reduced Japan itself to a pile of ashes. The year 1946 was opened by the emperor's "Humanity Declaration" (January 1). In the postwar constitution (1946), Japan began to speak a universally meaningful, human language that rejected the myth of imperial transcendence.

Myths abound in India and China. Japanese myths are fertility-centered. The sun, water, and growth of rice are their cardinal symbols. Sexual images, as an expression of nature's reproductive power, are profusely used. In order to confer the quality of transcendence upon the person of the emperor, the fertility myth of sun, water, and rice were transformed to political myth of transcendent power. Classical China philosophized a transcendent "heaven" from which the earthly ruler derives a "heavenly mandate." Heavenly mandate, however, is temporal and impermanent. It is conditional. As long as one rules well, the mandate resides with the ruler. Japan made use of the concept of an eternal "heaven," but discarded the temporal concept attached to the "mandate." The Japanese emperor's mandate is not temporal, as stated in the opening sentence of the 1941 Declaration of War, "We, by the grace of Heaven, Emperor of Japan seated on the throne of a line unbroken for ages eternal. . . ." Ascribing eternal continuity—the "line unbroken for ages eternal"—to a human condition, "something essentially conditioned is taken as unconditional"[5] and violence emerged.

This line of analysis is supported by Masao Maruyama in his *Ancient Layer of History Consciousness (Rekishi Ishiki no Koso,* 1972). He observes that the idea of continuity is an ancient layer of Japanese historical awareness. Continuity is the form and substance of salvation, while discontinuity is damnation. The word "next-next" *(tsugi-tsugi)* without the disturbance of a cutting point embodies happiness. This emotional commitment to continuity survived through Hiroshima, the unconditional surrender, the emperor's humanity declaration, and the International Military Tribunal for the Far East (Seven A-class war criminals were hanged on December 23, 1948. More than 1,000 B- and C-class criminals were executed in various former war locations). The Japanese emotional attachment to continuity has made possible a passage from fertility myth to political myth of imperial absolutism. As heaven, the ultimate source of fertility, continues without fail, so does the imperial glory of the emperor, the son of heaven. The prestige of continuity—"seated on the throne of a line unbroken for ages eternal"—confers the political quality of absolute authority.

War and Guilt (*Senso to Zaiseki*, 1998) by Masaaki Noda, a scholar in comparative cultures and psychologies, observes the persistent tendency to suppress guilt awareness among Japanese. Guilt consciousness and emotional attachment to continuity do not form a good combination. Noda significantly points out that this suppression is done in the context of a psychological swing between inferiority and superiority complexes. The swing often is accompanied by the psychology of *amae*, the strategic use of the psychology of dependence to force an injured party to be lenient to the guilty self. Seen in this way, the Japanese *psyche* may be considered structurally irresponsible. Noda pursues this theme in his many revealing (and shocking!) dialogues with former soldiers who personally committed atrocities in China during the war years. This clinical sociopsychology of the Japanese people caught nationwide attention, much as *Silence* by Shusaku Endo did three decades ago. Both critically explored the encounter between the Japanese *psyche* and the biblical commandment of discontinuity and negation: "You shall have no other gods before me." Saburo Ienaga's *Development of the Logic of Negation* (*Hitei no Ronri no Hattatsu*, 1983) says that the logic of negation first came to Japanese people through Buddhism. Continuity optimism, however, has remained a stronger force in Japanese social and psychological history.

David Kwang-sun Suh writes of his preacher father,

> My father truly believed that Shinto worship or the thought that the Japanese emperor was divine was wrong because it was idol worship. He himself refused to attend Shinto shrine worship with other preachers in town. He was taken by the Japanese police and beaten up. I remember my father saying that the Japanese police asked him, Who is higher, the Christian God or the Japanese emperor? His answer was clear and stubborn: Of course the Christian God is much higher than any human being, and the Japanese emperor is just a human being.

Then he concludes,

> To bow down to the Shinto shrine was not only a religious act of idol worship, like worshipping woods, stones, or graven images, it was also a political

act of idol worship—like heiling Hitler. Refusal of the Shinto shrine was a matter of *status confessionis* for Korean Christians under Japanese occupation.[6]

When "something essentially conditioned is taken as unconditional," idolatry appears, and from it emerges violence. The rejection of such idolatry was the *status confessionis* of Korean Christians under the Japanese occupation. I wish to make a few observations.

First, how is it that pantheistic/polytheistic Japan, far distanced from the "you shall have no other gods before me" of Judaism, Christianity, and Islam, *can* commit the sin of idolatry? *Can* a nation commit idolatry without knowing the true God? The response to this may be deceptively simple. It is possible to reap the destructive result of idolatry without knowing its theological structure. Twentieth-century Japan is the case in point.

"Who is higher, the Christian God or the Japanese emperor?" In Japan the same question sent many Christians to prison. In 1942, one hundred sixteen members of the Japan Holiness Church were arrested, eighty-one of them were indicted, and twenty-nine were imprisoned, some of whom died in prison.[7] It is especially significant, however, that people of other religions in Japan were suppressed also. The leaders of *Ohmotokyo* were arrested, tortured, and imprisoned in 1921 and 1935 for rejecting the imperial cult.[8] The question "Who is higher, the Christian God or the Japanese emperor?" hits Christians directly, but other religious leaders were also critical of the imperial cult on the basis of human freedom. The *status confessionis* can be shared with people of conscience.

Second, I would name the imperial cult of twentieth-century Japan a wretched fact of history comparable to the ancient Roman imperial cult and the contemporary Heil Hitler cult. The Japanese cult was a phenomena of the swing between inferiority and superiority complexes, which is an expression of Japanese insular parochialism. The swing makes this parochialism feverish and toxic in international relationships. It exposes the demonic side of the continuity metaphysics. For more than three hundred years, from 1622 when fifty-five Japanese Catholics or *kirishitans* suffered martyrdom in Nagasaki to 1945 when Nagasaki was blasted by the nuclear bomb, Japan lived in a lamentable deficiency in the education of internationality. Between 1910 and 1945, Japanese fanatic inferiority/superiority swing was directed to its ancient cultural mother, Korea, and Korea was ravaged. Parochialism is, by nature, violent. It tends to breed false transcendence.

Third, while universality—"In everything do to others as you would have them do to you; for this is the law and the prophets" (Matt. 7:12, Luke 6:31)—may make a significant appeal to individual personal consciences, collective groups, such as nations, as Reinhold Niebuhr observed, are impervious to such appeal. Surely some Japanese personally lamented the atro-

41

cious Japanese rule over Korea, as some did with the 1937 Rape of Nan-jing, but as a nation, Japan went through these times without a hint of compunction. Nations behave immorally and egocentrically. Political power thrives as it ignores the golden rule. The higher continental civilization taught the early Japanese about the philosophy of the golden rule as reflected in the Article 17 of the Constitution of 604 of Prince Shotoku. But not until the experience of unconditional surrender in 1945, more than thirteen centuries later, did Japan for the first time speak a universal language, meaningful to the international community—"We believe that no nation is responsible to itself alone, but that laws of political morality are universal" (Preamble, the 1946 Constitution of Japan). At the cost of enormous destruction in Asian nations, Japan finally came to this principle of universality. History, however, continues. Their own words must now remain as a direct challenge to the Japanese conscience—its collective national conscience.

History continues, obviously, but I feel that the experience of history in Japan has become thin and flimsy after August 15, 1945. There must be two kinds of history, as there are two kinds of religion—authentic and inauthentic. True religion desires true history. False religion colludes with false history. Salvation for humanity is in the former, not in the latter. In order to reject false history, we need a true religion that creates "a truth and reconciliation commission" to judge false, hence violent, history, as demonstrated recently in the Republic of South Africa. When false history is judged—when Japan repents for what she has done to Korea—then authenticity will return to Japanese history. In 1995, the fiftieth year of the ending of the Japanese colonialism, the Korean people were disappointed in not hearing an official word of apology from Tokyo. The *status confessionis* has an ecumenical mission of bringing truth and reconciliation into the world.

Finally, though the Roman, German, and Japanese examples of imperial cult are drastic, the logic of the emperor cult is universally present in the political life of many human groupings. It is a tragic dimension of human civilization that idolatry is inevitably present in civilization as long as there is power in human society. All civilizations are dangerously ambiguous. The studies of history and of a theology of *status confessionis* go together.

––––––

Since the life of Jesus, as narrated in the apostolic tradition, came to end in the violence of crucifixion, the Christian faith tradition has a special proximity to the reality of violence in the world. The crucified Christ, a scandalous symbol of righteous judgment (1 Cor. 1:18–25), exposes the sin of fabricated transcendence. Here we may have a glimpse of the *true* transcendence. False transcendence terrorizes people.

The Terror of History and the Memory of Redemption: Engaging the Ambiguities of the Christian Past

Dale T. Irvin

For our purpose, only one question concerns us: How can the "terror of history" be tolerated from the viewpoint of historicism? Justification of a historical event by the simple fact that it is a historical event, in other words, by the simple fact that it "happened that way," will not go far toward freeing humanity from the terror that the event inspires. Be it understood that we are not here concerned with the problem of evil, which, from whatever angle it be viewed, remains a philosophical and religious problem; we are concerned with the problem of history as history, of the "evil" that is bound up not with man's condition but with his behavior toward others.

Mircea Eliade[1]

In a series of "Theses on the Philosophy of History" first published in 1940, Walter Benjamin, who was German and Jewish, wrestled with questions of the meaning of history while living through the crisis of the Nazi occupation of Europe. Thesis nine referred to a work by Paul Klee entitled "Angelus Novus," a painting of a celestial being whom Benjamin interprets as the angel of history. The face of the angel is turned toward the past, Benjamin tells us, its gaze fixed upon the catastrophes of human history that have piled up before it in a single, continuous heap of wreckage at its feet. The angel itself is helpless to act, its wings fixed open by the winds of a storm that blows across the ages from humanity's originating paradise. These winds propel the angel unwillingly into the future toward which its back is turned, as the pile of debris before it continues to mount toward the sky. "This storm is what we call progress," Benjamin concludes.[2]

The image is arresting. Progress, that great liberating dream of the modern era, turns out to be a windstorm of destructive proportions piling high the debris of ruined lives and cultures across the historical landscape. In one sense the destruction of the past five centuries has been all the greater precisely because of the grip that the myth of progress has held over so many. Yet it is not only the modern era that has experienced such winds. Indeed, one could argue with Eliade that it is "history as history," the collective experience of humanity's behavior toward itself in its multifaceted dimensions, that is the storm. The winds originated from paradise, but they blow across the landscape of the ages. Any religious or philosophical movement that has filled its sails with these winds and cast its lot with salvation in history has shared in the ambivalence of their power.

This is certainly true for the history of Christianity. For two millennia the winds of Christian salvation have blown across regions and cultures throughout the world, sweeping much away in its advance toward the kingdom of God. At times the winds have been refreshing, but they have just as often been winds of carnage and destruction. At times the storm of Christianity has approached terrorizing proportions, adding to the victims and catastrophes piled before the angel's feet. Yet just as frequently Christians have been among those working to end the violence and mend the destruction unleashed upon history by these forces. Quite often Christians have been numbered among those victims of history piled at the angel's feet.

R. Scott Appleby has recently grappled with these ambiguities, suggesting that this "paradoxical legacy" of religion lies not so much in the nature of the sacred as it does in the "ambivalent character of human responses to it."[3] Drawing upon Rudolf Otto's *The Idea of the Holy,* Appleby argues that the sacred is a mystery that transcends the categories of historical experience. As such, it encompasses both life and death and manifests itself in ways that are both creative and destructive. The sacred is *mysterium tremendum,* a mystery that is "awesome" in both senses of inspiring dread and fascination.[4] Religion, a collective human endeavor shaped in response to the sacred amidst the contingency of history, reflects the ambiguity of that experience.[5] Appleby points out:

> Most religious societies, in fact, have interpreted their experience of the sacred in such a way as to give religion a paradoxical role in human affairs—as the bearer of peace *and* the sword. These apparently contradictory orientations reflect a continuing struggle within religions—and within the heart of each believer—over the meaning and character of the power encountered in the

sacred and its relationship to coercive force or violence. . . . Rather than a direct translation of the "mind of God" into human action, religion is a far more ambiguous enterprise, containing *within itself* the authority to kill and to heal, to unleash savagery, or to bless humankind with healing and wholeness,[6]

Having said that, Appleby does not simply abandon his readers to the ambiguities of history, but calls upon us to make an option for reconciliation amidst the struggle. "Within each of these great traditions, notwithstanding their profound substantive differences, one can trace a moral trajectory challenging adherents to greater acts of compassion, forgiveness, and reconciliation," he writes.[7] The ambivalence of religious traditions provides him with an invitation and an opportunity to work against the terrors of history, doing so by strengthening the moral trajectories of peacemaking and justice.

The Moral Trajectory of Christianity

Among the religious traditions of the world, the moral trajectory of Christianity is unique in finding its starting point in the experience of Jesus of Nazareth, who was a crucified one. His contemporaries knew him first as a healer who brought a word of hope to those outside the boundaries of moral society in his day, yet a confrontation with the main custodians of religious tradition led to his arrest. Accused of making a terroristic threat against the temple, the institution at the center of the religious economy of Jewish life, Jesus was handed over to the Roman authorities who had him tortured and crucified on a cross.[8] No angel of history intervened to stop the terror that descended on Jesus, who was numbered among the victims of history.

The moral trajectory of the Christian movement thus begins with a victim of terror; but it then moves to transform victimhood into triumph. Three days later, the early Christian witness tells us, angels stood at the mouth of an empty tomb, announcing to the three women who had come to anoint Jesus' body that he was not there. Torture and death had been overcome in the resurrection, which is a sign of God's ultimate intentions for human history. God had raised up the one who was crucified, the early Christian *kerygma* announced, pointing the way into the future that those who sought to follow his moral trajectory were to tread. They could not do so, however, without starting with the memory of one who had experienced terror on a cross.

In this regard it is telling that the early Christian witness did not erase the memory of betrayal and terror, but on the contrary lodged it at the very heart of Christian ritual practices. In their eucharistic meals, Christians continued to recall that "On the night he was betrayed, our Lord Jesus Christ took bread . . ." The creeds Christians learned to recite prior to baptism found their historical reference point in the person of Pontius Pilate, the Roman governor under whom Jesus suffered and died. The cross itself, a powerful symbol of Roman political terror, became a symbol of divine activity and redemption in history for Christians.

The first years of the Christian movement continued to be ones lived in the shadow of violence that was cast by the cross. Christians made a public witness (*marturion* in Greek) in their faith and practice, for which they were exposed to political violence. Persecution at the hands of the authorities was interpreted as a means of purifying belief, validating faith, and participating in the life of Jesus. By the second century, martyrdom, that ultimate form of witness in the face of a hostile state, was playing a significant role in the formation of Christian identity.[9] Christians in the Roman world became targets of violence because of their refusal to join in the worship of the imperial gods. The charge against them was "atheism," which, in light of the role that these gods were perceived to play in maintaining the cohesion and well-being of the empire, was nothing short of "terrorism." Imperial officials thus felt perfectly justified in administering torture and death to people such as Christians who had endangered the welfare of the state. Those who suffered at the hands of their persecutors perceived things to be otherwise, of course.

Persecution and martyrdoms were local and sporadic at first in the Roman empire. Only after the year 200 were empire-wide efforts launched to eradicate the Christian religion, and even then they were of short duration. When persecution and martyrdoms did occur, they served to strengthen the movement overall. One reason that is often given is the courage that Christian martyrs displayed in the face of the "counter-terrorist" measures launched against them by imperial Rome. Such martyrs were more than inspirational figures of Christian virtue. They were considered holy people because of the violence they had endured and overcome. Since they shared in Christ's suffering, they shared in his glory, a spiritual endowment that often raised them above bishops in the hierarchy of holiness in the church.[10] Hippolytus's *Apostolic Constitutions,* a handbook on church discipline written early in the third century after a period of persecution in Rome, informs us that, regarding ordination to the priesthood, those who had suffered for the faith but were not put to death (the "confessors") were not to have hands laid on them, for they had already been ordained by their suffering.

It is important to note here that suffering itself was not seen as redemptive. Suffering that was experienced apart from Christ had little Christian value. Tribulation might be the fire that burned away the dross and thereby allowed the gold to shine pure, but it was not necessarily in and of itself a thing that was good. Only suffering that was endured on account of one's Christian confession or identity was theologically meaningful, because it had been transformed.[11] Such suffering for the sake of Christ provided an opportunity for one's confession of Christ to be tested. Endurance to the point of death demonstrated Christ to be greater than the violence of the world. The triumph of Christ over evil was thereby demonstrated in each occasion where Christians suffered for their faith but maintained their confession. This political terror transformed into a means by which God's triumph in history was made manifest.

Stories of martyrdom in early Christian experience were means of creating faithfulness in their readers and hearers. Through these narratives, others vicariously shared in the transformation of terror into glory to be experienced in the life to come. With their supporters, martyrs approached their own death as if it were a sacred liturgy, providing the community with ongoing symbols of self-sacrifice.[12] The cult of the martyrs located its followers within a perspective gained from the victims of political violence, thereby exposing the ideological dimensions of imperial terror.[13] In doing so, it inscribed their subjectivity and agency in the process of redemption, opening up a new Christian moral trajectory in history.

Given the authority the early Christian cult of the martyrs exercised within churches, it is all the more surprising how quickly a majority of Christian leaders in the Mediterranean region succeeded in transforming this religion into a vehicle of Roman imperial power. The story is familiar to students of church history. Persecution failed to stem the growth of the Christian movement in the third century in the Greco-Roman world. Included among the ranks of the believers were an increasing number of members from the upper classes. Churches became more visible, and clergy even began to be gain respect as public figures. A last effort to stem the growing tide was launched in the first decade of the fourth century amidst a period of severe internal crisis in the empire. Into this situation stepped Constantine, who first legalized, and then over the course of three decades came increasingly to embrace, Christianity as the official faith of the imperial household. Not only were churches granted legal permission to own property, but clergy began to receive support from the imperial treasury. Bishops were empowered to act as judges to hear civil cases, while one of their number was elevated to the ranks of a close imperial advisor.

Barely six months after legalizing the Christian religion, Constantine was asked to intervene directly in a controversy disrupting the churches in Roman North Africa. The immediate occasion was the disputed election of a new senior bishop in Carthage. Behind it was a divide opening up within the churches between those who welcomed the new arrangements and those who held steadfast to the memory and morality of the generations of martyrs before them. There were a host of other factors involved in the dispute between the Catholic and Donatist parties (as they came to be respectively known in North Africa). At the heart was the issue, how-

47

ever, of the memory of terror. Since their first days, Christians had maintained their life through an ethic of resistance and imperial opposition. The Donatists were merely continuing that tradition. The Catholic party did not abandon the memory of martyrdoms, but took the position that the opposition it represented could give way to accommodation. As historian Maureen A. Tilley notes, "The attitude of the Catholic Church to the Roman Empire was modified after 312, while the Donatists retained the antithesis preached by Tertullian and Cyprian."[14]

Ironically, it was the Donatist party who appealed first to the emperor to intervene in the case. Constantine turned to other church leaders, most notably the bishop of Rome, to decide on the matter. On the advice of councils held on two different occasions, the emperor sided against the Donatists. Before long he had dispatched imperial troops to suppress them for disturbing the peace, confiscating their properties and exiling their leaders. Violence and even death were now for the first time employed in the name of Christian unity, on behalf of a Christian imperial state.

By the end of the fourth century the transformation was complete. A new imperial Roman Christian order was firmly in place. Jews and other religious people became the targets of state-sanctioned terrorism for practicing their faith. Leaders of various Christian parties who were judged to be deficient in their Christian teaching or practice—heretics and schismatics—were stripped of their offices and forced into exile. Theologians of the church began to debate the sanctioned use of violence to achieve ends that were considered justified and compatible with the ultimate ends that God intended for creation.

What is startling in this history is the rapidity with which the church leadership of all persuasions succumbed to the seductions of imperial power. Within a generation Catholic church leaders who had faced persecution and death were praying for the welfare of the emperor and his armies. Exceptions can be found, but by the end of the fourth century most bishops and theologians in the Roman world had embraced the use of exile and even death as a justified means for securing orthodox belief. Nor was it only the Catholic church leaders who did so. Many among the dissenters who were being labeled heretics appealed to the same emperors and were ready to embrace the same mechanisms of violence to further their cause. The fact that the formerly-persecuted so easily turned to embrace persecution while the persecuted themselves did not shrink from the exercise of violence only serves to bolster Appleby's thesis regarding the ambivalence of the sacred and the manner in which contradictory impulses for and against violence are so intertwined within religion.

It is this same ambivalence, and the fact that Christian tradition is internally plural, that provides us an invitation to read the Christian historical archive for its alternative trajectories. The memory of early Christian martyrdom continued to inform several of these trajectories under changing historical conditions after the fourth century. One of these trajectories was in the rapidly expanding ranks of monasticism, the first alternative I will sketch out here. Asceticism had grown in concert with martyrdom in the early centuries of Christian experience. Those who denied the desires of the flesh in order to follow Christ, or who abandoned wealth and family in order to serve the community as a whole, were models of living sacrifice. After physical martyrdoms ended among Catholic communities under the Roman empire in the fourth century, the spiritual practices of monastic self-sacrifice accelerated in growth. Monasticism carried on this vision of self-sacrifice and virtue that was capable of transforming the sufferings of this world into glory. Women and men in great numbers and in every branch of the Christian movement after the fourth century devoted themselves to such practices that were intended to crucify the desires of the flesh in order to gain one access to a higher level of spiritual life.

Christianity and Other Religions

Not all Christians lived in regions of the world that fell within Roman imperial boundaries in the fourth century. Significant communities of Christians had formed within the Persian empire where they experienced a relative degree of toleration during their first years. A new Persian dynasty, known as the Sassanids, came to power in 225, however, and moved to reestablish Zoroastrianism as the national religion. The Sassanids paid little attention to Christians at first, but following Constantine's conversion, persecution in the Persian empire began.[15] For several centuries Christians lived under varying conditions of hostility and violence in this eastern empire. Nevertheless, by the time of the Arab conquest in the seventh century, Christians had grown (by some accounts) to number a majority of those living in Persia.

The Arab conquest and Islamic government brought new challenges not only to Christians in Persia but in Syria, Palestine, Egypt, and eventually Anatolia, and even Greece. As a "protected people" *(dhimmi)*, Christians had legal status under Islam, allowing them to practice their faith under restricted conditions. Among the restrictions were prohibitions against evangelizing and against uttering statements that were considered blasphemous against Muhammad. While conversion from Christianity to Islam was usually welcomed by Islamic rulers, conversion from Islam to Christianity was punishable by death. Muslim rulers publicly denounced Christian belief in the Trinity and the divine nature of Jesus Christ, but Christians and Jews were forbidden to disparage Muhammad or the Islamic faith pain of death. Around the twin practices of evangelism and public confession of faith a new tradition of martyrdom emerged in the Christian communities living under

49

Islamic rule. These new practices maintained a tradition of witness against the coercive power of a state acting on behalf of a universal religious belief.[16] This second moral trajectory, constituted by Christian communities living under hostile political regimes and exposed to periods of persecution, has emerged anew in the past century in various parts of the world as a living spiritual practice.

After the fourth century, imperial Christendom in the Roman world in both of its major branches (the Latin-Germanic West and the Byzantine East) continued to support the use of political measures of violence and even terror as a means of securing orthodox adherence to faith. Both continued to be home to Christian traditions that deviated from the majority orthodox consensus (in other words, heresies) as well as other religions (most notably, Judaism). Heretics and Jews within Christendom were continuously targets of violence and terror. Laws were issued and popular riots fomented against them. The reasons were not just economic or political, but were spiritual and theological in nature. At stake was the question of the possibility of ever attaining a truly Christian society, a Christian kingdom, a Christian land.

The last decade of the eleventh century opened a new chapter in what had already by then been a long, bloody tale of sacralized violence in the West. Pope Urban II had just concluded presiding over a regional synod at Clermont, France, in November of 1095 when he called for a crusade to recapure the Holy Land. A number of historical factors converged in the call. Iberia and Palestine were both perceived to be lands that once were Christian and had belonged to the Christian political empire on earth. The call for a crusade was literally the call to put these lands once again under the dominion of the cross of Jesus Christ ("crusade" comes from the Latin word *crux, cruzada* in Spanish). For a generation, popes had been engaged in a struggle with Christian kings across western Europe regarding the proper ordering of a Christian society, specifically whether or not Christian kings (who were members of the laity) could invest ecclesiastical appointments with the symbols of power and authority in their spiritual offices. For Urban II and the reforming popes of his period, power flowed from God through the priestly offices of the church and into the wider temporal world of kings and rulers. The violence that the kings and warriors exercised could be infused with sacred meaning by the church. Crusading meant warfare conducted under the authority of (and thus sanctified by) the cross. The terror of Holy War was the result.

Islam in its own way had sanctioned organized practices of violence prior to the Crusades. The Qu'ran itself instructed believers to use force to defend and extend the rule of divine law. The exercise of force for such ends, called *jihad* in Arabic (meaning "strife" or "effort"), could be nonviolent in character, as when one strove against wicked desires within oneself or when one strove to convince others of the error of their ways. The Qu'ran drew no line between violent and nonviolent methods for practicing *jihad*, however, nor did it suggest that such violence should only be understood metaphorically. The distinction that emerged within Islam between dimensions of political rule and community practice of religious life, conceptualized as the *dar al-Islam* ("the house of Islam") and *ummah* ("community"), served this purpose instead. Muhammad and his first successors institutionalized violence as a political practice and interpreted their military victories as a sign of divine favor. They distinguished the imposition of Islamic law upon a society from the practices of the community worshipping God, however, leaving the latter relatively uninstitutionalized. Within Sunni Islam (the majority tradition), Imams, who serve as leaders of the community that gathers at the mosque for prayer, had little occasion to be instruments of terror.

Over time these distinctions within Islam tended to break down or were disregarded by rulers who did not shy away from using holy means to incite violence. By the twelfth century of the Christian era, the mantle of *jihad* was as easy to spread as the cloak of Crusading. Muslims could respond, of course, that the Crusades were an unprovoked invasion of territory that had been liberated from corrupt Christian rulers six hundred years before. Muslims were only acting in self-defense. Little in the way of religious incentive was needed to stir Islamic defenders of their territory.

The Crusades had relatively little impact upon Islam in the long run. Far more decisive for shifting the meaning of *jihad* in the direction of terror was the advance of Western colonial rule and the accompanying impact of modern Western culture upon the Islamic world in the nineteenth century. By contrast, the Crusades had a tremendous impact upon Western European life in all of its dimensions: political, social, cultural, commercial, and religious. By fusing pilgrimage with militaristic violence, they recast the meaning of both. Those who would be pilgrims and missionaries thereafter found it necessary to defend why either should be conducted without violence. The Crusade proclaimed by Pope Urban II was invisioned as a two-pronged attack against the Muslims who ruled Spain and Palestine. Indulgences were granted equally to those who went into each arena of holy warfare. A century later, the cover of crusading, with the necessary arrangements for indulgences, was provided to justify a war of aggression launched against non-Christian Wends living in lands adjacent to Western Christian kings. Four hundred years after Urban II preached his memorable sermon, Europeans were still on a Crusade when they landed in the Caribbean and opened up a new chapter in the history of the world.

Within European society the first Crusade turned out also to be a war on Jews in the Rhineland. A century later the mechanisms of Crusade were used to launch a civil war against the Cathars in southern France. An estimated twenty thousand innocent victims were killed, mostly for holding religious beliefs the church deemed heretical. Once the concept of the Crusade at home

51

was in place, it was easy to establish it as a permanent factor in religious and social life. Thus was born the Inquisition, an institution that was a permanent vehicle for the Crusade against unbelief within Christendom. Heretics were its permanent obsession. Some suffered mutilation, others underwent trials by ordeal, and still others were eventually burned at the stake.

The tradition of persecution and terror within Western Christendom did not end with the period of the Renaissance and Reformation. The city councils and ruling princes of the territories that adopted evangelical reforms did not hesitate to enforce their new orthodoxies with exile and executions. Not even the emergence of the secular state following the Enlightenment stemmed the ever-flowing tides of organized violence carried out in the name of God. New reigns of terror were unleashed by so-called Christian powers in the conquests of the Americas, justified on religious as well as political and economic grounds. The African slave trade was defended in part as a potential means for Christianizing heathens. The new colonial enterprises Europeans undertook in the nineteenth century did the same. Christian terror against Jews reached its demonic depths in the Holocaust of the twentieth century.

Read against the background of the memory of Jesus in the New Testament and the martyrs of early Christian experience, the history of the victims of Christendom's terror over seventeen centuries of time carries with it a profound moral judgment that disturbs any triumphal notion of Christian progress or achievement today. The voices of the victims of Christendom cry out too loudly not to be heard. The moral trajectory of the victims of Christian violence might seem at first to be an unwarranted source upon which to draw for contemporary Christian reflection, yet it is precisely because of the ambivalence of the Christian response to the sacred that we not only can but must do so. The witness of Christendom's victims, of its "others" who have been rendered the object of its violence and terror, provides the standpoint for moral judgment against the dominant traditions, which means also its redemption. Christendom did not seek to erase the memory of its victims; on the contrary, it often maintained it triumphantly as part of its historiography of victory over disbelief. Ironically, the victims of Christendom's collective terror witness against it by occupying the moral place in which Jesus, who was crucified "outside the city gate" (Heb. 13:12–13), stood. That same memory and witness must continue to be maintained if Christian history is to find its redemption and to prove itself to be in any way redemptive.

Finding Meaning for Today

Recognizing the ambiguities of the Christian past but seeking to follow a moral trajectory of reconciliation and peace, I suggest three historiographical principles to inform our historical interpretations and practices today. The first is a commitment to refuse to sanction violence as a holy act. Whenever violence is sacralized, such as when it is regarded as an expression of divine justice, the pathway to terror is opened up. Too often religion has provided ideological justification of violence by ascribing sacred connotations to it.[17] Christendom's rulers often justified the punishment of those perceived to be the historical enemies of Christ by making recourse to the biblical images of Christ the king, for instance. The triumph of Christ in eternity over evil was cited to justify attempts to realize the triumph of his rule over those who opposed him in history. Any who denied the divine person Jesus Christ were by definition his enemies, as were any who denied the authority of those to whom Jesus entrusted on earth the rule of his kingdom.

Christian ethicists have long struggled with the question of whether the use of violence can be justified under certain historical conditions where the good of preserving innocent life will be realized. Debates such as these over "just war" are far too extensive to rehearse here.[18] Suffice it to note that one can advance arguments for the justified use of force and violence, such as in cases of legitimate self-defense, without seeking to deny the ambiguity that attends them. Indeed, it has often been noted that society itself is impossible apart from fundamental acts of self-surrender, and that human community cannot be constituted and sustained apart from the gestures of renunciation by which human beings defer to one another.[19] These are acts that constitute a degree of violence directed by the self against one's self or against those who are considered constitutive of one's self. Violence and punishment in this sense need to be analytically distinguished from the self-discipline and self-sacrifice by which the overall well-being of a community is advanced. The equation changes drastically whenever these acts are no longer voluntary gestures, but are imposed. When the latter becomes translated into transcendent dimensions, a different understanding of divine life and well-being emerges. God now appears to be saving the world by punishing evildoers rather than saving the world through acts of self-giving.

The second historiographical principle to be observed is that one needs to hold on to what Reinhold Niebuhr termed an "ironic view" of history, or what Cornel West calls the "tragic sensibility" of African-American thought.[20] The ironic or tragic sensibility is not that of Greek drama where a fatal moral flaw within the character of the protagonist evoked sympathy for the hero who was crushed. Suffering in such cases is rendered meaningful by the application of an equation of moral balance. The same moral equation is often found in the biblical tradition as a justification for suffering. But alongside this, one finds in the Bible another tradition that wrestles more emphatically with the question of undeserved suffering. It is here that Niebuhr and West both find their reference point: for Niebuhr, the transformation of divine judgment into divine mercy; for West, the "African slaves' search for collective identity" that found "historical purpose in the exodus of Israel out of slavery and personal meaning in the bold identification of Jesus Christ with the lowly."[21]

Such an interpretive move invites one to take up an activist stance against suffering in the world without succumbing to nihilism or despair when suffering is not overcome. Revolutionary patience, says West, is a required accompaniment of a tragic sensibility. Progress is taken out of human hands, but in its place is found a promise amidst the piled catastrophes of history. It is God who judges with mercy and promises to deliver the oppressed from the violence of their history, thereby allowing us to act and hope from within the confines of the ambiguities of our particular age.

Hope must always be coupled with remembrance, the third historiographical principle I would suggest as a necessary component for those who would seek to mend the terror of their historical ways. For Christians, faithful remembrance of the past is a spiritual exercise freighted with eucharistic overtones ("do this in remembrance of me"). The "real presence" of Christ in history is found in such acts of remembrance. On the one hand, the greater part of Christian tradition would push us toward remembering one who was like us but different, and whose "otherness" becomes continuously inscribed within social life at its margins. This in itself is reason to remember the plurality of Christian histories, and especially those "little traditions" that have maintained a vital witness against violence and terror.[22] One thinks here of Mennonites, Quakers, and others within the wider Christian community that have maintained an active witness on behalf of Christian pacifism over the centuries. Moreover, we who are Christians are compelled to remember those who were the victims of our chosen religion's violence in the past. Anamnestic solidarity with the victims of Christian terror forms part of the practice of overcoming the terror of Christian history.

I began this essay with a quotation from Mircea Eliade. Eliade suggested that historical consciousness itself is a product of the terror of history, of the disorientation caused by humanity being thrown out of Eden and into the land of Nod. As a historical faith, Christianity enabled one to live in a fallen world where terror reigned, doing so by offering a vigorous doctrine of sin, he believed. Eliade hinted that he believed the terror of history could be overcome only by a return to an archaic human consciousness of mythical proportions, one that offered transhistorical valuation in the form of cosmic or eternal return. Here I would respectfully disagree with Eliade, not regarding the terror that an unmitigated encounter with history brings with it, but that the means of overcoming terror lies beyond history.

Terror holds the human captive by denying the transcendence that is found within life. The purpose of political acts of terrorism is often explained as being to disrupt existing systems of power, to instill fear in others, or (in the case of state terrorism) to attempt to deter further actions on the part of dissident or deviant individuals. These explanations do not fathom the full depths of such acts. The practice of terror seeks not only to inflict severe pain, but to eradicate the humanity and to erase the memory of its victims. This is why it is so often practiced in secret, its victims disappearing in the night without a public trace; or why it is so often practiced anonymously, its victims randomly selected. Torture is inflicted upon human beings not only (and quite often not at all) to gain desired information or to satisfy depraved sadistic desires. Torture is usually designed to destroy the will, the freedom, and thereby the humanity of those against whom it is directed. So it is with all acts of terror.

Those who died on Roman crosses often had their bodies thrown to the dogs to be eaten. The manner in which the Gospels record Joseph of Arimathea wrapping the body and laying it in his own tomb and the women coming later to anoint the body already witnesses against the terror of the cross and prefigures the experience of Christ's resurrection. Those who were executed for their confession of faith at the hands of hostile governments were expected to serve as a warning to others who might likewise challenge political authority. The manner in which the memory of the martyrs stirred others to faithfulness directly contradicted the intentions of the executioners. Those who were burned at the stake as heretics often had their ashes scattered to prevent their followers from collecting their bones and making a shrine out of them. The manner in which we continue to search the historical records of Christendom for the names of such heretics suggests a faithfulness that transcends that of the tradition itself.

In each of these cases it is finally the act of faithfully remembering the suffering of the past that points the way toward redemption in history. Freedom from terror is impossible apart from such redemption. Its promise thus takes us back to the terrors of history continuously. Our hope is not found in terror in the end, but in the humanity we discover amidst those whose lives have been shaped by it. This is why in the Gospel of Luke, when Jesus showed his scarred hands and feet, his disciples responded with joy (Luke 24:40–41). "Progress" might well be the winds of the storm that propels the angel of history helplessly backwards into the future, but hope is found in the scarred lives piled before it, those victims of the catastrophes of history whom we continue to name and remember.

Troubled
but Not Destroyed:
A Reflection on Terror
and Redemption
in Contemporary Africa

Akintunde E. Akinade

Introduction

It is not mere happenstance that the central theme of the seventh General Assembly of the All Africa Conference of Churches, in October 1997, in Addis Ababa, Ethiopia was "Troubled, But Not Destroyed." This compelling theme vigorously invokes what Cornel West has aptly described as the "tragic predicament"[1] that bedevils people from the underside of history. The contemporary African continent is saddled with many manifestations and symptoms of the wretched of the earth. This is why the *New York Times Review of Books* can write without any cant that Sierra Leone is the worst place on earth,[2] and the *Economist* can unequivocally label Africa as "the hopeless continent."[3] A cursory look at the situation in many African countries will reveal many mysterious imponderables and many societal conundrums that will amaze anyone used to the normal order of logic. Many countries in sub-Saharan Africa are caught in the vicious circle of corruption, sociopolitical inertia, economic retrogression, and senseless ethnic and religious conflagration.

Any Christian theologian is bound to ask the nerve-wracking question: What's the role of the good news amid this situation of death and misery? Is it possible to envisage or conceptualize any symphony of hope out of the cacophony of terror within the African continent? My paper takes a look at some of the issues that are germane to an authentic prophetic theology in African today. I posit that in spite of the fact that Africans are confronted with what Emmanuel Lévinas has called "useless suffering," they are giving new and radical meaning to the words of Romans 8:18: "The sufferings of this present time are not worth comparing with the glory about to be revealed to us." This is not a fatalistic disposition but a persistent struggle to transform the horrors of servitude into a symphony of freedom and wholeness.

The Cry for Life

It seems to me that the African cry for life from the belly of the whale has consistently fallen on deaf ears. I am using the belly of the whale as a metaphor for the suffocating sociopolitical and economic situation in Africa today. In the political sphere, many African countries continue to serve as the expendable pawn in the political chessboard of Western powers. In terms of the economic situation, they are caught up in the economic manipulations of the World Bank and the International Monetary Fund (IMF). Foreign aid has become the monster that gives even viable African nations stupendous nightmares and trepidation. It has been used as the bait that will enable African people to be constantly tied to the apron strings of the "venerable" Western powers. In essence, foreign aid has inevitably converted many African nations to perpetual babies that must be spoon-fed and taught how to walk.

Africans are under the tight and unrelenting grip of a market economy that is being directly monitored and controlled by the financial giants of the powerful countries. It is clear that under that kind of debilitating economic arrangement, the situation of the poor will not become better. The economic indenture of the IMF and the World Bank have pulverized many African nations, and many of them are just yearning to breathe free.

It is appropriate to add here that the liberation struggle in Africa is not only against the hydra-headed monster of external forces of exploitation; it is also a constant struggle against internal forces of oppression. The oppression of Africans by Africans is a living reality in many countries in Africa today. Military leaders and political elites in many countries continue to plunder their national resources and subject their own people to unimaginable hardship and poverty. Their crass recklessness and myopia have plunged many countries into the abyss of anarchy and horror. Archbishop Desmond Tutu has correctly affirmed that

> too many of our (African) countries are ruled by unrepresentative, corrupt and self-perpetuating, self-enriching authoritarian oligarchies, often main-

tained in power by a military that does nothing to protect the people from external aggression or even from internal insurrection, but are past masters at repression and inequalities of all sorts . . . . They have an enormous appetite for power and once they have tasted it, they are very reluctant to give it up, and find all kinds of excuses to postpone return to civilian rule.[4]

The African renaissance demands that we purge ourselves of the internal diabolical forces that continue to suck the blood of the people. In order not to revisit the horror of the decapitated people of Rwanda, Liberia, Sierra Leone, and Somalia, African people muster the courage to fight and resist all the internal purveyors of death and dehumanization all over Africa.

Terror, Tears, and Torture

In his classic work *Cosmos and History,* Mircea Eliade offers a poignant description of the victims of history as those who know the terror of history firsthand. This is tantalizingly real in the life of African peoples past and present. No doubt, the onslaught of genocidal colonization and neo-colonization has had negative repercussions on the state of African nations and personhood. The "African Report" of the Ecumenical Association of Third World Theologian's Second General Assembly at Oaxtepec gives a comprehensive analysis of the African predicament:

> The social underdevelopment of Africa represents a fundamental aspect of the anthropological pauperization of the African person. If we define pauperization as the fact of becoming or making poor, namely being deprived of all that we have acquired, all that we are and all that we can do, we shall recognize that Africa is subjugated to structures which result in complete pauperization: political, economic, and social. When it is not a matter of being deprived of all that we own, but rather of all that we are—our human identity, our social roots, our history, our culture, our dignity, our rights, our hopes, and our plans—then pauperization becomes anthropological. It then affects religious and cultural life at its very roots.[5]

The pauperization of the African person has been defined in the theological parlance as anthropological poverty. This affects African people at the politicosocioeconomic level and also at the religiocultural level. It is simply an overwhelming assault on the African psyche. I believe that anthropological poverty is analogous to what Orlando Patterson has described as social death.[6] This is borne out of negative self-image of the oppressed. Africans as victims of history have been systematically brutalized and terrorized by forces from within and outside. The struggle against this fundamental problem is the foundation for any prophetic theology in

58

Africa today. This is a task that calls for a holistic analysis of some of the issues and problems in Africa.

The stark reality is that African victims are reeling in a pungent cesspool of dehumanizing poverty, incessant and meaningless *coups d'état*, internecine civil wars, endemic corruption, and economic stagnation. African children are not immune to this reign of terror. Thabo Mbeki once said that "the children of Africa continue to be consumed by death as their limbs are too weak to run away from the rage of adults."[7] The rage of adults in the African situation is an euphemism for madness and tyranny. We continue to witness this show of shame in the large number of children refugees in many parts of Africa. African theologians in the Ecumenical Association of Third World Theologians have further concluded that:

> Among the Third World continents, Africa appears essentially as a land of domination and exploitation, quartered, torn apart, divided, atomized, trampled under foot. It is the continent where frequently the people have no dignity, no rights, and no hope. These challenges are becoming more intolerable considering that natural catastrophes—which are desperately repeated—are added to evils caused by human mischief and injustice.[8]

It is rather unfortunate that the church, which should be the bastion of hope for the people, is also saddled with many problems and contradictions. In order for the churches in Africa to serve as the fountain of hope for the people, it must overcome the problem of *eccelesia militans,* that is, the church in conflict with itself. The African church must be a "listening" church, to borrow a metaphor from the Nigerian Catholic theologian Elochukwu E. Uzukwu, it must have a clear vision, and it must exorcise its own demons. The church must speak out against all forms of oppression that keep people in everlasting bondage. Church leaders cannot afford to keep quiet on issues that have grave implications for the well-being of the people. The church that is also called the body of Christ cannot straddle the fence on matters that are dehumanizing and oppressive. The church has to confidently speak out and defend the poor, the weak, and the exploited. To heal the wounds of Africa, the church must be a credible and competent agent of change by reading the signs of the times and responding prophetically. The African church must embrace the idea that the church should be the *ecclesia reformanda,* the church always in process of being transformed. The third World Council of Churches (WCC) assembly in New Delhi in 1961 said that:

> The assembly wishes only to urge that those who know themselves to be called to the responsibility of Christian witness in their own locality should examine afresh the structures of their church life with a view to meeting the challenge and opportunity of a new day. In a spirit of penitence and of will-

ingness to be led by the Spirit of God into new ways of witness, the whole church must recognize that its divine mission calls for the most dynamic and costly flexibility. . . . Thus the church may become the pilgrim church, which goes forth boldly like Abraham did into the unknown future, not afraid to leave behind the securities of its conventional structures, glad to dwell in the tent of perpetual adaptation, looking to the city whose builder and maker is God.[9]

Rising from the Ashes

At the WCC General Assembly in Harare in 1998, there was an overwhelming affirmation that Africa has started a new agenda of hope. This is a telling testimony to the fact that all is not lost. Africa is bent but not broken! This strong affirmation also confirms the prophetic stance that "We are afflicted in every way, but not crushed; perplexed, but not driven to despair; persecuted, but not forsaken; struck down, but not destroyed; always carrying in the body the death of Jesus, so that the life of Jesus may also be made visible in our bodies . . . so we do not lose heart" (2 Cor. 4:8–10, 16a). Africans are sustained by the christological hope that Jesus is the author of life and he is the only one who has the power over death. The Akan people of Ghana will say that "it is not easy to fell a tree that leans against a rock." The eternal rock in the African situation is Jesus Christ, who is always on the side of the oppressed. This positive perspective is very helpful for an authentic selfhood in Africa. It will inevitably contribute to the development of anthropological dignity or the image of the self that is not catacombed in the moribund categories of inferiority, nihilism, self-hate, and psychological fragmentation. I agree with Jurgen Moltmann that "the missionary proclamation of the cross of the resurrected one is not an opium of the people which intoxicates and anticipates, but the ferment of new freedom."[10] This vision of hope and freedom is not an idyllic "pie in the sky" or a kind of a mysterious *deux ex machina,* but concrete well-being, harmony, and prosperity granted to all and sundry in the community—young and old, poor and affluent. The influence of Jesus is not rigidly confined to the first century; he is active in the struggle of millions of Lazaruses in Africa. He is very active in the tireless efforts of Africans to "make and to keep human life human."[11]

God is with the oppressed in the struggle to cast away the bondage of terror. In Jesus Christ, God takes sides with the forgotten and faceless people of the world. God "has brought down the powerful from their thrones, and lifted up the lowly" (Luke 1:52). The essence of life does not consist in the glorification of mammon and selfish political aggrandizement, but of struggling with God for justice among all peoples. God is vehemently against the forces of death and misery. In Jesus Christ, God provides the power of life over death. "I am the resurrection and the life" (John 11:25). In other words, we can affirm that Jesus Christ as the embodiment of God's justice is our only impetus in the struggle for justice. The gospel story of the life, death, and resurrection of Jesus Christ must serve as the substantive *fons et origo* of hope in the context of the persistent struggle for justice, peace, wholeness, and redemption. Jesus affirmed in word and deed that the primary purpose of his coming was to give life in abundance and fullness to everyone. Jesus came to make the blind see and the lame walk. He also came to bring dignity to the outcast, to set free the downtrodden, and to fight the forces of darkness and terror. "The light shines in the darkness, and the darkness did not overcome it" (John 1:5).

In the New Testament, the cross symbolizes the titanic moral clash with the principalities and powers of this world. The cross also reveals the unavoidable confrontation between the world system of exploitation and the kingdom of God—a confrontation that becomes liberating for the poor and the oppressed. African prophetic theology must be grounded in the amazing assurance that the power of God will overcome and destroy the principalities and powers of this world.

As we encounter situations of poverty and the plethora of other societal problems in Africa, our faith in Jesus Christ compels us to act and do justice. This is a radical faith that compels us to transcend our myopic vision and engage in the liberation of the poor and oppressed. God's redemptive acts performed for the well-being of humanity ought to call forth people whose lives also exhibit that kind of commitment and service—totally dedicated and fully involved. It is imperative for the Christian community to be at the center of the struggle against the wretched of the earth in Africa. Our faith must challenge all the forces and manifestations of death. This means that our faith, which is a gift of God's grace, must move beyond the soporific solidarity with the victims of terror and become the quintessential expression of resistance against terror, misery, and death. Here I can utilize the Tillichian phrase "in spite of" to better capture the resilience of African people. That means that in spite of the pain and meaninglessness in many parts of Africa today, Christians still hold on to a stubborn hope that all is not lost. They are echoing the words of Ernest Bloch that reality or the world is always in a state of flux, it is always changing or becoming otherwise.

The Jubilee Dimension

The biblical understanding of jubilee stipulates that God ordered the protection of the weak, the widow, the vulnerable, and the poor (Exod.

61

23:21–24). The order was unequivocal: You shall not pervert justice (Deut. 16:18). The jubilee command in Leviticus 25:10 demands that in every fiftieth year, slaves were to be freed, debts forgiven, and land given back to their owners. A jubilee year of such grand design has never been witnessed in any place. However, this does not obliterate the idea that the biblical jubilee is based on the idea that God is the absolute controller of everything in the universe. The sovereign source and Lord of life is God. All life ultimately belongs to God. The crux of the issue is that it is very hard for people to fully accept this biblical perspective. Musimbi Kanyoro has rightly observed that "we all claim ownership of something and center our lives on defending the things we think we own."[12] Thus we have arrogated to ourselves the prerogatives of God. A radical *metanoia* must affirm the integrity of God's sovereignty.

The language of jubilee is still very relevant in our world today. Jubilee is the restoration of justice and human wholeness. Walter Brueggemann has rightly observed that the "central vision of world history in the Bible is that all of creation is one, every culture in community with each other, living in harmony and security toward the joy and well-being of every other creature."[13] This is a vision that is much needed in Africa today. The jubilee demands that all slaves must be set free. What are the forms of slavery in contemporary Africa? Musimbi Kanyoro points out:

> The market economy has turned people into commodities. The global trade in children for labour and the entertainment industries is a horrendous form of slavery. The rampant abuse of women in the home through spouse violence or in cultures which deny their personal development are versions of slavery. Women's unvalued and unqualified labour in the home is slavery. The violence in our societies enslaves the mentality of men and keeps them chained to wrongful actions. African families are under constant slavery due to lack of education, shelter, water, health care, food, and, for a large majority, the right to decide their destiny.[14]

The jubilee year invokes a time of renewal, a time of sharing life as God's abundant gift. This is a proclamation of liberation, joy, and justice. It is a time for Africans to turn to God and rejoice in hope. It is also the auspicious time for African people to ask how the continent can overcome a series of perennial problems—starvation, the AIDS epidemic, internecine warfare, political instability, refugee problems, and many others. It is a time to refocus on the problems of the needy in African societies.

It is indeed the Kairos moment that can enable Africans to think about ways to be self-reliant and stop depending on peanuts from the Western world. Jubilee will be irrelevant if Africa cannot get rid of the shackles of dependency and perpetual slavery. The life and ministry of Jesus Christ compels us to live every year as a jubilee year full of grace and pregnant with purpose and possibilities. This will enable us to boldly respond to the gargantuan challenges of living in Africa today. I believe that this is the essence of the good news. In Jesus' jubilee, those normally denied access to joy and celebration can partake in the blessings of the society. In fact, when Jesus feasted with the "rich and powerful" of his day, he invited them to offer a jubilee experience to the downtrodden (Luke 14:12–14). Without any equivocation, the biblical vision of jubilee gives hope to people struggling for justice and the affirmation of life.

A New Anthropology

The call for a prophetic theology in Africa demands a new theological anthropology. We need a new understanding of the *imago Dei* and the meaning of community. In order to achieve any form of anthropological dignity, Africans have to fully come to terms with what it means to be human and to be created in the image of God. I believe that in our quest to establish a new identity for ourselves and our society, we must revisit our African values and ethos as well as the basic teachings of the Christian faith. We need to resuscitate the African values of love, justice, and togetherness. Traditionally, African societies are based on what Kwesi Dickson has described as communal equilibrium.

> A society (community) is in equilibrium when its customs are maintained, its goals attained and spirits powers given regular and adequate recognition. Members of society (community) are expected to live and to act in such a way as to promote society's (community's) well-being; to do otherwise is to court disaster, not only for the individual actor but for the (community) as a whole. Any act that detracts from the soundness of a (community) is looked upon with disfavour, and (the community) takes remedial measures to reverse the evil consequences set in motion.[15]

The South African ethos and philosophy of *Ubuntu* (humanity) evokes the African ideal of community and interrelationships. Communality, relationality, and fundamental connectedness undergird the African mode of seeing and being in the world. To be is to live in community and work for the total well-being of that community. There is no gainsaying the fact that the onslaught of Western industrial capitalism has undermined the traditional African sense of community, but there must be a concerted effort to regain and reclaim the African model of redemptive harmony. Robert Bellah has provided some credence to the viability and importance of retrieving communal ethos and moral ideals. He believes that

63

communities in the sense in which we are using the term, have a history—in an important sense they are constituted by their past—and for this reason we can speak of a real community as a "community of memory," one that does not forget its past. In order not to forget that past, a community is involved in retelling its story, its constitutive narrative, and in so doing, it offers examples for men and women who have embodied and exemplified the meaning of community. These stories of collective history and exemplary individuals are an important part of the tradition that is so central to a community of history.[16]

The process of developing a new sense of faith *(sensus fidei)* in Africa must be grounded in our African traditional ideals and ethos. According to Mercy Amba Oduyoye, "Africans recognize life as life in community. We can truly know ourselves if we remain true to our community, past and present. The concept of individual success or failure is secondary. The ethnic group, the village, the locality are crucial in one's estimation of oneself."[17] The African communitarian ethos can empower people to come together to fight the forces of dehumanization and terror. Social ecology is based on the fact that human beings are interrelated and our actions have tremendous implications for others. African people must seek to restore relationships and thus build community. The Akan people of Ghana will say that "it is because one antelope will blow the dust from the other's eye that two antelopes can work together." This proverb from Ghana underscores the importance of communal solidarity and interdependence. Solidarity is the union of people "arising from the common responsibilities and interests, as between classes, people, or groups; community of interests, feelings, purpose, or action; social cohesion."[18] Solidarity transcends any false notion of disinterest or altruism. It is rather based on "common responsibilities and interests, which necessarily arouse shared feelings and lead to joint action."[19]

The Christian gospel affirms that the goal of solidarity is to participate in the ongoing process of liberation through which we can become active agents in the unfolding of the reign of God. The overarching obstacle to the unfolding of the reign of God is the estrangement from God and from one another experienced through the oppressive institutionalized structures that engender and perpetuate pain and terror. This estrangement has been defined in many theological circles as both personal sin and structural sin. There is no gainsaying the fact that sin affects the well-being of people and the society as a whole. Gustavo Gutiérrez has rightly affirmed that "sin appears, therefore, as the fundamental alienation, the root of a situation of injustice and exploitation."[20] In order to be able to win the constant battle against injustice, sin, and oppression, African people have to use the best resources within the African culture and in Christianity.

64

African prophetic theology must also take a cue from the struggles of our brothers and sisters in Latin America and Asia. The theologies from these two contexts have been acclaimed for their unrelenting and radical commitment to the struggles of the poor in search of wholeness and liberation. Within the context of the Ecumenical Association of Third World Theologians, theologians from the so-called Third World have learned to forge connections, solidarity, and alliances without disregarding important differences. Ecumenical solidarity among Third World theologians is imperative because of the similarity of the context and situations with which they are dealing. For instance, the litany of prayer by the Christian Conference of Asia written some time ago looks like the prayer that is being recited by African Christians.

> Wasted by hunger, torture, deprivation of rights. Wasted by exploitation, racial and ethnic discrimination, sexual oppression. Wasted by loneliness, non-relation, non-community. That people are not to be wasted, people are valuable, made in God's image, redeemed by the Christ who died for them, people have his promise of abundant life, not wasted life. Therefore we affirm that God is a living God, the God of love and acceptance. That the Spirit of God works with his people in freeing and uniting them. This is our message. To share our new life by Word and action, to share His Lifestyle, to offer His hope by offering ourselves in proclaiming the Gospel.[21]

Conclusion

The good news of liberating Africans from the clutches of terror and all forms of oppression is a message of hope that is a nonnegotiable aspect of the gospel of Jesus Christ. The paradigms of a prophetic theology in Africa must not be considered as merely theological rhetoric, but as veritable tools for instituting the reign of God here on earth. Africans must cry out that terror is indeed "a slap in the face of God's sovereignty."[22]

"The Lord is king, let the earth rejoice" (Ps. 97:1).

Dethroning Violence and Terror: An Undercurrent in the Hebrew Bible

Jin Hee Han

> . . . no one shall make them afraid;
> for the mouth of the Lord of hosts has spoken.
>
> Micah 4:4b

Religious traditions are commonly presumed to inculcate peace and serenity by bridging humanity and divinity. In the same way, the Hebrew Bible, also known as the First Testament, is often used as the basis of efforts toward peace and reconciliation. A close reading, however, reveals that the biblical literature uncovers the paths strewn with struggle, violence, and terror in the life of the believing communities with the frequency and intensity that may conjure up the illusion of the reign of terror in biblical times.

Danger and peril were indeed no strangers to the biblical world, but the Hebrew Bible does not let fear be the final word. It lays bare the social and political manifestations of evil and features voices that hold renegade magistrates and nobles accountable for what they have done to the poor and powerless. Underneath the whirling notes of the reign of terror all around, there is a steady biblical undercurrent that runs in the Hebrew Bible, flowing steadily toward the dethronement of terror and toward the dream of peace. That undercurrent emerges, as the biblical traditions deconstruct the grip of terror in the world, explores measures to bring the reign of terror to an end, and envisions the state of *shalom* that shines upon not only the liberated oppressed but also the redeemed oppressors.

Some Sore Stories

The biblical literature has no shortage of violent stories. In the very beginning of the Hebrew Bible, the stage on which the biblical story unfolds is good enough to impress God. While the first week of creation is misleadingly calm,[1] the pages turn and the plot turns violent with betrayal, expulsion, and fratricide.[2] Violence grows, and God regrets that God has created the humans at all and sends a flood to wipe out all the living things along with the earth. God's violent judgment wreaks terror in the world.

Genesis 12 marks a new beginning of the relationship of God and humans in a world in which a threat of death hangs over the wandering matriarchs and the perishing patriarchs (cf. Deut. 26:5). When Abraham and Sarah flee from famine, they fear the notoriety of Pharaoh for lawlessness and violence. There are rumors and reports of war. Cities are incinerated completely in spite of Abraham's prayer. In the name of God's promise, Ishmael and Hagar are thrown out into a near-death experience. Isaac experiences his father brandishing a knife at his only son's neck on Mount Moriah. Esau and Jacob are caught up in sibling enmity serious enough to make their mother fear losing one or both sons. In the wake of the rape of Dinah, Israel's children reveal their susceptibility to raw violence as they massacre the people of Shechem. The whole incident casts doubt on whether different peoples can live together peacefully in the land of Canaan. A few chapters later, the brothers of Joseph lay their hands on their brother, their own flesh and blood.[3]

The birth of the people of Israel in Exodus takes place through God's powerful acts against the bondage of the house of Pharaoh. In the story of deliverance, which has been dubbed as holy,[4] the foundational event of Exodus leaves behind wailing Egyptian mothers in the spiral of violence, as the Talmud[5] (Meg. 10b; San. 39b) notes:

> God does not rejoice at the death of sinners. On seeing the destruction of the Egyptians the angels wanted to break forth in song. But God silenced them saying: "The work of My hands is drowning in the sea, and you desire to sing songs!"

The settlement of Israel cannot be told without the bloody battles and wars for survival, either. When the concubine of a Levite in Judges 19 is victimized in a town of Israel (cf. Judg. 19:12), the Israelites' effort to mend the wrong plunges the tribes of Israel into an ever deepening helix of violence upon violence. At last, the monarchy comes to Israel under the shadow of the Philistine military threat and delivers the people of Israel from the roaring enemies right into the royal abuses. Efforts to hold on to the land mean repeated battle cries until the demise of the kingdoms of

Israel in 722 B.C.E. and of Judah in 587 B.C.E. In the days of the Babylonian exile, a mourner mourns: "Judah has gone into exile with suffering and hard servitude" (Lam. 1:3), and a psalmist weaves a imprecatory line against Babylonian invaders: "Happy shall they be who take your little ones and dash them against the rock!" (Ps. 137:9).

Cyrus's edict in 538 B.C.E. marks a new era of restoration, but the project of reconstruction turns out to be burdened with greater challenges than the prophet of Isaiah 40 envisioned. Ezra and his group of returnees face the danger of ambush, and Nehemiah has to arm his workers with swords. The people who remained in the land during the exile do not necessarily welcome the changes the returnees are bringing.[6] Samaritans, Ammonites, and others try to discourage the work of the Jewish restoration through allurement, intimidation, and bribery.

The book of Daniel, at the end of the Old Testament period, witnesses the world turning more beastly than ever. The book begins with stories about a colonial situation in which young men are being deported, dissidents thrown into a fiery furnace, and a victim of political conspiracy locked in the lions' den. The book is completed at the time of Antiochus IV (Epiphanes), the Hellenistic king, who commits the first pogrom against the Jewish people in history. He attacks Jerusalem, massacres the people, outlaws the religion of Israel, and desecrates the temple. The apocryphal/deuterocanonical story of the martyrdom of seven sons before the eyes of their mother (2 Maccabees 7) takes place in this repressive time. These stories bear testimony to the biblical times whose canvas is painted in the color of terror, inviting the readers to delve into the origin of *the reign of terror* all around.

Terror on the Throne

Defining the contour of the terror in the Hebrew Bible may be compared with drawing a boundary line of the stormy sea. Such a task is properly reserved for the Almighty (Jer. 5:22; Job 38:11). For Jeremiah, terror is not something he could study *in vitro*. He experiences it *in vivo*, and cries "terror all around" *(magor missabib)*,[7] which can function as a paradigmatic statement of human condition. These words make "almost a Leitmotif in the Jeremiah tradition."[8] Using the same phrase, in Jeremiah 20:3, the prophet renames the priest Pashhur as "Terror-all-around." Since Pashhur is in charge of order in the temple, the navel of the universe, one could argue that Jeremiah's prophetic pronouncement exposes the terror that has replaced order at the foundation of creation. William Holladay[9] regards it as a reversal of God's creation and of the promise of protection given to the patriarchs. The phrase recurs in one of Jeremiah's laments, and it seems that he said it so often that it has become his trademark and his opponents taunt him as a man of terror all around (20:10). Jeremiah could feel to the bone the overwhelming power of terror all around.[10]

A little more than a century earlier another prophet who was going to exert a great influence upon Jeremiah pronounced a prophetic indictment of the powerful members who had lost the sense of urgency when the society was facing God's impending doom. Amos said, "O you that put far away the evil day, and bring near a reign of violence" (6:3). The Hebrew word behind the NRSV translation of "a reign of violence" *(shebet chamas)* refers to the royal seat that violence has taken up in society.[11] It is a metaphor based on the less than rewarding experience with the kingship, whether it was from the days of the Pharaoh, or under the Canaanite city state kings, or with the native kings of Israel. Like a monarch that has an oppressive grip on the land and the people, violence has seized the power over the land.

How did the oppressive situations of terror begin? Demonstrating brutal candor in the face of violence and terror, the biblical literature tries to capture the provenance of the beast of terror in human life and history in five major ways: (1) human propensity toward violence; (2) demand of the *Lebensraum;* (3) stated-sponsored violence; (4) terror as a social means of control; and (5) divine violence.

Human Propensity Toward Violence

The biblical corpus traces the origin of violence and terror all the way back to the primeval history in the book of Genesis. As soon as the genealogy of the descendants of Adam celebrates the blessing of multiplication, the biblical writer reports bluntly that the earth is "filled with violence" (Gen. 6:11). The human propensity toward violence is to blame: "The LORD saw that the wickedness of humankind was great in the earth, and that every inclination of the thoughts of their hearts was only evil continually" (Gen. 6:5). The ubiquity of violence stems from the innate nature of human beings.

The Talmud (Ber. 61a) locates a textual foreshadowing of it in the creation of human beings in Genesis 2:7. "Then the LORD God formed *(wyytzr)* man from the dust of the ground, and breathed into his nostrils the breath of life; and the man became a living being." The Hebrew text has the verb "to form" written with two of the Hebrew letter *yodh* instead of one, from which the rabbinical eyes deduced the creation of two of the object that starts with the same letter, *yetzer,* meaning "disposition." In other words, God gave humans two dispositions: one good *(yetzer ha-tob)* and the other

69

evil *(yetzer ha-ra')*. In the thesis of the good and evil inclinations in human nature, each person becomes a moral agent.

While the stories of Genesis place a moral responsibility upon the shoulders of individual human beings, humans prove to be capable of escalating violence instead of bringing it under control. In the most violent chapter in the primeval history, Cain is responsible for Abel's blood, but the guilty conscience does not prevent the spiral of violence in the primeval history from growing from a tragic fratricide to the boastful celebration of violence by Lamech.

> I have killed a man for wounding me,
> a young man for striking me.
> If Cain is avenged sevenfold,
> truly Lamech seventy-sevenfold (Gen. 4:23b–24).

The progressive—or regressive—story line from Cain to Lamech duplicates itself among families, the king, the people, and the nations, threatening the fabric of the created world.

Demand of the Lebensraum

Violence takes a new dimension as the anomaly becomes a part of the struggle for survival, in other words, a matter of necessity rather than that of choice. In an effort to secure the *Lebensraum* (living space), Joshua's army conducts military campaigns "to take possession of the land that the Lord your God gives you to possess" (Josh. 1:11) and the land is to be "a place of rest" for the people of Israel (cf. 1:13). The book of Joshua is followed by the book of Judges, which continues to record the efforts of individual tribes to secure the land with details sometimes difficult to reconcile with the reports in the book of Joshua.

Extrabiblical sources shed light on the picture of the struggle Israel had to go through. In the Egyptian Mer-ne-Pta Stela of about 1230 b.c.e. (*ANET*, pp. 376–8) one reads: "Israel is laid waste, his seed is not; Hurru is become a widow for Egypt!" In this ancient Near Eastern text in which Israel is mentioned for the first time, the word Israel is marked with a determinative that indicates it is a name of a group of people. It is not yet the land of Israel. It is the land of Hurru (cf. Horites). Historians doubt that the inscription is based on a historical event, but it illustrates challenges the people of Israel had to face in order to have their living space.[12]

The struggle for the *Lebensraum* continues into the monarchic period. The ninth-century inscription of the Moabite Stone (*ANET*, pp. 320–1) offers a window through which one can observe the nature of the struggle for survival during the monarchic period.

70

I (am) Mesha, son of Chemosh-[. . .], king of Moab. . . . As for Omri, king of Israel, he humbled Moab many years (lit., days), for Chemosh was angry at his land. And his son followed him and he also said, "I will humble Moab." In my time he spoke (thus), but I have triumphed over him and over his house, while Israel hath perished for ever!

It appears Mesha's claim was exaggerated, for Israel did not perish forever, but the neighboring nations went through vicious wars, as one endeavored to exist at the expense of another. The rules of engagement as in Deuteronomy 20:16–17 suggests that the annihilation was part of the military objective in war in antiquity.[13]

As the people are fighting for their life and well-being of their children, the demand of the living space has a power to generate a mythical façade of a just war and to inspire a will to fight at any cost. The theological claim of the gift of the land adds to the entrenched nature of the demand of the *Lebensraum,* for as the land is perceived as a gift from God, the war for survival turns into a religious obligation. The demand the *Lebensraum* places upon the people leaves one to wonder whether violence can ever stop as long as the people have yet to learn how to live with those whom they define as others.

State-Sponsored Violence

The people of Israel, who experienced a great deal of violence in the process of settlement, found that it required a great deal of conflict to stay in the land. During the time of the judges, the threat of enemies was only intermittent, and the charismatic leadership of temporary military leaders seemed to suffice. All of that changed with the Philistines, who arrived about the same time but with a superior material culture. They posed a constant threat and standing crisis. The Hebrew Bible recollects that the rise of the monarchy had to do with the Philistine crisis.

Given the situation, the monarchy was a matter of urgent necessity. According to the promonarchic tradition preserved in 1 Samuel 9:15–17, it is God who sets aside Saul as one that shall rule over the people of Israel, and commands Samuel to anoint him. "He shall save my people from the hand of the Philistines; for I have seen the suffering of my people, because their outcry has come to me" (v. 16b). The monarchy is introduced to counter the violent advance of the Philistines that threatens the survival of Israel in the land of Canaan. The throne delivers its promise in the days of David, who removes the threat of the Philistines.

David's reign, at least in the early part, is characterized by justice and equity (2 Sam. 8:15). However, the so-called Succession Narrative of 2 Samuel 9–20 and 1 Kings 1–2 is filled with abuses in the palace and violence throughout the nation. While the literary integrity of the narrative, as well as its presumed purpose, has been disputed, Hans Jensen[14] identifies its unifying theme as "desire (objective and mimetic), rivalry, collective violence and scapegoating." The monarchy undoubtedly brought its many blessings to the nation, but was also a mixed bag of blessings. The premonarchic time is known for lawlessness, as the people did whatever was right in their own eyes (Judg. 17:6; 18:1; 19:1; 21:25); if it was a violent time because there was no king, the monarchic period was violent partly because there was a king.

Under the Davidic monarchy beset with the corruption on the throne and the violence in the royal family, war takes upon a new characteristic as well. This transformation of war is hinted in 2 Samuel 11:1, which begins the report of the king's exploitation of the people whose well-being he should have sought instead of his own. The superscription to the moral bankruptcy of the Davidic regime reads, "In the spring of the year, the time when kings go out to battle, David sent Joab with his officers and all Israel with him" (2 Sam. 11:1). Now war has become a royal institution in Israel. David sends his warriors to war because that is what kings do.

David's war is now an imperial measure to take control over the surrounding region. As Susan Niditch[15] points out, "Many scholars have noted that for ancient Israelite authors, peace, the state of shalom, also implied Israel's dominance over all nations who might threaten her and often their coming to accept Israel's own world-view and her God (e.g. Zech. 8:20–23)." Israel adopted the monarchy to seek protection from terror, but ended up being wedded to terror now sponsored by the state.[16] Israel was no longer concerned about survival, but now was seeking the role of the benefactor of the subjugated peoples. In the United Monarchy Israel saw the fulfillment of the promise of God to Abraham: "I will make of you a great nation, and I will bless you, and make your name great, so that you will be a blessing. I will bless those who bless you, and the one who curses you I will curse; and in you all the families of the earth shall be blessed" (Gen. 12:2–3). Now the power of the Davidic empire could bring either blessing or destruction for all the families of the earth.

The state-sponsored violence did not wield its sword upon the foreign enemies only. It touched upon the life of the people of Israel as well, as Samuel had warned in 1 Samuel 8:11–18.

> These will be the ways of the king who will reign over you: he will take your sons and appoint them to his chariots and to be his horsemen, and to run before his chariots; and he will appoint for himself commanders of thousands and commanders of fifties, and some to plow his ground and to reap his harvest, and to make his implements of war and the equipment of his chariots. He will take your daughters to be perfumers and cooks and bakers. He will

take the best of your fields and vineyards and olive orchards and give them to his courtiers. He will take one-tenth of your grain and of your vineyards and give it to his officers and his courtiers. He will take your male and female slaves, and the best of your cattle and donkeys, and put them to his work. He will take one-tenth of your flocks, and you shall be his slaves. And in that day you will cry out because of your king, whom you have chosen for your-selves; but the LORD will not answer you in that day.

Samuel's warning of the royal highways uses the verb "to take" repeat-edly. In taking from the people, the kings practice the traditional form of royal abuse, i.e., confiscation, as if it were a royal prerogative.

A classic example of royal confiscation in the Hebrew Bible is the story of Naboth's vineyard in 1 Kings 21. The story features a negotiation between a farmer and the palace, which ended in the death of the farmer. Beneath the story, two economic systems clash head-on. Naboth's notion of econ-omy centers on the integrity of ancestral inheritance, which even the king is expected to honor. King Ahab understands the constraint of tradition that governs the transaction of land in Israel. Queen Jezebel, however, rep-resents a different economic system, according to which one who dares to disagree with the duce deserves to die. As a shrewd strategist, she stages a masquerade to preclude the public unrest. The story ends with violence with Naboth being stoned to death; however, the impact of the story does not end there. The royal violence calls for the prophetic response, and Eli-jah says to Ahab, "Thus says the LORD: In the place where dogs licked up the blood of Naboth, dogs will lick up your blood" (1 Kings 21:19). State-sponsored violence summons violence back to the palace.

While 1 Kings 21 offers a sensational narrative on the royal abuse, the prophets' witness reveals that confiscatory taxation becomes a part of social structure under the predatory leadership. Micah condemns, "They covet fields, and seize them; houses, and take them away; they oppress house-holder and house, people and their inheritance" (Micah 2:2). The struc-tural abuse by the leadership is the constant target "the prophetic tradi-tions do not tire of condemning,"[17] and the prophets diligently attest to the abuses by the state that sought expansion and exploitation while promis-ing protection from anarchy.

Terror as a Social Means of Control

Situations of terror portrayed in the Hebrew Bible are not limited to the aberrations caused by the less than perfect nature of human society. In terms of the nature of the beast, the state as an institution knows how to protect its interests, and in the biblical world those who hold power have found in terror an effective means to control the people of the kingdom.

The Golden Age of Israel under King Solomon provides an example of a time of totalitarian control in biblical proportions. His reign starts with the elimination of the political undesirables. He rearranges the map of the nation, turning the twelve tribes into the twelve administrative districts. The wisest king in the East reorganizes the kingdom into the supplier of forced labor for his building projects. In his glorious days, "Solomon was sovereign over all the kingdoms from the Euphrates to the land of the Philistines, even to the border of Egypt; they brought tribute and served Solomon all the days of his life" (1 Kings 4:21). Solomon's daily provision in 4:22–28 pales the modern capitalistic culture of consumption, as the king lives the life of a luxurious despot off the fat and lean of the land. Against the backdrop of the glittering picture of luxury and abundance, apart from the sharp criticism by the Deuteronomistic Historian in 1 Kings 11, there is the prophetic silence throughout the reign of Solomon.[18]

After the death of Solomon, one begins to see what it was like under his reign. When Rehoboam succeeds him, the elders of Israel make one petition to the new king in a preelection session: "Your father made our yoke heavy. Now therefore lighten the hard service of your father and his heavy yoke that he placed on us, and we will serve you" (12:4). Rehoboam, who knew the Solomon that the people mourned but not the Solomon whose death the people celebrated, listens to the hard liners ("the young men who had grown up with him," 12:8). He responds to the people, "Now, whereas my father laid on you a heavy yoke, I will add to your yoke. My father disciplined you with whips, but I will discipline you with scorpions" (12:11). Whips hurt, scorpions kill. Solomon's reign was maintained with violence, and Rehoboam promises terror. The seed of revolution that was sown in the days of Solomon sprouts after the death of the king. Rehoboam's attempt of control by terror aborts.

The secession of the northern tribes leaves Israel and Judah two petty kingdoms in the Fertile Crescent, until the Assyrian advance destroys Samaria. It is in the Assyrians that one finds the well-known example of the reign of terror in the international arena in the history of the Near East. They waged cruel wars as a means of empire building, and habitually scattered the subjugated people in various parts of the empire.[19] Assyria maintained its empire by "calculated frightfulness," as A. Olmstead[20] put it. While the Babylonian kings and the Persian overlords are occasionally given human touch in the Hebrew Bible, it is a struggle to find any positive note on the Assyrians. One may be enticed to find an exception to this in the book of Jonah, which goes on to place the people of Nineveh on the level of "many animals" (Jon. 4:11; cf. 3:8).

The Assyrian reign of terror left a deep imprint in the history of Israel and Judah. In a study on the political function of the terrifying discourse in the Joshua narrative, Lori Rowlett[21] argues that King Josiah was also

74

affected by the Assyrian reign of terror. She finds the book of Joshua, whose publication Josiah sponsors as part of his Deuteronomistic reform, indebted to the rhetoric of violence in the Assyrian war oracles. Josiah pursues centralization of power in Jerusalem, destroys the local sanctuaries, expands the kingdom, and applies measures of his reform vigorously, more diligently in what used to be the territory of the northern kingdom than he did in Judah. Rowlett[22] regards Joshua as the narrative of violence designed "to establish the lines of inclusion, authority and hierarchy desired by the central government whose control was far from secure."[23] In the rhetoric of violence, the king offers "calculated frightfulness," for "the post-imperial power of the central government could and would be unleashed upon any who resisted its assertion of control."[24] Canonical portrayals of Josiah make it difficult to reconstruct Josiah the Terrible. Yet, as part of the Deuteronomistic History prepared under the guidelines of the Josianic reform, the narrative of violence in Joshua could well have had the effect of violence as a means of Foucaultian social control.

Since Josiah's reform was a last-ditch effort to save the declining nation, should one excuse Josiah for holding a tight rein on the nation? The question is swallowed up by the rapid deterioration in the fate of Judah until it meets its end in 587 B.C.E. at the hand of the Babylonians.

Divine Violence

The biblical literature is clear about the individual responsibility for his or her violent behavior and the societal responsibility for corporate acts of violence. Brothers who did not learn to live with one another were not the only ones who could create violence in the biblical world, however. Kings, nobles, and invading armies were not the only ones capable of wreaking terror either. The Hebrew Bible points out that God is responsible for some of the violence inside its scrolls.

Concerning the advance of foreign powers beyond their control, prophets of the First Testament charge the leaders and the people with rebellious life styles. They will answer to a higher power, God who is in charge of the course of history. For the prophets, God's reign gives a sense of totality to the disparate events in history, which seem to be individually meaningless but take their place in the meaningful history led by God. Klaus Koch[25] calls the prophets' version of history a metahistory, comparing it with "what Isaiah calls 'Yahweh's work' and Jeremiah 'Yahweh's way.'"[26] According to the metahistory, God directs the historical process so that the people of God may fulfill their destiny.

The monistic production of meaning exacts a toll, however, as it becomes difficult to exonerate God from being significantly responsible for the vio-

lent affairs of the world. The God of the Hebrew Bible is capable of dis-
solving the heavens and the earth, and under certain circumstances, it is
not clear if God would refrain from doing just that. While the leaders and
the people could write their history in blood, God can wipe out their memory altogether from the face of the earth.

God, as portrayed in the First Testament, does not maintain comfortable
distance from violence, nor does violence stay away from the people of
God. In Psalm 44:8–11, a passage that Abraham Heschel cites to dedicate
his book on the prophets to the martyrs of 1940–45, the psalmist lodges
charge of oppression in God as much as in the enemies.

> In God we have boasted continually,
> and we will give thanks to your name forever. *Selah*
> Yet you have rejected us and abased us,
> and have not gone out with our armies.
> You made us turn back from the foe,
> and our enemies have gotten spoil.
> You have made us like sheep for slaughter,
> and have scattered us among the nations.

In the story of Hagar and Ishmael in Genesis 16 and 21, one of Phyllis Trible's *Texts of Terror*,[27] it is not clear who is the bigger oppressor: Sarah or
God. Since God supports Sarah, Trible concludes, "The deity identifies here
not with the suffering slave but with her oppressors."[28] God is involved in
the act of oppression, for "in protecting the heirs of his promise from a rival,
God endangers the life of the defenceless, the socially weak!"[29]

When God shows care for the poor, the biblical world sees more, not
less, terror, as God appears as a prosecutor, judge, and executioner. God
sponsors wars in judgment over the sinful people.[30] The day that God
demands justice is expected to leave the earth devastated.[31] "Those slain
by the LORD on that day shall extend from one end of the earth to the other.
They shall not be lamented, or gathered, or buried; they shall become dung
on the surface of the ground" (Jer. 25:33).

In wars of judgment, "Yahweh's great weapon was the divine terror
(Exod. 23:27; Deut. 7:23; Josh. 10:10; Judg. 4:15; 7:22; 1 Sam. 5:11; 7:10;
14:15)."[32] The avenging God brandishes a sword for slaughter (Ezek. 21:15),
and threatens expulsion: "I will scatter you among the nations and disperse
you through the countries, and I will purge your filthiness out of you" (Ezek.
22:15). A heavy concentration of Yahweh's anger in the biblical literature
invokes the notion of God as a vengeful, jealous, and violent God. Schwager[33] offers a stunning statistic: "Approximately *one thousand passages* speak
of Yahweh's blazing anger, of his punishments by death and destruction,
and how like a consuming fire he passes judgment, takes revenge, and threat-

ens annihilation." Is peace a possibility in a world inhabited by fallible human beings and yet run by a God prone to anger and destruction?

Any attempt to shield God from all charges of violence seems to be doomed, as one of the most ancient texts in the Hebrew Bible declares, "The Lord is a warrior; the Lord is his name" (Exod. 15:3). The divine warrior does not hesitate to demolish the opponents of Israel, and sometimes the warrior's wrath is unleashed upon Israel under judgment. When the people of Israel set out for the land of Canaan from Sinai, "Moses would say, 'Arise, O Lord, let your enemies be scattered, and your foes flee before you'" (Num. 10:35). The divine warrior marches before the people of God, and in an even more gruesome picture, "The Lord has a sword; it is sated with blood, it is gorged with fat, with the blood of lambs and goats, with the fat of the kidneys of rams. For the Lord has a sacrifice in Bozrah, a great slaughter in the land of Edom" (Isa. 34:6).

The *Gottesbild* of the divine warrior is potentially a troublesome image of God, for it is hard to dissociate a warrior from the violence of war. Grant that the people wage war, but why does God lead it? "The main problem is not that the people of God were warriors, but that the Old Testament affirms that God is a warrior."[34] God of the Hebrew Bible neither offers a unilateral *shalom*, nor refrains from violence in order to destroy the enemies of God, mythical or historical.

From time to time, the divine warrior is referred to as a God who comes to the rescue of those who have nowhere else to turn. God wages the holy war to defend the defenseless, from whom the divine warrior demands absolute faith. The most serious blunder the people can commit is "not so much the cultic infidelity of bowing to graven images as it is the political infidelity of trusting Egypt or Assyria instead of yhwh as the guarantor of national *shalom*."[35] Israel is entangled in wars not because they could not grow out of the tradition of the divine warrior but precisely because they did. God is there to fight the battle on behalf of God's people, and the people are there only to witness the victory and deliverance. While the immediate context of Exodus 15 may portray a picture of a defensive holy war, however, other parts of the Hebrew Bible do not fit the prescribed contour of the holy war. The stories of conquest as told in the book of Joshua are by any count offensive maneuvers, unless one reads them as a historicized fiction of the people who had no fighting power but a set of writing instruments and fertile imaginations. The army of Joshua 6 resorts to peculiar machinery of war with seven trumpets of rams' horns and an even more peculiar strategy of marching around the city once a day for six days and seven times on the seventh day. The liturgical assault, however, is followed by a report that says, "Then they devoted to destruction by the edge of the sword all in the city, both men and women, young and old, oxen, sheep, and donkeys" (Josh. 6:21).

The image of the divine warrior, which appears in various parts of the Hebrew Bible, is deeply embedded in the religious tradition of Israel, and the stories of the divine bloody battle deal a blow to the argument that the biblical tradition does not foster enmity at all. The objection of Carol Christ[36] does not necessarily require a feminist perspective: "The God of Exodus and the Prophets is a warrior God. My rejection of this God as a liberating image for feminist theology is based on my understanding of the symbolic function of a warrior God in cultures where warfare is glorified as a symbol of manhood and power." God of the biblical literature can be quite frightful.

In the Hebrew Bible, the appearance of God is a frightening experience prefaced by the formula of "Do not fear" *('al tira')*.[37] Since Joachim Begrich,[38] the formula has been considered part of the oracle of salvation pronounced by the priests in the cultic setting "to guarantee to suppliants the all-powerful protection of Yahweh."[39] Second Isaiah ran with it to proclaim the message of encouragement (Isa. 41:10, 13, 14; 43:1, 5; 44:2, 8; 54:4). It has been part and parcel of homiletic tradition to read this line as the powerful statement to the effect that the divine presence promises to set the people free from the terror of harsh reality. Yet, in the distant background, the formula had to do with the great threat the divine appearance presents, especially in the light of the motif that no one can survive seeing God.[40] There are many reasons to have fear, and above all, God is to be feared most.

Where, O Terror, Is Your Sting?

The biblical writers do not always offer a clear-cut moral directive for situations that involve violence and terror. From time to time, religious tradition found in the First Testament is not only an unsuspecting trespasser in the process but also an active participant in the promotion and execution of violent measures in life. Even God does not hesitate to resort to violence when there is a justifiable cause. Many parts of the Hebrew Bible offer an all too honest description of brutal realities of human existence in the ambience of terror—with the kind of integrity that could well breed the impression that the Hebrew Bible either endorses or capitulates to violence and terror. However, the biblical literature resists the grip of violence and terror in God's world as it allows the victims of violence speak up, as it permits protest against the demands of the state and God, and as it seeks healing and reconciliation in the broken world. While the Hebrew Bible contains images of the terrifying deity, it brings out the picture of a God who participates in the suffering of the people of God.[41] In a world where oppression appears to be a fact of life, the First Testament reaches out for a dream of a world that knows no more terror.

Voice of Victims

The greatest contribution René Girard, the French anthropologist, has made to the biblical studies is that he has identified as one of the distinctive features of the biblical literature *voice given to the victims of violence*. Girard privileges the Second Testament for this insight, calling Christ "the God of victims primarily because he shared their lot until the end"[42] and calls the First Testament the text in travail that cranes toward the resolution of violence. Girard's program still gives an important place to the Hebrew Bible in the process since birth comes after labor. Meanwhile, the First Testament offers a fertile field for locating the voice given to the victims of the pain and suffering that continued to be part of human experience both in the B.C.E. and the C.E.[43]

Girard locates the origin of violence in the notion of *mimesis,* meaning "imitation." Just as culture, music, and art are all products of duly processed mimicry, so violence is born as human beings develop a desire to be like each other in desiring the same object and fight over it. Human beings imitate and irritate.

The more they become alike, the more intense the conflict grows. A conflict of a few escalates into a larger conflict of many. The more serious it becomes, the more people it will draw into conflict. As an Asian proverb says, a clash of shrimps turns into a war of whales. When the mimetic rivalry reaches the level of epidemic and the society faces a possible self-destruction, the blame is focused on someone, and as that person bears the guilt and gets condemned, violence disappears, and mysteriously, peace comes back. Girard summarizes this process: *"The victim is a scapegoat."*[44]

The violent execution of the victim does not take place without the complicity of those who participate in the act of violence. Accomplices feel they have to look out for each other, and if anybody speaks up in protest, they lynch that person too, for such a voice challenges the whole social mechanism of scapegoating. As they conspire to develop a means to reaffirm their unity, a ritual is shaped. As they share stories, a myth is generated as a device to maintain secrecy.[45] They introduce a system of sacrifice, an institutionalized form of violence, to prevent "the recurrence of reciprocal violence."[46] They pad their efforts to protect themselves against their own violence by projecting their stories into the realms of religion.[47]

Girard observes the same process operative in the violence and killing in many cultures, but there is a distinctive feature of the biblical narrative. It is a voice given to the victims, while in rituals of violence in other societies the victims are typically gagged so that they may not be able to unravel the irrational behavior of the collective. The clearest example of the biblical distinctive feature is found in the first fratricide in Genesis 4. Cain kills Abel, whose most important identity is Cain's brother,[48] and his mimetic double. Both Cain and Abel wanted God's approval. One got it, but the other did not. As the mimetic rivalry starts, conflict takes its own life apart from why and how it started. Cain's mimesis turns into Abel's nemesis. The whole chapter of Genesis 4 follows the typical scenario in Girard's anthropological theory (or hypothesis, as he preferred) on violence along with a significant twist. Usually, the rest of the world does not get to hear from the victim. Victims and the dead share the fate of silence. In Genesis 4:10, the victim does not go away silently, but is given voice, as God says, "Listen; the blood of your brother Abel is crying out to me from the ground!" The creation of civilization may be credited with Cain, but the victim's voice cannot be silenced.

Sometimes the biblical literature has the victims of violence go through a further transformation and become agents of salvation for many, including the perpetrators. As a significant example of this, Joseph was also victim of collective violence of his brothers. They threw him into the pit, a symbol of death, but in the end he turns out to be a means of salvation of many. As part of the scene of reconciliation, Joseph says to his brothers, "And now do not be distressed, or angry with yourselves, because you sold me here; for God sent me before you to preserve life" (Gen. 45:5; cf. 50:20). Moses is denied access to the promised land (Deut. 1:37–27; 3:26–27; 4:21), as he is forced to bear on behalf of the people of Israel.[49] The same dynamic is operative in the Song of the Suffering Servant in Isaiah 52:13–53:12,[50] in which the burden of guilt is completely dissociated from the sufferer.

> Surely he has borne our infirmities and carried our diseases;
> yet we accounted him stricken, struck down by God, and afflicted.
> But he was wounded for our transgressions, crushed for our inquities
> (Isa. 53:4–5a).

The song does not stop at lamenting the injustice done to the servant of Yahweh. The servant's suffering has a significant impact upon the rest of the world, for

> upon him was the punishment that made us whole,
> and by his bruises we are healed (53:5b).

The sufferer has become the agent of *shalom*.

Protest and Resistance

The people in the biblical times knew the reality of pain and suffering in a less than perfect world. The biblical literature, in which Girard saw efforts to escape from the realms of violence, not only laments over the sad situations but sponsors acts of defiance—not only against the human rulers but also against God. In his essay on the spirituality of protest in the book of Job, U. Kaufmann[51] captures another major distinctive feature of the biblical literature: "The Greeks, by and large, did not expostulate with the Divine: the Hebrews did. Oedipus confronts his fate with horror, but he does not dispute its justice with Apollo or Zeus. . . . But in Hebrew tradition, expostulation with the Divine is characteristic." It is not an exaggeration that the Hebrew Bible is filled with the people who put up a good fight with God. In Genesis 18, Abraham refuses to accept God's pronouncement of judgment as a final answer. Abraham drags God through the slippery path of the deal-making of the Near East, even though he regrettably stops at asking for ten righteous people in an utterly corrupt place. Lamenting voices in the book of Psalms cry "out of the depths" (Ps. 130:1) to the LORD, whom they trust as capable of bringing about the reversal of fortune. Another protester, Jonah, defies God's directive and lives on. The only thing that is destroyed in this wonderful story is the plant of *qiqayon*.

The biblical traditions, which take on God in demand for changes, are not about to easily submit to the forces of oppression. Social institutions of power are eager to protect their invested interest and to justify their actions in the name of peace and order; however, the biblical literature reports what the protesters have done to challenge the regime's self-serving measures. Alicia Winters[52] finds a powerful example of the subversive response of the oppressed in 2 Samuel 21. It happened in the third year of the famine, which means that the famine reached its critical stage and began dipping into the reserve of seeds set aside for the next year's planting. Through a religious device, the blame is placed on the house of Saul, the previous king, and the seven sons of Saul are executed under the permission or aegis of King David. The mother of two of the seven sons slaughtered in the name of peace attends to the bodies in a most provocative way.

> Then Rizpah the daughter of Aiah took sackcloth, and spread it on a rock for herself, from the beginning of harvest until rain fell on them from the heavens; she did not allow the birds of the air to come on the bodies by day, or the wild animals by night (2 Sam. 21:10).

By her action, she preserves the memory of her sons who died in the state-sponsored act of violence. "This woman did not submit to the eradication

81

that threatened the victims of the massacre."[53] The regime may have thought that it had silenced the victims along with the complaint of the populace, but the mother of the victimized children kept their memory alive by protesting against the brutal act of violence by the throne.

It would not be surprising to expect to find a multimillennial support for social criticism in the prophets from Elijah through Nathan, Hosea and Amos to Malachi. Walter Brueggemann[54] sees the prophetic task with three parts: (1) the formulation of symbols that lay bare the terror that exists in a pervasive manner; (2) the search for metaphors that strike a chord in the heart of the people in various forms of suffering; and (3) the call for the cessation of godless alienation through the language of grief. As they carry out these tasks, the prophets are seen with the people who experience fear, suffering, and grief. During the famine, Elijah stays with the widow, who has nothing to eat. Nathan's fury speaks volumes about how the king's misconduct affected him. Amos refuses any privileged status, as he declares *"lo'-nabi' 'anoki"*, which is a nominal clause that could be translated either as "I am no prophet" or "I was no prophet" (7:14). When there is a war in the land, the prophets expose the terrible reality of war with colorful metaphors and symbolic actions.[55]

Building upon the prophetic spirit of protest along with other religious traditions of Israel, the apocalyptic writer of the Hebrew Bible nearly gives up on the possibility that the present time is redeemable (cf. Dan. 2:44–45). "The nature of apocalyptic vision," Jon Berquist[56] states, "demonstrates an inherent pessimism about human ability to choose new options for society." In the harsh reality in which the lamenting prayer goes unanswered, the apocalyptist sees no hope of historical repair but locates hope beyond the confines of history. In the apocalyptic scenario, human efforts will never be enough to inaugurate the kingdom of God.

It is not just in the caustic words of prophetic or apocalyptic writers that one finds subversive elements. While snuggly camouflaged as the sayings of the royal voice, the book of Ecclesiastes challenges every basic premise in the religious tradition of ancient Israel, questioning the very possibility of any coherent systematization of principles that govern life and history. The book of Job challenges the traditional wisdom and questions the character of God who does not seem to recognize the innocent.[57] Job's arguments with his friends do away with the claims of wisdom as universal or useful truth.

One may expect the clearest case of structural legitimation in the book of Proverbs. Nevertheless, the sages did not fail to include a few words about a wicked ruler who oppresses the poor (28:15) and a cruel oppressor who lacks understanding (28:16). A king is looked up to as a source of blessing, but "a ruler who oppresses the poor is a beating rain that leaves no food" (28:3). A king is capable of bringing about stability in the land

and of ruining it with confiscatory taxation (29:4). The royal wisdom sorts out the wicked, but does not preclude the king from adopting a violent measure as needed (20:26). The teachers of wisdom, while familiar with the elite class in society, do not issue a unilateral approval of the *status quo*, even if they make their living off the existing power structure.

The Yahwist, who presumably worked at the court of the United Monarchy, may not have been totally approving of the monarchic society either. In the Garden of Eden the first human beings are invited to enjoy the bountifulness of the land, but are placed off-limits to the tree in the center of the garden. As two trees are located in the proscribed center, the divine directive points to the tree of knowledge of good and evil. In an almost predictable manner the humans eat of the tree, and the narrative possibilities of death and deathliness open up *agape*. In this intriguing biblical passage, James Kennedy[58] finds a political allegory of peasants (symbolized by Adam and Eve) revolting against the king (represented by God) who owns the estate and needs the peasants' labor to tend the royal manor. The king is the provider (adumbrated under the image of the tree of life), but "the fact that the text does not portray Yahweh Elohim as specifically leading the couple to the tree casts doubt on the benevolence of the king."[59] The eating of the forbidden tree is an act of defiance against the royal claim, and the king expels the rebels who dare to know more than they are supposed to instead of remaining obedient, and keeps them outside of the bliss of the royal garden. The Yahwist has inserted his political critique in the legendary story of Adam and Eve.

The other creation text from the priestly writer has its own fight to put up, as it offers an alternative cosmology in the land of exile, where the Babylonian myth represents a dominant worldview. The Babylonian creation epic of *Enuma Elish* functions as a concealment of violence embedded in the origin of the universe and latent in the undercurrent of the world. In order to bring an order into the world, Marduk must kill Tiamat. In its western equivalent, Baal has to kill Prince Yamm and Judge Nahar. Against the dominant cosmology of violence, God in Genesis 1 orders the heavens and earth without violent battles. The priestly vision competes with the superpower's policy of empire building by violence and imperial maintenance by terror. In the rest of the Torah, the priestly writer makes no reference to violence or war, which has resulted from "a deliberate redactional policy" adopted "in order to envision an earthly utopia."[60] The priestly writer gropes for a world free of violence, living in a world constructed with violence.

Heal and Mend

In the biblical literature, terror is indeed part of life, but is not so engrained in human condition that nothing can be done about it. Where no change is possible, no prayer avails. Historical events threaten life situations of the believing communities; however, the reign of terror will not have the last say in the world God created, for the First Testament persists to give voice to victims, chide the oppressors, protest injustice, and resist religious legitimation of exploitation. Furthermore, it plans the life after destruction.

The people who survived the Babylonian exile faced a challenge of envisioning continuing existence after the destruction of Jerusalem and the temple. That involved a valiant religious imagination that addressed the problem of guilt. In the Tetrateuch, the redactor modulates the burden of punishment with the theology of grace, forgiveness, and everlasting covenant. No matter what may happen in history, God abides with the people of Israel, as in the wilderness God journeyed with them in the tabernacle, a portable sanctuary. No matter what wrong they may have done, God's covenant with the people of God remains valid, for it is an everlasting covenant unbreakable by human sinful behavior (Gen. 9:16; 17:7, 13, 19; Exod. 31:16). Concerning the exile, Jeremiah declares, "The people who survived the sword found grace in the wilderness" (31:2a). Resonating with Jeremiah 31:29–30, Ezekiel 18 deconstructs the theology of communal guilt. The generation of the exile were repeating the fatalistic proverb that said, "The parents have eaten sour grapes, and the children's teeth are set on edge" (Ezek. 18:2). Ezekiel announces that the proverb no longer applies to the exilic situation. They no longer will be forced to pay for the guilt of their previous generation, for "it is only the person who sins that shall die" (18:4). Those who pursue righteousness will be given another chance to live. "For I have no pleasure in the death of anyone, says the Lord God. Turn, then, and live" (18:32). Toward the end of the exile, 2 Isaiah comes and challenges the notion that there exists a relation of equation between guilt and punishment. "Speak tenderly to Jerusalem . . . that she has received from the LORD's hand double for all her sins" (Isa. 40:2). The prophetic mode of revisionism continues to offer life in a world shattered by violence.

Leviticus 16, a passage that strangely did not draw much of Girard's attention, establishes a liturgical means of grace that lifts up the burden of guilt and makes life possible on an annual basis. Two goats are chosen for a sin offering of the people. One is to be slaughtered. The other live goat is sent away into the wilderness, bearing all the iniquities of the people to a barren land, so that the sinful people may continue to live. The price the scapegoat has to pay for atonement receives a stark expression in the Mishnah, which instructs the high priest to bind a thread of crimson wool on the head of the scapegoat.[61] After the first goat was slaughtered, "He divided the thread of crimson wool and tied one half to the rock and the other half between its horns, and he pushed it from behind; and it went rolling down,

84

and before it had reached half the way down the hill it was broken in pieces."[62] On Yom Kippur, the Day of Atonement, the innocent victim dies, and the atoned sinners are permitted to live on.

The biblical literature takes a step even further than accommodating those who committed unintentional acts of violence. It extends the invitation of *shalom* to the oppressors. Significantly, the city whose *shalom* Jeremiah promoted in 29:7 was not Jerusalem but Babylon. In the vision of the peaceable kingdom, Isaiah envisions a world in which the wolf dwells with the lamb, the leopard with the kid, the calf and the young lion and the fatling, gentle enough to be led by a little child (Isa. 11:6–8). The peaceable kingdom is designed to include the formerly violent, who will have to unlearn their ways of terror if this dream were to come true.

Until the enemies are embraced, reconciliation will continue to struggle to find a place to take hold. Niditch[63] finds in the biblical war accounts the brutality of war, especially in "the naked brutality with which enemies are treated."[64] As long as there are enemies—whether they are there to hate or to love, violence remains viable.

The biblical literature bears witness to a violent world in which no one is shielded from expulsion, bloodshed, war, and annihilation, and as Noah learned, "even perfect obedience offers no proof against violence."[65] Yet, after the flood, God "has set aside the bow of war and laid it in the clouds," which signifies that "God will tolerate this world of violence with infinite patience."[66] War has passed away, and now it is time to heal, time to mend, and time to plant peace together.[67] Hosea had a dream:

> I will make for you a covenant on that day
> with the wild animals, the birds of the air,
> and the creeping things of the ground;
> and I will abolish the bow, the sword, and war from the land;
> and I will make you lie down in safety (Hosea 2:18).

Conclusion

The Hebrew Bible may not offer a blueprint of revolution that would inaugurate the dream world of peace at the stroke of midnight. It may not issue an immediate action plan that would bring peace and justice in a torrential flood. Rather, it carries the voice of innocent victims. It sounds alarm against injustice and oppression. It seeks to heal and mend brokenness in the world. One has only to look underneath the surface of the text and feel the stream of the biblical undercurrent that flows to dethrone the terror and violence in God's world.

A Jewish Midrash tells a story that values human cooperation at the Tower of Babel, even when it was a misguided project.

> Why was the generation of the Flood destroyed while that of Babel was merely dispersed? The Babylonians said to one another: Come let *us* build [Gen. 11:4]. They worked together, in peace and harmony. This distinguished them from the people of the Flood who committed violence against one another and were, therefore, destroyed. The generation of the Tower defied God openly, yet, because they practiced brotherhood toward each other, they were merely scattered.[68]

What then would be the impact of the effort of brothers and sisters to plant peace for all? The new millennium presents modern and postmodern readers of the Hebrew Bible with a time to hope for the world of *shalom*, which Professor David Kwang-Sun Suh has pursued in the *minjung,* through the *minjung,* and for the *minjung.*

Prophecy and Patriotism: A Tragic Dilemma from the Cross of Terror

Luis N. Rivera-Pagán

The Spanish Crown and the Evangelization of America

Fernando and Isabel, Catholic monarchs of Spain, gave Christopher Columbus, in 1493, the following instructions, when the now Viceroy of the Indies and Admiral of the Ocean Sea was to initiate the conquest and colonization of the lands and peoples found during his first expedition:

> Wishing that our holy Catholic faith be increased and augmented, we order and charge the said admiral . . . that by every means and ways possible he should try to persuade the inhabitants of said islands and mainlands to be converted to our Catholic faith . . .[1]

To that end, the monarchs sent a group of religious and friars to evangelize the natives, thus laying the foundations for the world expansion of the Christian faith as the religious counterpart of European colonial outreach.[2] The missionaries, however, were too few and were not able to escape the tensions, hostilities, and finally the crisis that besieged the Columbus administration of the Antilles from 1494 to 1500.

The first shattering of illusions happened at the arrival in Hispaniola, when all thirty-nine men left behind by Columbus in January of 1493 were found killed, a clear sign that the paradise described by the admiral in his earlier reports existed only in his mind.[3] The natives were not as timorous as he had asserted; they were quite willing to defend their patrimony, culture, and freedom. Nor did the islands seem to be Ophir, the biblical region where King Solomon had obtained the gold to build the temple of Jerusalem. Neither was the conversion of the native communities a simple matter to be entrusted to a small band on unprepared friars. The natives also attested to many abuses on the part of the Spanish garrison, an ominous anticipation of the predatory conduct of the first generation of colonists, almost unrestrained by juridical norms. Those norms would begin to be established, at least in the lawgivers' books, in 1512 and 1513, two decades after the colonizing process had begun, a lawless period that proved to be lethal for the Caribbean communities.[4]

The conquest and colonization of the Americas proceeded at a very slow pace. Its christianization was even slower. In spite of the many pious expressions of the *Christum ferens,* evangelizing the Native Americans was never in the forefront of Columbus's colonial projects. During those very difficult six years, his main objective was not to proselytize the native communities but to provide political stability and economic prosperity to the colony, aims that eluded him totally. When he failed to create even the appearance of civic control, he was unceremoniously chained and expelled from the lands he had found and inscribed in the history of Western civilization.[5]

In 1504, in the codicil to her will and testament, the dying queen Isabel included the following clause, a forceful reminder to her husband, Fernando, her daughter Juana, and her son-in-law Felipe, of the unfulfilled goal to christianize the new world as the main purpose of the Spanish arrogation of sovereignty:

> From the time when the Holy Apostolic See granted us the isles and mainlands of the Ocean Sea which have been or will be discovered, our principal intention . . . was to try to lead and bring the peoples of the said areas and convert them to our Holy Catholic faith. . . . Therefore, I beg the King, my Lord . . . and I charge and command the Princess, my daughter, and the Prince, her husband, to carry out and fulfill this charge and that this be their principal aim . . . for this is what is enjoined on us by the Apostolic letter of the aforementioned grant . . .[6]

King Fernando, for his part, commanded Diego Columbus, son of the admiral and new Viceroy of the Indies, to make certain that the natives be instructed "in the matters of the Catholic faith, since this is the principal basis for the conquest of those regions . . ."[7] This kind of ordinance proliferates under the dynasty of Carlos V and Felipe II. The former "Ordinances About the good treatment of the Indians,"[8] decreed in 1526, and the latter "Ordinances regarding new discoveries,"[9] enacted in 1573, stress the conversion of the Native Americans as the main objective of the conquest and colonization of America. The 1573 Ordinances insist that: "The zeal and wish that we have is that all that is yet to be discovered be discovered, so that our holy Gospel be made public and the natives come to the knowledge of our holy Catholic faith   "[10]

In summary, despite the many changes in political strategies of conquest and colonization, in the century that goes from Isabel and Fernando to Carlos V and Felipe II, the evangelization of the natives and their conversion to the Christian faith was continually made explicit as the transcendental goal of Spain's political, economic, and cultural dominion over America. It was explicitly and self-consciously an imperial expansion understood as a missionary enterprise.[11] It failed totally in the Antilles but was able to produce the Franciscan mission to Mexico and the Jesuit Reductions in different parts of South America, two of the most exceptional and exciting chapters in the history of the expansion of Christianity.[12]

Despite several attempts to conceive the colonization of America in what they perceived to be the Old Testament pattern of the "extermination of the infidels" (whose presence and existence defiled the promised land and thus they deserved, because their abominable sins, to disappear from history), the prevailing and official model was missionary, whereby the military actions were perceived as paradoxical ways of fulfilling Christ's last commandment: "Go to all nations and make them my disciples." When references are made to Juan Ginés de Sepúlveda and his book on the justice of the wars against the Indians, a work in which Aristotle's concept of the barbarians who are by nature serfs converge with the Old Testament vision of the God-commanded Israelite destruction of the peoples of Canaan, we should not forget that it was explicitly repudiated by a good number of Spanish theologians and was not printed for lack of official authorization.[13] It did not receive the imprimatur from the juridical and theological authorities who reviewed the manuscript.[14]

Thus genocide, which undeniably occurred in many parts of Spanish America, was never official policy. When and where it tragically happened, as quite different sixteenth-century Spanish historians like the Dominican Bartolomé de Las Casas[15] and the Franciscan Gerónimo de Mendieta stressed, it went against the explicit policy of the crown to preserve and evangelize the natives. Both Las Casas and Mendieta attempt to distinguish the lethal actions of conquerors and colonizers from the official policy of the crown. This policy, adopted either for religious and humanitarian reasons or for the obvious inconvenience that represents the death of the servile workers, means, at least for me, that it is incorrect to ascribe to the Spanish conquest the Canaanite model that could better explain other colonial endeavors in America.[16]

This is not to say that the evangelization was devoid of military coercion. As the Jesuit José de Acosta states in the prologue to his important

1589 missionary treatise *De procuranda indorum salute,* military coercion and religious conversion in America went as a general rule hand by hand, with exceptions that do not invalidate the norm.[17] The insistence of Las Casas in his own missionary work, *De unico vocationis modo omnium gentium ad veram religionem,* that the use of military force and compulsion should be *a priori* excluded from the process of evangelization, although the basis for some interesting isolated experiments, was in general unheeded.[18]

The linkage of conquest and christianization was dialectically conceived. On the one hand, the first was always and everywhere formally perceived in conjunction with the second; on the other, the second was considered viable and fruitful only on the basis of the first.

Conquest and Christianization

Even the ambitious and violent Hernán Cortés insists on the christianization of the American lands and peoples as the principal purpose of his military endeavors. He conquers the native communities, in his words, "to attract them so that they would come to the knowledge of our holy Catholic faith. . . ."[19] Cortés launches the attack against Tenochtitlán, probably the most violent military confrontation in the whole epic conquest of America, only after publicly, officially, and formally declaring his war a crusade, a religious and missionary enterprise. His Tlaxcala military ordinances constitute probably the most forceful statement of the paradoxical identification between conquest and christianization.

> In as much . . . the natives of these regions have a culture and veneration of idols, which is a great disservice to God Our Lord, and the devil blinds and deceives them . . . I propose to bring them to the knowledge of our Holy Catholic faith. . . . Let us go to uproot the native of these regions from those idolatries . . . so that they will come to the knowledge of God and of His Holy Catholic faith . . . because if war is carried out with any other intention it would be unjust. . . . And therefore . . . I affirm that my principal motive in undertaking this war . . . is to bring the natives to the knowledge of our Holy Catholic faith.[20]

He is not slow to add that if his army were devoid of such a "right intention," then the wealth and properties to be acquired according to the ancient military tradition of the booty would be unjust and subject to restitution. Cortés applies the tradition of the Spanish *Reconquista,* whereby the lands and goods of the conquered infidels, the Moors, were considered rightly distributed between the triumphant troops as long as the conflict is perceived as a holy war, a religious confrontation. Only *post facto,* after the

Nahuatl culture had been destroyed, would critics like Bartolomé de Las Casas call attention to the obvious difference between the *Reconquista* model and the invasion of other peoples' lands and societies.[21]

God and gold are inextricably linked. Only if the war is undertaken for the sake of God is the gold obtained rightfully preserved. Also in Columbus we find a constant conjunction of gold and God. He wants the gold of America to finance a new and last crusade, which he would lead, to recover the Holy Land and the Lord's sepulchre.[22] In Cortés' case, God and gold (as well as glory) are distinct but inseparable goals of one and the same historical process of conquest. Modern historians, however, are mistaken when they, from the standpoint of their secularity, cynically understand this kind of statement as a textbook case of hypocrisy.[23]

The unity of God and gold, religion and avarice, is perhaps nowhere more strikingly expressed as in the May 1512 Capitulations of Burgos. It is the first formal agreement between the crown and the initial Bishops of America before they were transferred to their dioceses.[24] The commandment to the future bishops of America to take care of the well-being and conversion of the natives is emphasized. Immediately afterwards, however, they are charged, in the same capitulations, with the peculiar episcopal duty of convincing the Indians to work even harder in the gold mines, suggesting to the reluctant miners that the product of their work was to be used to make war against infidels, the old crusading ideal, and for other undefined purposes, all of which would allegedly be for their spiritual benefit.

It is significant, as well as clearly allusive to the story of the Roman emperor Constantine, that Cortés had a cross in his military banner accompanied by a Latin inscription that declared, *Amici, sequamur crucem, et si nos fidem habemus, vere in hoc signo vincemus* ("Friends, let us follow the cross, and if we have faith, in the name of this symbol we will conquer"). The presentation of a cross was, as noted by some scholars, one of the symbolic paraphernalia of a crusade required by medieval canon law.[25]

The conquest of America takes place after the *Reconquista*, the long military struggle between the Iberian Christians and the Iberian Muslims. I say Iberian Muslims because the great majority of the defeated followers of Allah were born, as were their parents, the parents of their parents, and the parents of the parents of their parents, in Iberian lands. It is no mere coincidence that Cortés refers to the Aztecs temples as "mosques," evoking in his army the honored tradition of the holy war against the infidels "enemies of the Cross." The battle against Tenochtitlan becomes an ideological crusade, a holy war, in which the most powerful God defeats the lesser deities.[26]

The conquest of America also took place after the expulsion of the Iberian Jews, followers of the Law of Moses, who also for generations and generations had considered as their home the same land and nation that now the Christians claim to be only theirs. In the history of philosophy, immortal names of the Arab Averroës and the Jew Maimonides (both of whom were born in the same city, Cordoba, Spain, also the birth place of the Latin Seneca, and of many Christian writers, artists, and thinkers) constitute eloquent evidence of the common Spanish ancestry of the followers of the three great universal monotheistic religions, as the Spanish scholar Américo Castro insisted upon several years ago.[27]

The linkage between the *Reconquista,* the expulsion of the Jews, and the expansion to new lands, to America, is recognized by Columbus himself, in the prologue to his diary of the first journey.[28] National identity becomes one with religious orthodoxy, which at the same time transforms itself into an imperial crusade. Fernando de los Ríos has clearly shown how, in Spain, "the central dominating force of the will of the nation was a transcendental idea . . . a religious conception of life, incarnated in the Catholic Church."[29]

This peculiar Spanish history gives birth to an exceptional identification between confession and nationality, religion and nation, which is the hermeneutical key to understanding the faith and praxis of conquerors like Hernán Cortés, who commands that the first thing to happen every morning in the camp of his invading army is a Mass, the enactment of the sacrifice of Christ; who has no scruples in accepting women as gifts of subordination by the Mexican caciques and to use them carnally, but only after ordering them baptized; who has no qualms about torturing and executing the brave Cuauhtemoc, but humbles himself in front of the Franciscan friars who arrive in Nueva España to start the christianization of the conquered people.[30]

When Cortés began his final assault of Tenochtitlán (1521), Western Christianity was undergoing the first agonizing signs of the process of division and antagonism that soon would fragment it and transform the *communio sanctorum* into a field of warring armies in which Protestant and Catholic communities would violently face each other with opposing dogmas and opposing weapons. The Spanish crown and church decided to "protect" America from the contamination of the European heresies, giving birth to a history of ecclesiastical repression still waiting to be narrated in its totality.

The Jesuit historian Pedro de Leturia has written: "The crusade of Granada continues in the Indies. . . ."[31] We might add, in the Indies also continues the expulsion of the Jews and the persecution of those who defy traditional ecclesiastical dogmas. Even the prophetic Las Casas officially requested, in 1516, the establishment of an American counterpart to the dreaded Spanish Inquisition.[32] The medieval dictum—*extra ecclesiam nulla salus*—which was meant as a theological judgement, becomes a political condemnation of all kinds of heterodoxies, including the native creeds and religions. Historians and scholars differ pointedly in their evaluations whether it was fundamentally a case of an ecclesiastical state or of a state church. The difference might be significant, but not for the victims of the repressive violence that usually accompanies such an intimate conjunction of material and spiritual ends.[33]

Providential Messianism

Gerónimo de Mendieta, the Franciscan scholar who, at the end of the sixteenth century, wrote a most important history of the conquest and christianization of Mexico, *Historia Eclesiástica Indiana* (a work similar in scope to the patristic *Ecclesiastical History* of Eusebius) asserts that Hernán Cortés was born the same year, 1485, as Martin Luther, emissary of the devil, and the same year that the Aztec Templo Mayor was consecrated with the human sacrifice of more than 80,000 persons (truly a hyperbolic figure). The birth of Cortés thus becomes a providential event, an extremely significant element in the cosmic struggle between Christ and Satan, manifest both in the attempt to eradicate the Protestant heresy and to eliminate the Native American religions. Mendieta praises the Spanish crown for being the only European state that has firmly stood up against "Muslim falseness," "Judaic perfidy," the "household malice of heretics," and "idolatrous blindness." He goes one step forward in the discernment of God's providence, as he boldly asserts that the discovery and conquest of America is a particular divine reward for the strict manner in which Spain has kept the faith uncontaminated.[34] The notion of the elected nation, to which God has conceded a providential and transcendent mission, becomes the hermeneutical key to understand the conquest of America.

It is an idea forwarded also by Friar Toribio de Benavente (Motolinia), one of the twelve Franciscan missionaries that since 1524 forged the monumental christianization of the vast Mexican territory. Motolinia's history of the conquest and evangelization of Nueva España narrates that process as an apocalyptic divine intervention that expresses both God's wrath against the many devilish traditions of the natives and God's merciful redemption of the peoples blinded by Satan.[35]

It was thus ideologically impossible for the Spanish crown to conceive the conquest and colonization of America in terms other than missionary evangelization. It could not articulate the legitimacy of its colonial dominion exclusively from a political or economic perspective. What for other modern empires has been possible, namely, to claim control of the instruments of political and economic power and allowing the dominated peoples spiritual solace for their troubled subjectivity in their native religiosity, was absolutely out of the question for sixteenth-century Spain.

The first law of the 1680 *Recopilation of the Laws of the Kingdom of the Indies* makes unequivocally clear the theological legitimacy of the Spanish domin-

93

ion. It states that the great Spanish empire is a divine grant that imposes a missionary task: "To work so as to make God known and adored in the whole world. . . ."[36]

The understanding of the discovery and conquest of America cannot proceed apart from the analysis of the providential messianism that narrates those events in the light of a transcendental and universal confrontation between true faith and infidelity. This providentialism can be perceived very early in the writings and correspondence of Christopher Columbus himself.[37] In one instance he writes: "It was Our Lord who clearly opened my understanding . . . and who opened my will. . . . Who shall doubt that this light was from the Holy Spirit?"[38] This messianic consciousness is particularly sharp at times of crisis and despair. In the midst of a fearful Atlantic hurricane on his way home after the first expedition, or lost and forsaken in the Caribbean in his fateful fourth journey and seemingly on the verge of collapsing, he undergoes profound spiritual crisis from which he is strengthened in his belief of his God-given providential mission.[39] He even compares himself favorably with the main biblical heroes.

> Oh foolish one and slow to believe and serve your God. . . . Could he have done any more for Moses or for David. . . . From your birth, God has always taken great care of you. . . . The Indies, such rich regions of the world, he has given to you. . . .[40]

This messianic providentialism is even more intense in Cortés. I do not consider his many expressions that attribute his war victories to divine guidance and protection to be merely rhetorical. An example: "As we carried the banner of the cross, and were fighting for the faith. . . . God gave us so great a victory that we killed many of them without our people suffering any harm."[41]

Such messianic devotion is recognized by Pope Clement VII, who after receiving a very generous gift indeed by the conqueror of Mexico, grants him, in 1529, a plenary bull of indulgence forgiving all guilt and penalties of his sins because, according to the Holy Father, Cortés had exposed his life to every danger "for the yoke of Christ and obedience to the Holy Roman Church. . . ."[42]

In this context it is important to note something that many students of the christianization of America fail to perceive. Hernán Cortés pioneers the concept of the new church as an essential element of the new world. Even before the arrival of the twelve Franciscan missionaries, the conqueror of Mexico conceives the linkage of the two eschatological notions: *novus mundus—nova ecclesia.*

Shortly after defeating Tenochtitlan, as a crucial element of his project of colonization, he asks the emperor Carlos V to send missionaries from the mendicant orders. He specifically requests Franciscan friars, renown for the fidelity to the most stringent vows of poverty. The missionaries shall devote themselves solely to the spiritual well-being and redemption of the peoples of the conquered territory. It is not merely a game of words to perceive as key elements of the founding policy of Mexico's colonization what has been called the Franciscanism of Cortés and the Cortesianism of the Franciscans.[43]

Cortés explicitly rejects a former suggestion that the evangelization of Mexico be given to the secular clergy and diocesan hierarchies. The repudiation of the secular church and clergy is abrupt and reveals his opinion, not uncommon in his time, of the moral decadence of the Renaissance church. "Having bishops and other prelates they would follow the customs which they have acquired . . . of disposing of the goods of the Church by wasting them on luxuries and other vices . . ."

The preference of the mendicant orders over the diocesan church that anticipates the intense battles between both ecclesiastical structures later in the sixteenth century is not arbitrary. Only those wholly devoid of material preoccupations could bear the immense challenge poised by millions of conquered infidels. Cortés knew that the Aztec priests could be more austere and chaste than their Catholic European counterparts. He feared that if the natives were exposed to the worldliness of the secular clergy it might prove impossible to demonstrate them the ethical and spiritual superiority of the Gospel. As he writes to Carlos V,

> If they were to see the things of the Church in the hands of the clergy and other ecclesiastical authorities, and were to see them in the profanities and vices in which they indulge in Europe, they would have our faith as worthless. . . . And since the main objective of your Highness is and should be the conversion of these peoples . . . Your Majesty should supplicate the Pope to have as His delegates in this region two religious persons, one from the order of Saint Francis, and the other from the order of Santo Domingo. . . .[44]

Only if these precautions are carefully taken, Cortés asserts, could in the new world be established a new church, in which God, more than in any other, be exalted and glorified.

> It could be with certainty asserted that in a very brief period of time, it will be raised in these lands a new church, in which God will be more praised than in any other in the whole world . . .[45]

Thus, the violent, ambitious, and lascivious conqueror shows himself also to be an apostle of the infidels. But beware; immediately after writing this paean to the new church to be developed in the new world, Cortés recommends that the natives of Michoacán, who refuse to submit to the Spanish conquerors, be enslaved.

> We should make them war and take them as slaves. . . . Bringing these savages as slaves, to work in the gold mines, would produce to your Majesty and the Spanish people benefits, and it might even happen that thanks to such a familiarity with us some might even be redeemed.[46]

The new apostle to the infidels might be their enslaver. Cortés's messianic providentialism does not tolerate any insurmountable obstacle, especially if it comes from the infidels. In the Antilles, and thus in America, the first to propose the slavery of the natives and the first to institute the slave trade was none other than the *Christum ferens* himself, Christopher Columbus.[47]

A Theological Critique

Cortés's messianic and militaristic providentialism does not represent the sole attitude of the Spanish protagonists of the conquest of America. Indeed, the sixteenth century abounds with many different and contradictory voices and perspectives. It truly constitutes a polyphony, and not always symphonic. Many participants of the choir are able not only to make their dissident voices heard but in the case of some of them, like Bartolomé de las Casas, to become quite strident soloists. The basic failure of the perennial followers of the black legend is their inability to perceive the critical and important participation of the prophetic voice, of the prophetic church, in the conquest of America.

Some readers of my book *A Violent Evangelism: The Political and Religious Conquest of the Americas,* which deals with the theological debates in the sixteenth century related to the discovery and conquest of America, have wrongly asserted that my critical evaluation of those events suffers the methodological vice of anachronism, of interjecting into the sixteenth century the ethical sensitivities of the twentieth. That is not the case. Besides the reasonable doubts that one may have with respect to an alleged advanced moral sensitivity of a century that has produced Auschwitz and Hiroshima, Hitler and Stalin, we find here a underestimation of the richness and amplitude of the theological debates in the sixteenth century. As the North American scholar Lewis Hanke so aptly insisted upon several decades ago, sixteenth-century Spain vibrates intensively with disputes and debates about the legitimacy and justice of the conquest.[48] No official colonial axiom was left unquestioned or debated. I am even willing to advance the thesis that no other empire has scrutinized so critically its colonial actions as sixteenth-century Spain did.

When exactly did the debates begin? Maybe the disgust of Father Bernard Boyl, who accompanied Columbus in the second journey and left the expedition in discomfiture, had something to do with the attempt of the Admiral to initiate a transatlantic Indian slave trade to compete with the Portuguese African slave trade.

It is also possible that the sharp repudiation given in 1500 by Queen Isabel to such slave trade was not an impromptu solitary reaction of an ethically sensitive woman. She probably had received some unknown theological advice adverse to Columbus's slave initiatives. The record, I must admit, is not altogether clear. Some feet-upon-earth historians interpret Isabel's outburst—"Who does the Admiral think he is to dare distribute my vassals?"—as rather a clever political maneuver designed to inhibit the development in America of a powerful feudal class with extensive private holdings of lands and slaves.[49] That might be, but I doubt it was the only, or even the main, reason. It was probably the obvious doubts about the theological legitimacy of enslaving infidels who had not injured in any way Christian lands or nations. For the Catholic monarchs of fifteenth- and sixteenth-century Spain, theological arguments did count;[50] they were not perceived as mere ideological tools even when, as always happens in history, kings and queens have a clear proclivity to harmonize their theological views with their material and political interests.

It is also probable that the criticisms of the second decade of the sixteenth century may have been preceded by serious and deep soul searching.[51] That is clear at least with respect to Las Casas. What the scholar Felipe Fernández-Armesto calls the "sudden revelation" of Las Casas was, in my opinion, not so "sudden."[52] His *Historia de las Indias* gives us a portrait of a man of faith, conscience, and courage, who, between 1502 to 1514, underwent a very slow spiritual transformation from being another wealthy *encomendero* to the irate prophet who would denounce to the church, the state, the whole world, and God the oppression of, ironically, the Godless infidels by the God-fearing Christians.

It is Las Casas who preserves in his *Historia* the first clear, unequivocal, and loud voice of Christian[53] prophetic protest. By the end of 1511, the Dominican monks of the Hispaniola were disgusted with the treatment received by the native Americans. They became convinced that such a mistreatment constituted a violation of Pope Alexander's 1493 "donation bulls." The papal decrees had recognized Spanish sovereignty over the lands discovered in order that the native communities be converted to the Christian faith, and the Dominican friars were not fool enough to confuse evangelization with slavery and, worse, demographic elimination. They also came to the conclusion that the European Christians in America were,

97

according to the ecclesiastical norms, in mortal sin on the basis of their cruel conduct. The destiny of the Indians' bodies and of the Europeans' souls weighed heavily in the minds of the friars and they concluded that they could not keep silence anymore. They felt impelled to protest by their religious vows. It is a religious imperative, not any alternative political or social conception, that promotes the first strong prophetic challenge of the conquest.

The narration of Las Casas acquires dramatic overtones.[54] The Dominican priests warn the most prominent members of the colonial establishment of Hispaniola, at that moment the principal focus of Spanish colonization, that they should all go to church the second Sunday of Advent. They obeyed, only to receive the moral shock of their lives. After reading the biblical passage of John the Baptist, *ego vox clamantis in deserto,* friar Antonio de Montesinos, selected by his brethren for his homiletical faculties, said to the audience of respected white European Christians the following piercing words:

> You are in mortal sin . . . for the cruelty and tyranny you use in dealing with these innocent people. Tell me, by what right or justice do you keep these Indians in such a cruel and horrible servitude? On what authority have you waged a detestable war against these people, who dwelt quietly and peaceably on their own land? . . . Why do you keep them so oppressed and weary, not giving them enough to eat nor taking care of them in their illness? For with the excessive work you demand of them they fall ill and die, or rather you kill them with your desire to extract and acquire gold every day. . . . Are not these people also human beings? Have they not rational souls? Be certain that in such a state as this you can be no more saved than a Moor or a Turk. . . .[55]

The final sentence, according to the record of Las Casas, had to sound like an exceptionally terrible indictment to the ears of a Spanish Christian of the epoch, for whom the Islamics—be they Arabs or Turks—were nothing but the most hideous and hated enemies.

Only to a community that cares for the salvation of the soul but is unable to perceive the insidious ways it has been snared into mortal sin could these last words have the strong impact they had that Sunday. The commotion was such that the principal authorities of the Dominican order in Spain and King Fernando himself intervened with threatening admonitions of silence and obedience to the small band of friars. The King requested a copy of the homily, which he read with irate attention. The royal order was categorical: "They [the Dominican friars] should never speak about this subject; neither in public, nor in private, neither directly, nor indirectly shall they ever refer to it."[56] The Dominican prior in Spain commanded silence to the rebel brethren: "*Sumittere intellectum vestrum*" ("Submit your intellect").[57]

But it would not be so. The first prophetic voice had been uttered in the unquenchable style of John the Baptist. The Montesinos homily created the first theological conflict in America. It can also be considered the origin of Latin American liberation theology. From then on, the voice of the prophetic church will never cease to claim for justice and mercy.[58] Those who in the Anglosaxon Protestant tradition have internalized the "black legend" and who think that Bartolomé de las Casas is an exception in an ocean of cruelty and injustice deprive themselves of learning and enjoying the many and diverse ways in which the prophetic voice expressed itself in the sixteenth century. It began with Montesinos. It never ceased.

The main exponent of the prophetic tradition was certainly Bartolomé de Las Casas.[59] We have mentioned him so many times because the story of his discovery and conquest of America can not be narrated without constant reference to him. He was directly responsible for the preservation and transmission of the diary of Columbus's first journey.[60] His *Historia de las Indias* is probably the best source for the first three decades of colonization and christianization,[61] and during more than five decades between 1514 and 1566 he filled the air with his strong comminations and the printing press with his burning treatises.[62] He was here and there, ubiquitous in all debates and disputes.

From his many writings let us choose two of the latest, brief but incendiary. His last letter to the Council of Indies summarizes and culminates his denunciation of five decades. It is brief, only eight sharp statements, but its condemning prophetic tone could hardly be matched:

> 1. All conquests are unjust and tyrannical; 2. we have illegally usurped the kingdoms of the Indies; 3. all encomiendas are bad per se; 4. those who possess them and those who distribute them are in mortal sin; 5. the king has no more right to justify the conquests and encomiendas than the Ottoman Turk to make war against Christians; 6. all fortunes made in the Indies are iniquitous; 7. if the guilty do not make restitution, they will not be saved; 8. the Indian nations have the right, which will be their till doomsday, to make us just war and erase us from the face of the earth.[63]

That strong statement was followed by an epistle to Pope Pius V.[64] Las Casas requests from the *Vicarius Christi* the promulgation of a decree that would: (a) anathematize all those who justify military conquest on the basis of the infidelity of the natives or their alleged rational inferiority; (b) order all bishops and ecclesiastical authorities to defend the powerless from the aggression and oppression of the powerful, the lambs from the wolves, even to lay down their lives in their protection; and, (c) enforce the vows of ecclesiastical poverty and make restitution of the wealth already accumulated by the young American church, thus cutting short its participation in the exploitation of the native peoples.

This denunciatory type of writing made Las Casas an extremely controversial figure, the most polemical protagonist of the conquest of America. He was harshly censored by the Franciscan Motolinia and eulogized by the also Franciscan Mendieta. Oviedo and López de Gomara, the two great chroniclers, were his personal adversaries, but Herrera y Tordesillas, as well as numberless other historians, were indebted to his research. Cortés considered him his enemy, but Carlos V respected him so much that he wanted to make him Bishop of Cuzco, probably the wealthiest American bishopric of the time (Las Casas finally accepted the bishopric of Chiapas, a poor region between Guatemala and Mexico).[65]

He has been extolled by people like the Cuban patriot José Martí, who in his *Edad de oro* considered him a paradigmatic figure at the same level with the Latin American liberators Hidalgo, San Martin, and Bolivar.[66] Simon Bolivar, on his part, once suggested that a new capitol city be built for his vision of a great unified Colombia. The name of the city? Las Casas.[67] Spanish scholars and patricians have either anathematized or canonized Las Casas. Manuel Giménez Fernández dedicated many years and scholarly efforts to his monumental biography of Las Casas[68] and the great Ramón Menéndez Pidal wrote a stinging book lambasting Las Casas.[69]

Many of these opposite evaluations, be they positive or negative, miss the essential mystery of this man. Las Casas was a man educated in the spirit and style of the biblical prophets. His conversion to the freedom of the American communities was intimately linked, as in Saint Augustine's case, to a biblical text. In the case of Las Casas, the text was *Ecclesiasticus* 34:24–25:

> To offer a sacrifice from the
> possessions of the poor
> is like killing a son
> before his father's eyes.
> Bread is life to the destitute,
> and to deprive them of it is murder.[70]

The Latin text used by La Casas was even stronger. "To offer a sacrifice from the possessions of the poor is like killing a son before his father's eyes" is rendered: *"Qui offert sacrificium ex substantia pauperum, quasi qui victimat filium in conspectu patris sui."*[71] The expression *"ex substantia pauperum,"* "from the substance of the poor," implies that what is taken from the dispossessed is decisive for their existence. The crux of the matter is indeed the life or death of the native American peoples.

The old discussion about Las Casas and Spanish national identity can be settled only from the perspective of the prophetic understanding of the relationship between nation and mission. The prophets of the Old Testament have a peculiar love of Israel, their nation. It is a scorching and ethically demanding love. It is a love that requires justice and rightfulness. This is the school of love and justice in which Las Casas learned his particular historical role. To consider Las Casas anti-Spanish, as some have dared to suggest, would be like accusing Jeremiah, Isaiah, or Amos of anti-Semitism.

Las Casas, like Columbus or Cortés, developed a messianic providential concept of himself. He was not, however, a believer in God as the transcendent hypostasis of the nation. His messianic consciousness compelled him to consider himself the chosen prophet who would chastise his nation in the name of the God of justice and mercy. His patriotism reveals itself not in chauvinistic eulogies to the fatherland but in the courage to speak the word of God against those who dare to destroy the poor and powerless, forgetting that they might be, in their destitution and poverty, the predilect creatures of God.

To some this might seem to be a somewhat Protestant interpretation of Las Casas, but as Professor Sylvest has rightly emphasized, the Bible was the main source of authority and inspiration for the mendicant orders of the pre-Counterreformation period.[72] The biblical prophets, not an abstract concept of human rights, provided the paradigmatic model for Las Casas' understanding of his providential role *vis-a-vis* his nation. His readings of the prophets led him into the tragic dilemma of prophetism and patriotism.

Part 2

Politics and Sociology of Terror

The Terror in Ourselves

Donald W. Shriver Jr.

The opposite of the human is not the animal. The opposite of the human is the demonic.

Just to be is blessing. Just to live is holy.

The prophet is a person who suffers the harm done to others.

Abraham Joshua Heschel[1]

The city of Weimar was declared the "cultural capital" of Europe for the year 1999. Goethe and Schiller made their homes there, and the city honors their legacies in numerous museums, libraries, theaters, and wall plaques. When one crosses the street from the train station to the bus stop, one finds two upright signs, written in German and English. This is the site of Germany's greatest artistic contribution to world culture, says one sign. But, says the other, be aware that several miles from here was the death camp Buchenwald.

Goethe's own greatest work, *Faust,* portrays the voluntary fall of a scholar into the hands of the Devil. The signs in front of the Bahnhof seem to say: "You are now close to the best and the worst of human history. Which will win out in our future remains an open question."

Uniquely among modern countries, Germans have attempted to put on permanent display emblems of *die Nazizeit* as warnings to themselves and the world of the evils that lurk in even the most "civilized" cultures. Buchenwald is now a museum visited by thousands of Germans and others every year. There, spread out, are the remnants of the terror that swept Germany and Europe from 1933 to 1945: the foundations of the blocks where prisoners lived; the stakes where they were whipped; the mounds where they were shot; the laboratories where their pain was "scientifically" measured;

the furnaces where their bodies were cremated. The Nazis hoped to obliterate the remnants of these camps after their victories. Modern Germans have decided on public preservation of their negative history.

Invariably, foreign visitors tour these places and emerge with the agonizing question: "How could they?" But the domestic German visitor is likely to change the pronoun: "How could we?"

In easy refusal of that latter pronoun, all such visitors can project the Nazi terror onto mostly dead criminals. A certain fascination with horror can draw some of us to the sites of such atrocities, such as the level field near the crematoria of Auschwitz where the ashes of some one million humans are scattered, making it the largest known graveyard on earth. All of this can be pondered with a certain shiver in the spine that some of us experience in viewing horror movies. But one crosses the boundary from observation *of* evil into vulnerability *to* evil once one begins to entertain the change from "they" to "we." Fight as we will against that change, it creeps up on us when we immerse ourselves in the flood of literature now available on the mass murders that made the twentieth century the most deadly in human history. The names alone betoken a huge cast of demons haunting the century: The Somme, Babi Yar, Gulag, comfort women, Hiroshima, Great Leap Forward, Pol Pot, Bosnia, Rwanda. In war alone, the twentieth century saw the death of humans at an average of one hundred *every hour*.[2]

If the question, "How could we do it?" does not capture us in a grip of despair about human capacities for evil, we must ask it for the purpose of learning answers to the twin question: "How could we stop doing it?" Answers to the first question can possibly serve as answers to the second. One of the evils of evil is its uncanny escape from the yearning of intelligence. Even were we able to understand, we would not thereby necessarily change anything. In the century just past, intelligence was coopted to the service of terror. In the hope that it might yet be recruited to the service of life, however, it is important at least to try to understand.

The Quest for Understanding: Social Psychology

Jonathan Glover's recent study, *Humanity*, ends with the summary sentences: "The means for expressing cruelty and carrying out mass killing have been fully developed. It is too late to stop the technology. It is to the psychology that we should now turn."[3] Glover's book says to philosophers, historians, and theologians that their disciplines must get over the famous distinction between fact and value in human affairs. Instead we all must allow fact and value to "interrogate" each other. The historical facts of human cruelty to fellow humans are ethically important to examine. The ethics of human life must reckon with its allies and enemies in the empirically discernable world.

One courageous student of this mixture is Robert Lifton, who has spent his career inquiring into the origins of human violence. One of his studies concentrates on a group of people who were members of his own profession: medical doctors employed at Auschwitz to conduct obscene experiments on living men, women, and children. Throughout this harrowing study Lifton asks, "How could they do it?" His general conclusion is that the human mind has a capacity for "doubling," for living part of their lives in one mental compartment by one set of rules while living in another compartment simultaneously by another. The Nazi doctors put their medical skills and professional medical commitments to the service of Nazi ideology of racial cleansing. Ranked in a hierarchy of more-to-less valuable people, Auschwitz prisoners were classified as *lebensunwertes Leben*—life unworthy of life. Once defined so, prisoners were easier to torture, mutilate, and kill by physicians who went to their camp homes at night, played with their children, loved their wives, and listened to Mozart. Month after month they endured this dualism with no signs of insanity.

Late in the book, Lifton poses the question that he and his readers would both like to avoid: Do we all have the potential for becoming like these parodies of the medical profession? A prompt "no" rises protectively in most of us. Anyone who has pondered the violent history of the twentieth century, however, should resist the rush to personal denial. Lifton and other students of politically organized terror come to a dreaded conclusion: "Just about anyone can join a collective call to eliminate every last one of the alleged group of carriers of the 'germ of death.'"[4] Almost every study of the guards and other agents of the Nazi genocide points to the fact that the majority of them were ordinary people persuaded by their leaders to "do a job." Members of Police Battalion 101, assigned to kill Jews in Poland and the Ukraine, disliked the work of spattering the brains of victims on the ground with guns held close to the head, but most got used to it.[5] Out of five hundred battalion members, only a dozen took up the offer of the commanding officer to exempt themselves from this grisly work, underscoring Christopher Browning's insistence that the Nazi leaders understood social group pressures well enough but continued to respect the role of individual decision in the choreography of terror.[6] The Nazis knew that vertical obedience to commands, combined with horizontal conformity to a peer group, constitute powerful pressures on individual behavior.

Legal scholar Mark Osiel has coined the term "administrative massacre" to describe mass murders undertaken organizationally at the behest of leadership.[7] Minus bureaucratic organization, how could six million Jews be killed by the Nazis? Without careful orchestration by a government plan, how could eight hundred thousand Rwandan Tutsis be slaughtered more efficiently in two months than were the inmates of Auschwitz?

Lifton's term for human capacity for becoming agents of these atrocities is "psychic numbing." One must also speak of moral numbing. Anyone who has ever gone through basic training in the military will remember that one aim of that process is to break down resistance to killing that most civilians bring with them to the experience. If the work of armed police and soldiers is to be accorded ethical legitimacy, of course, they must retain some of that resistance. Their job is to protect life at the cost, if necessary, of destroying it. This is not an easy psychic combination. During the Battle of Fredericksburg, with its eighteen thousand casualties, most of them Federal, Robert E. Lee remarked to Longstreet, "It is well that war is so terrible—we should grow too fond of it."[8] One senses from this remark Lee's awareness that killing can become an only-too-tolerable human activity. A line officer of the U.S. Navy remarked once to Chaplain Arnold Resnicoff, "My job on occasion is to kill people. Your job is to keep me uncomfortable about it." Reinhold Niebuhr would have agreed: "It may be possible for Christians to carry a gun, but they must carry it with a heavy heart."

The trouble with these formulations, however, is that they approach the very edge of Lifton's psychic numbing. Pacifists know this, and their argument for swearing off all use of violence is compelling. Are we asking for the impossible when we expect soldiers to do double duty to society by killing (or curbing) its enemies while still preserving moral respect for life? Civilians have an easier time tolerating violence when they delegate duties of killing to their official military agents. Civilian comfort with war at a distance can thus be preserved, but this psychology is deceptive. It ignores the implication of all members of modern society in the destructive powers of our governments and the destructive policies that receive our majority approval actively or passively. Indeed, civilian rage against enemies sometimes outdoes that of soldiers. The distance of the former from the bloody work of the latter makes the *idea* of killing more tolerable.[9]

In great unflinching honesty, Lifton ends his book on the Nazi doctors with a warning against a form of "doubling" that afflicts virtually every modern American: our toleration of weapons able to kill every human on earth. He calls this the mind of "nuclearism." It has seeped into us all. For fifty years the world has held back from nuclear war under the threat of nuclear war. We keep the peace—so goes the policy of "Mutually Assured Destruction"—by preparations for instant total annihilation. We assume that leaders of governments antagonistic to us love their own people too much to risk their destruction as the cost of destroying us, so we hold at bay vast new levels of administrative massacre by equipping our society for undertaking it.

No one knows if Americans would someday undertake it. Anxiety that we might do so rises from the fact that, in our collective name, we—our military—did once do so. The best that can be said of Hiroshima is that perhaps it put all the world, including Americans, on the alert against another Hiroshima geometrically multiplied. That is the hope alongside the horror with which Lifton concludes his great study of the Nazi doctors. Those who survive mass terror witness to their experience in the hope that it will never be repeated in the lives of others. But listening to that witness requires special inner moral discipline, for one is likely to hear

> . . . what Loren Eiseley called "the dark murmur that rises from the abyss beneath us, and that draws us with uncanny fascination," and realizes that the murmur is our own, a whisper of danger that must be heard before it becomes a hopeless genocidal scream.[10]

Are we brave enough to listen to that "dark murmur"? And is there another voice somewhere—in our history, our spirits, our prayers—that beckons us away from hopelessness to life? These are the two questions that have haunted me as I have tried to write this essay.

A Necessary Parenthetical Disclaimer

Not long ago, Elie Wiesel, who has probably written more eloquently about the Holocaust than any other survivor, said to his interviewer: "One writes for the silences between words, and one writes against the words, for words can never really express the horrors we have witnessed."[11] As another writer on this subject, a person like me must, *a fortiori,* confess my inability to speak as the subject deserves to be spoken about. The deficiency here is twofold: not only can a nonvictim not truly understand the agonies of the victims, but neither can our thought or our words move readers or author to acts that will prevent the repetition of these awful events. Nevertheless, the authorial excuse for putting such words to paper is akin to that of Augustine for the inadequate but necessary wordage we call theology: "We speak in order not to be silent."

On Being Brave Enough to Face the Terror

When we hear these days about "the problem of terrorism," we think of people out there who prey on the rest of us with guns, bombs, and lethal microbes. We shrink in horror from one more story of vicious human cruelty. In rehearsing a series of atrocities from the World War II era, for example, teachers will discover that students have limited capacity for digesting it all. German high school students will tell you, "We have had it up to here with the Holocaust." If they ever came close to learning the full horrors of the African slave trade and the slaughter of Native Americans, many American students would make similar protest. In fact, the real resistance in American schools comes from teachers and administrators who feel bound by their political sponsors to hide many of the atrocious crimes of our ancestors. A Mississippi history textbook cowritten by James Loewen, for example, included a grisly photograph of two dozen white men and women circling around a burning black man. Such photos of lynching, said members of the state textbook board, would cause a riot in classrooms of young people. Eventually accepted for school use, the photo did not evoke a riot. Instead, the incident demonstrated the adults' fear of facing the evil sides of American history.[12]

No one can be blamed for turning away in horror from pictures of bodies piled up in Dachau in 1945, the church floor full of corpses in Rwanda in 1994, and the mound of skulls in the Cambodia massacres. To be sure, images of violence in fact or in film can be entertaining. For reasons that elude the most moral of us, we all are vulnerable to curiosity about killing so long as we can view it from the safe distance of a TV screen. Keeping it "out there" is our way of coping with it. Terror is something that other people do.

To think so is to be deaf to Eiseley's "dark murmur." Listening to that murmur *in here,* in our own selves, is the ultimate terror, companion to the terror of remembering the pain that one once endured at the hands of the perpetrators. Individual survivors of great violence do not return readily to memories of their pain. Consoling forgetfulness may be their balm of choice, even though their minds may involuntarily gravitate back to the old unspeakable suffering. Some survivors of the Nazi camps testified that dreams took them regularly back there. For years, many a Vietnam veteran revisited the jungle every night. Their memories proved all the more indelible because friends and family often refused to listen to their stories. To listen is to taste some of the pain of another human being. We all shrink naturally from even a taste.

But the heart of our natural resistance to tales of vast suffering stems not from our difficulty in empathizing with victims. Our problem is our suspicion that everyone is a potential victimizer. *I* could be the Police Battalion 101 member who shot Jews in the fields of Poland. *I* could have wielded the machetes that killed eight hundred thousand Tutsis in Rwanda. *I* could have been a Serbian soldier who helped kill seven thousand Muslim prisoners in Srebrenica. *I* could have raped those Muslim women. *I* could be the soldier who would be only doing his duty by pressing the buttons that release nuclear missiles that would kill three hundred million Chinese people.

I blame no reader of this paragraph who calls its author an "alarmist." After all, not all Germans became Nazis, and not all Nazis pulled the trigger on Jews. Well that we should identify hopefully with those who resisted the evil-doing that someone in authority ordered, but the burden of reassurance here is hard to sustain. Would we resist to the point of dying on behalf of resistance? No one knows for sure. Heroism is unpredictable. What we do know, from the experience of others who have survived totalitarian systems, is that the influence of social authority, social conformity, and punitive threat can wring out the human potential for resistence.

A few years ago, Dr. Fulbert Stefensky, professor in the teacher-education school of Hamburg University, conducted an experiment with students in a class. "If a gang of young Nazis tried to burn down a synagogue in your city, would you protest?" A large majority of hands went up. "If Gestapo police took your father off to jail, would you protest?" Somewhat fewer hands went up. "If they required every young person in the school to join the Hitler Youth, would you refuse to join?" Fewer hands went up. "If they threatened you with deportation to a camp if you refused to inform on a fellow student, would you refuse?" One or two hands went up. "And if they were about to torture you to death . . . ?" No hands went up.

In the spring of 1994 in Rwanda, Hutu organizers of the genocide informed their educated Hutu comrades that unless they joined in the killing of Tutsi neighbors, they too would be killed. A few preferred to be killed. Most joined reluctantly in the massacre. Even more reluctantly, after the six weeks of mass murder were over, they confided that their second murder was easier, the third easier yet. After they had ushered ten thousand inmates into the gas chambers, did the guards in Auschwitz have second thoughts about it? When American bomber crews returned from Dresden and Tokyo in February–March 1945, did many suffer mental disturbance? Were their hearts heavy?

We cannot be sure of the answers to any of these questions, but the more we ponder them the less sure we can be that, in the same times and places, we ourselves would act differently from the majority of these, our fellow human beings. This is one of most depressing thoughts that can come to any human who stands on this rim of the twenty-first century. We have inherited the most violent century in human history. Many of us are more than inheritors—we participated, in one way or another, in the violence. Anyone who wants to claim that they did not participate must be prepared to answer questions like:

What taxes did you refuse to pay for the financing of nuclear missiles?

When did you write a letter to Congress protesting CIA support of training of death squads in El Salvador or torturers in Chad?

How often during the Cold War did you pray for the welfare of the Soviet people?

Have you ever pondered the argument that the atomic bomb was not necessary for ending the Pacific War in 1945?

Would it be worth risking a hundred American lives to save the lives of ten thousand people in Africa?

To ask such questions is to reckon with the limits of human virtue that afflict most of us. It is also to raise up one's defense: "better a bystander to terror than a perpetrator."

Is it really better? Midnight of May 10, 1997, was the deadline for filing of amnesty applications by South Africans willing to confess to "crimes against humanity" during the apartheid era. Just before midnight, a group of six black youths walked into the Truth and Reconciliation Commission office in Cape Town and asked for amnesty applications. "What did you do?" asked the official. "Nothing," they answered. That was our crime, they said. "We neglected to take part in the liberation struggle. So, here we stand as a small group representative of millions of apathetic people who didn't do the right thing."[13]

A long spectrum of human sin spreads from high-profile evildoing to low-lying apathy. Were we to quantify it, the human capacity for apathy would probably exceed our capacity for killing. One saves a fragment of self-respect in thinking that, caught up in a lynch mob, one might stand by as another struck the match to the fire. One might just go home. But one would never. . . . Oh, never? *How can the devil of human violence be exorcised if the majority of us simply let others become the agents of that devil?*

Beyond this rhetorical question, I want to examine what, if any, spiritual forces are at work in our world to defeat this devil's rampage through our history and in ourselves.

The Spirit of Life Against the Spirit of Murder

Discussion of this subject runs headlong into theology. Some secularists may doubt this inevitability, but the issues of violence in our recent times hurl issues of ultimate meaning at us, and in one form or another this means theology. One of the great contributors to world discussion of these matters is Jonathan Schell. His 1982 book, *The Fate of the Earth,* posed the question in theological terms. Many of his secular critics scoffed at his turn from politics to religion. Schell suggested that the Creator of the world meant for the human race to survive its own propensity for murder. He even invoked, as an image of ultimacy in the universe, the love of God expressed in the Christian concept of Trinity.

Writing in 1940, Kenneth Patchen proposed that the question of the twentieth century is not, "Do we believe in God? But rather: Does God believe in us?"[14] That may be a clumsy way of putting one of the agonies of ancient Israel, but the prophets Amos and Hosea come to mind. Like his predecessors, Amos believed that the Creator of Israel, who called a people out of Egyptian slavery, had special reason to be *angry* with the sins of this supposedly chosen people. "You only have I known of all the families of earth; therefore I will punish you for all your iniquities" (Amos 3:2). It was anger rooted in care.

Whether or not punishment falls on the head of the iniquitous is a great theological question for lots of us in the twenty-first century. We would like to see more divine anger! We survey the horrors of organized evil in our time, and we ask if God was present in any of it. Where was the divine *wrath* in Auschwitz? When even a human parent is angry at the conduct of a child, we understand the anger as love for the good of that child. Ignoring evil is a sure sign of lovelessness. A certain practical atheism haunts us: If God exists, is it a remote existence unrelated to us? Is God apathetic to the suffering of creatures?

Aristotle thought so, but we must assume that Aristotle was not apathetic to the suffering of his own wife and children. Twentieth-century theologians have warned us against trusting much in human experience as a doorway into experience of our Creator, and it does seem that only in some revelation—a door opened from the other side—can the conviction dawn that God really does believe in us. Hosea's great clarity about God's "belief" in Israel, however, came to focus in his own experience of love for his own faithless wife, and practical atheism will make its inroads into our intellect and our spirits if we never feel the presence of One whose love will not let us go. So to experience God is not to convey theological "proof" to our skeptical neighbors, but it is to have a reason for believing, deep down, that the world of humanity is not exclusively under the rule of the Devil. Gomer's behavior brought tears to Hosea, and he dared to believe that the God of Israel could weep, too. This Creator suffers in the suffering of creatures. Divine anger is the cloak for divine love, "for I am God and no mortal, the Holy One in your midst, and I will not come in wrath" (Hosea 11:9).

It is time, I think, for religious people around the world to take seriously this evil "in your midst." Christian theologians have sometimes supposed that if they can just demonstrate how evil humans are, they can then demonstrate how good God is in saving us from our evil. Not only does that proposal defy logic, it also feeds the cynicism that W. H. Auden put on the lips of King Herod, a corrupt king who resorted habitually to violence and vengeance. Let this Jesus come to power, Herod muses, and

> Justice will be replaced by Pity, as the cardinal human virtue, and all fear of retribution will vanish. Every corner-boy will congratulate himself: "I'm such a sinner that God had to come down in person to save me. I must be a devil of a fellow." Every crook will argue: "I like committing crimes. God likes forgiving them. Really the world is admirably arranged."[15]

Early in the oratorio the narrator sets the stage for this drama of theological agony befitting the experience of all who have asked if God could possibly be present in the world of twentieth century terror:

> We are afraid
> Of pain but more afraid of silence; for no nightmare
> Of hostile objects could be as terrible as this Void.
> This is the Abomination. This is the wrath of God.[16]

The theology is doubtless debatable, but the question of *where* God is present in today's earthly world needs to be answered in terms of demonstrated *human* potentials *if* we are to believe that human existence is worth our deep continuing affirmation. Theologians and ethicists in the Jewish and Christian traditions will disagree on questions of "general" revelation, but—to put it crudely—God's presence in the realm of humanity generally is now a hope on which the persistence of our specie may critically depend. Contrary to some critics of a theological basis for moral law, moral invitations in the Bible are very much down-to-earth. Was it only to Israel that the following assurances were delivered?

> . . . this commandment that I am commanding you this day is not too hard for you, nor is it too far away . . . No, the word is very near to you; it is in your mouth and in your heart for you to observe. See, I have set before you today life and prosperity, death and adversity. . . . Choose life so that you and your descendants may live . . . (Deuteronomy 30:11, 14, 15, 19).

The greatest precis of ethics some of us know is Micah 6:8: "[God] has shown you, O mortal, what is good; and what does the LORD require of you but to do justice, and to love kindness, and to walk humbly with your God?" The words are addressed to "man," to our specie. If this core of morality has been revealed only to humans who call themselves Jews and Christians, our specie really is on shaky grounds for survival.

The bridges between affirming this ethic and practicing it may be rare and shaky, but the time is at hand when we must search more diligently than Diogenes for traces of honest justice and kindness in the human community worldwide. Wherever found, justice and kindness are evidences of the presence of a Holy Spirit in human affairs. That Spirit surely is not in evidence everywhere. But if the Spirit does not live somewhere, in some of us some of the time, we really are a threatened specie. Reluctantly but realistically, I have to agree with Gordon Kaufman, who some years ago wrote that those who believe in God's sovereignty over human history must now take with unprecedented seriousness the sovereignty that humans have now grasped for committing specie-suicide. The real sentimentalists of our time are those who want to treat the trenches of World War I, the city-killing of World War II, and the train of genocides from the Armenians to the Stalinists to the Cambodians as mere diversions from an otherwise hopeful history of *homo sapiens*. Human sapience has regularly served human annihilation. In an unprecedented, terrifying sense, "to be or not to be" really is the question. *Do we love our unborn descendents enough to do what we can to make their birth possible?* What in fact can we do? What are our shared capacities for reversing the inertias of violence in the future history of humanity?

Evoking the Best in Us to Curb the Worst: Reading the Signals of Hope

This question came home to me, literally, on the weekend of October 26–28, 1962. All who have seen the movie *Thirteen Days* will remember that this was the date of the Cuban Missile Crisis. That weekend saw me, my wife Peggy, and our three children traveling to my hometown, Norfolk, Virginia, for the celebration of my parents' thirty-seventh wedding anniversary and my recent completion of graduate work in preparation for taking a new job in North Carolina. As we traveled the New Jersey Turnpike, the world's nearest approach to nuclear war was gathering, and we were about to visit the city with the largest naval base on earth, quite within the nine hundred-mile range of nuclear missiles stationed in Cuba.

The most poignant autobiographical note about that October 28, for me, is the fact that in exactly thirty years to the day, our younger son, then aged twenty months, would become the father of his own first child. But for that event to come in 1992, something momentous had to intervene that very weekend of 1962. We may call it political wisdom. The chief practitioners of that wisdom, it turns out, were an officially atheistic communist named Nikita Krushchev and a Catholic American president, John F. Kennedy.

Early in his presidency, Kennedy had attended a meeting of senior American military officers who laid out to him the probable devastations of a nuclear war. After the meeting, reported Dean Rusk, Kennedy returned to his office "with a strange look on his face," and to Rusk he said, "And we call ourselves the human race." We know that on being similarly informed by his own military, Krushchev said that he could not sleep until, several nights later, he concluded that nuclear weapons could not ever really be used. Something of this wisdom was obvious in the letter which he wrote to Kennedy on Friday, October 26:

> Should war break out, it would not be in our power to contain or stop it, for such is the logic of war. I have taken part in two wars, and I know that war ends only when it has rolled through cities and villages, sowing death and destruction everywhere. . . . If people do not display wisdom, they will eventually reach the point where they will clash, like blind moles, and then mutual annihilation will commence. . . .

On his side, in the same week, Kennedy said to his brother Robert that he had read the recently published book by historian Barbara Tuchman, *The Guns of August.* "I am not going to follow a course which will allow anyone to write a comparable book about this time, *The Missiles of October.* If anybody is around to write after this, they are going to understand that we made every effort to give our adversary room to move. I am not going to push the Russians an inch beyond what is necessary." Kennedy was not sure that his own military advisors took seriously the dangers of violent push on each side. Emerging from a meeting with them, he said to his press secretary: "Do you think the people in that room realize that if we make a mistake, there may be 200 million dead?"

"Room to move" meant room to back down, to back away from looming disaster. Afterwards, Krushchev himself put the moral-political lesson in another letter to Kennedy: "We had to step over our pride, both you and we, in order to reach this agreement."[17]

What were the human capacities that enabled these two statesmen to "step over their pride" and to save the lives of perhaps millions of people? Jonathan Glover contends that there are at least two such capacities, both of which were finally activated on both sides of this momentous conflict: *respect* for other human beings and *empathy* for their thinking, feeling, and living.

Are human beings respectable? Most world religions say so. Hunger for respect from our neighbors seems high among human hungers. Youth in urban ghettos require respect, and being "dissed" (disrespected) prompts some to murder. Street culture encourages many such youth to live by the rule: "Trust no one. Everyone is out to get you." Given the ease with which we countenance killing on all sides of modern civilization, one has to wonder if the facts echo the amoralism, "People are no damn good." Political ideologies have maintained that as truth about at least some people. If about some, why not all?

Religion stubbornly continues to tell us that we humans have extraordinary value—from the red soul-spot on Hindu foreheads to Muslim transcendence of racial identities to Jewish and Christian claims that we all bear in ourselves the image of our Creator. The Hebrew law "love your neighbor as yourself" implies equal value of all human neighbors, and the great parable of the Last Judgment of Jesus (Matthew 25:31–46) asserts the value of "the least of these" as an identification of them all with the person of Jesus himself. The implication is radical: those who kill a fellow human are murdering God.

Of all the Christian assertions of this radical view, the most radical is what we say about the crucifixion of Jesus. Following Rene Girard, Gil Baillie says that in the death of Jesus the world got put on notice that when human "justice" overwhelms respect for both God and fellow humans, death ensues. A world in which holiness can no longer be attributed to human beings—not to speak of other beings—is a world on the road to destruction. Christian faith sees the cross and resurrection of Jesus as constituting the Creator's break with the corruptions of the old violent world of Cain and Herod, the inbreaking of a new order beginning with the removal of sanctity from all human violence. The divine Spirit is now at work "in our midst" to restore the divine image to every one of us. A great reversal is afoot: "forgive them, for they know not what they do"; and a great new power portending the final defeat of the Devil: "he is risen!"

Baillie believes that the death-knell of deadly violence has been struck in the cross of Jesus, however visibly violence continues to haunt our history past and present. Religion now has abundant reason in history to abolish all sense of sanctity in its own symbols that have often legitimated violence. From time immemorial, "sacrifice" has been at the core of much religious ritual. Devilish sanctity still cloaks many a contemporary act of political violence, but it is a mere cloak. If one wanted to see demonry remembered in photographs on display in the year 2000, one had only to visit a museum displaying the faces of white people gathered for one of the five thousand lynchings in the United States from 1890 to 1930. The visages of these white witnesses are frightening: smiles, eyes alight with revenge, and even little children caught up in a kind of unholy, shared glee. They are all stand-ins of the witnesses who mocked the crucifixion of Jesus.[18]

If Baillie is right, gradually, in many a time and place, it is becoming harder for humans to claim that violence can ever be perceived as sacred. Whatever else murder is, it is not an act of piety. Ever and again, societies rediscover that killing is not holy. Soldiers went off to World War I in an euphoria of patriotism, but the realities of the Western Front become anything but an experience of the motto on German belt buckles: "Gott mit uns." World War II evokes mostly grim loyalty among Americans. The Korean and Vietnam Wars become grimmer yet. And, in spite of the triumphalism of a president, the Gulf War of 1991 leaves a trail of guilt in the minds of many Americans over the news that filtered through Pentagon censorship that many a surrendering Iraqi soldier was blown away. Whatever else we can say to justify modern war, we Christians have to say that never again will we call war a "crusade," nor will we sing, as we pick up a gun, "Onward Christian Soldiers." The time is over when Christian Americans can tolerate "Corpus Christi" as an appropriate name for a nuclear submarine.[19]

But these ambiguous cultural winds are not the best examples of what Baillie calls experiences of "the gust of grace that makes a loving and forgiving God plausible." Moralism tempts all of us in our spiritual battle against our own propensities for violence. Like moralists of every age, notes Baillie, John the Baptist "passionately enjoined his listeners to renounce their evil ways." But Jesus' way was different: he *inhabited* a sphere of God's presence "on earth as it is in heaven." He "made it a palpable reality for others by forgiving sins, restoring faith and hope to those around him, and bringing people he touched fully alive."[20]

Some of our neighbors, past and present, inhabit the same sphere. They are the heroes and heroines of God's New Age. They are God's witnesses that the Lord's Prayer is not prayed in vain. Without their embodiment of the respect and empathy that makes a human community human, all our hope in ourselves might perish. Skeptical as he is of any religious basis for retrieving a robust, life-preserving morality for the world of modern politics, Jonathan Glover peppers his book with signs and examples of the other side of human nature at work to overcome the murderous side: a flash of empathy for a soldier already in one's gunsight, a Jewish child saved by a Nazi soldier, a village in France (Le Chambon) whose populace organized around its Reformed Church pastor to save five thousand Jews from capture by the Gestapo. The religious among us must be free to claim that the Spirit of God moved in our midst in the lives of a Martin Luther King Jr., a Dietrich Bonhoeffer, a Mother Teresa, a Mahatma Gandhi, a Nelson Mandela, a Kim Dae Jung, and a David Kwang-sun Suh. Not only has their faithfulness to life against death, respect against contempt, and empathy against cruelty provided us with personal examples, but their leadership has attracted many anonymous followers whose collective impact is a world more conducive to our redemption from violence than it might have been. Deep in the minds of Nikita Krushchev and John F. Kennedy was anxious concern for the lives of millions. If we cannot find reason to thank God for such endowments of wisdom and goodness that save us from self-destruction, for what on earth might we be thankful? The word that can save us had better be very near. If it is not, we remain horribly endangered by our over-equipped capacities for killing.

Toward the end of his book, Gil Baillie has two powerful illustrations of the humanity that wonderfully survives attempts to destroy it in the lives of some of our persecuted neighbors. One is the story of a nameless Jew killed in Buchenwald. Before his death he left behind a testament of hope that read, in part:

> Peace to all men of evil will! Let there be an end to all vengeance, to all demands for punishment and retribution. . . . Lay not their sufferings to the torturer's charge to exact a terrible reckoning from them, Lord. Instead, put down in favor of all men of evil will, the courage, humility, dignity, love and spiritual strength of the others. Let it be laid before Thee for the forgiveness of sins. . . . And may we remain in your enemies' memory not as their victims . . . not as haunting spectres, but as helpers in their striving to destroy the fury of their criminal passions. There is nothing more that we want for them.

That murdered Buchenwald prisoner was a world-class saint. Such a person is the hope of our self-beleaguered human specie.

Baillie's other illustration is a young woman who died in the massacre of El Mozote in El Salvador. Government soldiers, bent on killing the whole village, raped many of the women. On a hill called La Cruz ("The Cross"), they repeatedly raped a young woman and then shot her in the chest. Not yet dying, she kept singing an evangelical hymn, which struck the soldiers with such fear that to stop the singing they took machetes to her neck.[21]

Another story, from 1994, belongs with these two: a Rwandan Tutsi woman named Alexia watched machete-wielding Hutus murder her neighbors, her husband, and her children. She then endured rape and a miscarriage. In the midst of this horror, she drew out her copy of the Bible and said to her attackers: "Take this Bible, because it is our memory, and because you do not know what you are doing."[22]

We have to wonder if they ever read it, if they ever came to the place which was the source of her own dying words: "Forgive them, for they know not what they do."

Baillie's somber, hopeful conclusion is one that none of us his readers can ever forget. It is my own: violence in human hands can never be more than a simulation of sanctity. In fact, it is the instrument of a devil. Our ultimate question is: Will Evil Spirit or Holy Spirit win out in the history of humankind?

> However shrill and bombastic the voices of the victors and victimizers may grow, there is now something at work in history that endows the faintist gestures of the victim with a *lasting* moral power that will sooner or later be all

the world remembers. . . . Most of us, therefore, can thank God that we live in the vast middle ground of history, where the choice between sanctity and savagery is never this stark. But ultimately, we live in a world that will be ordered and made coherent by one or the other of the two forms of religious transcendence that struggle with one another so pitiably on *La Cruz*."[23]

. . . and at Buchenwald, in Rwanda, in New York, and every place on this inhabited planet.

Terror and Hope in the Minds of Russians[1]

Tony Carnes

Catastrophe, terror, and hope are a litany of Russian history. Today, many Russians feel that they have been through the double catastrophe and terror of both the communist and the Yeltsin reformist periods. Yet, Russians have persisted with patience and hope.[2] In the past, religion and noncommunist secular hopes were officially suppressed. Though the Soviet masses had largely distanced themselves from official ideology by the 1980s, they had not yet seen the opportunity to believe in an alternative society-transforming ideology. In 1991, many Russians started to try out religions as a way to make sense of their catastrophes and terrors.[3]

Faith, half of religious Russians today say, helps them overcome their fears. Indeed, according to our surveys, more Russians cite faith than anything else as an effective resource during these catastrophic times.

Terror and fear pose a question of authority, about who or what will rule us. The Bible portrays God surrounded by a terrifying glory.[4] All the false gods flee before God in his awe-inspiring glory. However, the Bible also notes that idols, sometimes called "Fears," have their own glories to betwitch and terrify their worshippers. In this sense, any kind of terror is evidence of a numbing or awesomeness that surrounds someone or something that seeks to dominate our seeing, thinking, feeling, and acting. The terror claims the authority's right and power to begin and end life, to determine the boundaries of its own reach, of nature and spirit and of the mundane order that comprehends our lives. Terror says that all other authorities need to be put aside and ignored in the presence of the terrorizing authority. Terror legitimizes, authorizes, the reordering of life, action, and world. In the face of a terror a stronger authority is needed to sustain oneself.

Social surveys over the last ten years seem to indicate that Russians have brought to bear two cultural mentalities on the terrifying chaos of the 1990s and the more distant past. Consequently, persistence and hope have arisen in two different ways in today's Russia. On the one hand, there was the worldview, more predominate among Russian Orthodox, that saw the world as being undone, as an overwhelming, contaminating force. One can only be passively patient before catastrophe and terror, adherents of this view said, marshalling and maintaining one's small circle of trusted friends. On the other hand, a group of younger, more educated Russians had a more activist *zweckrational* worldview. They also saw the world as being undone but were more likely to feel that they could manage the chaos and their fears. However, by August of 1998 many were beginning to flinch and, if possible, flee Russia. Since then, the Russian situation has stabilized and slowly improved. However, these two worldviews continue to act as deep structures in influencing every day life and public policy, particularly during catastrophes.

Russians today have also thrown themselves into their work and have structured their relations to the social world so as to minimize the terrors of their catastrophes. Because most Russians believe that the big world is beyond control and trustworthiness and is deteriorating further, they have retreated to the redoubt of their private world. Many believe that while the bigger world is going to the dogs, in their private life they still have some control, trust, and hope. The most characteristic structure of emotions may well be a layer cake of emotions: fear in the big world and cheerfulness in the private world. This explains how Russians can report terrible circumstances and psychological disturbances but 44 percent can still say that they remain cheerful and content.

National Catastrophes, Fears, and Terrors in Russia

In Russian history, remembered or expected national catastrophes have reinforced an apocalyptic mood in Russian thinking and action. Indeed, the study of Russia cannot be accomplished without a study of the role of catastrophes (Ivan the Terrible, pogroms, World Wars I and II, the Great Depression, totalitarian rises and falls, etc.), the intensification of catastrophic thinking, and the emotions of fear and terror.

The causes of most terror is usually related to some sort of extreme catastrophe—real, remembered, or imagined—that seems to throw down all other stable national authorities in life, dissolves all boundaries, and then lives on as a vivid, terrifying memory. The catastrophe and its terror may also be buried in memory only to explode into consciousness later, or it may apocalyptically loom in the future.

Also, most social scientists have said that "terror" is when the ones terrified say that they have experienced terror. For example, Juergensmeyer says, ". . . terror is meant to terrify. The word comes from the Latin *terrere*, 'to cause to tremble,' . . . Hence the public response to the violence—the trembling that terrorism effects—is part of the meaning of the term. It is appropriate, then, that the definition of a terrorist act is provided by us, the witnesses—the ones terrified—and not by the party committing the act. It is we—or more often our public agents, the news media—who affix the label on acts of violence that makes them terrorism."[5] Sociologically, this seems to make sense, and our surveys have included this subjective element. However, we have also compared our respondents' feelings to external events and conditions.

However, Juergensmeyer's definition excludes the existential terror that many people feel when confronted with the incongruity between their feelings of hopes and significance and the meaninglessness of existence. Indeed, in *Man's Fate*, Andre Malraux says that terror is one way that an actor can existentially fight back against the terrifying meaninglessness and amorality of life so that in one shining moment of a terrorist act meaning and purity are intensely realized by the human actor.

Russians themselves have believed that existence was overshadowed by terror, whether of the soul or from causes external to the individual. Usually, the idea of a terror-hardened life was joined by a feeling that one could only be passive in waiting for terrible things to occur. So, in the messianic "Story of the White Cowl" the millennium and its judgments are sent down, not brought on by the active preparations of believers.[6] If not passive, Russians have often thrown themselves into futile attempts against the terror-causing agents: anarchist terrorists' suicide against a terrorist state. Some state and political terrorists, however, like Lenin and Stalin, effectively used terrorism as an adjunct to revolutionary war and to create a culture of terror that kept the masses atomized and thus powerless.[7]

From Ivan the Terrible to Stalin, Russians have experienced state terror and terrorist reactions to the state, as well as natural and social calamities that were thought to be terrors sent by God, hostile nature, or fate.[8] Like the English writers after World War I portrayed in Paul Fussel's *The War and Modern Memory*, Russian intellectuals have traced the impact of fearsome catastrophes and their aftermath. The early twentieth century Russian intellectual culture has featured such an apocalyptic mood. Poets like Valerii Brivsov, Alexander Blok, Dmitrii Merezhkovskii, Andrei Belyi, novelists like Fedor Dostoyevskii, and philosophers like Vladimir Soloviev prophesied catastrophic events in Russia. Modernizing movements in Russia have also battled against the terror that collective Russian society (*sobornost'*) imposed on independent thinking and on those people defined as "outsiders."[9] Consequently, traditionalists and others have warned of the terrible consequences.

On the other hand, modernizing movements themselves have threatened or created their own terror. Modernist movements like Leninism created new collective terrorism.[10] The political elite in totalitarian U.S.S.R embedded terror in official ideology and created it by their use of power. At times the sheer randomness of terror in which everyone lived created an atmosphere of fear.[11]

Certain groups were targeted with coercion and stigmatized to such an extent that they became fear objects: peasants during collectivization, capitalists and various ethnic groups like Poles, Koreans, and Greeks before World War II, Germans, Crimean Tartars, Kalmyks, Chechens, and several other North Caucasian peoples during the war and Jews after the war. After a massive explosion in the southeastern working district of Moscow on September 8, 1999, and two more subsequent explosions, one in Moscow and the other in Volgodonsk in the Rostov region, the Chechens have become those who are feared and hated.[12] Religion was particularly targeted and almost wiped out.[13] Ironically, in some ways the memory of the fearsomeness of Czarist Russian Orthodoxy was wiped out and by the 1990s replaced with a memory of Christian hope.

Bolshevism itself was a veritable religion with sacred rituals and an apocalyptic mood. One of the most popular revolutionary songs during the revolution and civil war expressed this religiously ultimate mood with the line, "And all of us will die for our cause." In fact, the most important reason that Marxist Communism has been called totalitarianism is that it demanded control of the interior consciousness and conscience of the Soviet citizen.[14] From the beginning this was seen as an internal terrorism. The Kronstadt sailors revolted in 1921 against this dictatorship of the conscience, not against political Bolshevist dictatorship. Their manifesto proclaimed: "But most infamous and criminal of all is the moral servitude which the Communists have inaugurated: They have laid their hands also on the inner world of the toilers, forcing them to think in the Communist way."[15]

Today, it is hard to convey the intensity with which Russians felt that their very minds and consciences had been violated and polluted first by Soviet terror and then by Soviet decadence. A major theme of the dissident writers was the need to clear the internal consciousness and free them from fear. Alexander Solzhenitsyn's exhortation "Do not lie! Do not take part in the lie! Do not support the lie!"[16] found widespread reverberation.

These catastrophic events have become part of the memory and common sense of Russians.[17] When a momentous event happens, Russians may rejoice if it is a happy occasion, but dark images from the past are never far away. At the collapse of the Soviet Union, the intelligentsia resurrected images of distant events such as the feudal strife in Russia and the "Time

124

of Trouble" in the beginning of the seventeenth century. Both the intelligentsia and the common people interpreted the events of 1991 and after with symbolism drawn from the 1918–20 Civil War, the famine of the early 1930s, and Stalin's mass repressions.[18] In 1999, most Russians thought of the following events in the distant past as the most tragic, catastrophic, and terrifying:

World War I	27%
Patriotic War with Napoleon in 1812	11%
Russian-Japanese War 1904–1905	9%
Tartar-Mongolian conquest	9%
Periods of epidemics and famines	6%

However, even looking back to 1930, Russians remembered fifty of the last seventy years as "bad catastrophic times." Russians most often ranked war with Nazi Germany as a bad time (11%), followed by "life in the 1990s (11%)."

Authoritarian terror and apocalyptic thinking[19] again looms now that contemporary liberal democrats have been stuck in a terrible no-man's land of incomplete transition to a stable democratic capitalist society.[20] Even some liberal democrats in Russia favor the imposition of order from outside.[21] Vainshtein claims that this actually is the continuation of the old totalitarianism "at the psychological level."[22] Biryukov and Sergeyev place the new authoritarianism as an inheritance from prerevolutionary, cognitive traditions of anti-individualism and collectivism.[23]

Since 1989, the semitotics of fear and terror, particularly the memory of terror, has been used by both democratic and authoritarian politicians. A salient feature of the politics of the Russian Communist Party headed by Gennadi Zyuganov has been a focus on a future global ecological catastrophe and the mortal conflict between "the North" and "the South" for resources. Recently, the party has raised the fear of Semites. Russian liberals have also been active in producing fear. The entire presidential campaign of President Yeltsin in the summer of 1996 was based on the suggestion that a Communist victory would lead the country to catastrophe and a new terror.[24]

The symbolic manipulations of contemporary catastrophes and their terrors are also accompanied by conspiracy theories that are widely popularized in contemporary Russia. For example, an influential nationalist weekly Zavtra (Tomorrow) devoted many articles to various conspiracy theories in 1991–1996, including descriptions of Western and Zionist plans to destroy Russia, its economy, culture, ethnicity, and population.

However, the manipulation of fears represented a callous arrogance of the political elites about the masses and their emotions. The liberal reforms

125

of the early Russian Republic mostly ignored the need for addressing the everyday terrors of Russian people. The assumption was that big political and economic structural changes would change fears of everyday hearts. For all the talk of civil society, there was relatively little done about it. Government officials acted as if they were independent of actual politics and social forces, and thus exacerbated problems.[25]

Some intellectuals see the degradation of Russia as part of a general slide of the whole world toward an abyss. The writer Victor Astafiev has written, "Bitterness and sadness, consternation and disappointment, because the aggressive and animal elements of the human being at the end of the millennium, as was predicted in Revelations, push mankind into chasm and arouses in it primitive instincts."[26]

Contemporary Russian Catastrophes and Their Terrors

In 1985, the number of Soviet people who believed in impending catastrophe was insignificant. Even intellectuals who were very critical of the regime felt quite negative but not apocalyptic about their times. They believed that their existing state of life, though bad, would survive for decades without any cataclysm.[27]

By 1992–1994 Russians certainly believed that they were living in catastrophe. Two-thirds described the situation in their country as gloomy with little optimism about the future. When asked, at the end of 1994, if hard times were behind us or in the future, 9 percent said "in the past" and 52 percent said "in the future."[28] According to a survey conducted by the Institute of Marketing, Moscow, based on a national sample of 2,205 Russians (March 1995), almost half of them (46 percent) said that they "do not plan their life and the lives of their family for the future. There is no sense to do it."[29] By June 1999 only 20 percent of Russians expressed certainty about their future. Over half of Russians were dissatisfied with their lives and only 13 percent were more or less satisfied. A majority lived on poverty level incomes.

The main reason for this late twentieth-century growth of a sense of impending doom was the troubles and dashed hopes following the collapse of the Soviet Union. In 1996 we asked Russians, "How long have you felt anxiety about the danger you consider the most significant for you?" Forty percent of the respondents said "the last several years," and 26% said "since the beginning of the reforms in the country."[30] Almost two-thirds (61%) of Russians said that their fear and terror had arisen from concrete personal experiences.[31]

126

In many ways the Russians at the end of the twentieth century were overwhelmingly past-oriented. They often remarked that the past was better, the present terrible, and the future—don't even think about it.

In the face of the precipitous fall in the Russian standard of living in 1992, past historical experience and many sociological theories would seem to indicate the immediate rise of mass movements.[32] In 1992, probably over half of all Russian workers stopped receiving their salary.[33] By the end of the year, 70 percent of individual savings were lost, according to official figures.[34] Public services drastically deteriorated and the protection from criminals collapsed. By 1994 about one third of the population was "poor."[35] Conditions continued to deteriorate. Then, in August of 1998, a sudden devaluation wiped out the savings of the middle class. Yet, through all these catastrophes and terrors, Russian people did not form a mass social movement of rebellion or revolution. The standard theories of modernization, development, and the rise of revolutions seem not to hold. The fault may lie in an over-reliance on rationalistic theories of development and decline that discount catastrophes and their terrors as strategic research sites.

Contemporary analysis of catastrophes and their terrors has two important antecedents: the Greek mythological idea of cycles and the biblical idea of intrusions upon a settled people or situation by God. These two strands of thought were brought together by Augustine into the idea of linear progress. The ideas of cycles versus the idea of stasis punctuated by intrusions and consequent responses account for most of the theories of social change and catastrophe today.[36]

The Greek cyclical idea has typically generated two ideas of catastrophe and terror. On the one hand, according to Aristotle, catastrophes are seen as fearsome monstrosities that are interferences or accidents to natural *(physis)* development (cf. his *Politics* I & II and *Physics* I & II). American secularization and modernization theories of the 1950s institutionalized linear progressive ideas as an intellectual norm. However, both Marxists and capitalists have used versions of the same model to explain Russia and the Soviet Union. To this way of thinking, catastrophe is anything that derails economic or social development. So-called antimodern movements like extreme nationalism or religion are irrational, ineffective responses to the terror of the catastrophes.

On the other hand, catastrophic monstrosities can also be evidence of the decline of a polity to the end of its cycle—a sign of senescence and a fever of the dying. Both interpretations discount catastrophic events, their terrors, and their rationalizations as significant rational historical developments. They are symptoms to be lived through but not truly causal events or processes. In this view, the revival of past religious values or ideologies, reactions against change, extreme environmentalism or antitechnologism, etc., themselves constitute signs of social death and should even eventually intensify catastrophes. The triumph of secular rationality and modernism is assumed.[37]

In analyses of Soviet and Russian social life the Greek cyclical ideas or linear variants have found expression in convergence theories, decline theories, communism as a monstrous interference in Russian national development or, contrawise, communism as a culmination of Russian national and international development. Today, some would emphasize that Russia's troubles and its terrors represent the pangs of death before a new cycle of nation-building begins or the pangs of birth to inevitable democratization, capitalism, and a new Great Russia. Others may say that the reforms were a monstrous intrusion on Russian development as a great nation perpetrated by the beast (Mikhael Gorbachev) or the evil cowboy (Ronald Reagan), and that a reunified Russia will—must—continue its inevitable expansion and triumph.

These rationalistic models have too often hindered clear analysis of Russia.[38] In a spirited series of public forums in the fall of 1993, Carnes and Shlapentokh warned Yuri Levada and others that they were letting their democratic ideology wed their ideas of rationality to the detriment of objective understanding. They consistently painted an overly optimistic picture of the development of the Russian economy in particular and social conditions in general. They denigrated fears and terrors as irrational impediments to democratic capitalist development and predicted that undecided voters in the December elections could not possibly, if rational, vote for the extreme nationalist Zhironovsky group. So, the democratic public opinion specialists were shocked by Zhironovsky's strong showing. Democracy and capitalist economic development are not objective, "rational" trends of history as Fukuyama has claimed, but valued ideals that may win the affirmation of the thinking masses or may lose to autocratic national ideals.

To its credit, Russian social science has often been more concerned with the role of fears and terrors in social life than Western social science. For example, Russian social surveys regularly have monitored fears in society. Since 1989, VTSIOM under Yuri Levada has systematically collected such data. However, Levada and his colleagues have often maintained a cheery progressive outlook on Russia despite severe criticism by sociologists like Boris Grushin (who always sees no hope for the future).[39] Most Russian and East European studies of catastrophe, fear, and terror are products of our catastrophe project.[40]

Western social surveys have mostly ignored the role of fear and terror in human life. Pitirim Sorokin's famous book *Man and Society in Calamity* was mostly theoretical in its approach.[41] Besides this work, there were only a few other publications that were concerned with the sociology of fear in general, particularly the works of Enrico Quarantelli.[42] Most studies were concerned with postcatastrophic situations such as the way societies, organizations, and communities respond to technological or ecological disasters[43] or how individuals and the public adapt to disasters.[44] Only in the specialized studies of irrational crowd behavior (including panic) and disaster research does fear and terror as a significant social problem emerges as a main issue. Quality of life studies have not usually dealt with fear or terror.[45] Risk and decision analysis usually involves rational actor models without a well-developed social theory of emotions, though they do focus on how people and institutions handle uncertainty, often giving rise to fear.[46] Barry Glassner's *The Culture of Fear* is more of an opinion piece than analysis.[47] Samuel Prince's statement from seven decades ago remains an adequate summary: The study of catastrophe and its terrors is still "a virgin field in sociology."[48]

On the other hand, the biblical idea of fixity and catastrophe emphasizes that peoples tend to stay the same, clinging to custom and habit, unless intruded upon from the outside by God, prophets, deliverance, invasions, migrations, or disasters. The intrusions are experienced as catastrophes to settled thought, habit, and custom. Fear and terror arise, motivating people to subversiveness or motion. People are then forced to choose between rejection or acceptance of change, synthetic development or collapse under the weight of crushing events.[49]

"In the past ten years students of social movements have rediscovered the importance of culture," James Jaspers wrote in *The Art of Moral Protest*.[50] This also means that the social processes for discounting catastrophe and terror may also be cultural, not just material and political. Erich Goode and Nachman Ben-Yehuda have brought a recognition of the intrusive effects of religion in their *Moral Panics* (1994), though it deals only with single cases concerning fears that result as a result of moral crusades organized mainly by "moral entrepreneurs."[51] David C. Rapport has examined biblical ideas of terror in relation to the intrusion of God, prophets, and Holy Scripture.[52]

To theorists in this line of thought, the sudden collapse of Russia is not surprising. Some would argue that Reagan or Gorbachev was the individual intrusion that undermined the settled order and demanded new responses. However, catastrophe and social change may result in unpredictable outcomes. In Russia, the outcome has been determined by two worldviews: one emphasizing patience and immobility, and one seeing the catastrophe as an opportunity to create a new society.

Religious and Social Responses to Catastrophe

Russians are relying on three resources to see them through their catastrophes and terrors. A majority of Russians believe that religion is a resource in their catastrophe.

129

Only a small minority fear that catastrophe and terror will come in the form of a religious occurrence. Russians are pouring themselves into work, partly out of sheer necessity and partly because they believe that is where their future hope lies. Finally, Russians also have created a certain type of social world that insulates them from the environment.

Russians would probably rate the importance of these three resources inversely from how I have listed them.[53] They started developing their shock-proof social world at least thirty years ago, long before free enterprise or religion was widely available. Professionals under the Soviet regime valued work, but after 1990 everyone refocused on the value of work, particularly in the private market, because they had to. At about the same time, Russians developed a widespread belief in God and interest in religion. Politics has also been a hope, but most Russians are disillusioned. In the back of their minds most Russians believe that they must become what they call a "normal, civilized country" like European nations or the United States, as well as a "Great Nation." While their political leaders try to sort things out, most people look for family, friends, work, and religion to see them through.

At the end of the twentieth century, Russians reported terrible, catastrophic circumstances and psychological disturbances. In 1999, 69 percent of Russians were not confident about their own future, yet an incredible 44 percent still said that they were cheerful and content. In 1996, while the Russian economy continued to deteriorate, only 23 percent of the public thought that by the end of 1995 the economy was "in crisis—a significant decline in comparison with previous years."[54] How could this be?

Russian perseverance continued with 67 percent saying that "it is necessary to endure all danger and hardship." In fact, this patience often assumed a more decision-making quality than common stereotypes would have one believe. In Russia, a significant number of people said that they would actively manage their fears through attempts to remove their source of their fears. About 40 percent of Russians believed that they themselves could take action to alleviate catastrophe and about 60 percent did not. From where did the Russians get the resources to endure, even to gradually flourish amidst catastrophe and terror?

The Social Resource against Catastrophe and Terror

Part of the answer is that Russians have structured their relations to the social world so as to minimize the terror of their catastrophe. Emotions can be seen as simple, hyphenated, layered, or unstable. Fear would be a simple emotion. Melancholy-fear would be a hyphenated emotion. In Russia today, the most characteristic structure of emotions may well be layered emotions: fear in the big world and cheerfulness in the private world. Because most Russians believe that the big world is beyond control and trustworthiness and is deteriorating further, they have retreated to the redoubt of their private world. Many believe that while the bigger world is going to the dogs, in their private life they still have some control, trust, and hope. Even the 25–28 percent who were confident about their future were mostly confident about their own personal lives or that of their relatives. This bifurcated social orientation explains how Russians can report terrible circumstances and psychological disturbances, but 44 percent can still say that they remain cheerful and content. Each individual makes a distinction between the future for himself and the future of his group and society. This is an interesting contrast to Stalin's time in which people combined high optimism about the future of the nation with pessimistic feelings about their personal future.

Until 1998, the combination was a moderate optimism about one's individual fate with quite a pessimistic outlook on the future of the nation. Such a combination of the attitudes toward "my present life and my future" and "the present life and the future of others" is an adaptive mechanism exercised at the individual and small group level, but to some degree at the macro-social level also.[55] According to the All-Russian Center of Public Opinion Studies (VTSCIOM) surveys, while 46 percent of Russians in 1995 assessed their life as "average" or better, only 29 percent ascribed a similar positive rating to life in their city or village. Even fewer (12 percent) ascribed a positive rating to life in the country.[56] After the catastrophic devaluation in August of 1998, Russians temporarily lost their moderate optimism. However, their optimism about their personal lives seems to have returned.

Other surveys have found a shriveling circle of trust. This process started in the Soviet Era and has continued. Trust was a casualty of Soviet life. Vladimir Shlapentokh has found that, starting in the 1970s, a significant number of people withdrew positive emotional connection with public institutions, particularly political ones, and narrowed their trust to the private sphere, particularly family and circles of friends.[57]

Unfortunately, the conditions in the age of democratic reform have deteriorated trust further.[58] Most Russians have come to trust only their family, fewer close friends, and a narrower group of "decent people." Over time, trust in family has tended to narrow down to trust in nuclear family members.[59] The social space of civil society is not a web of intermediary institutions creating webs of trust as springs against the shocks of catastrophes and terrors.[60] Rather, Russians, particularly new entrepreneurs, believe and experience social space as filled with intriguing coalitions and Macheviallean moments. Mikhail Khodorkovsky and Leonid Nevzlin, managers of Menatep (one of the first commercial banks in Russia), are typical. In their book *A*

131

Man With Rubles (Chelovet s rubles) they proclaimed, "A person can count only on himself. We don't deal with the needs of our employees."

Also, the moderate personal optimism is not thoroughly shared by everyone. In 1999 Russians who were older than sixty-five or younger than twenty or poor felt more deeply the terrors of catastrophe and less able to handle them. According to our 1996 survey, among Russians, terrors and fears of catastrophe were more often found among the youngest and the oldest. For example, the number of people older than fifty-nine who said they were in "permanent fear" about various threats was about 10 percent, compared to only 3 percent for people aged thirty to thirty-nine. Seven percent of people younger than twenty years of age had "permanent fear." We also have some evidence that class affected the perception of dangers. For example, in Chernobyl, poor people ignored the dangers of radiation and stayed. People of higher status recognized the dangers and fled.

The Religious Resource against Catastrophe and Terror

In Russia, beyond oneself and immediate family and work, hope is most often vested in religious faith. However, the "nonreligious" (hereafter referred to as the "Nons"), who make up about a third of Russia, are religious in the sense of adhering to certain worldview commitments as if they were a religion. Both Russian Orthodox and "Nons" have many inconsistencies of belief, mixing religion and irreligion. Many Russian social scientists believe that the degree and intensity of the contradictions in their mentality is the result of no firm replacement for the failed Soviet ideology.

Many Russian scholars of a democratic inclination consider religion an "irrational" response to catastrophe, a response similar to believing in flying saucers, Communism, and Jewish conspiracies. They envision religious people as harmless at best and dangerous Rasputins at worst. One of our project participants even defined religion as irrational and seems to have had a disinclination to study it. Early in the project, he devoted quite a bit of space to discussing religion and catastrophic thinking, but when it came to operating the survey, he paid only cursory attention to conceptualizing religion itself. This is exactly the lack of empathy that leads one to misunderstand the actual social situation. Too many sociologists have declared "religion" (or "ideology") as a passing irrationality only to be surprised by religious revitalizations and desecularizations of the late modern world.

In light of religion's persistent importance in the modern world, it may be useful to reconceptualize religions and ideologies as directive authorities that project images of the world and paths of salvation from catastrophe and terror. In this sense "rationality" can also become a religion in the form of "rationalism," science as "scientism," and technology as "technologicalism" or "techism" (Jacques Ellul). This reconceptualization would allow us to more systematically and coherently understand Russian rationalities, including the "rationalism" that can't fathom "irrationality" in others.

We shall build a portrait of the Russian Orthodox in comparison to the nonreligious as they were in 1998–1999. Then we will examine the way Russian Orthodox and the nonreligious are psychologically, socially, and politically positioning themselves in the catastrophic Russian situation.

The Religious and Nonreligious

The Nonreligious

In 1998, we found that 34 percent of the population said that they are "nonreligious" (Nons). This is a little bit higher than we observed in our 1994 Moscow population survey.[61]

In 1998, in comparison to the general population and Russian Orthodox, the "Nons" were more likely to be male, slightly younger, and more likely to have a professional degree (particularly in a technical field). In 1994 in Moscow we found an identical pattern.

The relatively few new Protestants that we interviewed look a lot like the Nons. They were more likely to be male and less likely to be female than were the Russian Orthodox, were younger and more likely to have a professional degree. Although our sample of Protestants was too small to analyze, much of what we found about the Nons probably applies to the new Protestants.[62]

Additionally, our 1994 Moscow survey covered some areas not covered by our 1998 general population survey. Based on how closely the Nons of the two samples match on many socioeconomic measures, it is reasonable to imagine that the measures in Moscow in 1994 are reflective of the Nons of the general population, at least in magnitude.

Of course, the Nons of 1994 Moscow seldom say that religion plays an important role in their lives (3.6 percent). However, they are equally likely as the religious to believe in God and even more often say that Jesus is the Son of God (48 percent) in comparison to the general public (41 percent). Their attitudes toward the Bible are similar to those of the general population, believers in God, and the Russian Orthodox.

Also, in 1994 the Nons were more likely (46 percent) than even believers (41 percent of Russian Orthodox for example) to trust a believer. The Nons have pretty much the same view of clergy and religious leaders as the general population and Russian Orthodox.

It seems that the nonreligious in general are not particularly hostile or disbelieving of the religious doctrines and institutions we asked them about.

They may even have a deep belief in the sacredness of the soul or the desirability of religion. The boundary between most of the Nons and the religious doesn't seem psychologically rigid.

The Russian Orthodox

Most Russians say that faith sustains them against their fears and terrors. Since the most commonly cited faith is Russian Orthodoxy, we will evaluate the role of Russian Orthodoxy in dealing with catastrophe and terror. Indeed, our most recent surveys indicate that for the first time since 1989 most Russians identify their religion as Russian Orthodox.

Is this an indication of an increasing turn to Russian Orthodoxy during Russia's deepening crisis? Unfortunately, at the present time we can't say for sure because the way we worded the "religion question" may have skewed the results. Our question offered only four religions as choices (not religious, Russian Orthodox, Catholic, and Muslim) with a write-in option that is not usually chosen in surveys by Russians.

We interviewed too few adherents of other religions than Russian Orthodox to be able to say much about them. Still, we can examine and compare the Russian Orthodox with the nonreligious to gain a better understanding of religion's role in dealing with fears during catastrophe.

Although most Russian Orthodox say that their faith helps them overcome fears of catastrophes, only about half (48 percent) definitely affirm this. Even this number is surprisingly high in light of the empty content of most contemporary Russian Orthodox. What most Russian Orthodox mean by "being religious" is to believe in God, identify Russianness with Russian Orthodoxy, and to practice certain national rituals on ceremonial days. Today, Russian Orthodox laity live on the "spiritual afterimages," to use Clifford Geertz's term, of Russian Orthodoxy before the Revolution. According to well-known writer Priest Innokentyi, Russian Orthodox people seldom attend church or live within the norms and values of Christian morality. Social surveys consistently show that very few Russian Orthodox practice of their religion. "Faith" helps overcome fears, but it is a rather vague feeling rather than a rational conviction about the logic of the universe. Undoubtedly, many "religious" people have only this type of faith, a vague emotional conviction.

However, the meaningful role of Russian Orthodoxy in its adherents' lives may be increasing. In Moscow in 1994 only 38 percent of the Russian Orthodox, about the same as the general population, said that religion played an important role in their lives. The Russian Orthodox are more likely than the general population to say that religion plays an important role in their lives, perhaps due to the rise in personal religiosity related to personal experiences with the harsh nature of economic life. Russian Orthodox people are much more likely to be terrified by the threat of growing secularization and materialism.

In comparison to the Nons, the Russian Orthodox are slightly older, more often employed as a political party worker or in a collective farm, and much more likely to be female. They are much less likely to have a professional degree, be employed as a scientist, technical specialist, artist, etc., or to have a high income. Consequently, they are less certain about their own future and more likely to think that economic or political catastrophes are probable.

Russian Orthodox of all ages, genders, professions, and incomes are similar in their expectations of catastrophe, fears, and terrors and what they should do about them. Likewise, the Nons are also pretty consistent on these issues, though in a markedly different way from the Orthodox.

Fears, Terrors, and Mentalities

In qualitative interviews and content analysis of mass media, Russians talk about their fears and terrors as rational responses to objective catastrophes and as a result of a general social corruption that threatens to contaminate and overcome them all. The Nons are more likely to couch their fears and terrors as the emotions that accompany rationality and its drive to overcome catastrophes. Catastrophic corruption, on the other hand, is the feeling that dark, mysterious forces may unpredicatably come over passive victims. Here, the response to catastrophe is more like a cleansing process that one can obtain through rituals of purification. Russian Orthodox are more likely to talk about corruption and contamination and to have a more passive approach to catastrophes and their fears and terrors.

Russians most often report that they fear natural catastrophes and their corruptions will touch and overcome them. Second, they report fears of political catastrophic corruptions. Third, they are concerned over the socio-economic corruptions deteriorating their lives and that of their families. Fourth, Russians fear international catastrophes.

Ecological catastrophes loom more dangerous to Russians than anything else. Twenty-seven percent say that such a disaster would be absolutely devastating for themselves and their families. In contrast, only 4 percent affirm the same absolute importance to sudden, unpredicted economic or political chaos.

Ecology looms so much more important to Russians than many imagine. The Soviet regime's ecological acid bath has left deep scars, both environmentally and psychologically. Persistently, the Russians are worried about their polluted environment. In varying numbers Russians may feel just as deeply about other issues, but most Russians come together in their alarm over their environment. Their concern is the concrete pollution they see around them, not broad, less tangible concerns about the depletion of ozone. Russians also fear the extinction of animal species, the destruction of forests, catastrophic crop failures and other tangible concerns. AIDS and mass epidemics are also a pollution, a corruption by actions. Interestingly, Russian immigrants are also concerned about toxic contamination, but are less concerned about the depletion of forests and waste accumulation. Individual Russians (53 percent) believe that other Russians must be more concerned with economic or political chaos. It seems that the constant media attention on politics has gotten Russians to believe that their ecological concerns are not shared.

All fear environmental catastrophes, but Russian Orthodox have an intensified sense of general degradation and chaos. Russian Orthodox are much more likely than anyone else to feel that they are being overwhelmed and contaminated by waste, AIDS, and genetic degradation. All vitality seems to be leaking out, they think. They are almost twice as likely as Nons to worry about leaks in the ozone layer.

Russian Orthodox have a special reverence for nature and are profoundly and religiously disturbed by its pollution. For them, apocalypses will likely come in the form of holocausts of the earth. Russian Orthodox are seven times more likely than Nons to fear or be terrified by the prospect of the annihilation of the planet.

Of course, almost all Russians fear economic and political chaos and, indeed, expect it to come. Over three-quarters are extremely fearful, even terrified, at the prospect. There is a similar fear of unemployment and civil war.

The political profile is that a majority of Russians want to support market reforms and the international system. Russian nationalism comes in three types: xenophobic nationalism, Great Russian chauvinism, and superpower nationalism, which is the desire to be respected in the world of nations. This survey indicates that the third type of nationalism is the most prevalent, though undoubtedly it is mixed in volatile combinations with other attitudes.

Perhaps with good reason, Russian Orthodox fear the Communists and counterrevolution. Russian Orthodox also seem to interpret the political situation not so much in terms of events but in terms of a generalized chaos as part of a corrosive socioeconomic catastrophic situation.

Russian Orthodox are the most likely to think that political castastrophes are probable. More than any other group, Russian Orthodox see conspiracies against Russians behind national politics. This is partly explained by their fear of corrupt international influences. Russian Orthodox are more boundary- and hierarchy-orientated, and social chaos appears to them to corrupt everything, including politics.

The Mentalities

Russian Orthodox feel weak and helpless, threatened by outsiders and the world's chaos. Their emotional state is similar to Weber's *affektual* type of action: a pervasive emotional state that has not yet been linked to purposeful action. They are moralistic in their fears and favor the *status quo*. Their sense of overall degradation and chaos leads them to eschatological interpretations. Russian Orthodox people are thirteen times more likely to say that the end of the world is coming. They focus many of their fears around moral problems like AIDS, crime, corruption, and lawlessness.

Russian Orthodox people fear outside forces but not specific foes. They feel weak and fear, even expect, dangers from the outside. They are twice as likely as the Nons to feel that invasions and genocide are probable. They are not against their old foes, the Americans, but would react against intrusions, like NATO, from the outside that highlight their sense of weakness. In fact, this happened during the Kosovo conflict.

The Nons feel stronger and more independent. They are more focused on perils to their specific ends, fearing economic woes and criminalization. Their fears are more linked to *zweckrational* social action.

Still, one out of five Russians believe that occult forces are a threat. Russian Orthodox people are slightly more conspiratorial in their view of the world.

Fears and Personality

About half of Russians say that their deep sense of foreboding only came in the last few years. Both the religious and nonreligious had things to be joyful about during the early reform years. The religious could celebrate a rebirth of religious freedom, and the nonreligious celebrated the general freedoms that came. In the last few years, however, fear has become pervasive through all groups regardless of religious beliefs.

Generally, the Nons are somewhat more content and cheerful (47 percent) than the Russian Orthodox (43 percent) or the general population (44 percent). The Nons are significantly less likely to have psychological fallout from their fears. Russian Orthodox are twice as likely as the nonreligious to report that they have become critical and hostile and have nightmares and insomnia.

The better psychological well-being of the Nons goes along with a somewhat higher sense of individual efficacy. Fifty percent of the Nons, in comparison to 42 percent of the Russian Orthodox, say that they will act on the disaster that most concerns them. This not a huge difference, but Nons consistently report a more confident, activist attitude toward catastrophe than do the Russian Orthodox or general population. For example, while 42 percent of the Russian Orthodox admit that they wouldn't take every action possible to defend themselves against crime, only 27 percent of the Nons take a similar passive attitude.

Russian Orthodox are much more likely than the Nons or the general population to have retreated from society amidst the chaos in Russia. Seventy-three percent of the Russian Orthodox in comparison to 65 percent of the Nons say that they wouldn't unite with others to defend against crime. Both groups have alarmingly high rates of retreat from society. Seventy-six percent of Russian Orthodox people say that they would not defend the people in Russia against crime in comparison to 64 percent of the Nons. A staggering 37 percent of the Russian Orthodox would not defend their relatives against crime. Here, the Nons are barely holding the line with only 21 percent giving up this social space to the predators.

However, the Russian response to catastrophe is more like a retreat than an endurance in a storm. For example, only about one-third of Russians say that all they can do is to endure the crime wave of Russia. The common image of Russian Orthodox people as endurers is only partly right. They do feel overwhelmed, but their response is not so much endurance as a retreat from almost all social space. The Nons have also retreated, but are still holding onto solidarity with an extended network of relatives. The Nons are not yet emotionally exhausted and still feel that they can fight back.

Conclusion

Almost half of all Russians are nervous and agitated. About one-third are psychological wrecks largely because of their uncertainty about employment and are on the brink of breaking under the stress. Thirty-one percent find it difficult to deal with hardship. They are prone to hostility, argumentation, and dreams interrupted by insomnia and nightmares.

The emotions range from a deep sense of overwhelming contamination to a feeling of deadness or a feeling of hyper-real existence. Even the cycle of nature (meaning that all will pass) is not available as an emotional reassurance since Russians believe that the environment is a dangerously contaminated cesspool. The president flees to his *dacha* only to flee back. That leaves two-thirds who still feel that they can prevail. Are two-thirds enough to provide leadership? Will they provide leadership?

A breakdown leads to anarchical thinking. The broken grab onto anything that promises to be a vehicle of their salvation. Even the confident unbroken Russians limit themselves to smaller spheres of action and social interaction. Although most will take strong measures to defend their relatives against crime, about one-third say that they wouldn't even do that.

At the end of the twentieth century the conditions were ripe for a new *czar*. President Putin has certainly tried to exercise a sterner hand. However, Russians' repugnance for the past totalitarianism has also continued. Though many longed for "a strong hand," most don't the trust higher authorities. In Russia today leaders have a hard time rising above the chaos of little gangs. If a new *czar* arises, he is likely to be ineffective and quickly overwhelmed. Consequently, Putin has been focused on reigning in the powers of the regional bosses and the economic oligarchs.

Believers say that Russian Orthodoxy helps them to deal with their fears of catastrophe, but their faith seems to be more of a turning inward than a renewed confidence to take on the world. Of course, this is a restructuring of personal social reality that evidently offers great resilience to Russians and its attempt to democratize. In Russia today there are two worldviews that give rise to two competing sets of opinions. On the one hand, there is the worldview, more predominate among Russian Orthodox, that sees the world as being undone, as an overwhelming, contaminating force. One can only be passively patient, adherents of this view say, marshalling and maintaining one's small circle of trusted friends.

On the other hand, a group of younger, more educated, secular Russians have a more activist *zweckrational* worldview. They also see the world as being undone but are more likely to feel that they can manage the chaos. They have a harsh, even savage, edge in dealing with catastrophic terrors and a soul that feels hardened even to themselves. What will Russia's future be—inert icon or fearsome ax? Will a new double blessed Russia emerge with both a transcendent vision and a domesticated ax?

Mapping Love and Terror: Walking the Terrain of I AM Who Is Being-There[1]

A Sociology for Pastoral Engagement with Terror

Victoria Lee Erickson

[God hears the cry of the Children of Israel who were oppressed by the Egyptians, and in response, God goes to Moses with a plan for deliverance.] Moshe said to God: Who am I that I should go to Pharaoh, that I should bring the Children of Israel out of Egypt? He said: Indeed, I will be-there with you, and this is the sign for you that I myself have sent you: when you have brought the people out of Egypt, you will (all) serve God by this mountain. Moshe said to God: Here, I will come to the Children of Israel and will say to them: The God of your fathers has sent me to you, and they will say to me: What is his name?—what shall I say to them? God said to Moshe: YAHWEH ASHER YAHWEH/I will be-there howsoever I will be-there. Thus, you will say to the Children of Israel: YAHWEH/I-will-be-there sends me to you.

> Exodus 3:11–14
> Everett Fox[2]

"Do not let your hearts be troubled. Trust in God; trust also in me. In my Father's house are many rooms; if it were not so, I would have told you. I am going there to prepare a place for you. And if I go and prepare a place for you, I will come back and take you to be with me that you also may be where I am. You know the way to the place where I am going." Thomas said to him, "Lord, we don't know where you are going, so how can we know the way?" Jesus answered, "I am the way and the truth and the life. No one comes to the Father except through me. If you really knew me, you would know my Father as well. From now on, you do know him and have seen him."

> John 14:1–7 (NIV)

The Map

This chapter will begin to map the social process that seeks to become terror itself. It will be a small map. I will skip over much territory: why one comes to hate, why one decides that degrading another is appropriate action to settle one's argument, and the like. I will explore a terrain marked out by our response to terror and to the terrorized. Terror is its own *being*; perhaps it is Satan or evil in its most complete manifestation. Terror's method is to degrade the other, erasing the human face of its target so that it is free to destroy the target. Death is the goal. Terror is not a rational activity. Terror is the destructive work of people who, and timeless forces that, are jealous of God's creative action. Terror seeks to destroy God's creation so that it owns the material resources with which to recreate the world in its own image. What terror has not learned is that only God can call life up out of the ashes. Life is the product of our response to the voice of God who calls us to care for the oppressed in history by reversing the processes of degradation and terror. We call this response "religious action." Religion and praxis are *one*.

Keys

‡ Terror is the lived experience of a kind of chaos that disrupts, fragments, and scatters the ongoing interactions that produce human life.

‡ Lost to terror is power; power is replaced with violence.

‡ The antidote to terror is love, a particular kind of love generated by religion.

‡ Religion creates the love that empowers one to face the other. Face-to-face, the one is called to embrace the pain of the other; so compelled, the one takes on this pain as one's own pain, therein dismissing the fear of what is strange because the strange is now the familiar.

‡ Love, after all of that, transcends religion itself. It will not be held captive to the bounded social institution that was the means by which the Holy entered human life.

Terror and Violence Defined

Terror is not the same as violence; it is, rather, the form of government that comes into being when violence, having destroyed power, does not abdicate but, on the contrary, remains in full control. It has been noticed that the effectiveness of terror depends almost entirely on the degree of social atomization. Every kind of organized opposition must disappear before the full force of terror can be let loose. This atomization—an outrageously pale, academic word for the horror it implies—is maintained and intensified through the ubiquity of the informer, who can be literally omnipresent because he no longer is merely a professional agent in the pay of the police but potentially every person one comes into contact with . . . [this is Stalin]. . . . The decisive difference between totalitarian domination, based on terror, and tyrannies and dictatorships established by violence, is that the former turns not only against its enemies but against its friends and supporters as well, being afraid of all power, even the power of its friends.

Violence is not power. Violence and power are opposites.

Hannah Arendt[3]

Love and Christian Love Defined

Finally, consider the inner reality which, in this emotional phenomenon, is always a single entity: *one* fate, *one* result, *one* act. . . . It is the inner mode of being—in itself, completely indivisible—that we call love.

Georg Simmel[4]

Christianity produces the great axial revolution. In a reversal, love becomes an ultimate central point—as a result of which it really becomes "love" for the first time—and life with its religious energies is summoned for the realization of this point. Subsequently, of course it can react upon life and be assimilated into it. In that case, however, it remains an assimilated content that stems from a sphere of its own validity, not from life itself. There is no sense in which life itself decides the distinctive form of love. The proto-form of love is indeed an element or a product of the religious life, just as it is an element or product of biological life. But when it really becomes Christian love and a constituent of dogma, it also transcends this mode or domain of the dynamic life. Once again incorporated into life, it discloses its trans-vital nature by virtue of the fact that it frees itself from the selective and individualistic determinations of life as such, its discontinuities, limits, and susceptibilities, and those of the religious life as well.

Georg Simmel[5]

Neighbor Defined

Anyone who shows up.

God Self-defined

The One who is Being-There.

142

Social Life Requires Boundary Crossing

The social world seeks to manage its diversity of actors through constructing a shared set of morally good behaviors and an ethical code for living them out. This rule set is held in common by all actors and is that to which we appeal when the "bad/not desired" behaviors appear. Our multiple sets of associations form webs of expectations[6] that are at times in conflict with one another.

By and large, though, the social world tends to be a good place. People form associations that produce rewarding results: strong economies, good schools, hospitals, entertainment, and the like. To reach the pleasurable end that we call "sociability" or the "compassionate society," humans have, for thousands of years, taught each other how to behave ethically and how to negotiate conflicting ethical systems. Because we don't always remember what we have learned and because heaven seems so far off, we often evaluate our ethical failures in the comment, "we are on a journey." Below I will briefly examine Jewish and Christian "journey strategies" for producing "right behavior" and "the holy community." These strategies start by introducing us to the one who stands next to us, our neighbor.[7]

Emmanuel Lévinas

"I see myself, and I am seen, in the face of the stranger." Lévinas presents us with "the human face" and calls "the face" the source of human ethical reasoning. When we look at the human face, we are confronted with "naked immortality" and the "precariousness of the stranger." Exposed in the face is humanity's "summoning" of us in a "primal language" toward peace. The face calls the self deeply into it, Lévinas argues, and asks the self to be concerned with the death it sees in it. "In this reminder of my responsibilities by means of a face that has a claim on my selfhood, the stranger is my neighbour."[8]

The stranger's face brings to the self a voice, "Thou shalt not kill." In this voice Lévinas hears an appeal for peace that waits for the promise of peace.

> The impossibility of leaving that person to face the mystery of death alone . . . entails a willingness to die for him. That is the momentous implication of loving one's neighbor with selfless love. The peace attained by loving one's neighbor is not that of pure rest . . . rather it represents a continuous challenge to pure selfhood, its limitless freedom and its power.

Buber's "All in Israel are responsible for one another,"[9] is the third, other, absent face found in the voice that is the start of ethical action before one encounters the face. Before I meet my neighbor, I have been told how to respond to my neighbor.

THE TRIAD

Israel is the NAME, the second party in the God-and-Me dialogue. My *I* acts out chosenness (hears its name Israel) when I respond I-Thou (subject to subject) to the face (the third party, the stranger). If my *I* does not hear "Israel," my *I* does not respond I-Thou. The triadic relationship of God, Israel, and the Stranger is where ethical relationality is produced. It is the foundation for praxis. The *ME* that responds to the face is at once God-Israel-Stranger.

NINE TALMUDIC LESSONS

In Lévinas we find ethics to be the first philosophy.[10] "But this is also how the presence of God is to be glimpsed in daily life itself, in the exchange between people . . . it is the embodied truth—the truth in action—that conveys meaning."[11] For Lévinas, the meaning of "God" is expressed when Israel takes an ethical stance (goes beyond justice and judgment of the State) and refuses to abandon the one who is being crushed in order for (the State) to achieve its goal. *"Respect for the stranger and the sanctification of the name of the Eternal are strangely equivalent."*[12]

Israel and God are a stable dyad in this triadic social relationship. The stranger comes and goes, but the stranger has an important role to play in the dyad. Israel is forever reaffirming its own identity (its own *NAME*) when it responds to the stranger as if it cannot respond in any other way. The stabilized Israel is the source of a stable dyad. The stranger threatens the dyad at the same time: Israel might not hear its name and choose I-It, it may choose to treat the stranger like an object—therein threatening the very meaning of God. The triad is at peace, strong and powerful, when Israel discovers in the stranger's tears its own tears and the tears of God.

Pain is the organizing center for ethical action. Israel's response is at once humanly empathetic and divine. Pain breaks down the boundary between You and I. Pain creates a we, a shared identity that seeks to end suffering. This action is a movement toward *Being-There*.

Georg Simmel

Georg Simmel[13] argues that the dyad is the absence of the group. The third party makes society, it expands the love relationship of the dyad past "contentment" to "collectivity."[14] The triad, then, brings activity into the dyad that has a tendency to drift of into a "triviality" that is desperate and fatal to the relationship.

LOVE

Love is contentment, for Georg Simmel. Contentment arrives through adjustment and adjustment is itself an agreed upon activity that insures compatibility. If we cannot adjust to each other, there is no contentment and hence no dyad. Israel's story is one of a God who is continually adjusting to Israel. Israel agrees to try to live by the rules, the Ten Commandments, and God agrees to love the Israelites intensely. Intense love, argues Simmel, is only found in the dyad. The power of love, he observes, stabilizes the group, while withdrawing love from the dyad destabilizes the group.

PASSION IN THE DYAD

The goal of passion, argues Simmel, is to tear down the ego. In a marriage dyad, the "I" of each person disappears as they are bridged into a shared identity. Simmel argues that it is society that requires this work of the dyad. Society wants a suspended ego that is free to be confronted by the collectivity. When the boundaries of the "I" are transcended, a social "we" is possible by adding a third party to the dyad—frequently a child. In order for society to receive this child as a socializable resource, it must be able to impact the dyad. It does this through its passionate appeal to see suffering as a result of, e.g., not immunizing the child, not sending him/her to school, etc.

Howard Becker's early work on Simmel noted his interesting observation that the dyad meets face-to-face and over time and comes to develop a patterned and mutual interaction that, if it grows limited in meaning, will break up.[15] Meaning is constructed out of our continued engagement with others. Broken dyads are mended or prevented by reference to the outside. Likewise, the outside, the community, the stranger, requires the aggregate of dyads in order to stabilize life and to develop a sense of belonging that produces pro-social engagement. These dyads must be in continual engagement with the outside just as God and Israel are a strong dyad when engaged with the stranger, the other.

PASSION IN THE TRIAD

If intense love is the property of the dyad, then the triad is continually at risk of destabilization. What maintains the equilibrium of the triad is a face-to-face meeting where pivotal political alliances are "watched" and "dissolved" or "affirmed." The tendency of the sociological triad is to separate into a pair with an "other." The pair, made up of the two weakest members, often finds common solidarity with an object of opposition. The third is the intruder, the outsider, the scapegoat, the common enemy, and the "cement" that either holds the pair together or "disturbs" the pair.

145

KINDS OF TRIADS

Caplow[16] and Mills's[17] early work to "systematize" Simmel's dyad/triad observations appears to be an accepted project. In Simmel we find six types of triads.

Type 1: Simple case, all three are equal in strength. AB, BC, AC are all likely combinations of equal strength. The triad is stronger than the dyads because they can indeed recombine equally.

Types 2–6: Complex dyads of unequal strength. In 2–6, the dyads favor the weakest, leaving the strongest the isolated, therein the weakest, member of the triad. Dyads combine for political and status security, forming coalitions of strength. Destabilizing the triad is a key element of coalition maintenance within the dyad.

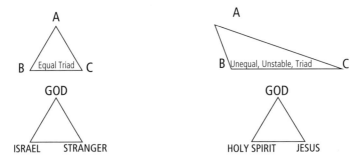

The triadic structure of Judaism and Christianity resists destabilization through a simple formula: We are One. Stabilization depends upon Israel's remembering and embracing the stranger, and in Christianity, through remembering and embracing Jesus, the one who was strange to society, the one who calls us to embrace our neighbor.

Creating a conversation between Simmel and Lévinas allows us to experience more deeply the simple triad of shared identity as a divine action of sharing the task of holding each other's pain. The destabilized sociological triads are dyadically controlled by creating separation and lack of relationality, by inflicting pain or by not addressing it. In all triadic structures, however, pain is a relationship expressed in ethical or unethical communicative action.

Terror Is the [Pain-Filled] Destruction of the Sociological "Me"

Research has shown that, in the stress of combat, most soldiers fight less for the cause of the country or hatred of the enemy than for their buddies.

Henry Frank Guggenheim Review[18]

In the following I will be using Charles Norton Cooley's and Erving Goffman's notions of the self. Along these lines, we might argue that what is happening in the combat scene described above is the self's protection of the self. The sociological "me" that fights for my "buddy" is the expected "I" engaged with the "you." The violent context of the battlefield finds the sociological and moral community attachments to others, friends and buddies, intact. Their collective will to be one-for-the-other is their power—dying for your buddy is an act of love. There is something right and familiar about this. Even if we do not agree that war is correct political action, we never condemn soldiers for their love, for their "humanness." To not defend each other would be an internal act of violence and at the same time an act of "terror." Stories of friends/colleagues/soldiers abandoned by other friends/colleagues/soldiers causes fear and moral indignation in the social network. Moral indignation is a reference back to what Lévinas calls the foundational source of ethical action: my response to the face that is precariously close to death and that needs me to live. Yet Lévinas is calling us to remember a deeper obligation. The people of God are to respond to the stranger, to the one who is not colleague/friend/comrade. Israel is not to separate its own identity from the identity of the other. Israel is by divine definition "we."

Terror, in Hannah Arendt's framework, is the ability of violence to "atomize," to break apart the sociological "me" from the "we," therein leaving isolated "I's." The face does not see the face. This isolation is horror itself. It is the breaking apart of what it means to be human, and at the very least it is the breaking apart of commonsense: soldiers protect each other. In the midst of terror, the rules no longer apply, friends turn against friends, love is gone. Yet more than that, more than being for one's friends, Israel is to love the enemy, the stranger, the one who is not the friend.

Any threat to the common and life-giving actions necessary to the divine kingdom of peacefully coexisting strangers and nonstrangers is to bring Israel's moral indignation—a corrective force that attempts to control behavior through a restating of the rules for human interaction. If people respond to this corrective action, terror is diverted. In the following I will look at moments when "the rules no longer apply." We will look at times when society or individuals felt or claimed to be "terrorized." We will begin to chart the boundaries that, when transgressed, dissolve love and the ability to control each other through moral indignation, therein opening the way to terror.

The Sociology of Moral Indignation[19]

Sociologists have long established that shame, guilt, and boredom are ways society uses to address moral issues by changing individuals through the removal of particular behaviors from them while, at the same time, keeping their egos intact. The act of *remembering to retain* the social-psychological integrity of the person holds society accountable to its moral obligations to the offensive actor. Society wants to minimize and control the level of sociopsychological pain inflicted on those perceived as needing "correction." Sociological concern for pain keeps society on an "ethical path" of action that finds all parties equal and deserving of respect.

There are times when particular people decide that a person, group of persons, or an identity (and the memory of them) has to be totally destroyed and rebuilt. In these cases, shaming, producing guilt, or promoting boredom are not sufficient acts of transformation to achieve the desired end, which is *a radically new identity*. Totally replacing actions, identities, a person, or a cluster of persons outside of the normally ongoing corrective social systems requires a special kind of status degradation work. Harold Garfinkel calls the work of status degradation "ritual" and "ceremonial" activity that maintains its own set of specialized actions.[20] Status degradation ceremonies serve to ritualistically replace the old with the new through carefully orchestrated events. Garfinkel found that all of the social structures and conditions for the degradation of identity are available to society. Degradation rituals were seen by him as a kind of secular "communion" that brings to the denouncing party a reinforced group solidarity. The denouncing party is empowered as the degraded person is literally destroyed and then becomes a totally new person in the eyes of the condemners, whose values and virtues are successfully defended by the perpetrator's loss of identity and status.

In the Lévinas and Simmel frameworks, degradation is a willful lack of concern for the pain of the other. In the case of Lévinas, if Israel degrades, Israel has decided not hear its *NAME* in the crying of the other (or see its face in the face of the other). In Simmel, degradation is evidence that the degrader's very being, his or her soul (who the degrader really is), has dissolved, become damaged, and is fragmented—is not whole. The will to degrade, with no regard to the healing and reconstructing processes that must follow, is evidence of a destabilized ethical system. Actions coming from this system are designed to generate "the other" who is targeted for destruction. However, in both of these frameworks, the one who degrades the third party, the stranger, is degrading the whole ethical system that includes the degrader.

Christian theology, having roots in Judaism, also has a triad. Christians call it the Trinity: God the Father, God the Son, and God the Holy Spirit. It is very much like Simmel's simple case triad of equal membership, free to combine A, B, and C with equality among the membership. It's perfect triangle shape in religious symbolism dramatizes the equal distance between the members of the triad. Over the course of Christian history, various

Christian theologies understand the members of this triad to form dyads, leaving the third present but not of equal interest for the moment. For example, God the Holy Spirit is found historically minimized in much of Lutheran theology and is only in recent decades of much interest. As interest grows, so too does interest in Mary, the Mother of Jesus. However, one cannot argue that God the Holy Spirit was a destabilized member of this triad. One might argue that a revived interest in the Holy Spirit is in fact the people's act of keeping the triad stable in their own thinking and acting. The most well-known example of the triad's move to stabilize itself, as told theologically in the story format found in the Bible, occurred when Jesus cries out from the cross: "My God, My God, why have you forsaken me?" The cry to see the self in the pain of the other (I am you, you and I are me) is a cry to be seen and known, face to face. God heard *his NAME* called, answered the cry, and raised Jesus from the dead by the work of the Holy Spirit. God and Spirit become the dyad that rescues the third, the one found to be a stranger in human life. That is why Christians say that no one can come to God except through the *ONE* who was strange to human society.

Likewise, Jesus gives life to the Father by directing the people's attention to God. The Spirit directs people to remember Jesus. This constant recombining of the dyadic relationships keeps the possibility of divine community alive, therein teaching the faithful how to create equitable community amongst themselves.

Violence and Degradation Are Problems, Terror Is Worse Than That

To help unpack the constellations of overlapping ethical systems involved in the degeneration of human community into terror, I have applied the theoretical observations of Garfinkel, Cooley, and Goffman. This particular collection of social theorists find "common sense, everyday" activity as a credible site for indigenous theory production, and all three document the moral work of society found in everyday accounting practices.[21] Note in the following something not yet noted in Garfinkel's work: his work on successful degradation ceremonies is itself a mapping of a destabilized triad between the victim (the stranger whose face pleads against death), the perpetrator (the one who has not heard the plea from the depths of humanity), and the moral community (who must judge this act even if they failed earlier to prevent it).

CONDITIONS FOR SUCCESSFUL STATUS DEGRADATION

Garfinkel's ethnomethodological study of moral indignation charts the conditions necessary for successful degradation ceremonies to occur.

149

a. The steps toward a successful degradation are intended to announce that:

    i. the old identity was an accident and the new identity was there all along;

    ii. the rightful identity has been established in the eyes of witnesses; and

    iii. the old identity is not changed, but it is reconstituted.

b. A good denunciation requires:

    i. a denouncer,

    ii. a person the denouncers see as a perpetrator (the denouncer's victim), and

    iii. an event where witnesses agree with the denouncer.

c. Timing:

The event can take place quickly, as in a one time court appearance or an afternoon spent before the tribal elders, or it can take place across time and be carried out through newspapers and television reports. The event itself calls upon the witnesses to choose an alternative identity as a morally required action.

THE STEPS TO SUCCESSFUL ACTION

a. Both the event and the perpetrator are removed from their everyday character and made to stand "out of the ordinary."

b. The event and the perpetrator are treated as instances of uniformity, as ongoing possibility. The witnesses must appreciate the characteristics of the person and the event as dialectical counterparts—as profane and sacred, for example.

c. Then, the denouncing agent must be identified as publicly known actor(s) who participate in the witnesses' lives—feel what they feel, see what they see, know what they know.

d. The denouncer then makes the values of the witnesses superpersonal and

e. delivers the denunciation in their name.

f. The denouncer arranges beforehand to speak in the name of these values as one of their greatest supporters.

g. The denouncer leads the witnesses to experience the distance from the perpetrator.

h. The denounced are then ritualistically separated from the legitimate order and placed outside of it as opposed to it and are made "strange."

If these conditions are not met, the denunciation fails. Garfinkel found that not only do these elements create a successful ceremony, they also tell us how to "render denunciation useless."[22]

Robert Gephardt's study[23] of the successful forced succession status degradation ritual within an organization's succession events extends Garfinkel's observations to include the denouncer's use of social rules and the importance of the denouncer's knowledge of "the organization" in the success of the attempted degradation. What interests Gephardt is that the denouncing actors must display a knowledge of that which they want to replace. In other words, the actors who create degradation events know what they are doing and know themselves to be potentially capable of enforcing a new organizational reality.

The power to force a new reality, the lowering of a social status, is found in language. In order to degrade, we must speak degradation into being. Types of degradation ceremonies abound. Gephardt's example is the thirteen month long succession ceremony in which he was the targeted student government leader who was removed from office. The following is a condensed version of the ceremony.[24]

1. Six student government leaders had overlapping dyadic friendships. Two of the students did not consider Gephardt their friend, although Gephardt socialized in their circles. The six are never able to stabilize the group relationship.
2. Gephardt was chosen the informal chair of a graduate student event with a sizable budget. His "talking" pushed his colleagues into establishing a formal committee, so that "people will listen to us."
3. The transition from an informal to a formal organization was rocky and everybody made mistakes. Gephardt's ability to operate as the chair was reigned in by the committee who would not let him act without their permission. Gephardt did act to obtain a sum of money for a manager in the student activities arena.
4. A dispute over his right to act on behalf of the group and the continued displeasure stemming from their disorganization precipitated a struggle to which Gephardt managed to bring a semblance order. A formal organization begins to emerge out of the chaos.
5. The committee was not sure that it wanted this order. A nomination to remove him from office was spontaneously brought to the floor of the committee meeting. Some resisted, others rallied behind dismissal. Friends and nonfriends argued. In the same meeting in which he protested his dismissal, he was voted out and a new president was voted into office.

This may seem like a trivial story. It is the mundane nature of it, however, that makes it a critical story. All degradation ceremonies are critical stories in which others decide the fate of the target. These ceremonies are called into being countless times a day and we all participate in them as defenders or degraders. Degradation ceremonies are peopled events in which the defenders of the target and the target lose the struggle to retain status. Are degradation ceremonies good or bad, necessary or unnecessary?

Degradation is a broadly used concept in scholarship and in everyday life. Ecologists use the term to describe what humans have done to the earth.[25] Marxists have used the term to describe what capitalist culture does to workers,[26] and feminists use the term to describe what patriarchy does to women.[27] Only in special cases does the literature report degradation in itself to be a positive thing. The results of degradation are almost always what commonsense actors seek to amend, control, heal, or resist. However, there are cases in which degradation is seen to happen for "the public good." For example, degrading the driving status of a city bus driver from "fit to drive" to that of "unfit to drive" so that his license is removed, thereby preventing him from injuring people, is called a "public good." However, recognized in the act of "bus driver status degradation" is the negative result to his psychological well-being.[28] The literature also documents the social expectation that the degraded party will resist degradation.

Response and Resistance to Degradation

Below, I will sample the literature's discussion of the results of degradation by asking: How do people targeted by others as the perpetrators (their victims) respond to degradation rituals and a degraded self?

LABOR AND ECONOMICS

Neitzel[29] documents efforts in the 1800s by Catholic clergy who organized journeymen associations in order to resist the degradation and poverty brought on by German industrialization. Increasing the religious and moral resources in the journeymen communities was seen as a key ingredient for resistance degradation. Their goal was to create an economically independent class of journeymen. This example of organizing against the source of degradation in order to create independence from it, while simultaneously reconstructing the depreciated moral self, can be expanded past Neitzel's historical moment and said to be a summary of what Marxists would most likely say about their praxis.[30]

However, against the Marxist problematic, Trice argues that it is important to realize that people do not see themselves as operating in a mass of humanity. Trice finds that workers "make sense" of the work experience and its particular ceremonial activity by locating the self in a "clustered" work context and by comparing one subculture to another.[31] In the Trice framework, the supportive clustering of "Catholic journeymen" would be an expected response to degradation. Trice further argues that the dysfunctional consequences of degradation are met with functional responses that act to renew, integrate, and enhance work life.[32]

ETHNICITY AND RACE

In sociologies of race and ethnicity, social and personal degradation within ethnic and racial constructs have been well documented internationally. Mathiesen documents a Norwegian example of ethnic degradation that is very much like the North American degradation of indigenous peoples. The Sami of Norway experienced degradation when housing projects did not make room for their legal participation in the program designed, for the most part, to be for them.[33] Having no legal process or status required informal networking. As the American civil rights struggle has taught us, the power of law is the cornerstone of an equitable society. The power to bring about a desired life is a power for which people are willing to die.

Martin Luther King Jr. and Mahatma Gandhi's struggle for a nonviolent accomplishment of civil rights was a struggle against the grain of the majority sentiment. Malcolm X would have understood Rai Gandhi's sentiment that ethnic conflict and communal violence are "inevitable" in India's caste system.[34] Violence then is an expected outcome of alienated and degraded ethnic identity. Enhancing the capacity to do violence or to prevent violence is a pivotal decision degraded groups make—one that will shape their advocacy agenda as well as their theoretical, ideological, and theological thinking.

People like King and Gandhi worked against the "violence as normal natural" response mechanism. Similar to Trice's clustering argument, DeVos discusses what has become a rather well-known technique of youth workers.[35] In order to resist the inclination toward violence, which only brings the degraded a harsher reality (often imprisonment or death), "peer groups" or "support groups" are established to make conscious the denial and repression that happens within the degraded person and people. When rejected by the dominant culture as a favorable partner in the building of social life, the peer group provides what DeVos called "compensatory socialization." However, this compensation is not ideal. It is always better to be accepted by those in authority as a competent moral agent in society. DeVos's Japanese data conclude that a young person could experience a healthier psychocultural life if past cultural traditions and ways of learning are valued in the classroom. In other words, life is always better without the experience of degradation.

Degradation intends the social, cultural, and psychological death of the targeted perpetrator. Gabel's linking of racism and racist false consciousness to schizophrenia and autistic character disorders further details the descriptions of Orlando Patterson's slavery as social death analysis.[36] There is nothing whole, healthy, positive, nice, or good intended by those who construct systems of racial or ethnic degradation. Researchers who target the young with educational inventions appear to be on the right track toward reversing and maybe even healing some of the damage. The degradation of values degrades a whole people, their history and their theology. Once the targets are ideationally degraded, it is easier to degrade their bodies.

The collapse of values that allows a person or a group of persons to use degradation rituals in the reconstruction of social life is the very collapse of values they seek in the degraded target. Ulrich's study of East German youth finds that the collapse of value systems increases the nonparticipation in political life. The Ulrich survey of 3,905 youth documents what happens when the young have limited opportunities to develop identity in social life: materialism increases as a sense of social responsibility decreases.[37] Post-Holocaust sociology is teaching us that there is perhaps no stronger social attack on the psycho-social-cultural identity of the young than is found in the degradation of the history of an ongoing society. Without a future that makes sense of the narrated and experienced past, society is robbed of the creativity of the young who not only need the past but who need to be forgiven/relieved of the responsibility for a past they did not live in as they create a future that is accountable to the ongoing realities of the past.

Robbing society of the passion of the young is effective degradation. This degradation can occur in the way we analyze social actions. For example, the history of intermarriage analysis is summarized by Porterfield to be in dynamic transition from an understanding of intermarriage to be a search for the exotic or an expression of self-hate and degradation toward an understanding that intermarriage is for the couple what marriage is for same-ethnic couples: a search for love and companionship. Porterfield links the growing acceptance of black-white marriage with an "inevitable" positive effect on race relations.[38] This positive effect will come none too soon for the children produced by interracial marriages.

As we have seen in Africa-centered theory and practice among African-Americans, the search for an originating place and mythic structure is key to claiming, constructing, and reconstructing identity. Corzni and Dubois find this search elemental to recovery from the trauma of degradation.[39] The recovery of mythic life then is elemental to resisting the effects of degradation.

154

Women, Men, Sex, and Gender

Perhaps the surest way to achieve public disagreement around issues of the degradation of women is to discuss pornography. Although there are well-known dissenters, there is growing worldwide challenge to the "pornography as a social good" argument.[40] In the United States, much activism has sought to ensure limited access to pornography and the conversion of the pornographic mind.[41] Feminist resistance to pornography is resistance primarily to declared outcomes of pornography consumption: violence and aggression toward women. There is growing awareness that male pornography is also degrading of men,[42] and, one would suspect, is not helpful in a context of male violence.[43]

Sheffield's study finds that obscenity brings with it feelings of anger, degradation, and abuse.[44] Her study is important in that she details the level of women's response to this degradation. Women who have experienced male violence prior to the obscene act or women who are in deep life stress respond with the greatest levels of fear. Prior experience of violence teaches women to fear the denouncer and the degradation rituals. Regardless of how one views the pornography debate, one can understand antipornography advocacy as an attempt to protect women against violence and as an act of resistance against the degradation of women.

Ecology

Issues of degraded labor power and the female body surface in ecological degradation of the earth analyses.[45] From international development to household structure, images of work, body, and earth merge in feminist analyses.[46] The resurrections of the idea of moral animal life in contrast to the immoral way humans treat them documents a developing ideological shift that merges development economics with earth and sexuality themes.[47] As appears to be the case, the ritual elements of degradation that lead to plant and animal deaths are the targets of analyses that seek to reverse degradation.

Degradation as Worse than Death

Women who kill their male abuser frequently report that the emotional and psychological degradation that led up to the act of violence ending in death was worse than the physical battering itself.[48] Women who kill the abuser are also likely to kill themselves.

Aggression toward the self in the context of degradation is documentable. Zivkovic's study of Yugoslavian elderly finds that more than 50 percent of suicides are committed by the elderly—a doubled percentage from twenty years earlier.[49] Zivkovic finds gerontology to have become a "militant" science in the effort to advocate for the elderly. However, in

155

advanced medical societies the expanded length of life as a result of medical attention might not be the answer advocates seek either. Living a degraded quality of life is described by the Pearlman, et. al., study as "worse than death."[50]

Resisting degradation itself and its negative impact is expected in social life. For example, if one is the advocate for safer driving, one develops an action strategy around the expectation that each bus driver will resist degraded status. In a similar way, social degradation is resisted by ethnic and racial minorities who work against racism and the ethnocentrism of the majority in order to hold family and cultural traditions intact.[51]

Paradoxically, the seekers of public good may require the pain of group degradation. A group may be asked to experience public degradation as the lesser evil in the context of impending violence. For example, Kallen and Lam's study of anti-Semitic hate trials in Canada document the degradation individual Jews experienced watching the public trials on television. Individual and group degradation was experienced in the same moment. The study argues however, that it is for the good of the public that hate crimes are prosecuted publicly as a long-term violence prevention strategy.[52]

Regardless of why social degradation happens, it is understood in these studies that the result brings undesirable ends to that which is degraded. There are times when the denouncer has not adequately realized that degradation has lasting negative effects for everyone, including the denouncer.[53] Correcting the effects of wrongful degradation is just as complicated as organizing the degradation in the first place.

Self-assertion, whether by the individual or by the group, and regardless of context (university life, medical attention, public antihate actions), is a critical tool for empowerment and resistance of the effects of degradation. Without self-assertion, degradation is complete and people mentally, socially, culturally, and physically die—they become invisible.[54] Neutralizing the effects of degradation is also, then, a step made toward halting the degradation process. Jacobs's study of neutralization indicates that the resistance mechanisms are just as present and known in culture as the mechanisms for degradation itself.[55]

Another observational response is that people with operative ethical and moral frameworks will surrender themselves before they harm others. Built into human responsiveness is a restraint on the kinds of response moral people will produce and a sense of "reality" about the chances of survival. When no one stands up against the denouncer, a successful degradation is well on its way.

Terror Seeks the Destruction of the Simple Triadic Community of Voices that Call the *NAME*

Terror is the ultimate form of degradation. Degradation disfigures the face, terror eliminates the face. People withstand tremendous acts of aggression against the body and soul. Jews and Christians have a moral obligation see through terror; we are to "see the face" even when the face is "not seen." God's voice and the ancient voices of Israel refer to the face. To hear is enough for us. Terror is only successful in the community of faith when it is able to separate the faithful from their obligation to hear, see, and act responsibly even in the midst of intense pain. Degradation and terror are sociological tools crafted for the purpose of separating the person(s) from the moral community. Whether or not the effort is successful, the disrupted lives of the targeted individuals or community must be addressed and healing sought.

We End Terror by Fearlessly Telling the Truth about Terror's Agents

Creelan sees himself treading on ground where few of Cooley and Goffman's students were interested enough or brave enough to go. He argued that they saw the degradation of the sacred to include the rise of self-interest and the decline of self-transcendence. He found that this collective process produces "only fragments of the original, more expansive ideals."[56]

Creelan argues that for Cooley and Goffman, the loss of a generous self-giving moral framework represents a loss of self-transcendence. Self-transcendence in Garfinkel's ethnomethodological framework is the most important ongoing work of society. Society seeks to connect the member with divine ideals regardless of the strength of the countervailing arguments. The divine ideal that is the larger idea of which the self-loving person is but a fragment, is disinterested love. Disinterested love is neighbor-relational love; it is an ongoing quality in social relations that society seeks to protect.[57]

Cooley found the self-interested, self-loving person not a "grand" accomplishment of modern life but an "intellectual and spiritual failure of the highest order."[58] Others have called this failed person "the oppressor." The oppressor seeks to destroy intellectual and spiritual life that helps members transcend the self and reach the very center of moral life.[59] Degradation rituals became taken-for-granted acts of violence and exclusion in communities that wished to maintain and develop self-love. In order to justify accruing privilege unto the self at the expense of others, society's sacred, disinterested relational love, its divine ideal, must be destroyed and replaced. As Patterson, a theorist of race and racism, has taught us,[60] there is no better way to destroy ideas than to destroy the people who hold them.

Yet all of these theorists believe that terror itself can be diffused through acts of disinterested, other-relational love. Ultimately divine love is available for the reestablishment of relationality because society has at one time experienced its own *soul* and it remembers that therein is reserved space for the divine ideal, a space that cannot be taken over by self-love.[61] When we embrace the divine love that we remember, we are called to serve this memory by embracing the one who stands next to us. This smallest of relational spaces is the seed bed for healing and new life.

Being-There Is Advance Preparation of a Healing Place

Working within the people's method for healing is simultaneously a working within the people's response to the divine ideal. In the Gospel of John, Jesus tells the people that they know the pathway home. In the Book of Exodus, God tells Moses, a leader of the people, that they will know God when they see each other serving God. Serving people and serving God are to be equivalent practices. When we divinely serve people, we reside in God's home. Anthropologist Gay Becker, in *Disrupted Lives*,[62] documented how people respond morally to the pain of others who have experienced great suffering. She discovered that people seek to help others reorder their lives by helping them into conversations about death, home, and the spiritual community. Remembering the literature we have just read and combining Becker's invaluable observations produced the following list of activities that people engage in as they seek healing through moralizing narratives that make judgments on everyday practices. The ordinary conversational input of people who respond to pain seeks to stop the degradation, and it seeks to enter into disruption with practical solutions that heal people. Terror is diverted by encouraging the targeted person, the victim, the one in pain, or the object of hate to:

1. Find common ground with others.
2. Materialize memories.
3. Seek to understand wholeness.
4. Search for who one really is.
5. Seek knowledge of what is not home.
6. Seek tradition and order.
7. Seek continuity in metaphor, pictures, art, and vision.
8. Organize our stories into a linear account that turns chaos into order.
9. Seek to establish a connection with a moral authority that explains their lives.
10. Listen to their bodies, which are a conduit for emotions.

11. Feel normal and not different, and establish a template experience even through we know that we are not cookie-cutter people.
12. Map culture, making sense of the local world.
13. Create statements of resistence: who I am and who I am not.
14. Create a story plot in our imaginations of how we got here.
15. Reconcile order, push people to talk about good and evil.
16. Rework meaning by establishing values.
17. Seek not to be trapped in the present.
18. Seek hope, which brings continuity and regret and therefore responsibility.
19. Seek restoration through continuity (listen to the body).
20. Understand healing and discover that it is performative.
21. Seek satisfaction with the narrative that makes sense of suffering.
22. Anchor it in memory (selective memory is natural and okay).
23. Seek to symbolize memory to keep continuity.
24. Create a new plot, a third thing that sits between order and chaos.
25. Forever live with distrust: the body remembers; seek transformation of body knowledge. Forgive, let go, live in a new way with memories.

The people who are the healing hands of God for others in pain, others who live disrupted lives or who are living in or who have survived terror, have their specific tasks as well. Those called to heal are to work within the people's story and:

26. Hold their stories of pain, desire, and memory and suggest moral authorities for interpreting these.
27. Try to prevent fragmentation and resist the tearing apart of the story on the behalf of the suffering.
28. See the whole picture.
29. Tell them that the people know "what this is."
30. Seek to nudge them on to a new way of being whole and promising to remember their journey that you help them narrate.

Reversing the degradation process and healing the effects of disrupted lives is the moral praxis of neighbors who are called to be there to lead the oppressed out of bondage and into a life of freedom. This new life is gloriously free to pledge itself to *Being-There* for the one who needs freedom. The one who is there holds the power of the One Who Is Being-There, a power that pulls life up out of the ashes.

The Sexual Politics of Terror

Katharine H. S. Moon

About once every two months, an [Japanese] army surgeon gave us check-ups . . . . The surgeon would insert an instrument that looked like a trumpet or a duck's beak and with this he examined us. If we had any disease we would be given the "No. 606" injection, but I was never diagnosed as needing such an injection. Yet, even though I had no venereal disease, I had to have treatment, because I kept bleeding and couldn't pass water. . . . There were some women whose vaginas were so swollen and were bleeding so profusely that there was no space for a needle to be inserted inside. How could one expect anything to be otherwise when an innocent girl was subjected to such torture day and night? None of us had children, but I heard that some became pregnant and were forced to abort with an injection or drugs. Even though I had no disease, I was told at a recent check-up that my womb is malformed from the abuse it received in my youth.

Kim Tokchin,
Korean survivor of the Japanese "comfort system" in World War II[1]

In October, 1992, the landlord of Yun Kum-I found her body "naked, bloody, and covered with bruises and contusions—with laundry detergent sprinkled over the crime site. In addition, a coke bottle was embedded in Yun's uterus and the trunk of an umbrella driven 27cm into her rectum. [Private Kenneth Markle of the U.S. Army was convicted of murder by the South Korean courts.]

Rainbow Center Newsletter #3, January, 1994[2]

I saw a young woman crouched in a corner below the neighbor's kitchen window. Around one of her legs was a long chain (normally used to restrict the movement of house pets that are let loose in backyards) attached to the kitchen's sliding metal door. I asked her who she was since I did not recognize her as a member of the neighbor's family. She cried as she said that she was the family's Filipina servant. Her female employer, who was going out to shop for groceries in a nearby farmer's market, had chained her to the back of the house to ensure that she would not eat the family's food in her absence. . . . I quickly realized that the phenomenon of employer-abuse of foreign servants is not restricted to Malaysia. Many employers throughout Asia, the Middle East, and the West are implicated similarly in abusing foreign servants.

Christine Chin, author, *In Service and Servitude*[3]

India, in fact, has been gaga over beauty contests since 1994, the year of that first astonishing Miss World-Miss Universe twin triumph. Awakened was something that might be called patriotic vanity. . . . Indian women, many say, are discovering their sexuality; some are also discovering bulimia and anorexia . . . . "There is a sense that we can be a contender . . . . That's why we became obsessed with these beauty contests. We thought they brought us a victory over the world."

New York Times, December 13, 2000

Why is it that women's bodies, Asian women's bodies, have been so up for grabs by those with or seeking power? What is involved in the logic of military and economic competition that drags women's bodies into an intimate system of violence, abuse, and exploitation? How does the rivalry for international status and power among nation-states "normalize" the feminization and sexualization of women? Why has it been so easy to sacrifice women's bodies, dignity, and abilities for some "higher good" such as national security, economic growth, religion, or national pride?

In *Fear and Trembling,* Kierkegaard contemplates the terror, doubt, transcendence, and reconciliation that unfold through and around the faith-act of sacrifice, both of Abraham and of God (Gen. 22). He emphasizes Abraham's responsible and dutiful fulfillment of God's calling, and in the end, Abraham gets to have it all: his son, his Yahweh, and his immortality as the progenitor of Israel, Jesus, and the masses of the faithful. But what of Isaac and *his* fear and trembling? What of his horror at witnessing the determined brutality of his father? What of his despair at Yahweh, who was requiring him to serve as a mere instrument of Abraham's faith? Did God call Isaac aside and inform him of his role? Did he make clear the charge to Isaac? Did God grant Isaac time and space to exercise his agency? In this story no physical harm came to the father or to the son, and whatever the psychological damage to either, we can trust that their sense of relief, renewed awe at the mercy of Yahweh, and the fulfillment of their side of the covenant with God might have helped them leave behind the fear and trembling at Mount Moriah and get on with living.

161

Like Isaac, many Korean and other Asian women have been put up for sacrifice at the altar of a higher call: war, political competition, military alliances, economic development and restructuring, newfound pride in the "Pacific Century," or globalization. Some have marched to their own downfall on their own two feet, reaping the benefits of new wealth and consumer freedoms; many, such as those enslaved by traffickers and brothel owners, have been stripped physically and figuratively of their will and dignity. But have these sacrifices been part of faith-acts or acts of exploitation and abuse? Does the "larger good" have any kind of redemptive or transcendent qualities for the individual woman and the greater society? If we can imagine that Isaac might have screamed and wailed and squirmed within the constraints of being bound by Abraham, what of these women? How many of us hear them, let alone see them? How many of us are aware that they are living beside us, not isolated on the top of a mountain? As in the story of Abraham and Isaac at the altar of God, are there possibilities for collective reconciliation, forgiveness, reparation, and renewal?

Military Power and Terror

Korea occupies a key geostrategic and cultural place in East Asia, historically serving as a bridge between the islands of Japan and the continental powerhouse, China. Since World War II, the Korean peninsula has become the common preoccupation of China, Japan, the Soviet Union/ Russia, and the United States. In this context, Korea can teach us important lessons about the impact of military power on women's lives. The kind of exploitation, oppression, and terror that Koreans have grown accustomed to in the last century can be characterized largely as victimization by more potent political, military, and economic forces (e.g., China, Japan, the U.S., or the International Monetary Fund)—what Koreans and others refer to as a "shrimp among whales" syndrome. Korean nationalism has also reflected this power asymmetry: G. Cameron Hurst has noted that Korean nationalism exhibits "a xenophobia that relishes the image of Korea, past and present, as victim of an outside world intent only upon its exploitation."[4] Such nationalism has colored the ways in which foreign domination and abuse of women are understood. In the 1970s, Korean women's protests against Japanese *kisaeng*-tourism (sex tours to South Korea) resounded with anti-Japanese sentiments that recalled the humiliation of the colonial period.

Power asymmetry also applies to state-society relations within Korea. For four decades since the establishment of the republic (1948), South Koreans had their political voice, physical mobility, freedom of association, educational environments, and religious expression tightly controlled by

162

military authoritarian regimes. It is commonly noted that the first generation of labor activists (1970s) were primarily women, fighting for better work conditions and treatment as human beings by their primarily male bosses, whose interests were safeguarded by the brute force of the national police. These women in low-paying, low-skilled, labor-intensive manufacturing firms that promised national prosperity through the export of cheap textiles, clothing, and shoes were deemed by the Korean government as essential to the economic development and political viability of South Korea.

The nation was the be-all and end-all of women's existence, whether as restorer of pride and dignity from foreign domination or as organizer and beneficiary of women's skills, energy, and labor power. In what follows, I examine the role of nationalism as both enabling those who seek to confront/resist terror *and* facilitating new forms of terror and violence against women. I argue that Koreans and others in this expanding world society need to recognize and resist the transnationalization of terror in the context of globalization, and that constructive action requires honest self-examination and reflection as individuals and nations and the forgoing of holier-than-thou stances. We will need to confess that we are all implicated in the web of human rights violations and abuse of women, and that reconciliation among peoples and the redemption of individuals require mutual admission of self-interest, wrongdoing, and forgiveness.

The national and international movement to confront the realities of and demand reparations for those Korean women among the estimated 80,000–200,000 who survived the system of Japanese militarized sexual slavery (*chongsindae* in Korean) during the Pacific War (World War II) is an example of how nationalism and transnationalism can respectively distort and empower women's relationship to militarized terror. The *chongsindae* experiences of Korean and other women from the Asia-Pacific and Europe reveal an egregious example of organized, large-scale sexual slavery/forced prostitution under government sanction that we know of in modern history. It is a classic example of how imperialism and colonialism forcibly enlisted the bodies of women from the conquered society to raise and sustain the morale of the conquering troops and how, as many feminist scholars have observed, women's bodies became the battleground for warring among men. Some Koreans have even suggested that the abuse of young Korean women's bodies as sexual receptacles of Japanese power was a means to preempt/eliminate the next generation of Koreans, tantamount to genocide. The *chongsindae* movement for official apology and individual reparation has benefited from and reinforced the anti-Japanese sentiments among Koreans. I have argued elsewhere that in the international arena the "comfort women" movement is a movement for women's human rights, but within Korea it has been primarily a post-colonial, nationalist,

163

anti-Japanese movement.[5] From the perspective of social movement theory, the *chongsindae* movement's appeal to nationalism makes sense because it provides the context for "frame alignment" of the social movement, particularly the "nature of the belief system held by potential participants" and the "extent to which the framing resonates within the 'life world' of potential participants."[6] According to one leader of the *chongsindae* movement, there was enough "anti-Japanism" in the society to fuel the cause of the survivors.[7]

But the human rights-nationalist distinction is also important analytically and morally because it helps us question how one cause on behalf of oppressed women affects others. At least in the short term, the *chongsindae* movement within Korea has had a narrowing rather than broadening effect on other efforts to address the status and needs of women in various forms of sexual slavery or servitude because the rhetorical framework of the movement has established innocence-*cum*-virginity as the cornerstone of constructing claims for the recognition of human rights and the redress of past crimes. The movement has emphasized repeatedly that the Korean "comfort women" were young virgins who were drafted by force or fraud and therefore are innocent victims of colonial domination. Most of the survivors and leaders have refused to acknowledge the concerns of *kijich'on* women (prostitutes/sex workers near the U.S. military bases in Korea)[8] and their advocates as having anything in common with their own. The *kijich'on* women were deemed immoral, based on the common assumption that the women were willing providers of sexual services, in contrast to the innocence of *chongsindae* victims. Although the two women's movements originally began together in the late 1980s as part of a larger Asian women's movement against sexual exploitation, they soon went their separate ways because they could not reconcile their differences over the "legitimacy" of *kijich'on* women's needs and interests.

Even though *kijich'on* prostitution is a system of sexual indentured servitude (and in some instances outright slavery) that is directly regulated by the Korean government at the national and local levels and indirectly by the U.S. military,[9] the burden of legitimacy over the claims of the *kijich'on* movement for basic protection from physical harm, economic exploitation, and social condemnation has hinged on women's innocence. Although there are countless *kijich'on* women who were kidnapped, raped, and/or beaten into and during sexual labor in the bars and brothels that cater to U.S. servicemen, virginity, not human rights, has endured as the social marker of women's dignity, value, and status. This in turn has helped reinforce the long-standing Confucianist valuation of women as "virgin girl–obedient wife–moral mother" in determining women's political legitimacy. Such politicized value judgements also help sustain a particularly gendered Korean nationalism, one that puts the burden of maintaining the integrity of the (extended) family, home, and nation on women. In *Measured Excess,* Laura Nelson discusses how and why the South Korean government's *kwasobi ch'ubang* (anti-excessive consumption) campaign of the 1980s both blamed women as destroyers of national well-being and targeted them as would-be patriots through national social reform:

> The imagined inability of women, as a class, to restrain their desires is seen as leading to the social disharmonies of conspicuous consumption, the financial ruin of spending beyond one's means, and the corrupting adoption of foreign ways and things. . . . This sense that the nation is made vulnerable through its women-as-consumers seems almost sexual, metaphorically related to the idea that the nation's women need to be protected from the predations, or temptations, of foreign men.[10] . . . Kwasobi ch'ubang was not just a governmental propaganda campaign. Existing ideas about the symbolic and material importance of household frugality as participation in the development of a healthy national economy formed the basis of a renewed discourse of economic consumer patriotism.[11]

Transferring Terror

Ironically, the very women who were marginalized by the *chongsindae* movement have themselves been discriminating against other women—Filipinas, Indonesians, East Europeans, and more—based on the category of "foreigner." Since the early 1990s, thousands of women from China, Southeast Asia, and the former Soviet bloc have traveled to South Korea as part of the expanding labor migration force in Asia. Many of these women have entered the *kijich'on* sex industry under the thumb of flesh traffickers and labor brokers. They are part of the trend toward globalization—the free movement of goods, services, capital—that includes labor migration across national borders. Korean owners and managers of the *kijich'on* sex and drinking establishments have eagerly "recruited" young foreign women, especially Filipinas, to "entertain" U.S. soldiers. For such entrepreneurs, this is an economic opportunity to reduce labor costs and maintain a docile workforce that appeals to American customers (American soldiers are known to prefer the Filipinas because they tend to be younger and better English-speakers than the Korean women).[12] For the Korean *kijich'on* women, the foreigners amount to economic competition. Fights and arguments between Korean and foreign women have broken out in several *kijich'on* areas, and the relationship between the two groups is tense. In American Town, the *kijich'on* near Kunsan U.S. Air Force Base, Korean prostitutes publicly protested the presence of foreign sex workers and called for people to "buy domestic-made." In my own conversations in Seoul in the spring of 1999 with a woman who is a former prostitute and an outspoken activist on behalf of Korean *kijich'on* women and their Amerasian children, I learned that economic competition was not the only cause of the resentment toward foreigners. This woman expressed her concern that with increasing numbers of foreign women in the *kijich'on,* Korean culture will become confused and corrupted.

There is irony in both these examples. Even though contemporary prostitutes urge men to buy flesh that is "domestic-made," their predecessors back in 1971 had staged public protests against the explicit commodification of their sexual services. Angered by a boycott organized by U.S. airmen, the "Do Not Buy Korean Commodities Campaign," the local prostitutes held rallies near various U.S. installations and "adopted a four-point resolution, calling for the withdrawal of the Korean commodity boycott drive and reverence for the human rights of the Korean people."[13] As part of the boycott, servicemen had compiled and circulated a list of prices they were willing to pay for various goods and services in town, including sex as just another object, like shoes. The women's public protests helped end this campaign in two short months and elicited an apology from the command.[14]

Additionally, the concern even among past and present prostitutes that foreign women will have negative effects on the national identity and cultural integrity of Korea reflects how deep nationalist sentiments run among everyday Koreans. The irony here is that Korean women who sold their flesh to U.S. soldiers themselves have been considered the lowest of the low in Korean society and even within the hierarchy of sex laborers in Korea. They have been deemed by the larger society as agents of moral corruption and bearers of national shame, for they have been with foreign men and mothered offspring of mixed blood. Sadly, the outsider status that has been attributed to Korean women in the *kijich'on* is expanding to include foreign nationals living and working in these areas. It speaks to the endless possibilities for constructing and reconstructing who belongs or is an outcast, who is authentic, and who is a pariah. The very women who have been stigmatized as pariahs by the larger Korean society are now using the shield of national identity to keep foreign women out. Terror, in this sense, is alienation, condemnation, and a conscious refusal to see others as like us, bound to one another in fear, vulnerability, and violence, as well as in hope for constructive change.

The tendency to let nationalism inform individual and community rights and pride seems to cut across gender and class divisions in Korea. After more than four decades of ignoring *kijich'on* women and the context of violence in which they live and work, the recent wave of anti-American protests and debates in Korea (since the early- to mid-1990s) includes the rapes, murders, and assaults on these women as proof of the unequal relations between South Korea and the United States, particularly the terms of the Status of Forces Agreement (SOFA) that governs the stationing of

U.S. military personnel and their dependents while in Korea. From grass-roots and student activists, lawyers and intellectuals, to high-ranking government officials and members of both ruling and opposition parties, Koreans have been calling for changes in the SOFA and the U.S.-Korea relationship toward one of equality and full exercise of Korean sovereignty. Since the brutal murder of Yun Kum-I in 1992 by a U.S. serviceman, the media and the public at large have become more aware of *kijich'on* women's lives, and civic organizations, like the National Campaign for the Eradication of Crimes by U.S. Troops in Korea, have emerged to document, monitor, and protest the criminal and other undesirable conduct of U.S. military personnel.

But the demonstrations and discourse that oppose U.S. troop violence are grounded in nationalism, with an emphasis on state sovereignty and national pride, not women's human rights and welfare. There is no public mention, and not much awareness, of the fact that *kijich'on* inhabitants now include more than a thousand Filipinas and other women from Indonesia, Sri Lanka, Eastern Europe, and more. Nor do some of these progressive activists address the human rights violations and sexual exploitation of these foreign women by Koreans, Americans, and traffickers of different nationalities. In contrast to the internationalizing and transnationalizing trends in labor migration and organized crime that require civic and policy responses that reach across national boundaries and recognize the interconnectedness of different issue areas, the terms of protest and policy redress remain bilateral. With increased migration into Korea, there will be more people who fall into a legal and normative vacuum unless the terms move beyond nationalism and state sovereignty to human and labor rights.

Weaker nations and victimized peoples need to acknowledge that they also generate, transfer, and sustain various forms of terror, not just receive the blows and indignities from the more powerful. With respect to Korea, its newly achieved economic wealth and status as an East Asian "Tiger" or "Dragon" abetted South Korean businessmen to travel to poorer countries and buy the flesh of Southeast Asian women. If Japanese sex tours to Korea in the 1970s were sustained by Japanese economic power over Korea and a lingering colonial attitude of sexual entitlement, then South Korean "sex-ploration" in Southeast Asia in the 1980s and 1990s has been based on a newly derived sense of consumption power and sexual acquisitiveness that crosses national boundaries.

Since democratization trends began in the late 1980s, individual Koreans and the media have, to their credit, been willing to investigate and reflect on their roles in past human rights abuses, namely the killings, rapes, and other atrocities toward Vietnamese civilians that Korean soldiers have reportedly perpetrated. Korean human rights groups have taken a lead role

167

in demanding that Seoul open its war archives and compensate Vietnamese victims, although both the Korean and Vietnamese governments prefer to keep this issue off the bilateral agenda. But even as some try to account for their nation's role in generating and transferring terror in other countries, there are many who fear that such confessions would damage national pride and international status. One *Newsweek* article reports that many Korean veterans of Vietnam "believe their younger critics are on a mistaken crusade that threatens the country's hard-won pride. 'This could be reported in The New York Times!' shouted an angry ex-marine. . . . Then what would foreigners think about Korea?"[15] Moreover, the situation is complicated further by the fact that many Korean soldiers believe they too were victims of the Vietnam War, namely the U.S. use of Agent Orange. Korean veterans are known to feel betrayed by their U.S. ally for having left them out of a 1984 settlement in which 253,000 Vietnam War veterans from the U.S., Australia, and New Zealand were monetarily compensated by U.S. manufacturers of the defoliant. Suh Jung Won, a former division captain in the war who now oversees the Agent Orange issue for the Korean Veterans Office, stated that he believes Korean soldiers "were ignored because of our (lack of) national strength."[16] Such a sense of national victimization and powerlessness blocks the ability to take stock of and responsibility for wrongdoing toward others. Similarly, many Japanese have a sense of victimization as the only nation-state and people who suffered the ultimate show of force, the U.S. dropping of two atomic bombs in 1945, and this reality in turn abets Japanese resistance to apologize and make amends to the people and nations it had victimized, particularly the former "comfort women" from Korea.

As politically sensitive and emotionally disturbing as it is to discover, place blame, and find ways to redress past acts of terror, recognizing and addressing current and future forms of terror are even more difficult. For one, attention to violence against women tends to be sporadic and focused on extremes. The media, international organizations like the United Nations, and major nongovernmental organizations tend to get busy when rape in war amounts to tens of thousands of women, as in women in Bosnia and Herzegovina; when sexual abuse of Asian women by U.S. servicemen gets enacted in the gang rape of a twelve-year-old girl in Okinawa; or when a renegade regime like the Taliban deprives girls and women of access to education and health care. But variations on these themes, in less sensational forms, take place every day but go unnoticed, overlooked, or simply ignored.

One such example involves North Korean women and girls. Most of the world does not know much about the realities of life in North Korea, and those who are in the know in the West—government officials, international agencies, nongovernmental organizations, and think tanks—focus almost exclusively on nuclear nonproliferation, military security on the Korean peninsula, and only recently, food assistance in the context of a devastating famine. Attention to women's realities is scant although their circumstances are urgent. While the North Korean leaders strive to maintain the military machine that sustains their power, people have died or grown weak and malnourished from a famine that the government refuses to acknowledge and have been forced into detention camps and self-exile as food migrants. International newspapers have also reported intermittently since the late 1990s that girls are being sold to traffickers by their parents in exchange for money or food. According to journalists and nongovernmental organizations—religious and secular—who are familiar with the plight of North Korean migrants in China, close to half of the estimated 150,000 who have fled to China are women, many of whom have been forced into prostitution or child marriage to Chinese farmers by ethnic Korean-Chinese in the Yanbian region.

Trafficking and the forced sexual labor of North Korean women and children in other countries are already taking place, even though the North is quite isolated. But this reality is made invisible as a matter of public policy because (1) the Chinese government does not want food migrants from North Korea to attract international attention and official refugee recognition; (2) public attention to the trafficking of North Korean girls and women would necessarily call attention to the increased trafficking of Chinese women and girls by Chinese nationals within and outside its borders; (3) the Korean government does not want to rock the boat of inter-Korea communication/cooperation that officially set sail in the summer of 2000 or take responsibility for migrants from the North; and (4) the U.S. government myopically focuses on one issue—North Korean nuclear and missile development—at the expense of others. In general, there has been no or little interest around the world in North Korean affairs (with the exception of the recent inter-Korea summit), while the little interest that has been paid has been based on North Korea as a regime rather than as a place with human beings struggling to survive and adapt. In contrast, recent efforts to resist and prevent the trafficking and forced sexual labor of Russian and Eastern European women have gained relatively fast momentum because of the European Union and the United States' ongoing interest in the former Soviet countries. The fact that North Korea is diplomatically isolated means that its citizens are shut off from or ignored by advocacy groups and governments. Their suffering therefore continues in silence.

Resisting Terror

As the "sins of the fathers" get transferred from generation to generation in the Hebrew Scriptures, so does hope and the possibility for renewal

169

and reconstruction of human beings' faith and covenant with God. Having been spared from death, Isaac became the father of Jacob, a feisty servant and strategist of human relations. In Korea, the suffering of earlier generations has left a resilient legacy of feisty activism to counter the new forms of exploitation and abuse of women and men. South Korea is noted not only for its authoritarian past and economic "miracle" but also for its more than four decades of resistance to military-authoritarian rule and the self-sacrifices for labor and human rights—the 1971 self-immolation of Chon Tae Il, a young garment district worker, who protested against the exploitation of factory girls/women with his own life is a well-known example. Korea is what Hagen Koo has labeled "strong state-contentious society."[17] For example, Koreans who had been dissident activists in the 1970s and 1980s have been raising consciousness about the plight of several hundred thousand legal and "illegal" migrant workers from South and Southeast Asia, China, former Soviet Union, and elsewhere who have been servicing the Korean economy since the early 1990s. They also have been leading demonstrations and lobbying government agencies so that human and labor rights violations are stopped and protection is extended.

For many of the leading Korean activists, both secular and clerical, their current struggle on behalf of the migrant workers is an extension of their participation in the labor and democracy movements of earlier decades. For example, the heads of the Association for Foreign Workers' Human Rights (the first secular advocacy group), the Songnam Migrant Workers' House, and the Ansan Migrant Workers' Center (two of the largest and most active counseling/advocacy centers near Seoul) had all been outspoken critics of military rule and labor repression in the 1970s and 1980s. The director of the Foreign Workers' Labor Counseling Office of the Catholic Archdiocese of Seoul has worked in the Catholic Church's labor advocacy/ministry programs since the 1970s. She also established the first counseling center for migrant workers in Korea in 1992, centered on the needs of Filipinas. This itself was an outgrowth of transnational cooperation: what began as a Catholic mass led by a nun from the Philippines and a nun from Korea for seven to eight Filipinas grew to a gathering of one hundred female migrant workers within a year and compelled the Korean Catholic Church to respond institutionally to the plight of migrant female workers.[18] In general, churches and other religious organizations in Korea have played a significant role by assisting with the welfare and health needs of migrant workers, and in the case of progressive religious activists, also with efforts to fight discrimination and exploitation and address the legal issues surrounding their visa status, marriage, paternity, and more. This reflects a learning curve for religious institutions. In contrast to the quiescence and passivity of mainstream churches during the earlier movements for democracy and labor rights in Korea, they and some Buddhist organizations are now taking on the needs of exploited and oppressed foreigners as part of their mission and service.

The Korean activists have transferred not only personnel but also public rhetoric and symbolism to the migrant workers' cause. The first ever public demonstration by foreign workers took place in 1995 in front of Myongdong Cathedral in Seoul, the traditional stage and refuge of antigovernment protesters during the decades of military rule. What started as a demonstration by thirteen Nepalese led to a meeting of more than thirty-eight grassroots and labor organizations to form "an association for the human rights protection of foreign industrial trainees."[19] During the early years, the migrant workers' movement in Korea perceived the government's treatment of the foreign nationals as a form of political authoritarianism. For example, their depiction of the government crackdowns on escaped industrial trainees and undocumented workers recalls the violence by the police and military against Korean dissident activists in the democracy movements of the 1970s and 1980s, and they have been challenging the Korean government to practice the democracy it has been touting since the early 1990s.[20]

The ability to recognize similar conditions across national, religious, and cultural boundaries is key to the constructive work of such organizations and activism. In personal terms, empathy is required. Kim Yonja, a former *kijich'on* prostitute and madam who is now an activist, told me that although the *chongsindae* and *kijich'on* movements do not work together, personally getting to know and sharing life stories with *chongsindae* survivors has helped bridge the misperceptions, misunderstandings, and value judgements about *kijich'on* women. She recounted how her own befriending of *chongsindae* survivors at international conferences and other gatherings on militarism and sexual violence allowed them to see their experiences of terror as comparable and related rather than as morally superior or inferior and politically legitimate or illegitimate.[21]

The younger generation who came of age during the turbulent 1980s are also playing leading roles in uncovering Korea's past in Vietnam and forging private attempts at reconciliation. For example, in March of 2000, the Dentists Association for a Healthy Society, based in Seoul, sent thirty-eight of its members as volunteers to Vietnam to offer free dental work to those who had been injured by Korean actions. *Newsweek* noted that "most participants, who treated 1,500 people in four days, were young professionals" and that the organizer of the trip, Chung Chang Gon (Kwon) reflected, "Our generation benefited from the Vietnam War, so we had a moral and ethical obligation to treat its people."[22] In an article he wrote for *People to People*, a human rights and peace magazine published by the Korea House for International Solidarity, Chung recounted that Korean clinicians and Vietnamese patients hugged and cried and held each other although they could not read-

171

ily communicate through words. There were those who expressed their anger and hatred of Koreans for having destroyed their families and their own lives but in the end were thankful for the treatment freely offered as a gesture of reconciliation. Many Vietnamese spoke words of forgiveness to the Koreans, and many Koreans apologized and begged forgiveness. By the end of the encounter, laughter and tears helped make peace among peoples whereas governments failed to take up the concern.[23] The Korea House for International Solidarity also sponsored and organized the first-ever cultural festival in the summer of 2000 to raise funds to assist Vietnamese victims of Korean atrocities and to "plant a new flame of peace in people's hearts."[24]

The world is growing more connected through the Internet, the exchange of pop culture—from U.S. films, to Japanese animation, to salsa—and the spread of norms about human rights in both peacetime and war. In a measure that directly penetrates the walls of national sovereignty, the United Nations is making it possible for women for the first time to "bypass their governments" and "complain directly to the United Nations about discrimination, sexual exploitation and other violations" as a part of the Convention on the Elimination of All forms of Discrimination Against Women. Even though bureaucratic, political, and economic obstacles will not make such direct access to the United Nations easy for all women, it is nevertheless an historic breakthrough. It recognizes states' inability or unwillingess to take women's claims about their experiences of discrimination and terror seriously, and it secures women's rights more firmly in the institutional and normative framework of international human rights. It also stands in contrast to the refusal of the United States to support and participate in the creation of an International Criminal Court of Justice to adjudicate cases of war crimes. It is an example of a genuine "larger good" supported by many governments and peoples around the world that the sole superpower and leading proponent of democracy opposes in order to prevent international moral and legal scrutiny of its own armed forces. On the one hand, the world is changing to move away from historical patterns of institutionalized terror toward establishing new patterns and practices of accountability and responsible exercise of power. On the other, powerful governments stand in the way. Resisting and redressing different forms of terror that Asian and other women experience confront both hope—in the progressive activism of civic organizations and international coalitions informed by international norms—and intransigence—in nations' pursuit of self-interest as "national security."

What constitutes the "higher call"? Who decides? And who will be required to lie atop the altar, bound and fear-stricken? Who will protect and redeem? The answer lies with us as individuals and communities. Nationalism, national security, and economic competition are not faith acts ordained by God. They are man-made. We need not blindly sacrifice one another to man-made calls for obedience.

Part 3

Theological Leadership through Terror

Calling the Oppressors to Account for Four Centuries of Terror

James H. Cone

> God is not dead,— nor is he an indifferent onlooker at what is going on in this world. One day He will make requisition for blood; He will call the oppressors to account. Justice may sleep, but it never dies. The individual, race, or nation which does wrong, which sets at defiance God's great law, especially God's great law of love, of brotherhood, will be sure, sooner or later, to pay the penalty. We reap as we sow. With what measure we mete, it will be measured to us again.[1]

This 1902 statement by Francis Grimke, an ex-slave and Princeton Theological Seminary graduate, is an apt summary of the major themes of justice, hope, and love in African-American religion from slavery to the present. These themes were created out of the African slaves' encounter with biblical religion (via the white missionaries and preachers) as they sought to make meaning in a strange world. To make meaning in any world is difficult because human beings, like other animals, are creatures of nature and history. We can never be what we can imagine, but to be slaves in a foreign land without the cultural and religious support of a loving family and a caring community limits human possibilities profoundly. Because Africans were prevented from freely practicing their native religion, they merged their knowledge of their cultural past with the white man's Christian religion. From these two sources, Africans created for themselves a world of meaning that enabled them to survive 246 years of slavery and 100 years of segregation—augmented by a reign of white terror that lynched more than 5,000 black people.

The black religious themes of justice, hope, and love are the product of black people's search for meaning in a white society that did not acknowledge their humanity. The most prominent theme in this trinity of divine virtues is the justice of God. Faith in God's righteousness is the starting point of black religion. African-Americans have always believed in the living presence of the God who establishes the right by punishing the wicked and liberating their victims from oppression. Everyone will be rewarded and punished according to their deeds, and no one—absolutely no one—can escape the judgment of God, who alone is the sovereign of the universe. Evildoers may get by for a time, and good people may suffer unjustly under oppression, but "sooner or later . . . we reap as we sow."

The "sooner" referred to contemporary historically observable events: punishment of the oppressors and liberation of the oppressed. The "later" referred to the divine establishment of justice in the "next world" where God "gwineter rain down fire" on the wicked and where the liberated righteous will "walk in Jerusalem just like John." In the religion of African slaves, God's justice was identical to the punishment of the oppressors, and divine liberation was synonymous with the deliverance of the oppressed from the bondage of slavery—if not "now" then in the "not yet." Because whites continued to prosper materially as they increased their victimization of African-Americans, black religion spoke more often of the "later" than the "sooner," more about justice in the next world than in this one.

The theme of justice is closely related to the idea of hope. The God who establishes the right and puts down the wrong is the sole basis of the hope that the suffering of the victims will be eliminated. Although African slaves used the term "heaven" to describe their experience of hope, its primary meaning for them must not be reduced to the "pie-in-the-sky," otherworldly affirmation that often characterized white evangelical Protestantism. The idea of heaven was the means by which slaves affirmed their humanity in a world that did not recognize them as human beings. It was their way of saying that they were made for freedom and not slavery.

> Oh Freedom! Oh Freedom!
> Oh Freedom, I love thee!
> And before I'll be a slave,
> I'll be buried in my grave,
> And go home to my Lord and be free.

Black slaves' hope was based on their faith in God's promise to "protect the needy" and to "defend the poor." Just as God delivered the Hebrew children from Egyptian bondage and raised Jesus from the dead, so God will also deliver African slaves from American slavery and will "soon" bestow upon them the gift of eternal life. That was why they sang:

Soon-a-will be done with the trouble of this world;
Soon-a-will be done with the trouble of this world;
Going home to live with God.

Black slaves' faith in the coming justice of God was the chief reason they could hold themselves together in servitude and sometimes fight back, even though the odds were against them.

The ideas of justice and hope should be seen in relation to the important theme of love. Theologically, God's love is prior to the other themes. But in order to separate love in the context of black religion from a similar theme in white religion, it is important to emphasize that love in black religion is usually linked with God's justice and hope. God's love is made known through divine righteousness, liberating the poor for a new future.

God's creation of all persons in the divine image bestows sacredness upon human beings and thus makes them the children of God. To violate any person's dignity is to transgress "God's great law of love." We must love the neighbor because God has first loved us. And because slavery and segregation are blatant denials of the dignity of the human person, divine justice means God "will call the oppressors to account."

Despite the power of black faith, belief in God's coming justice and liberation was not easy for African slaves and their descendants. Their continued suffering created the most serious challenge to their faith. If God is good, why did God permit millions of blacks to be stolen from Africa, to perish in the middle passage, and to be enslaved in a strange land? No black person has been able to escape the existential agony of that question.

In their attempt to resolve the existential and theological dilemma that slavery and segregation created, African-Americans in the nineteenth century turned to two texts: Exodus and Psalm 68:31. They derived from the Exodus text the belief that God is the liberator of the oppressed. They interpreted Psalm 68:31 as an obscure reference to God's promise to redeem Africa: "Princes shall come out of Egypt, and Ethiopia shall soon stretch forth her hands unto God" (KJV). Despite African-Americans' reflections on these texts, the contradictions remained between their sociopolitical oppression and their religious faith.

A free black woman named Nellie from Savannah, Georgia, expressed the challenged black suffering created for faith: "It has been a terrible mystery, to know why the good Lord should so long afflict my people, and keep them in bondage,—to be abused, and trampled down, without any rights of their own,— with no ray of light in the future. Some of my folks said there wasn't any God, for if there was he wouldn't let white folks do as they do for so many years."[2]

Throughout the twentieth century, African-Americans continued their struggle to reconcile their faith in the justice and love of God with the persistence of black suffering in the land of their birth. Writer James Baldwin expressed the feelings of most African-Americans: "If [God's] love was so great, and if He loved all His children, why were we, the blacks, cast down so far?"[3] It was Martin Luther King Jr., a twenty-six-year-old Baptist preacher, who, empowered by black faith, confronted the evil of white supremacy and condemned it as the greatest moral evil in American society. He organized a movement that broke the backbone of legal segregation in the South. From the beginning of his role as the leader of the yearlong Montgomery, Alabama, bus boycott (1955–56) to his tragic death in Memphis, Tennessee (April 4, 1968), King was a public embodiment of the ideas of love, justice, and hope. The meaning of each was dependent on the others. Though love may be placed appropriately at the center of King's faith, he interpreted love in the light of justice for the poor, liberation for all, and the certain hope that God has not left this world in the hands of evil men.

King took the American democratic tradition of freedom and combined it with the biblical tradition of liberation and justice as found in the Exodus and the prophets, then he integrated both traditions with the New Testament idea of love and hope as disclosed in Jesus' cross and resurrection. From these three sources, King developed a radical practice of nonviolence that was effective in challenging all Americans to create the beloved community in which all persons are equal. While it was Gandhi's method of nonviolence that provided the strategy for achieving justice, it was, as King said, "through the influence of the Negro Church" that "the way of nonviolence became an integral part of our struggle"[4] against the evil of white supremacy.

As a Christian whose faith was derived from the cross of Jesus, King believed that there could be no true liberation without suffering. Through nonviolent suffering, he contended, blacks would not only liberate themselves from the necessity of bitterness and feeling of inferiority toward whites but would also prick the consciences of whites and liberate them from a feeling of superiority. The mutual liberation of blacks and whites lays the foundation for both to work together toward the creation of an entirely new world.

In accordance with this theological vision, King initially rejected black power because of its connotations of revenge, hate, and violence. He believed that no beloved community of black and whites could be created out of bitterness. Only love, which he equated with nonviolence, can create justice. When black power militants turned away from nonviolence and openly preached self-defense and violence, King said that he would continue to preach nonviolence even if he became its only advocate.

He took a similar position regarding the war in Vietnam. In the tradition of the Hebrew prophets and against the advice of his closest associates in black and white communities, King stood before a capacity crowd at Riverside Church on April 4, 1967 and condemned America as "the greatest purveyor of violence in the world today."[5] He proclaimed God's judgment against America and insisted that God would break the backbone of U.S. power if this nation did not bring justice to the poor and peace to the world. God, King believed, was going to call America to account for its violence in Vietnam and in the ghettoes of U.S. cities.

During the crises of 1967–68, King turned to his own religious heritage for strength to keep on fighting for justice and for the courage to face the certain possibility of his own death. "It doesn't matter with me now," King proclaimed in a sermon the night before his assassination, "because I've been to the mountaintop . . . and I've seen the Promised Land."[6] It was the eschatological hope, derived from his slave grandparents and mediated through the black church, which sustained him in the midst of the trials and tribulations in the black freedom struggle. He combined the justice and love themes in the prophets and the cross with the message of hope in the resurrection of Jesus. For King, hope was based on his belief in the righteousness of God as defined by his reading of the Bible through the eyes of his slave foreparents. The result was one the most powerful faith responses to the theodicy question in African-American history.

> Centuries ago Jeremiah raised the question, "Is there no balm in Gilead? Is there no physician?" He raised it because he saw the good people suffering so often and the evil people prospering. Centuries later our slave foreparents came along and they too saw the injustice of life and had nothing to look forward to, morning after morning, but the rawhide whip of the overseer, long rows of cotton and the sizzling heat; but they did an amazing thing. They looked back across the centuries, and they took Jeremiah's question mark and straightened it into an exclamation point. And they could sing, "There is a balm in Gilead to make the wounded whole. There is a balm in Gilead to heal the sin-sick soul."[7]

King's approach to evil did not satisfy all blacks. There is another side in black religion that is rooted in blackness and its identity with Africa and its rejection of America and Christianity. From the time of its origin in slavery to the present, black religion has been faced with the question of whether to advocate integration into American society or separation from it. The majority of the participants in the black churches and the civil rights movement have promoted integration, and they have interpreted justice, hope, and love in the light of the goal of creating a society in which blacks and whites can live together in a beloved community.

While integrationists emphasized the American side of the identity of African-Americans, black nationalists rejected any association with the U.S.

and instead turned toward Africa for identity and hope for coping with suffering. Nationalists contended that blacks will never be accepted as equals in a white racist church and society. Black freedom can be achieved only by blacks separating themselves from whites—either by returning to Africa or by forcing the U.S. government to set aside a separate territory in the U.S. so blacks can build their own society.

The nationalist perspective on the black struggle for justice is deeply embedded in the history of black religion. Some of its proponents include Martin Delaney, often called the founder of black nationalism; Marcus Garvey, the founder of the Universal Negro Improvement Association; and Malcolm X of the religion of Islam. Black nationalism was centered on blackness and saw no value in white culture and religion.

The most persuasive interpreter of black nationalism during the 1960's was Malcolm X, who proclaimed a challenging critique of King's philosophy of integration, nonviolence, and love. Malcolm advocated black unity instead of the beloved community, self-defense in lieu of nonviolence, and self-love in place of turning the other cheek to whites.

Malcolm X rejected Christianity as the white man's religion. He became a convert initially to Elijah Muhammad's Nation of Islam and later to the worldwide Islamic community. His critique of Christianity and American society as white was so persuasive that many blacks followed him into the religion of Islam, and others accepted his criticisms even though they did not become Muslims. Malcolm pushed civil rights leaders to the left and caused many black Christians to reevaluate their interpretation of Christianity.

> Brothers and sisters, the white man has brainwashed us black people to fasten our gaze upon a blond-haired, blue-eyed Jesus! We're worshiping a Jesus that doesn't even *look* like us! Now just think of this. The blond-haired, blue-eyed white man has taught you and me to worship a *white* Jesus, and to shout and sing and pray to this God that's *his* God, the white man's God. The white man has taught us to shout and sing and pray until we *die*, to wait until *death*, for some dreamy heaven-in-the-hereafter, when we're *dead*, while this white man has his milk and honey in the streets paved with golden dollars right here on *this* earth![8]

During the first half of the 1960s, King's interpretation of justice as equality with whites, liberation as integration, and love as nonviolence dominated the thinking of the black religious community. However, after the riot in Watts (Los Angeles, August 1965) some black religious activists began to take another look at Malcolm X's philosophy, especially in regard to his criticisms of Christianity and American society. Malcolm X's contention that America was a nightmare and not a dream began to ring true to many black clergy as they watched their communities go up in flames.

The rise of black power in 1966 created a decisive turning point in black religion. Black power forced black clergy to raise the theological question about the relation between black faith and white religion. Although blacks have always recognized the ethical heresy of white Christians ("Everybody talking about heaven ain't going there"), they have not always extended their race critique to Euro-American theology. With its accent on the cultural heritage of Africa and political liberation "by any means necessary," black power shook black religious leaders out of their theological complacency.

Separating themselves from King's absolute commitment to nonviolence, a small group of black clergy, mostly from the North, addressed black power positively and critically. Like King and unlike black power advocates, black clergy were determined to remain within the Christian community. This was their dilemma: How could they reconcile Christianity and black power, Martin Luther King Jr. and Malcolm X?

Under the influence of Malcolm X and the political philosophy of black power, many black theologians began to advocate the necessity for the development of a black theology. They rejected the dominant theologies of Europe and North America as heretical. For the first time in the history of black religion, black clergy and theologians began to recognize the need for a completely new starting point in theology, and they insisted that it must be defined by people at the bottom and not from the top of the socio-economic ladder. To accomplish this task, black theologians focused on God's liberation of the poor as the central message of the gospel.

To explicate the theological significance of the liberation motif, black theologians began to reread the Bible through the eyes of their slave grandparents and started to speak of God's solidarity with the wretched of the earth. As the political liberation of the poor emerged as the dominant motif, justice, love, and hope were reinterpreted in its light. For the biblical meaning of liberation, black theologians turned to the Exodus, while the message of the prophets provided the theological content for the theme of justice. The gospel story of the life, death, and resurrection of Jesus served as the biblical foundation for a reinterpretation of love, suffering, and hope in the context of the black struggle for liberation and justice.

There are many blacks, however, who find no spiritual or intellectual consolation in the Christian answer to the problem of theodicy. After nearly four hundred years of black presence in what is now known as the United States of America, black people still have to contend with white supremacy in every segment of their lives. This evil is so powerful and pervasive that no blacks can escape it, but poor blacks bear the heaviest brunt of it. The

181

persistence of racism makes the creation of meaning difficult for blacks inside and outside the church.

Is God still going to call the oppressors to account? If so, when? Black churches seem to have no meaningful answer to these questions. They simply repeat worn-out religious cliches: "All things work out for the good for them who love the Lord." "God will make a way out of no way." "By and by when the morning comes, We'll understand it better by and by." Black suffering in America and throughout the world, however, seems to be a blatant contradiction of that faith claim. Black suffering is getting worse, not better, and we are more confused than ever about the reasons for it. White supremacy is so clever and evasive that we can hardly name it. It claims not to exist, even though black people are dying daily from its poison.

No people are more religious than blacks. We faithfully attend churches and other religious services, giving reverence and love to the One who called us into being. But how long must black people wait for God to call our oppressors to account? How long is it going to take for black people to get justice in America?

Theology's task is to give reasons for the Christian hope in the face of horrendous human suffering. How can Christians hope in the face of unspeakable evil? No one wants a hope that has not been tested in life's great agonies.

"Suffering precedes thinking," wrote Ludwig Feuerbach. It creates thought, forcing people to search their faith for meaning and purpose in a world of deep contradictions. If the massive suffering of black people does not cause them to think deeply and critically about the reasons for their absurd predicament, then what will shake them out of their spiritual complacency? What will it take for blacks to stop preaching pie-in-the-sky as an answer to worldwide black suffering? Whether in Harlem, New York, Chicago's South Side, or Nairobi, Kenya, "O Lord, how long shall I cry for help, and you will not listen? Or cry to you 'Violence!' and you will not save?" (Hab. 1:2).

There is no easy answer to this theological problem, no easy way to deal with the absurdities and indignities of American life. We must reflect theologically, probing the depth of our faith in our effort to deepen it. This is an urgent and necessary task because an uncritical faith cannot sustain you through life full with trouble.

Black and womanist theologians have no satisfactory answers for the theodicy question either—at least not for those blacks who, like Job, "will not put away [their] integrity" or "speak falsehood" (Job 27:5, 4, respectively) about what is happening to them in this world. We can write about God's justice and love from now to the end of time, but until our theological discourse engages white supremacy in a way that empowers poor people to believe that they can destroy the monster, then our theology is not worth the paper it is written on.

Most black churches preach a cheap spirituality, a "cheap grace," to use Bonhoeffer's classic language. It doesn't cost us much, except a little time on Sunday. Our preachers are well trained in the art of proclamation. They can open up the doors of heaven without leaving earth, giving people a transcendent entertainment that surpasses anything on Broadway in New York City.

Martin Luther King Jr. described "the existence of evil in the world . . . as the great enigma wrapped in mystery. . . ."[9] There is no intellectual or theoretical answer that will ease the pain of police brutality and the daily insults to black humanity woven into fabric of this society and its churches. The Christian answer to suffering is both practical and spiritual. We solve the mystery of evil's existence by fighting it, and faith is real only to the degree it endows us with the courage to fight.

On the one hand, suffering challenges faith, causing us to doubt and question faith's credibility and its authenticity in a world of trouble and sorrow. On the other hand, faith challenges suffering, refusing to let trouble have the last word, the final say about life's meaning and purpose. This is faith's stubborn tenacity grounded in its political struggle against the perpetrators of evil.

In 1903, W. E. B. Du Bois said: "The problem of the twentieth century is the problem of the color-line,—the relation of the darker to the lighter races of men in Asia and Africa, in America and the islands of the sea."[10] That message is as true today as it was when he uttered it. There is still no justice in the land for black people. "No justice, no peace" proclaimed blacks to whites during the 1992 Los Angeles riot and the years that followed. "No love, no justice" was Martin Luther King Jr.'s way of proclaiming to all who would listen. King's words are what whites want to hear when there is a racial disturbance, protesting the limits of black patience with white supremacy. But African-Americans want to know whether there is any reason to hope that the twenty-first century will be any less racist than the previous four centuries. Is there any reason to hope that we will be able to create a truly just society where justice and love flow freely between whites and blacks and among all peoples of the earth? Let us hope that enough people will bear witness to justice and love so as to inspire others to believe that with God and the practice of freedom fighters "all things are possible."

Systemic Theology: Preliminary Principles

Timothy Light

This essay is an attempt to articulate the basic principles of what appears to me to be a significant theological "movement" and one to which David Suh belongs. My suggestion that there may be a theological movement and the assumption that, if there is, it has not yet been widely discussed may simply be the product of my untutored ignorance. I am a lay person—both in the sense of not being ordained and in the sense of having done no study of theology beyond a couple of courses at Union Theological Seminary in the early 1960s. I trust that at least to specialists (if not to all readers) my lack of acquaintance with both traditional and current theological dialogue will be evident in every line of what follows. I have gone to the rashness of writing this both to honor an old and dear friend through attempting to intellectually situate his work, and because to me theology continues to serve its traditional function of helping faith to find understanding. Taken together, the thinkers to whom I refer herein have enabled me to remain a Christian in the midst of a life and career that had grown to the point where much of the Christianity with which I was familiar in North America had become less than irrelevant. In writing what follows, I have attempted to clarify in my own mind how an aging European-American white man can be touched across gaps of gender, culture, and race to have learned a renewed vision of God in Christ in the hope that one or two others in similar situations might also find solace in this understanding of how contemporary Christians might be able to think about their lives and their faith and still remain Christian in a pluralistic world.

The notion of "movement" to which I have alluded is not the typical conscious joining of minds around similar experiences and shaping of common thoughts that are mutually built upon by a relatively small group of thinkers who become defined as much by those with whom they do not associate as by what they say. At least some of those to whom I refer as "systemic theologians" apparently have less rather than more in common with each other. I doubt that many of them—if any at all—would refer to all of the others in their own work. The (perhaps spurious) idea that there is a movement is, thus, inductively arrived at through what a linguist (my original academic discipline) would call feature analysis. The end product is a set of abstractions that make up a proposed framework—for theology, not a theology itself, since theologies are highly particular stories that arise out of highly particular (often traumatic) circumstances. Further, the "induction" of these principles is based simply on my own reading over the past decade or so. That reading has been scattered and undisciplined and has followed my own needs rather than a systematic program.

Because this inductive method of outlining systemic theology is inherently derivational, it is not fair or accurate to pretend that any of the thinkers to whom I refer here would necessarily concur with all (or any) of the abstractions that I shall give below in the way in which I shall state them. Since my aim is not to *prove* (whatever that might mean) that they do form a movement, the format I use deviates a bit from the typical academic paper. That is, my references in what follows will be general pointings to a specific thinker or thinkers and, occasionally, to a particular book. I will not make specific reference beyond that. To go beyond this level of generality would end up requiring a book rather than an article. The thinkers to whom I am referring as "systemic theologians" include James H. Cone,[1] Diana Eck,[2] Francis L. Gross Jr.,[3] Gustavo Gutierrez,[4] Ralph Harper,[5] John Hick,[6] Kosuke Koyama,[7] Margaret R. Miles,[8] Sallie McFague,[9] Kathleen Norris,[10] C. S. Song,[11] David Suh,[12] and those whose essays are collected in the volume edited by Fabella, Lee, and Suh,[13] and the volumes edited by Sugirtharajah.[14] That list, I believe, is but a partial record of those whose thinking actually is abstracted in what follows, so it could be substantially expanded. I name just these thinkers because it has been with their work in mind that I have written what follows.

Preliminary Principles of Systemic Theology

The bulk of this essay consists in the following preliminary list of principles of systemic theology. Each of the principles is stated and then followed with as brief an explication as I can give and remain (hopefully) intelligible. There is an apparent incongruity in giving such a list. Principles are inherently propositions, and the wording of the preliminary principles given below are at least quasipropositional. Systemic theologians avoid propositional statements and lean much more towards analytic, descriptive, and narrative accounts of their experience with God. I use this form for the following reasons:

1. The propositional form allows the abstracting or epitomizing of a very disparate set of statements according to their common features. This is particularly important to do when the main mode of theologizing is in fact not propositional in nature, so long as it is understood that the principles of systemic theology are not in themselves specific theological propositions beyond what they actually say, for:

2. Taken together, the principles form a framework *for* engaging in theology, not a specific theology. These principles for doing systemic theology are not a surreptitious form of systematic theology. If there is systematic theology, that must come in the form of specific theologies tied to acknowledged circumstances.

3. Propositions of this sort are intellectually necessary in the effort to begin to sort out at what level of abstraction Christians can legitimately operate when discussing their common faith. Although stated simply and in a dry analytical form, this problem of working to ensure that we state overarching Christian statements in the appropriate amount of generality and specificity is the most difficult and probably at this point the most critical task for theology in a dynamic and pluralist environment. Received theology tends overwhelmingly to provide statements of purported universality. The reaction to that pretension to commonality on the part of those whom I am calling systemic theologians begins with the assumption that all thought arises out of a context, and that it is presuming to suprahuman status to claim ubiquitous validity for the products of highly vulnerable and contingent human thinking. We need some shared analytical generalities to figure out from time to time the field within which we are working when we call ourselves Christian thinkers. However, any time we try to take such analytical propositions beyond their analytical role, we run the immediate danger of overreaching. If what is given below is also overreaching, the explicitness of the propositional form will make the task of criticism far more transparent so that any or all of the principles can be readily discarded as needed.

4. The statements given below are preliminary principles. They are not suggested as having any staying power, but are offered as hypotheses for testing and examination. It is probable that such a framework as this determines that any principles will always remain preliminary, that is, always open to continuous (or at least intermittent) amendment.

1. Creation Is Integral; Human Responses to God Must Be Integrative

Systemic theology is based on the fundamental instinct that human experience, both individual and collective, should be as integrated as possible because creation is arranged to function best in harmony. Hence, the first principle of systemic theology opposes alienation of any sort. The goal of human life—to live with God, to work for the realization of God's kingdom, and to return to God at the end of our short span of life—is a goal that is governed by an ideal of harmony between humankind and God, amongst humankind, and amongst humankind and all other creatures. It is from this principle that the term "systemic" comes. Systemic theology—abstracting from a host of thinkers who have attempted to grapple with a multivariate world—begins with the conviction that the human experience of God is fundamentally congruent with and inextricably linked to the totality of our collective and individual experience. This holism is manifested, for instance, in Song's interpreting the gospel through traditional Chinese legends, through Koyama's establishment of God's cosmic time commonplace Asian metaphors, through Eck's linking her struggles with illness and family tragedy with an exegesis of God's presence as simultaneously one-and-many, through Harper's exemplification of the power of our natural capacity for synesthesia as the engine through which we sense Presence, and Miles's insistence that Christian thought rejoin our bodies and minds and souls in order to bring health to the Christian enterprise.

Many of the thinkers on whom I have drawn in this attempt to abstract some principles of systemic theology begin with an implicit or explicit assumption that the interpretations and/or institutional manifestations of Christianity that they have received are inherently alienating. For many thoughtful twentieth-century Christian thinkers, the thought of attempting to remain Christian within the mold that was handed to them is unbearably fragmenting. This experience is particularly pronounced amongst the vast majority of Christians or would-be Christians who are culturally, sociologically, and economically distant from the narrow band of humanity represented by Western European (male) experience, and whose own specific story has for several centuries been mistaken for the Christian framework from which Christian theology may actually emerge (consider Cone, Gutierrez, Miles, Song, Suh as examples).

For faithful Christians who are in such a condition, the initial cosmological alienation represented in the story of the fall and the doctrine of original sin has become supplanted by the far more painful alienation caused by human formulations of God's revelations that exclude and demean their own experience of God. When this has been even acknowledged by those of the (European) mainstream, it has been reduced to just ethical and psychological terms. That is, it is readily understandable to the "mainstream" that faithful Christian women who sense a sacramental vocation feel rejected by a church that denies them realization of that vocation. It is understandable that faithful Christian peasants in Mexico feel distanced from a church that remains silent (or, worse, complicit) when their families' livelihoods, the futures of their children, and the dignity of all their associations are compromised and destroyed by the economic and political structures within which they live. Further, is understandable that a Korean Christian might feel compelled to "inculturate" his or her Christianity by relating it to (and interpreting it from within) those pre-Christian ideas and practices that do not conflict with mainline Christian thought and practice (cf. Schreiter).

Adherence to Christianity has increasingly meant alienation to those whose authentic lives are in some sense denied or devalued by received and organizational expressions of Christianity. This feeling of alienation goes even beyond those specific ethical and psychological violations of their personhood, the communities embracing them, and their immediate brothers and sisters. It fundamentally does not allow them or anyone like them to become integrated persons, because in order to participate in the church, they must compartmentalize their experience to suspend awareness of their condition or the condition of others like them.

To some degree this alienation is analogous to the existential alienation to which Paul Tillich[16] spoke effectively two generations ago. Nevertheless, while all of the thinkers whom I am calling systemic theologians are influenced by Tillich, and while some explicitly draw significantly from his work (e.g. Eck), the alienation experienced by those who directly experience the contradictions inherent in today's very uncertain and fragmented world is of a different order and of a much greater magnitude than Tillich's quintessentially European imagination (magnificent as it was) could encompass. An attempt at an analysis of multipolar human experience to justify this claim would be endless. For this essay, let a bare list of four prominent reasons suffice to distinguish the alienation experienced by many of today's Christians from that to which mid-twentieth-century existentialism spoke so effectively for its own time:

> First, this alienation is *caused by,* not remedied by, the introduction of received Christianity (which includes theological formulations of the twentieth century) into the lives and communities of these faithful Christians. Their expressed disjunctive living and cognitive dissonance are a *result of their attempting to remain* Christian, not the result of their lives outside of Christianity. Second, this alienation is epistemological as well as existential in the sense that what these faithful Christians have been taught to "know" about the world and creation is not in alignment with what they know through their experience about their lives and their hopes. Third, this alienation is ontological

(and perhaps cosmological as well) because the source of being and the understanding of being which is taught through their experience validates their experience through God's participation in that experience as manifested in Christ as the historical Jesus irrespective of doctrine or interpretations of doctrines—which might say otherwise. Fourth, and perhaps most telling, the author and maintainer of a forced imposition on others is in the end as much a victim of that travesty as those whom he or she oppresses.

Stated as I have in the above paragraph, the alienation that I am trying to describe is characteristic not just of "liberation" theologians and others who base their understanding of Christ and God on an experience of injustice, but pertains as well with those whose experience hardly bumps into imperialist, colonial, economic, or sociological injustice, and whose religious vision is informed by mystical or meditational experience, as well as by those whose study and experience have forced them to assimilate truths from other religions (consider Gross, Hick, and Merton).[17] It is not accidental that the bibliographical list to which I refer throughout this essay includes African-Americans James Cone, Gayraud Wilmore, and James Washington, Asian C. S. Song, Latin Americans, feminist Sallie McFague, and British and American Caucasian Europeans John Cobb, Diana Eck, and John Hick (and the present lay writer). For the starting point for each of these thinkers and many others like them is the pull of a deep and unavoidable faith combined with a repulsion by formulations that deny the validity of their experience of God in Christ in the same way that members of the earliest church attempted to deny the authenticity and participation of new Christians from non-Jewish backgrounds who did not observe received behavioral codes.

Given this principle, the initial task of Christian theology is to define the field of theology in a way that exalts God and affirms God's presence within and among us as God's creatures by continuing to undergird the unavoidable requirement that more precise accounts of human experience with God come as just that, accounts of particular people's experience of God. We can remain whole in our faith only as long as that faith is described and symbolized in terms that are true to our circumstances. The remaining principles attempt to expand this notion.

2. God Is the Ineffable Creator of the Good

Most of what we feel about God and experience of God can be articulated only as the story of our experience because, in the Biblical tradition, one of the very few attributes of God that we can objectively know is that God is ineffable. Whether it is Moses before the burning bush, the delivery of God's name YHWH, the still small voice bringing Elijah to heel, the theophanies of Jesus and later Paul, or the experience of mystics through the ages, the first thing that is certain about God is that God is not directly knowable by human beings in any way that is familiar to us or similar to the way we know whether it is raining or sunny outside, that 2+2 = 4, that our hands have five fingers, etc. What follows from this principle is that those qualities that we can attribute to God beyond God's ineffability are severely limited by the difference between God and us. What follows is that our sense of knowing God is our experience with God, and when we talk of God, we rely on trust in our experience. We cannot attribute any exclusivity to our own experience. We do not know how many ways God chooses to speak with God's creation. None of us knows the full range of God's gift of experience with Christ. None of us knows the full range of God's gift of experience with God in forms that do not explicitly refer to Christ or even to God. God's ineffability is often misconstrued as absoluteness, omniscience, omnipotence, etc. From a human standpoint, it is more than likely that God is absolute, omniscient, omnipotent, as well as describable by other unique superlatives, however, there is no way for human beings to know that. If one thinks about the matter even for a little while, it becomes evident that our notions of superlatives and supremacies may be utterly meaningless. (After all, in a universe that might well have more than our familiar three dimensions, typical human notions of comparative and superlative would have to be inadequate for description, but human language—tied as it is to that very simple framework—is utterly inadequate to allow us even to imagine what omnipotent, omnipresent, omnipotent could possibly mean.) For this reason, all that human beings can do is to tell our stories of our encounters with God, remaining humble in regard to their complete particularity.

There are two other attributes that, from the biblical record, we Christians can commonly know about God. God is the Creator, Redeemer, and Sustainer of all of creation. And, as Creator, God continuously calls us into being and thereby calls creation into goodness. How God manifests God's presence is known to any of us only in very tiny measure. That paucity of knowledge is inherent in our relationship as creatures to our Creator. We are endowed with the ability to perceive God's presence in making and maintaining all that is (including us!). We are not endowed with the privilege of determining how many ways God chooses to do that. And any attempt to predetermine limits on God is an attempt to be God, which traditionally is called blasphemy. Additionally, as Christians, we are committed to God's not being indifferent to creation. Hence, as God's creatures, we are endowed with the ability to perceive the need for, and are obligated to undertake, participation in moving creation towards goodness.

Beyond these very general statements of conviction about God, there is little that we can say outside of the testimonies of our own experience. The

190

means through which God has established, renewed, and continues to maintain God's creation are known only through the emergent revelation of human experience throughout our histories. The ways of goodness that are appropriate for us in our own times and places are equally discoverable only through experience, except that, of course, immediately derivable from what we are able to know about the ineffable Creator are the two great commandments that we love God with all our being and our neighbors as ourselves.

This principle excises as presumptuous claims at finality of knowledge about God or creation and the relationship between them. Obviously this exclusion is an important caution from faith for biblical literalists who would shut Christians off from the vast majority of what we can know. It is an equally important caution for ideologists of science, who confuse the validation and verification of factual knowledge with all potential realms of knowledge.

3. We Humans Must Trust Faithful Experience to Lead to God

Following directly from the second principle, our trust in our experience implies both a collective and an individual trust. We rely on the record of experience of God's people as expressed in Scripture and the record of the church for received representation of our discourse about our experience with God. In keeping with the practices chronicled in that record and in accord with the first and second principles, we not only do not eschew voices that move us from outside of that record, but we embrace those experiences with God that enlighten and inform our own experience of God as revealed in Christ, irrespective of where those experiences come from. Thus for European thinking until the Enlightenment, it was inevitable that the received Hebrew story of God's involvement with God's people would be interpreted in terms of regular logic that must culminate in a single apex, a form of mental peregrination which would probably have baffled the patriarchs and prophets and most likely even many of the apostles. Similarly, it is inevitable that for (at least some in) the Korean Church, approaching Christ's God and understanding Christ's God must include historic practices of direct apperception of the Ultimate in shamanic form. As well, it is inevitable that contemporary theologians would explicitly exhibit the operation of principles 1, 2, and 3 through symbolizing God multivariately, as exemplified in Hick's notion of God having many names, Eck's phrase, "the manyness of God," McFague's acceptance of different "models of God," and Asian and African theologians telling each other and the West of the Asian and African faces of Jesus. What is most to be understood by these recent explications is that the act of formulating an explicit interpretation of God-revealed-through-Christ in terms that belong to cultures and times different from those of the New Testament or Renaissance Europe is by itself an act that is no different from the Johannine identification of Christ with the Greek Logos, Paul's deliberate abandonment of received canons of ritual behavior as a requirement for membership in the church, Aquinas's merger of the Christian story with Aristotelian logic, or the nineteenth- and twentieth-century attempts (up to now rather inexplicit and generally clumsy) to reconcile Christianity with the process of scientific discovery.

In fact, this principle is understood to be little more than an explicit acknowledgment of what God's people (including those portrayed in Scripture) have always done, namely, interpreted their direct experience of God in the terms given to them in their own times and places, both of which have always incorporated voices other than those received from within the tradition which used the familiar terms for God. While the church has at times almost acknowledged this natural human habit of borrowing, it has had great difficulty in admitting the necessary correlate: all human formulations of a Christian vision are cultural products, including canonically received traditions. That correlate is a necessary consequence of God's ineffability. While understanding this puts a severe limitation of humility on any human claims to the truth, it also liberates *all* of humanity to accept and live through the cultures that are our immediate homes. For the systemic theologian, insisting on this is not only a release from intellectual and spiritual bondage for himself or herself but also just as much for those from the historical "mainstream." Acceptance of the contingent world in which we live begins the recognition of the glory which we have as God's creatures.

4. Jesus' Identification with the Poor and Outcast and His Radical Ethic of Treating Human Beings as Embodiments of God Are Inextricable Evidences of Redeemership

Christ's manifestation of his divinity is evident not only in the church's experience of his sacrifice through crucifixion and his resurrection, but as well in his identification with the poor and dispossessed. He articulated his own behavior in the most radical of ethical codes when he insisted that we must treat each other as manifestations of himself. Christ's insistence on human reverence for the rest of creation, on human understanding that in our treatment of each other and ourselves we are thus treating God, is an ethic which points towards a reharmonization of creation. As such, ethics is not a subordinate branch of faith or doctrine (the only substantive key to which and first axiom of which is the definition of God), but

rather ethics is necessarily a completely inextricable part of the statement
of our highest experience of God. Put into traditional terms, this implies
that the doctrine of God must include and be defined by the ethics of Jesus.
Historically, the conviction that the signs of a truly saving God must include
strong presence of an ethic of insistent justice and not just narratives of life
triumphing over death was important because in classical times, the
Mediterranean basin was replete with many overlapping and competing
salvation cults, and the bases of their theophilosophical claims offered no
grounds for identifying God with one over the other. For modern theologians, principle 4 relates principles 1–3 to the explicit experience of the
oppressed. Hence, Suh's argument that the Korean Church has arisen
because of its oppression through Japanese colonialism, American hegemony, and internal dictatorship (after, one must add, a history which has
always placed Korea under the shadow of culturally overbearing China
and Japan) is more than just a strategic choice of an alien religion as a third
force with which to oppose the domineering power of the moment, a part
of the definition of Christianity and Christ's power amongst Korean Christians. This, I believe, is also what Cone refers to when he states that one
must be black to understand Christ. It is also what is being expressed in the
recent Roman Catholic doctrine of the "preferential option for the poor."
The essentiality of this principle should not be ignored. The imposed uniformity of thought and practice against which various recent theologians
have argued (and the accompanying political, military, and economic domination that have accompanied that imposition) is understood to be a violation of Jesus' insistence that we love each other and that it is only through
doing so that we love God. In short, we cannot have the Christian God
without Jesus' expressed notions of goodness. The two are of a piece and
inseparable.

5. No Epistemological Commitment Precedes Christian Faith in God

Christians have no specific epistemological commitment that precedes
their devotion to, and reliance upon, God. The most traditional consequence of this principle is that concern with "proofs of God" or proofs of
"God's existence" is at best tangential to any thoughtful response to having encountered God (perhaps notably, but not necessarily always, through
suffering). There are also longer-range consequences of this principle. An
ontological consequence (congruent with principle 1) is that perception of
the structure of beings and the relationships amongst beings precedes an
acquaintance with being *per se*. An empirical corollary is that the variety of
human psychology does not appear to yield a single response to the numinous; that is the principal problem in the study of religions to accepting

Otto's notion of *mysterium tremendum*. This differentiation in response to whatever may be considered suprahuman also calls into question related formulations such as Schleiermacher's absolute dependence and Tillich's Ultimate Concern. An epistemological-psychological corollary is that the study of cognitive science over the past two decades or so seems to have demonstrated that the mechanisms for knowing with which we are "hard-wired" are variegated and rather synchronous with objects of our perception, rather than being rigidly uniform irrespective of what happens to be in the human ken at any given moment (cf. Dennett,[18] Gardner,[19] Pinker,[20] Lawson and McCauley,[21] and Whitehouse[22]). While it is certain that we do have the capacity to determine and retain or know those objects of knowing that are verifiable, it is equally certain that we can determine and retain a huge (perhaps much larger) body of knowable objects that are utterly impervious to verifiability and reliability tests. A further corollary to this principle is that ethical thinking and judgments may create ways of knowing rather than being a necessary consequence of a prior epistemology. Carol Gilligan's study of women's ethical judgments in *In A Different Voice*[23] is a prominent illustration of how this is actually a regular occurrence. The Confucian psychology as evidenced in the *Analects* is a more ancient account of the same notion. When one rereads the Gospels in the light of modem feminist notions of epistemology and ancient Confucian notions of epistemology, it becomes far from obvious that Jesus' own stance did not also derive knowledge of God from ideals of goodness rather than the other way around.

Because so much of Western thinking has been bound up in epistemological enquiry, and because religion and ethics have been so long subordinated to questions of how we know whether there is a God and how we know what is good, this principle will probably require a book of explication to forestall the criticisms which will be made of it. For this essay, just a few directions of argument can be adduced. It was noted sometime ago by Langer[24] that aesthetic knowledge is simply different from replicable factual knowledge, and following Langer, Magee[25] cogently describes the dead end that Western epistemologically-centered thought eventually reached by the middle of the twentieth century. Kuhn[26] and others sometime ago made it eminently clear that even scientific discovery may have little to do with scientific method, as inspiration, sociology, and politics may be as influential in the new ideas of science as in any other field. Feyeraband[27] demonstrates the destructiveness which comes from applying to other areas of enquiry and judgment the canons and habits of scientific verification and knowledge accumulation. As exemplars, Steiner[28] and Harper demonstrate that transcendent knowledge (or, if one insists, the appearance of transcendent knowledge) emerges through the operations of the linked senses and particularly through synesthesia and not through the application of previously worked out rational axioms and postulates.

In short, with each passing year, it is more widely accepted that the capacity to know is related to the type of object known (cf. Gardner, Pinker, Lawson and McCauley). Reformulations of Christian theology that include works whose foundation is mystical, borrowings from other religions, intuitive, symbolic, and artistic, and correspondingly very little from the epistemologically centered "philosophical theology" that for long dominated Christian thought, turn out to have support from cognitive science.

6. God Is Directly Approachable by Human Beings

God's ineffability has seemed at times to some people a logical constraint on human approaches to God. That has always been a confusion of limitations that God's ineffability imposes on us and our knowledge (which is indeed limited) with God's openness to the approach of willing "humble and contrite hearts" (which appears to be limitless). The biblical record, the testimony of mystics, the Christian experience of worship, the sacramental tradition of the church—as well as simple logic—all suggest that God's presence is continuous within and amongst us. Further, that God is not describable or analyzable logically suggests nothing at all about whether humans can have a meaningful sense of God or can legitimately attest to have encountered God, particularly in the critical moments of their lives. For Christians, religious practice and theology must be seamlessly connected. Theology cannot be merely an intellectual pursuit. Much of the correction to mainline Christianity that has developed over the past three or four decades has come in the form of open and vibrant spirituality and intensive religious questing. The popularity of Thomas Merton and M. Basil Pennington,[29] the growth of retreat centers, the proliferation of meditation groups and practices, interest in meditational and mystical traditions outside of Christianity (Buddhist, Sufi), and, yes, the explosive growth of evangelical Christianity (cf. Dorrien)[30] all attest to the significance which faithful or would-be faithful people attach to finding ways to approach God directly. The effusion of spirituality is so great right now that its magnitude and its motivation stemming from the inadequacy of received church practice and behavior cannot be ignored. More important, however, even where a given "liberation" theologian does not explicitly deal with practices of spirituality, the fundamental principle of understanding God through the crucible of experience pertains equally to revolutionary liberationists and those whose mission is focused on contemplation. Indeed, as one probes more deeply into the actual practices of those who are collectively defining our theological age, one discovers at least a very trenchantly articulate subset of individuals and groups whose practices become more contemplative and prayerful and whose actions and words become more radical. This is perhaps made most readily apparent in a notable few amongst the profusion of prayer books that have emerged over the past decade or so. Striking examples of such books (which I have used in personal devotions) would be Daniel Berrigan's *Uncommon Prayer: A Book of Psalms*;[31] Edward Hays's *Prayers for a Planetary Pilgrim*;[32] Bishop Desmond Tutu's *An African Book of Prayer*,[33] and James M. Washington's *Conversations with God*.[34] Moreover, at least in Gross's extraordinary retreat diary, the self-knowledge that accompanies long decades of discipline in prayer yields a stunning candor in discussing actual prayer life, real meditation, and the actual behavior of mystics.

An important corollary to this principle is that religious participation and practice are generally aligned—explicitly so—with the theological notions that arise out of individual and group experiences with God. Systematic theology as taught a generation ago was kept quite distinct in the curriculum from matters of worship and especially from consideration of prayer and meditation. That distance was symbolized for me in the 1950s when I heard a thoughtful and sensitive clergyman muse, "Have you noticed how uncomfortable we all get [and here he included himself] when anyone talks openly about prayer?" But for many of those whom I am calling systemic theologians, formal theologizing, regular contemplating with God, and a radical ethic are intimately woven together.

7. Received Creeds and Doctrines Are Interpreted, Not Supplanted

Following the historical practices of the church (as opposed to some doctrinal commitments), as well as the preceding six principles, the received experience of the faithful community is accepted and reinterpreted for a new time but not supplanted. Nothing in what I am calling systemic theology is aimed at replacing the creeds of our various subtraditions; nothing is aimed at insisting on a reformulation of basic doctrines as they have been received within any or all of our Christian traditions. To be sure, part of this disinterest in rearguing questions that were in some form or other settled by church councils of much earlier ages stems from the explicit recognition that for the times and places (Mediterranean shore and later Western and Central Europe, both with tiny populations that were overwhelmingly Indo-European in ethnic and cultural background), the conciliar format and the propositional mode of discourse were the proper norms. Even where that is not true for many Christians today, the acknowledgment of the authenticity for its own time is necessary.

Beyond that recognition of cultural difference, however, is the more profound recognition and acceptance that it is only because of the received experience, only because of the transmitted record of human experience of God-in-Christ, that contemporary Christians would be Christians at all. That is a critical point. When one reflects on how Christianity was in fact transmitted during much of its history, this acknowledgment has an aura of the miraculous surrounding it. The majority of today's Christians today are resident in Africa, Asia, and Latin America. It is in Africa where the growth of Christianity is the most pronounced. The majority of Christians are not Caucasian. Christianity was delivered to most of these regions of the world through economic expansion enforced by military and political oppression. Imperialism, colonialism, slavery, opium trade, forced removal of local wealth in the form of natural resources, unjust monopolies and market controls—and all backed up with vicious brutality and violence—were the vehicles Christianity rode to many of those places where it is now in its greatest ascendance. In merely human terms, it is incomprehensible that any in such places would consider Christianity anything but an ideology of evil. It is necessary to recognize the ineluctable mystery of God's hand in the persistence of Christianity into our own time, and with that recognition, it is equally necessary to acknowledge how obviously reasonable it is that a principal concern for today's Christians who were long oppressed by Christian powers to insist that God's presence through Christ absolutely must mean continuous working for God's kingdom of justice and liberation. This is, of course, the relation of principle 4 to the acceptance of the past. Perhaps it is best stated most simply in the acknowledgment that our Christian brothers and sisters in lands that our European ancestors conquered and oppressed heard the gospel and heeded it despite those who brought the gospel.

For a European-American Christian such as myself to contemplate the vibrance of the Korean church, the faithfulness of Chinese and Burmese Christians, and the wonderful proliferation of Christian churches in Africa, there is indeed a sense of awe-filled *mysterium tremendum*. It is correspondingly obligatory for me as a European-American Christian to recognize any insistence on my part that Christianity continue to be defined only by the terms with which I am familiar is essentially an insistence on the continuation of the oppression that brought Christianity to non-European lands in the first place. Instead of such an evil insistence, my obligation as a European Christian is to give a continuously attentive ear to the articulation of Christianity that has emerged in those formerly (and some continuingly) oppressed lands, for it is from those voices that the voice of Christ is most likely to be heard.

Terror and the Context for David Suh's Korean Christian Theology

The principles abstracted above apply, I believe, entirely to David Suh's theology, which has been a theology both of explicit writing and of action in his society. In the following paragraphs, I will briefly describe his life and work as an example of systemic theology.

This collection honoring David Suh centers around the theme of terror. Among other things, *terror* refers to an original Christian condition. The church was born in a conquered land. The church grew and developed amidst all of the destructive ironies of imperial power. The consequence of imperialist conquest and rule is not only that the invading power may behave (and usually ends up actually behaving) with cruel brutality, but that imperialism itself fosters the raising up amongst subject peoples a class of collaborationist leadership that is marked by significant mediocrity, moral paucity, high ignorance, and constipated imagination. Terror, in short, comes from a world that human beings have turned upside down to the degree that their fellow human beings are left always uncertain as to what they may and may not do without incurring brutal and cruel retribution. While most develop strategies of subservient and cautious self-protection, a vicious minority of their own brothers and sisters transform those strategies of survival into oppression. Political, economic, and military oppression and submission virtually always lead to terror. They do so not just because the conquering or hegemonic power takes what is not his and subjects humans to inhumane treatment, but because the very act of conquest patterns and creates a vacuum for the emergence of demonic and illegitimate indigenous leadership and governance to arise not in response to the needs of the community but in response to the fact of having been conquered. If one is subjected to torture, imprisonment, death, or even just to the deprivation of basic civic rights, that occurs as frequently at the hands of one's immediate fellows as at the direct hands of a hegemonic power. In ancient Israel, Jesus was seldom, if ever, in conflict with Rome. It was the leadership of his own subjected people who engineered his execution.

It is, of course, just this that occurred in Korea from the end of World War II until the late 1980s. By the mid-twentieth century, Korea had a heritage of colonial rule. It was designated a battlefield for the forces and surrogate forces of the two superpowers, the Soviet Union and the United States. Then it became a pair of mirrored client-states standing as surrogates for their patrons. It is no wonder at all that the North developed a bizarre parody of the worst of communist excesses, and that the South just as quickly fell into that common abyss of client states to democratic powers—military dictatorship. For forty years—over a full generation—Koreans on both sides of the Thirty-Eighth Parallel were subjected to the possibility of terror. The foreign powers were seldom directly involved in the brutality. But because of the overreach of two powerful countries, an atmosphere of unrestrained mutual fear was created and sustained on both sides of the Parallel, and that atmosphere allowed the justification of any level of brutality in order to maintain order and prevent collapse.

David Suh, originally a north Korean, spent his early years in Manchuria, where his Christian minister father had been sent by the Japanese overlords of both Korea and Northeast China to be a pastor to Korean Christian communities whom the colonial power was using to intensify its hold on that part of China. The end of World War II allowed a return to Korea, but the immediate southward push of the Soviet Union at the moment of peace and the consequent catapult to power by Kim Il-Song resulted not in a freed land but in an even more insecure and hence even more brutal rule by client Koreans. David's father was killed along with many other Christian leaders, and David joined the throngs fleeing to the South. Once there, he was pressed into the South Korean navy, where he spent six years, being discharged only when he was able to obtain admission and a scholarship to Rocky Mountain College in Montana. While a desperately needed respite from the years of World War II and the Korean War, life for a rare Korean in the American Far West contained its own ironic particularities. A natural leader, in his senior year David was nominated for president of the student government. He was defeated in a campaign whose slogans and posters focused on the unacceptability of having a foreigner, particularly an Asian, leading the American students of that *Christian* college. From there, he went to the University of Illinois to do an M.A. in philosophy. By the 1950s Illinois had become a premier center of scientific research. Not surprisingly, the department of philosophy tended to ape the subject for which the University was justly famous, and David was thoroughly indoctrinated with the viewpoints of logical positivism and linguistic philosophy. When he arrived at Union Seminary in 1962, he was as deeply grounded in contemporary Anglo-American thought as any one of the ninety-member entering class. While his first two years in seminary naturally included courses in philosophy at which he excelled, the formative experiences occurred in New Testament and ethics classes and through deepening contact with the rapidly growing community of Korean Christians in and around New York. This was the first time in his life that David had been near large numbers of Koreans who, although they were obviously living as expatriates, were not creating lives largely in response to immediate oppression. The liberating sense of being around highly educated, professional Korean Christians was stunning. It gave David a chance to begin to sort out what was Korean and what was Christian, and to begin to deal with the multiple ironies in being free as a guest in the country that was the hegemonic power that backed up the governments oppressing his own people.

The class entering Union Seminary in 1962 was the first class at that institution of what later would be known in schools all over the country as the "'60s generation." Composed at least as much of seekers as of people convinced of a specific Christian formulation arising out of their denominational background—indeed containing a noticeable number of people who had not even been brought up in the church—this group questioned, doubted, and expressed itself in irreverent humor far more than in credos. In their first term, the collected class had a notorious set-to with the poor faculty member designated to direct their field work experiences. By their senior year, the whole student body was so similar to this group that the seminary president appointed a blue-ribbon committee of faculty to meet with small groups of students to try to figure out why the gap in experience, viewpoint, interest, and devotions between students and faculty had grown so wide. On graduation day in 1965, the president was appalled to learn from the registrar that just barely half of the entering ninety students were getting their degrees. Of the rest, many had simply left, and the remainder had postponed their final year in order to take an internship (often one far removed from typically recognizable internships in ministry) that would help them sort out the confusing waves, pulls, and attractions of their disparate backgrounds, the chaotic cultural, social, and intellectual currents crashing over their heads, and the consequent confusion they felt in their own faith. Being a part of this group for two years meant for David (as well as others) membership in late-night bull sessions, which, in their intensity and their explicit deviation from the then standard curriculum, proved at least as important a formal educational experience as what went on in the classrooms during the daylight hours. What this group represented was the collapse of what had seemed in colonial Korea to be an immutable synthesis between Christianity and American-European ways of life. If the message of Jesus seemed to promise a sense of liberation and legitimation for subjected peoples, and if even the citizens of a hegemonic power were distancing themselves from their own milieu, then clearly it all had to be rethought.

David was among that nearly half of the class who did not graduate in 1965. After his second year, David returned to Korea to marry Sunyong and to take up an internship in the chaplain's office of Ewha Women's University, Sunyong's *alma mater* and employer, where then she served as assistant to the president. The following year, David and Sunyong returned to Union for David to complete his M.Div. degree, and then then went to Vanderbilt University, where he completed his doctorate in theology, and then immediately returned to Ewha, where he ultimately served for thirty-two years in the department of Christian studies, as Dean of Liberal Arts, as graduate dean, and eventually as chaplain. The intern year and then the long years of his permanent commitment to Ewha dramatically reshaped his thought as he moved from being among the most Westernized of thinkers at Ewha to becoming a leading voice in articulating and advocating Korean Christianity through *minjung* theology. The South Korea to which David returned was a land still picking itself up and putting itself back together after the depredations of Japanese colonialism, World War II, and particularly the Korean War. It was a poor country and, caught in the Cold War, its military rulers were able to use politically apocalyptic scenarios as justification for suppression of free speech and free teaching in the universities, where the East Asian tradition of student protest always held the possibility of regime-threatening demonstrations like the ones that catalyzed the fall of Syngman Rhee in 1960. A frequent topic of conversation amongst professionals and intellectuals was how long people trained outside Korea would put up with the difficulties at home before returning to the United States or Europe. For David and Sunyong, the decision to remain in Korea and not return to the safer and more comfortable United States was tied to a repeatedly renewed commitment to truly becoming a part of South Korea and sharing in its difficulties and struggles. Attempting to consider Christianity with intelligent young women coming of age is challenging even under wholly benign circumstances. The Korea of the 1970s and '80s was hardly a haven for untrammeled thought about God. The military regime wanted religion to be a supportive servant of the state, which Korean Christianity would have been had it kept its focus on the preservation of what had been received in original evangelization. Some students wanted religion to give divine validation to every claim of injustice. Walking the line between extreme claims, joining the fight for justice against an increasingly irrational and oppressive regime, and coming to terms with what being a *Korean* Christian meant not unnaturally produced a lively and confusing time for faculty of faith and conscience.

For some faculty this meant imprisonment. For many, including David Suh, it meant years of telephones being tapped, being constantly followed by secret police, unpredictable arrests, and questioning which often involved torture. This period culminated in the governmental decision in 1980 to remove some four hundred unqualified faculty members from the faculty of the nation's universities. Buried amongst that long list of actually underprepared university employees were the names of fifteen to twenty conscientious professors of considerable unquestionable qualification and considerable scholarly eminence by whom the government had been irritated. David Suh was among those. For four years, he and the others of this tiny honorable group were prohibited from teaching or speaking in public, and were constantly harassed. Certainly the fellowship formed by those being most specifically suppressed helped sustain each of them.

In addition, for David, having a heroic university president during part of this period, Okgill Kim (whose own brother, a professor of history at Yonsei University, was jailed in a futile attempt to force her to betray her trust of courageous leadership) and a sympathetic denomination, which at that time chose to ordain him and assign him to a pastorate there, was also sustenance. It was during this period that he crystallized his understanding of the *minjung* theology to which he had already committed.

Developing this *minjung* theology meant simultaneously casting off and embracing. Abandoned were mainly the organizational and intellectual accouterments that had grown up around Christianity during its European and European-American phases. The hierarchical church, which, as an organization inevitably behaves like any other bureaucracy, was returned to its necessary and proper place. Humans need organizations, and organizations are necessarily self-protective, but the self-preservational instincts of organizations are not legitimately enshrinable in Christian doctrine. The organizational church is as likely as any other bureaucracy to become a collaborating partner to oppressive rule. The organizational church becomes the church of Christ only when it becomes the vehicle by which those seeking faith are actually enabled to approach God and when it becomes a prophetic beacon speaking and acting to represent Christ's presence in the world. Intellectually cast off was the intensity of focus on precision of verifiable language ("God-talk" in a world where only "scientifically" demonstrated language could be truthful).

Jesus' practice of identifying himself with the poor, the outcast, the denigrated, and the despised, and his insistence that those of us who claim that we seek God must do so through serving our fellow human beings, was embraced. Jesus' eclecticism of friendship and concern appears diametrically opposite to doctrines that draw lines of exclusion amongst peoples in the name of God. Recognizing this and realizing that Jesus' practice and insistence on loving behavior meant embodying that *in Korea,* David was driven toward support of students who protested governmental illigitimacy, toward ill-treated laborers, and toward women, whose position was distinctly second-class.

Further, Jesus' insistence that religious practices were made for human beings and not the other way around implies a catholicity of acceptance that would honor rather than denigrate religious modes that may be unpalatable to traditional (European-oriented) Christians, but that may be quite authentic for their practitioners and that may even move Christians once they become acquainted. Korean shamanic practice may not be everyone's notion of how to reach God, but then Plainsong and contrapuntal music in an eight-note scale and weekly sermons may not be either. These forms are cultural expressions that provide the only avenues through which humans from those cultures can reach God. It is impossible to rise above our culture, for we are not God. It is equally blasphemous to pretend that any one of our cultures is suitable for all of us. For many Korean Christians, the only forms of worship that resulted in a sense of oneness with God required ecstatic behavior derived from the shamanic tradition. (As is now being understood even in America, often the best cure for disease came through ancient shamanic rituals.)

Once David had recognized this, the political consequence of the monolithic notions of knowledge he had learned in American philosophy classes became disturbingly evident. Obviously, spending hours worrying about whether a given sentence about God was verifiably legitimate was an escape from engaging with God's kingdom in Korea, the place where he could most help to effect that kingdom. Moreover, copying Western philosophers in the notion that all significant knowledge was of *one* sort was simply wrong. One could not be an integrated Korean Christian and accept such nonsense, since the Korean tradition honored direct perception of the numinous and encouraged the development of epistemological principles from ethical understanding. Most alarmingly, he realized, following his American philosophy teachers in defining knowledge so narrowly was little better than an analogy to the geopolitical insistence of the two superpowers that either capitalist democracy or communism had to be chosen as each country's political system. In place of such mental imprisonment, David returned *as a Christian* to retrieve the Buddhist philosophy of compassionate assimilation and the Confucian belief that the role of the ruler and the state is to serve the people, and that it is the duty of intellectuals to criticize them and even work for their overthrow if they do not.

Confessional Conclusion

I am a twentieth- (and now twenty-first-) century Christian. I live in privilege in America, and I have little courage and no particular insightfulness. But, like a rapidly growing number of Americans and Europeans, I have been thrown in with a huge variety of people unlike myself and, while I have lived a safe and comfortable life, I have been witness to significant amounts of oppression and injustice. Sorting out what Christianity can mean for me and how I can remain a Christian in this milieu has been a concern virtually my whole adult life, which began forty years ago when I was working in Hong Kong, where I first encountered both colonialism and truly grinding poverty. I also encountered daily expressions of beautiful forms of Buddhism and religious Daoism (or, if one insists, popular Chinese religion), and at work I daily witnessed the administrative blessings of conscientious Confucianism, a philosophy that began with concern over how to rule and administer with effective humane benevolence.

Although I was never challenged by any threat to my freedom, survival, or health, through those years of working in Chinese society and subsequently teaching about China and the Chinese language, I grew to know that (in Phillips's phrase) "my God was too small." Attending church remained largely a habit, though increasingly with little enthusiasm. Eight years ago dumb luck put me in a department of comparative religion, and the reading I had to do to become prepared for that utterly unearned honor led me to those whom I have called systemic theologians. Through reading their work, I have experienced a long-term and persistent "strange warming of the heart," to use John Wesley's phrase. Through their widely different but equally courageous embrace of their own immediate circumstances, through their finding God in the peregrinations of typically dynamic and mobile modern lives, these Christian thinkers have imparted the courage to begin to see God-in-Christ in my own circumstances, along with the freedom and obligations that implies.

David Suh and I were roommates for our first two years at Union Seminary. We have remained devoted friends in the ensuing thirty-six years. I intellectually understood and vicariously grasped his anger at his government in the 1970s and 1980s, but I grasped nothing of his theological conversion to "the Korean *minjung* in Christ" until I stumbled on theological works by Eck, Harper, Cone, and Hick, and the comparative religion works of Eliade, Lawson and McCauley, Smart, Whitehouse, and many others. Because the stories of these thinkers were analogous to my own, the transformation of this dear friend suddenly became obvious, and the link in God between our utterly different experiences became clear as well.

My task in this essay has been analytical and abstract. I have attempted (however clumsily) to outline the principles that I believe underlie the dynamic theologies that arise from those parts of the world where Christianity has become the most dynamic, as well as theologies in Europe and America that speak from and to the honest fluctuations of our lives. Through this analysis, I have attempted to suggest how it is that even Western Christians can (actually must) learn from these very particularist Christian thinkers both elsewhere and even in our own home countries. To suit this purpose, I have used as flat and analytical a diction as I could. What I have tried to speak of, however, is a matter of passion, personally and religiously, for the Christian faith that is made possible through what I have been calling systemic theology. It has been, for me, truly life-giving. All of the thinkers to whom I have referred could state that immeasurably better than I could. I close with a striking statement of faithful passion from Ralph Harper (an American Episcopal priest) in his remarkable book *On Presence:*

A life that lives for itself, using its spontaneity only within its own bounds, makes no difference to the world. Whenever we sense a spontaneity that rejoices in breaking through the bounds, we may hope that its first act will be to listen to us before trying to impose itself on us. Real living is defined more by listening than by speaking, and the living God by his mercy more than by his indignation. Does she really hear us, we ask? Do I really hear her? Or has something been kept in reserve, secretive and evasive? Nothing is simpler than to thwart the extension of life's spontaneity, to give imitations of giving which are no more than pretenses of openness. Lying is meant to protect life from fully appearing, and we know enough from experience to be on the lookout for it. But to protect ourselves we deceive in return, even if only by keeping some part of us in reserve.[35]

Faith and Redemption Revisited in the Japanese Context

Hisashi Kajiwara

Introduction

In the preface of *Following in His Steps: The Faith of Martin Luther King*,[1] I wrote as follows:

> If physical death is the price I must pay to free my white brothers and sisters from the permanent death of the spirit, then nothing could be more redemptive.
>
> Martin Luther King Jr.[2]

The faith of redemption, preserved by Christianity through these twenty centuries, has the import that Jesus Christ was crucified for the redemption of humankind. Whoever commits oneself to God's redemptive love can be saved. And those who have been saved should bear witness to this redemptive love for the sake of others by "following in his steps" (1 Peter 2:21). It is the original meaning of the faith of redemption.

But unfortunately, in modern Euro-American Christianity this faith of redemption tended to be grasped only passively by each individual Christian. It was decisively lacking in the practical task of actively witnessing to others. For that reason, in North America Christians tended to view the system of segregation, which should be defined as the evil of separating people from each other, as a mere social problem rather than seriously viewing it as an essential problem *proper* to Christian faith. Consequently in a Christian country like America, especially in the Southern area known as the "Bible Belt," this "peculiar system" unashamedly existed even almost into the early Post-World War era.

However, in this America there was one man who channeled this faith of redemption for the good of the desegregation movement. He was Rev. Martin Luther King Jr. In this book the author tries to depict him from the perspective of *redemptive faith* as the inner driving force of his persistent struggle.

An unexpected number of people responded favorably to this small book, for which I felt very appreciative. But one of my friends, who usually was of the same mind as me on many points, was very critical about my view of redemptive faith. According to him, my emphasis on the practical task of actively bearing witness to God's redemptive love for others has a pitfall; that is, there is a danger of confusing human acts of love with the redemptive act of Jesus Christ itself. He strictly distinguishes human acts of neighborly love from God's redemptive work through Jesus Christ. He said, "the subject of saving others in your statement: 'the original point of redemptive faith as that which is to be witnessed by one's sacrificial suffering' (p. 86), should from start to finish be Jesus Christ himself and not any human being. Because human beings have no power to save themselves; they are only in dire need of Christ's redemption."

Although this was but one critical voice among the many otherwise appreciative, a response becomes necessary because it may highlight Christ's redemptive work in the Japanese context, where Christians are a small minority with only a little more than one percent of the whole population, by overcoming the futile controversy between Christian identity and social commitment.

From the turbulent days of the 1960s to the present day, those ministers, theologians, and lay Christians who insisted on the uniqueness of Christ's redemptive work have had an attitude of removing themselves from *social commitment.* And those religious people who have actively committed themselves to social participation have been rather apathetic to the faith of redemption and have had a tendency to avoid witnessing to the gospel truth as *Christians.* What we need urgently to do today, I believe, is to build a bridge across this dichotomy toward a horizon of making the gospel truth holistic and truly rooted in Japanese society, where the majority of people are unexposed to Christianity yet need its essential truth.

In the following sections I will expound on these points through my own autobiography.

My Encounters with Martin Luther King Jr. and Black Theology

I left Nishikata-machi Church in Tokyo, which belonged to the United Church of Christ in Japan (UCCJ), for my new post at Nagoya Gakuin University, Seto, Aichi, as lecturer of the science of religion in April of 1968.

At the same time I served the Owari-Ichinomiya Church of UCCJ as a minister. I was rather fascinated with the new jobs, but before long I was struck to the ground by the news that Martin Luther King Jr. was assassinated on April 4 in Memphis, Tennessee. My shock was beyond expression.

I had selected as a textbook for my religious study course the Japanese version of his first published book *Stride Toward Freedom: The Montgomery Story*.[3] This book elucidated dynamically the relationship between the problem of Christian identity and social commitment, which I had long groped for. His radical philosophy and strategy of nonviolence sounded persuasive enough for us to follow in our walk to the new world-community of love. It was all the more devastating for me to hear of his assassination.

However, this shocking experience led me to turn my theological concern from German dialectical theology that I had followed until then to the newly arising black theology in North America. It was a decisive turning point by which I had a chance to translate Dr. James H. Cone's *A Black Theology of Liberation*[4] into Japanese, published in 1973. This book was well received by Korean Christian residents in Japan in contrast to the apathetic reaction of Japanese theologians and Christians. Since then I have translated Dr. Cone's other books too, such as: *God of the Oppressed*;[5] *The Spirituals and the Blues: An Interpretation*;[6] *My Soul Looks Back*;[7] and *Martin & Malcolm & America: A Dream or a Nightmare*.[8] In addition to these works, I became personally acquainted with Dr. Cone himself and have communicated with black churches in the U. S. Besides having studied with him at Union Theological Seminary in 1977, I have invited him to Japan several times, as well as the black gospel choir of Canaan Baptist Church of Christ in Harlem, New York.

What moved me most about his theological work was his struggle in agony for a new way of doing theology in the face of a new situation. He confessed his agony during his graduate days when the civil rights movement reached its peak: How was I going to relate systematic theology to black people's fight for freedom in society? That was also one of my chief questions. Answering that question was not easy because there were no scholarly models for me to follow.[9]

We are, in a sense, always forming a new way of doing theology. Our problem is how to be satisfied by staying with some forms of established theology. This indolence is, I believe, an incessant temptation to "sin" for theologians. Cone describes such a theological indolence among American theologians in those days as follows:

> It seemed that the central problems in American theology were imported from Europe, especially Germany. Anyone who could speak German and who studied under one of the famous European theologians was always regarded as smarter than those who did not receive such academic privileges.

208

Even though the civil rights movement was the hottest news item in America and had been identified by most as the critical problem facing the churches as a central issue in theology, most North American theologians identified their task as keeping up with the problems defined by European theologians.[10]

This was and has been exactly the same situation in Japan, too. The reason I have been engaged in translating black theology and liberation theology is not merely to translate those English books into Japanese but rather to try to contextualize their theological enterprises into the Japanese situation. We faced essentially the same kind of problems in our context too, though in different forms. There were and have been serious minority issues like the Buraku people, Korean residents in Japan, the native Ainu, and Okinawans, who had to bear disproportionately the burden of living with American military bases on their land. Perhaps the problems of discrimination against women, negligence of children and the aged, and environmental issues should be added too.

If we confront these problems and try to tackle them theologically, we must begin to do theology in our own way. There is no set model before us. However, those thinkers who have been doing theology in their own contexts and facing their proper issues offer us a way to do creative agonizing and suffering. On this point one of the most suggestive words to me was expressed by Cone when he faced the difficulty of refuting an ideological black theologian, Joseph Washington.

In 1964 Joseph Washington published his well-known book, *Black Religion*, which many blacks regarded as combining poor scholarship and bad taste. But whites praised the book, apparently because Washington claimed the black religion was unchristian in that it identified the gospel with the struggle for justice in society. The gospel, he claimed, has to do with faith and creeds of the church, not with justice and the civil rights movement. Knowing that I had a Ph.D. in theology and that I was involved in the civil rights movement, several black preachers and teachers asked me to write a response to Washington's critique of the black church. Existentially I was against Washington, but intellectually I did not know at the time how to refute him.[11]

In my case, I have been almost constantly criticized and isolated among theologians and ministers because of my commitment to black theology and liberation theology. Even my concentration on Martin Luther King Jr. in my religion course at school had invited severe and sometimes ruthless criticisms against me because they thought that I was involved in too *particular* a field of Christianity rather than in more universal (?) Christianity.

Fortunately, I have found myself rather highly appreciated by the students whom I have taught. However, such an academic apathy has no small influence, especially upon the coming generations in terms of employment and position in the academic world.

My Commitment to the Citizens' Movement For Children

In the fall of 1970, a citizens' movement named "Ichinomiya Association for Protecting Children's Safety and Health" was organized in Ichinomiya, Aichi. I was asked to become the president of that association. This citizens' movement has steadily struggled for the life and the right of children for thirty years. There are many citizens' movements in Japan, but this is one among the longest in durability. The secret of this durability lies in that the members of the association have cooperated with each other by concentrating on one thing—the life and rights of children—and overcoming their differences in idea and creed.

In 1970 nine children lost their lives by drowning in fenceless rivers. The association worked to construct fences along dangerous rivers and has succeeded in the construction of 150 kilometers of fence (10 million dollars budgeted). With this initial effort we have also successfully gained city support to construct swimming pools and children's centers in all districts of the city. Additionally, we have been involved in problems of peace, education, and environment.

Although I was not a victim of a child's death myself, I have always kept a story of one of our association members in my mind.

> At about 6:20 p.m. yesterday the father of a drowned child, Tomomi (3 years old), found his dead body drifting down the Aoki River. Mr. Miruo Nakano immediately jumped in the water to pick him up. He asked a passer-by to call the police and his wife Mrs. Sachiko Nakano. He continually held the child's body in embrace until help came. The child had been the subject of search for some weeks until it was discontinued as being in vain. The police and others had tried all they could. But even after that Mr. and Mrs. Nakanos never gave up. They persisted to look for their lost child 70 kilometers a day by means of vehicle and vessel and on foot after their daily work, which was, indeed, sustained only by their parental love.[12]

The child's body was already decomposed and only the bones remained. Mr. Nakano was then a junior high school teacher of Japanese and also a Buddhist priest. Since that time I have struggled together with him for the rights of children. Among our members there were people of different religions and ideas. Nevertheless, we have struggled together in union for the same cause, and I find my life as a Christian minister, who is to bear witness to living "the light of the world" (Matt. 5:14), to be really worthwhile. I am now and then reminded of such words as Martin Luther King Jr.'s,

"This is the great new problem of mankind. We have inherited a large house, a great 'world house' in which we have to live together—black and white, Easterner and Westerner, Gentile and Jew, Catholic and Protestant, Moslem and Hindu—a family unduly separated in ideas, culture and interest, who, because we can never again live apart, must learn somehow to live with each other in peace."[13]

It is my conviction that living together among those who devote themselves to different ideas and religions is only possible by struggling together for the same cause of creating a more humane community rather than merely being engaged in abstract discussion. However, church people often find such ministerial work a deviation from the "genuine gospel truth." They think that the minister's primary job is to serve the membership's spiritual care needs and not to be distracted by notions of serving neighborhood problems.

In fact, my commitment to the citizens' movement further deepened my understanding of Jesus' gospel to a more *fundamental* level on one hand and to a more *universal* level on the other, but it was rather difficult for some leading members of my church to accept my way of doing theology. As a result, I had to resign from the church I worked for in the spring of 1976.

Thus I started a new congregation with those people who confessed the Christian faith along with having an active involvement in the citizens' movement. We named this new congregation Abel Bible Study Group, and we have continued to hold worship services for twenty-five years while continuing our social struggle. We hold up three simple and clear assertions of faith, as follows:

1. We deeply pursue the truth of the Bible.
2. We intend to take part in social activity.
3. We endeavor to form self-supporting faith.

These assertions may seem insignificant at first glance, but we believe that they point to a striking attitude about church activity that is in contrast to the established churches. The most characteristic of the three assertions is number 2. That one particular congregation holds up *social activism* as its manifest purpose means a significant decision under the present circumstances of Japanese Christianity. We intended to directly support the Ichinomiya Association for Protecting Children's Safety and Health, but we also take part in other movements for human rights, peace, environment, education, etc.

By taking up this basic stance, our way of reading the Bible should be distinguished from the traditional way. That is our primary assertion. We needed a new way of searching for the biblical truth in order to keep our manifest Christian identity while we engage ourselves in solidarity with those of different creeds.

The other assertion came as a matter of course. Without our self-supporting faith, we cannot maintain a Christian identity. Thus we continue on our way today as an independent congregation in Japan.

Toward the Development of Open Christology

One of the most urgent and important problems I faced in my involvement in the citizens' movement was how our divine revelation and salvation was related to the suffering and liberation of "non-Christians." This question may not be an urgent issue for those ministers and theologians who are only involved in increasing their Christian members and in the theology of church organization, but it is urgent for those who try to further deepen their Christian faith in the practice of social activism.

I came across the scene of a drowned little child quite a few times as the president of Ichinomiya Association for Protecting Children's Safety and Health. When his or her young parents cried out in sorrow before a small coffin, I groped in vain for some suitable words of consolation. However, I felt the reality of the biblical stories on those occasions. The story of a ruler of the synagogue, Jairus, whose little daughter was at the point of death, is an example (see Mark 5). As a matter of fact, those parents listened to me enthusiastically and were encouraged when I spoke to them: "Like the little girl who got up and walked when talked to 'Talitha cumi' by Jesus (v. 41), let us not try to forget the dead one as many Japanese usually do, but rather let her stand on our front step and with us keep our struggle for human life and rights." For me this was a realization of a biblical truth in our time.

The misgivings of the majority of Christians who think that the primary concern of the church is its promotion of the "gospel faith" become groundless when those Christians critique other Christians for their social activism. This criticism is nothing but a prejudice entrapped in a dichotomy of the holy and the secular. The original life of Jesus witnessed in the Gospels of the New Testament was filled with the flesh and blood of real men and women. When he was involved in human sufferings, he was not primarily concerned about any person's religious belonging, nor did he intend to form an organized church.

We who have questioned human survival itself should now get out of the dichotomous framework of "Christianity and heathenism," which is a residue of prejudice in these twenty centuries of Christian history. Rather, we should open our eyes to the original human-oriented way of living in Jesus. On this point, James H. Cone is instructive:

Indeed, if one's faith is true to life and is thus the defender of life, as the biblical faith most certainly is, then the faith itself forces one to remain open to life as it is lived anywhere. By listening to another who is not my faith, I am affirming my own faith insofar as it is the defender of life. Through this process, I am permitted to learn from another and to share with him the struggle of life. Indeed it is when we refuse to listen to another story that our own story becomes ideological, that is, a closed system incapable of hearing the truth.[14]

When we listen to another story, what is its essential element? I believe it is the human suffering that prevails the world over. It is not only Christians but all humans who suffer. Asians, Africans, and Latin Americans suffer, as well as Europeans and North Americans. Is not Jesus' crucifixion the prototype of all human suffering? In this connection, Kanzo Uchimura, a distinguished modern Japanese Christian thinker, was right when he characterized Christianity as "Crucifixianity."[15] The true meaning of the *universality* of Christian faith should be its *penetrating power* into human suffering.

Perhaps what we need most urgently today is this *deepened and extended level of Christology*, but according to the traditional Christology, even if the redemptive work of Jesus is interpreted as it reaches all humankind, as God's love revealed in Christ, those individuals who have a share in God's redemptive love are in reality limited to the persons who confess Jesus Christ as their Savior and are baptized in his name. Therefore, the traditional Christology cannot, after all, take up human sufferings of the innumerable people in the non-Christian world as a proper theological theme. On this point Dr. Choan-Seng Song, an Asian theologian, has a deep insight by introducing a new term, "people hermeneutics."[16]

Where these "inconceivably many, the whole host, all" are, where these people are, there Jesus is, whether two thousand years ago or two thousand years from now. In the midst of these people Jesus is to be found, yesterday, today, and tomorrow. This is the "historical" Jesus. Jesus is historical because people are historical. The life of Jesus is, in this way, linked with the life of people, with all that life means and brings—despair and hope, suffering and joy, fear and reality of death overcome with faith in resurrection. The history of Jesus becomes *historical* in the histories of people. In the meetings of these histories—Jesus' history and histories of people—the perimeter of God's saving power working in the whole of the world is broadened and deepened. Jesus is released from the captivity of the Christian church.[17]

I am here thinking of a young Japanese man whose name was Yuji Onodera. He died on April 30, 1997, after having lived in a vegetative state for twenty-four years. His mother and father had taken care of him in the hospital, changing his body position every two hours, day and night, for all those years.

213

Mr. Onodera was born in 1957 in Iwate Prefecture. He was a very healthy boy and was never absent throughout his primary school days. He entered Ichinoseki National Technical Junior College in April of 1973. He was the hope of the Onoderas, a poor farming family.

On May 22, 1973, only a little more than a month after his entrance to the college, he was forced to engage his Judo teacher in a practice match. He was thrown down and received a heavy blow to the head, then lost consciousness. He never regained consciousness, even after an emergency operation. He was supplied with food through a tube inserted into his stomach.

Nevertheless, the Judo teacher at first admitted his guilt but soon retracted his admission under pressure from a nationally instituted college. The Onodera family brought a suit against the teacher but lost their case at the first trial and the second. The judgment was that, despite the serious injury of Mr. Onodera, it was not decisively proved that his injury was the result of the teacher's careless behavior. Under the circumstance of not having eyewitness evidence, the Onodera family was left to prove the defendant's complicity or guilt.

During the eleven years of the lawsuit, quite a few people encouraged and helped the family, but they too withdrew their help as time went by. The family was eventually left alone to cope with caring for their son in a vegetative state.

My commitment to Mr. Yuji Onodera began with organizing the National Association for Protecting Children in 1978. Ever since then, the Abel Bible Study Group and I have supported the Onodera family both financially and spiritually. My persistent commitment to this young man has been always related to my theological concern. It is not only my concern of neighborly love but also my essentially theological concern—in particular, a christological one.

Mr. Onodera was an unconscious young man—breathing was his only sign of life—when I encountered him through the National Association for Protecting Children. He was not a Christian nor were his family members. Their religious creed was both Shintoist and Buddhist, as most Japanese follow, but he became a cross bearer by his accidental life of suffering just as it was with Simon of Cyrene (Matt. 27:32; Mark 15:21). In him I saw Job, a "man of the east" (Job 1:3), and I discerned him as the Lord's servant who "was despised, and shrank from the sight of men, tormented and humbled by [his] suffering" (Isa. 53:3 NEB), and in him I heard a voice of Jesus: "Eloi, Eloi, lema sabachthani?" (Mark 15:34; Matt. 27:46).

Is this insight not theologically right? Are not the words of Martin Luther King Jr. about unearned suffering being redemptive[18] really appropriate for him? Should we hesitate to take up this theme because he was not a Christian? It is very unfortunate that the traditional theology cannot make this theme come to the surface. It is, indeed, in the framework of liberation theology that we can tackle it properly. We must now open our heart to the construction of "open Christology," for it was a Gentile centurion who said, "Truly this man was the Son of God" (Mark 15:39) upon our Savior breathing his last.

Conclusion

In the context of the group-oriented society of Japan, even Christians are influenced by a group mentality, consciously or unconsciously. The tragedy of Japanese Christianity is that while it still remains a small minority among all other religions, it does not play a primary role as a *creative* minority. It has been four hundred and fifty years since Catholic Christianity was transmitted to this country and more than a hundred years since Protestantism was introduced to modernized Japan, but according to the *Religious Yearbook* issued by the Agency for Cultural Affairs of Japan (1998), the most recent number of Christians of both churches is only 1,761,835—a little more than one percent of the whole population (125,647,075).

The reason for this small number is primarily related to Christianity's intrinsic nature of nonconformity to this world (Rom. 12:2). Although the so-called dichotomy between the independent behavior of the West and the group-oriented behavior of the Japanese may be easily exaggerated,[19] one still must recognize that Japanese society tends to pressure each individual to conform to group wishes more coercively than do societies where individual freedom is idealized. However hard Japanese Christians have tried to be accepted by society, they have yet never been able to, and thus remain a social minority.

Our destined (or providential) mission is to challenge society as a creative religious minority. Bearing witness to "open Christology" in our confession and action is the most *proper* way of living as a church and as Christians in this country. This is, needless to say, a way of living in which we must necessarily expect isolation and persecution of all kinds, but it is the most hopeful way to realize true human solidarity here among us because we cannot escape to some kind of new abstract construct. Our only hope comes from the sincere and honest self-reflection of root confession or assertion of each group.

Korean Women's Christology: East Meets West

Michelle Lim Jones

". . . that you live in constant terror everyday because of the wrath of the oppressor, who is bent on destruction? For where is the wrath of the oppressor?"

Isaiah 51:13 (NIV)

". . . Terror will be far removed; it will not come near you."

Isaiah 54:14 (NIV)

Introduction

The word *terror* comes from the Latin, *terrere,* "to cause to tremble." *Webster's Ninth New Collegiate Dictionary* defines terror in several ways:

1. a state of intense fear 2.a: one that inspires fear b. a frightening aspect 3. reign of terror 4. violence committed by groups in order to intimidate a population or government into granting their demands.

The definitions "a state of intense fear" and "violence committed by groups in order to intimidate a population or government into granting their demands" especially draw my attention to this study of the subject of terror. In today's world, not only have many heard words of "terror" and "fear," but also many have constantly experienced terror in the midst of their daily lives. In this article, I will discuss my dear friend's experience of terror as a battered wife for ten years. I will describe how Korean women as immigrant women have experienced terror and fear as they struggle to root their lives in America. In unveiling Korean women's lives, I must describe their traditional upbringing in Korea. I will first explain how Korean-American women come to understand the concept of terror, experienced as a force on their body. Second, I will describe how they have internalized the violence committed against them by their oppressors. To explain the behavior of these women I must analyze traditional Korean Confucianism and ultraconservative Korean Christology. How have these two distinctive ideologies become a double-edged sword for certain women? What kind of reformation is needed for Korean-American women to reclaiming their full humanity?

A Battered Wife for Ten Years

Myung Ja[1] ended her thirteen years of marriage by signing a divorce agreement. She did not want to divorce, but she knew that she must do it for the sake of her two children. For her entire marriage life, her husband battered her. Until the end, she wondered how she stayed married to such a violent man. By tradition, many Korean mothers firmly believe that it is their ultimate duty to marry off their daughters to the most suitable Korean bachelors. Myung Ja's mother was not different. By this same social norm, mothers of Korean women have also faced pressure to ensure that their daughters are raised to become perfect wives. These mothers believed that a woman's happiness was dependent on her husband's success on his career path and his rank as a powerful person in Korean society.

Myung Ja was raised within this cultural setting. She went to a prestigious women's university in Korea. After graduating with a master's degree in fine arts, she came to America to be with her mother. Her own mother had divorced her father while Myung Ja was in college. This was another reason that her mother wanted her to marry to a man from well-to-do family—she assumed that character and wealth went hand-in-hand. Myung Ja met her current husband after numerous blind dates. He was a nice man who owned his own business and came from a strong Christian background. In fact, he was a *Gwon-sa-nim*[2] from a well-known Presbyterian church in the Korean-American community. After a six months courtship, Myung Ja decided to marry him. They were married and settled in a town in Long Island with excellent schools. The marriage seemed to be fine for the first few months.

Seven months into Myung Ja's marriage, it all began to unravel. Her husband began to curse her using the foulest Korean epithets. He started

217

to drink and display a violent temper. When she pleaded with him to stop drinking and cursing her, it only got worse. In her words:

> My husband came home after drinking heavily and called me names. He also started throwing things. I was scared and hid in the closet. He found me and demanded that I have sex with him. I tried to refuse, but he hit me a couple of times. I acquiesced hoping that things would get better, after we had children. I know that this was my biggest mistake. I thought that if I became a perfect wife to him, he would stop this absurd behavior.

A year later, they had a baby girl. At first her husband began to sober up and try to be a good husband and father. Things got worse a few months after the baby was born. He began to drink heavily and his beatings became more frequent. Divorce was out of the question because she had a baby and no resume or work experience. Myung Ja told her mother about her husband's drinking problem; however, she did not reveal his abusive behavior. Her mother told her that she should try harder to please him.

This marriage continued for twelve more years. I got involved when Myung Ja's first child turned twelve and her second, a boy, was ten. Late one night her husband came home drunk and threatened to kill her. He then got in the car and left. Myung Ja got scared and called her mother. Soon after, her husband returned, cursing and kicking the locked front door. The police arrived to take him into custody—they had been summoned by a neighbor's phone call. That morning I received a phone call from her mother asking me to take her into court to get an order of protection.

Myung Ja and her mother came to the conclusion that she would seek a divorce settlement. After twelve years of verbal, physical, and psychological abuse, she finally accepted that her children's lives were in jeopardy. She remembered one night of her husband's battering,

> He came home drunk at one or two o'clock in the morning and asked me to fix dinner for him. After I fixed dinner, he took a look at the table, and asked me to prepare different Ban-chan.[3] He also asked me to fix a new dinner. When I told him it was too late, he accused of me disobeying him. Then he started to throw dishes, beat and drag me by my hair up the stairs. The ironic thing was that I was more afraid that my children would see their father beating me than of the danger to me. I did not want my children to have a negative image of their father.

In the process of extending her order of protection and initiating a divorce proceeding, I learned from her mother and her divorce lawyer that she had had a broken nose and a fractured rib more than once during this marriage. During our trip to the Queens Family Court, numerous times she stated that she wanted to drop the charges against her husband and withdraw the divorce request. Although she suffered horrendously at the hands of her husband, she did not mention the pain in her own body. When I asked how she felt, she responded,

> When my husband hit me and pulled my hair, I did not think about the pain in my body. I thought I must have done something wrong to deserve this punishment from my husband. Maybe I was too stubborn, not obedient enough to my husband or not a sweet enough daughter-in-law to my mother-in-law. After all, I did not think I was entitled to claim my body for myself. It belonged to my husband and my children, although I knew that it was my body. I guess I am a traditional typical Korean woman. We always hear from our mothers, grandmothers, and aunts, that we have to become good mothers and perfect wives and sweet daughters-in-law. I often thought about rebelling against all these traditional norms, but I did not know how to do it.

She reluctantly filed for divorce. There were two reasons she had some reservations about her divorce. First, she was not confident whether she could earn enough money to support her children and herself. Second, she knew that she would not receive any support from the Korean community since she, not her husband, was the one who had filed for divorce. Divorce is still a taboo in the Korean society, although the number of divorce cases is increasing. In most cases, divorced women voluntarily withdraw from contact from their families and friends. Fully subscribing to the ideal of being the "perfect wife" (a "perfect wife" supports her husband with obedience, childbearing and childrearing, and being a model daughter-in-law), divorced women see themselves as failures. The image of the "perfect" Korean wife is deeply embedded in the Korean community.

While in the process of getting a divorce and renewing the order of protection numerous times, Myung Ja has received many phone calls from her husband and in-laws. Her husband tried to persuade her to withdraw the divorce suit, promising her that he would not harm her anymore, yet he threatened her in my presence to beat her again if he ever saw her. Her mother-in-law told her that she was not good enough for her son anyway, and said further that she will make sure that Myung Ja would not get custody of the children. The most difficult thing for Myung Ja is that her children, especially her son, want their father. Her son refused to believe that anything was wrong with his father. One day he screamed at his mother that it was her fault that their father had left home.

Another incident that shocked her severely was her pastor's response to her divorce. He told her that it is God's will for women to endure hardship because the husband is the glory of the wife while the husband's glory is Jesus Christ.[4] He added that suffering and patience were what Jesus Christ

219

showed during his ministry. The pastor said that as a good Christian daughter, she needed to learn to "bear the cross" that was her husband. Surprisingly, he said nothing about her husband's behavior and his violence toward her.

It was a long and lonely period for Myung Ja. In her journey of terror in silence, she internalized the anger, shame, and disappointment from her family, her in-laws, and her pastor. By the time the divorce agreement was settled, she did not know how to respond normally to people around her. She was numb, feeling degraded and humiliated.

Was it her family values or her upbringing that led her to stay in the relationship so long? Why do most Korean-American women still feel bound to this oppressive Korean tradition even though they no longer live in Korean society? Although there is great geographical distance between Korea and America, the authority of traditional values still has dramatic impact. The value system, based in Confucianism, deeply underlies the religious, political, and social structure of the Korean community in America. In the next section of this paper, I will discuss why it is extraordinarily difficult for most Korean-American women to break from traditional Korean values, especially those of family and of the image of the "perfect wife," even when their own lives are endangered.

The Prayer of Battered Women (1)[5]

Sook Ja Chung
Translated by Michelle Lim Jones

Psalm 13

O Lord, do you forget us?
Will you forget us forever?
How long will you turn away from "violence" we have experienced.

How long must your daughters persevere the "violence" inflicted on our
bodies and minds by men?
How long must our mothers endure suffering inflicted by battering
husbands?
How long will Korean women listen to Korean men's shouted demands?

O Lord, Look on us and answer,
O Lord,
Give light to our eyes, not to fall into the sleep of the death that is insensitivity and nonresistance, but to help us to see the reality of our situation.

We are afraid to hear,

Enemies who compete against battered women will say, "We have
  prevailed."
Our foes will rejoice,
When we tremble and fight hard to persevere the pain.

But we trust in your steadfast love;
Our hearts shall rejoice in our salvation.

We will sing to the Lord,
Because he has suffered with us.

Korean Traditional Family Values and the Image of the Ideal Korean Woman

Koreans are Confucianists by birth. Our social interaction is conducted on the basis of Confucius's ethical teachings. Dr. Young Taik Kim, the associate director at the Ignatius Spiritual Institute, states that the most conspicuous characteristic of the Korean mindset is its Confucianism. How are Confucius ethical codes embedded in the nature of Korean thought and action, and more specifically, how does Confucian ideology oppress Korean women?

The basic philosophy of Confucianism is as follows. Confucius (551–479 B.C.) was regarded as a sage in China, Japan, and Korea. He believed that the ruler of a nation should be benevolent towards his people in order to ensure that individuals become good and moral. According to D.C. Lau, Confucius believed that "politics is an extension of morals and provided the ruler is benevolent, the government will naturally work towards the good of the people."[6] Underpinning this vision of a benevolent nation are two distinctive themes, *choong* (loyalty) and *hyo* (filial duty) the basic principles in Confucian ethical teachings. *Choong* is the expected attitude of absolute dedication to a king or a nation leader by his subjects; *hyo* is the absolute obedience a son (or subordinate) shows to his father (or superior). For Confucius, the moral man is the gentleman of the society and the gentleman/moral man also will be an obedient son (or subordinate). The most important relationships are the relationships between father and son and between elder and younger brother. Confucius believed that moral men will become the leaders of the nation through learning. He stated that learning is the key to becoming a moral man, and therefore, to becoming a good son, father, and a loyal subject to his king. Therefore, a man's task is to cultivate and educate his mind. On the other hand, in Confucius's mind, a woman's task in society was limited to household management, to be a helper in raising good sons. A wife in this view is completely sub-

221

ject to her husband. These Confucian teachings of male hegemony over women first appeared during Yi Dynasty (1392–1910 A.D.).

Dr. Bae Yong Lee, a Korean history professor at Ewha Women's University, argues that Confucian moral teachings were used to legitimate the expansion of the Yi Dynasty. She states that the powerful men responsible for supporting the dynasty wanted to have a centralized authoritarian government run by the *Yangban* (aristocrat) class. Confucius's teaching provided the moral codes for this new Korean society.

The ruling class of this dynasty established a caste system according to *Sungrihak* (later Confucianism). This later Confucian caste system was based on *Samkang* (the three bonds) and *Oryun* (the five moral rules). The three bonds are *gun ui sin gang* (the loyalty must be kept between a king and subjects), *boo ui sin gang* (the trust must be kept between fathers and sons), and *boo ui boo kang* (the sincerity must be maintained between husbands and wives), which stipulate respectively the scope of the superior-subordinate relationships between a ruler and a subject, a father and a son, and a husband and wife. The five moral rules are *gun sin uoo ui* (loyalty must be kept in the relationship between a king and subjects), *bu ja uoo chin* (intimacy should be maintained between fathers and sons), *bu bu yu byeul* (difference between husbands and wives), *jang yu yu suh* (younger should give precedence to the older) and *boong woo yu sin* (confidence should be reigned in the relationship between friends), which indicate the hierarchical nature of societal relationships in their respective order of importance—ruler-subject, father-son, husband-wife, elder person-younger person, friend-friend. Therefore, as stated by Dr. Lee, the *samkang* and *Oryun* regulate the customs for social order with rulers, fathers, husbands, elders higher in importance than subjects, sons, wives, and the young.[7] This teaching of moral codes did not give women rights other than as dependents of husbands and rulers. A leading Korean scholar of Chinese culture and language, Dr. Kyung Il Kim, comments on the teachings of Confucius and its impact on Korean society today,

> Despite brilliant sayings, the moral teaching of Confucius is not for "people," but for the "politicians," for "men," for "adults," especially the "oppressors." Therefore, this moral teaching has brought the caste system to Korea, led to patriarchal tradition, and has prevented constructive discussion. Such moral teachings have harmed women's rights and emphasized the superiority of men, leading to an andocentric society. Its negative results also have showed in the education system as well. Teachers or professors actively discourage individual autonomy. The teachings of Confucius have become an obstacle for establishing equality among people and have stunted individual creativity. This teaching has been completely discredited.[8]

Dr. Lee discusses the image of women during the Yi Dynasty, describing how the moral codes have oppressed women and have prevented their participation in the public arena on the basis of "the law of husband and wife." This law enabled a man to confine his wife to the household. It was a law stemming from Confucian patriarchy.[9] A woman had to obey her husband's wishes, otherwise he had the right to divorce her and send her back to her family.[10] Korean law confined women to the household, limited to raising children and existing in subservience. Not only did it give women a lower status but also ensured an enhanced status for men by allowing them to have authority over women. The ideal image of woman was benevolent, gentle, still, submissive, chaste, and frugal. Her role was to constantly provide a harmonious household so that her husband could accomplish his professional goals. She was not to have professional goals that might complete with her husband's goals. Furthermore, there was an award system for women who served their mothers-in-law with respect and submission, as well as for those who kept their chastity after their husbands had died.

Dr. Lee indicates that it is obvious that "the law of husband and wife" and the ideal image of women were both written by male scholars. As young daughters, girls must keep their virginity and be absolutely submissive to their parents at all times, as well as provide the compassion and love towards siblings and relatives. When these young women get married, they have to serve their parents-in-law with absolute respect and tender care. On top of this, total submissiveness to her husband is required. As mothers, young women are to be focused on the education of their children.

This image of the perfect Korean woman has descended through generations. Many modern Korean women are challenging and rejecting this ideal. This portrayal of Korean women has been deeply embedded in the minds of Korean men and women for many centuries. Consequently, it is difficult to challenge such a merciless norm. This ideal is passed down in the oral tradition established between Korean women and Korean-American women and their grandmothers and mothers. This is why it is very hard for Koreans to break out of oppressive moral codes. Most Koreans conform to the social rules of the majority. Koreans and Korean-Americans are, in truth, one big family, closely related by birthplace, school alumnae, and numerous interpersonal relationships, especially those stemming from church participation. Therefore, conspicuous behavior aimed at challenging social roles, in the eyes of Koreans, is cause for the individuals' suffering the litanies of protest from relatives, friends, former teachers, and so on. For this reason, many Korean women are afraid of doing anything unusual or of seeking their own freedom. Ironically, many Korean-American women, including 1.5[11] and second generation, still hold on the image

223

of the ideal woman, although they have much more freedom and independence than women do in Korea.

In the next section of this article, I will discuss Christian fundamentalism's role in maintaining Confucian social norms for women both in Korea and in America.

The Fundamentalism of Korean Christianity and Its Christology

The Korean Christian community has been largely shaped solely by clergymen with a strong fundamentalistic view of the Bible. David Kwang-sun Suh, a Korean Christian theologian, points out that their fundamentalist view of salvation and theology was first influenced by earlier missionaries who came to Korea in the previous century. He states that one of the missionaries' goals at that time was to evangelize women and the poor. They realized that women and the poor were the least educated and the least powerful in society. In order to teach the gospel and evangelize them, the missionaries oversimplified their theological views and doctrines. Further, they implanted these theological views conservatively in the process of evangelization.[12] Dr. Suh describes the problem of this oversimplified theological view and its impact on Korean Christianity.

> Missionary policy was decided in 1895 after the war between China and Japan for working class and women of Yi Dynasty. At this time, the Yi Dynasty was about to fall into the hands of the Japanese government. Many Korean Christians wanted to use churches as the foundation for resisting and seeking independence from the Japanese. However, missionaries dismissed "shamanistic" Christianity, rather than have it be actively involved with political and social activities. . . . Korean Christianity began to emphasize empirical practices rather than be faith seeking understanding.[13]

Many Korean clergymen preach or teach the importance of Jesus Christ as their savior, with their ultimate goal being to lead people to confess Jesus Christ as a purely personal savior. The meaning of salvation for them is having a personal relationship with God. Consequently, in my view, most Korean Christians, including many women, only see Jesus Christ one-dimensionally as a sacrificial Son of God and as a suffering-servant figure totally obedient to God. This limited view of Jesus Christ led many Korean Christian women to be silent about the violence and suffering inflicted on their lives by men, specifically by their husbands. Too often many Korean clergymen emphasize obedience and the sacrificial life as the highest models for Christian women. They often preach about how Jesus was beaten, ridiculed, and humiliated by Roman soldiers, high priests, and the people of Israel. For many clergymen, as Jesus Christ, the Son of God, suffered for the sake of humanity's sinful nature, wives must also "bear the cross" as perfect mothers and ideal wives. It is for this reason that many Korean Churches have been silent on violence against women. They fail to preach the other half of the Confucian moral code that requires men to be educated and compassionate husbands and subjects of the king.

The interpretation of the Bible in the Korean and Korean-American Christian community still observes the early fundamentalistic views of American pietism. Most Korean clergymen believe that the Bible is the infallible word of God. Therefore, they believe that they are infallible interpreters of the Bible. The Bible becomes an object of their fundamentalistic theological proofs as well as an argument against any kind of "liberal" position, such as that favoring women's rights and equality. The Bible becomes a fundamentalist's instruction book for handling moral problems in the Christian community. David Kelsey states that "in the corporate experience of the Christian community the Bible is received as an awful and holy object and is used in a variety of ways: instructing the young, comforting the ill and dying, guiding the tempted."[14] However, the problem is not that they use the Bible as an instruction book, but that they refuse to accept the "hermeneutic of suspicion," or "hermeneutic of wisdom," as equally respectable methods to interpret the Scriptures. Their interpretation of God's words is andocentric and distorted. Their perspective discriminates against women's contributory role in church and in society. For instance, fundamentalist preachers often use the creation story in the Book of Genesis to argue against the order of God's creation that might suggest that women are equal partners of men. Their argument is simply that Adam was created first, and Eve second from Adam's rib, and furthermore, that she led Adam to disobey God.

Because of this notion of women as secondary and inferior to men, women have had to struggle to claim political and economical access. Women are expected not to get involved in politics, because that is man's arena, and are expected to stay home or be silent. This is why only a handful of women can be seen in Korean politics, and moreover, those that have made it into elected office have not lasted long. Economically, most women still depend fully on their husbands or, if they work, must accept earning one-third less income than men.

Yearning for Transformation

The later Confucianism teachings of the Yi Dynasty and the fundamentalism of Korean theology have become a double-edged sword for Korean women. It is a "marriage made in heaven" for fundamentalist and Confucian Korean Christian men, including clergymen, and one "made in hell" for most Korean Christian women. It is a mindset combining male-superior moral codes and male-dominant theology.

In a society where men have every right to rule over women, there is no concern for women's rights or their freedom. Specifically in the case of battered women, Korean traditional and Christian teachings have emphasized the virtues of the ideal women generation after generation. This is the reason that the battered woman I mentioned in section one of the article, Myung Ja, persevered through such a harsh married life. She did not think about her safety or the injuries inflicted on her body. Many battered women have internalized the shame and humiliation of spousal abuse and/or divorce into their emotional and psychological worlds.

Korean and Korean-American women have four critical tasks that must be performed for the cause of equality. The first is to reevaluate the two predominant value systems, Confucian and fundamentalist, and to simultaneously reject their androcentric teachings that stifle the basic rights of women. This must of necessity include liberation from the bondage of the image of the ideal Korean women. Women must liberate themselves from the traditional value system and fundamentalistic Christian doctrines that justify their silence and invisibility in churches and professional institutions. David Kwang-sun Suh states adamantly that "Korean women need to acquire the strength to liberate themselves from the bondage of oppressive religious practices. They should be focused on acquiring and then exercising their power. This power will lead Korean society towards more openness and creativity."[15]

The second crucial task is to utilize a critical feminist hermeneutic of liberation in interpreting and teaching the Bible. Feminist theologians must work to establish feminist liberation studies of the Bible. Every Korean Christian, both men and women, ought to know that there are many other theological discourses and methods of interpretation of the Bible. Korean Christians must perform this task because God gives every individual the mind to seek truth as well as the responsibility to participate in the kingdom of God on earth. Elisabeth Schussler Fiorenza states, "In our struggle for self-identity, survival, and liberation in a patriarchal society and church, Christian women have found that the Bible has been used as a weapon against us but at the same time it has been a resource for courage, hope, and commitment in this struggle.[16]

Korean women must reclaim our lost voices and throw off the cloak of invisibility in order "to call the whole church to a conversion that repents of the patriarchal church-structure which has marginalized and silenced women throughout the centuries and has denied us our baptismal right of being in church."[17]

Third, the final message of the Christian gospel is "the hope of trans-formation." Christians believe and hope to be renewed either by God's grace, or by faith, or by work. Our hope is an eschatological one. We believe God's promise that in God's holy sacrament, everything—the society, human beings, our relationship with each other, and our relationship with nature—will be a transforming work; we refuse to see all things as unchangeable. This hope for total transformation can be found in various theologies: feminist, liberation, womanist, and *minjung*. Sae Yoon Kim, professor of New Testament at Fuller Theological Seminary, says that it is time that Korean churches allow for further development of Korean Christianity, and points out that the problem of Korean Christianity is its theological fundamentalism and ecclesiastical authority. He posits, furthermore, that it is time for Korean churches to become sponsors for theological studies "in depth" as well as "in breadth."[18]

Lastly, a critical feminist hermeneutic of liberation is needed in this community as soon as possible to liberate and do justice for these women who are seriously hindered by the traditional fundamentalist Confucius and Christian value systems. In order to empower and demonstrate the other side of Jesus Christ to these women—focusing not only on the traditional suffering "Christ" but also on the human Jesus who takes the side of the oppressed and who wants to liberate them—the critical readings of the Bible and different methods of hermeneutics will aid in the true fulfillment of God's plan. Such new hermeneutics will help women find their own identities as children of God and allow them to gain self-respect.

As Rita Nakashima Brock sharply contends, the "hermeneutics of wisdom" will help Korean and Korean American women to understand their relationship to the past patriarchal tradition.[19] Her contention is that it is critically important for them to maintain their commitment to the Christian community and to pass down their cultural and traditional values without being victimized by this commitment to their culture and values. In her conclusion, she posits that the hermeneutic of wisdom will help these women to see the Bible not as an authoritative source but as a story of the suffering voices of many people. In this new enlightenment experience, they will begin to see the multiple perspectives of God's plan, the many different layers of interpretation of the Bible, and most of all they will "choose to be agents that nurture life, heal brokenness, and struggle against struggle."[20]

We must reevaluate the Confucianism ideology and fundamentalistic theology of the Korean and Korean-American mindset, challenging these value systems which have prevented women and men from being equal partners. We need to have constructive dialogues amongst ourselves, Korean women and men, in order to build a productive and proactive community of God, for ourselves and for the sake of future generations.

227

The Prayer of the Battered Woman (2)[21]

Translated by Michelle Lim Jones

Psalm 132

1. O God, Remember us,
   And remember our perseverance
   And all the hardships

2. Didn't we swear an oath to the Lord,
   And make a vow to the Mighty One of Jacob;

3. We will not enter the battering husband's house or go to bed with him.

4. We will not allow this in the name of wife,
   Nor forgive in the name of love.

5. Until all the violence and oppression will be eliminated in the name of
   God.

6. We heard the rest place is right here
   At "The Peace House of Women"
   We came upon it

7. "Let us go to his dwelling place.
   Let us worship at his footstool—

8. Arise, O Lord, and come to your resting place,
   To show your strength and direction.

9. May your servants be clothed with righteousness;
   May your daughters sing for joy."

10. For your loving daughters,
    For the sake of our mothers
    Do not reject your anointed one.

11. The Lord swore an oath to our mothers,
    "Your daughters will be liberated.

12. If your daughters keep my covenant and the statutes I teach them, then
    they will be freed ever forever."

13. For the Lord has chosen the house of daughters
    He has desired it for his dwelling;

228

14. "This is my resting place forever and ever; here I will sit enthroned, for I
    have desired it—

15. I will bless them with abundant provisions;
    Their poor will I satisfy with food.

16. I will clothe their priests with salvation,
    And their saints will ever sing for joy.

17. Here I will elect a great leader for suffering daughters and set up a lamp
    for my anointed one.

18. I will clothe their enemies with shame,
    But the crown on their head will be resplendent."

Part 4

The Gospel Is Life
in the Age of Terror

Threat and Terror in the New Testament

Robin Scroggs

All who want to live a godly life in Christ Jesus will be persecuted.

2 Timothy 3:12

Introduction

The classic Sunday-school picture of early Christianity facing political opposition is something like the following. A small group of believers, mostly outcasts of society, are huddled in a room, their faces filled with terror at the fear of arrests. A knock at the door fulfills their dread and Paul (or some other Jew) or Roman soldiers break down the door and haul off the Christians to prison, or worse. The basis for this picture is rooted in Paul's admission (or is it boasting?) of his persecution of believers, described in Acts 9:1–2, and images of imperial persecution taken from much later times, supported by the accounts of Nero's horrible acts against believers in the first century. Given this picture, there was opportunity for much terror in the early churches.

Scholarly judgment today about this picture is nearly unanimous: it is simply not true. Clearly there was some Jewish opposition and harrassment of the early Jesus movement. The accounts in Acts of the arrest and even execution of a few of the leaders have some credibility. The Gospels hint at opposition to this movement. Paul obviously did persecute groups of believers, but his acts cannot be defined by Acts 9:1–2, which is patently historically impossible.[1] The general picture of the Jesus movement in relation to the synagogue shows plenty of tension but not much cause for terror on the part of the followers of Jesus.[2]

Empire-wide persecution of Christianity did not begin until the third century.[3] Obviously there was much enmity earlier and some local persecution. Nero's brutality in 64 c.e. was an act of random violence not reported with pride by either Tacitus or Suetonius, the two early Roman reporters of the event.[4]

The earliest evidence of what could be called official persecution (c. 112 c.e.) is found in Pliny the Younger's correspondence with Trajan, material that is well-known and cannot be reported in detail here.[5] For our purposes a few things are significant. Christians are, at least in this instance, punished *because* they are Christians.[6] Some persecution, perhaps stemming from as much as twenty years prior to the letter, had already taken place. Trajan dictates that the government not seek out Christians. This follows the normal legal procedures in Roman law by which charges are brought by citizens against others and not by the government itself. This suggests a very important implication. When persecutions involving Roman authorities did occur during the early period, they were caused not by the government instigating legal actions, but by private citizens whose hostility against believers became so strong that they sought redress in the courts. It supports the judgments of many scholars that, until much later times, persecution against Christians was sporadic. During this early period, certainly during the time of the New Testament writings, believers lived among their pagan neighbors without the situation calling forth continuous terror.[7]

A Working Definition of Terror

Before we know what we are looking for, we need to define terms. I am sure that a number of definitions more sophisticated than mine are scattered throughout this volume; nevertheless I must struggle to find for myself a working definition of the term "terror," a term already bandied about in the paragraphs above, without any attempt at control. In what follows, I am heavily dependent upon a conversation with Dr. Paul Mestancik, a psychoanalyist who has read widely in philosophical and existential materials. I take full responsibility, however, for my judgments on the matter.

Terror is a primal emotion. Its primary causes are the threat of annihilation and hopelessness to defend against the annihilation. A person may be seized with terror when he or she is faced with death (which may be other than physical) and has no power to defend oneself. There is also, perhaps, a sense of the irrational in the situation. That is, the person filled with terror may not understand *why* the outside force involved is making the threat. The threat does not fit into the cognitive structure that forms the basis of a person's understanding of self and world.

Terror, as a primal emotion, erupts from underneath the cognitive structure of the person. It is likely to force aside that structure, overpower it at least temporarily, and in extreme cases actually destroy the structure of meaning that has formed the self-understanding of the person. This means that while a community might include in its "world" an explanation of possible terror to its members, in an attempt to keep its terrified members within its cognitive structure, such explanations might or might not suffice to control terror. It may be that terror cannot be contained by incorporating a rationale into the cognitive structure.

Terror can be distinguished from fear and panic. Fear can be said to be a range of anxieties about threat; indeed terror might be the extreme point on the line. One might then say that terror is an extreme fear of the sort that threatens the cognitive structure. I may fear that I may lose my job or that I may die due to a recently discovered malignancy, but I can easily incorporate that into my cognitive structure. I have read too much about downsizing not to know it could happen to me, and I know I will not live forever. Panic is related to terror in that it can be said to be a sudden irrational emotion, but one which is likely to subside or disappear; terror, while perhaps equally sudden, does not go away. It becomes a permanent threat— something that I cannot make disappear.

Methodological Necessities

If we apply the above suggestions to a study of early Christianity, how would it help us discover which texts are relevant and how would it give us perspective about interpreting such texts? Unfortunately, the leap is not easy.

It is usually conceded that early Christian documents do not reveal much about personal feelings—a feature that jolts the modern person who is so given to express feelings at the drop of a hat. This is not to say that persons in those days did not have feelings (though they may have been different from ours); it *is* to say that the writings do not often disclose in a specific way what those feelings were. Why there is such a large gap between that culture and our own is an interesting topic, but it cannot be explored here. No doubt, then as now, much could be assumed—and was assumed in the texts—about what people felt. If someone is in this or that situation, he or she is likely to be feeling this or that—unless it is otherwise pointed out. Alas, we dare not assume that the two cultures would have made the same assumptions. What caused terror in one would not necessarily cause terror in the other.

We are thus led to the following methodological reservation. Rarely does a New Testament text explicitly say one is, or may be, in terror. Obviously

235

we have no access to the emotion itself. And if almost no texts explicitly describe an emotion called "terror," how can we proceed? We are, it seems to me, only able to look for *situations* mentioned in the New Testament which *in us* would call forth terror. We need to accept the reservation, however, that that situation might not have caused terror in the early believers involved. To repeat: We have access neither to the emotions themselves nor to language which describes the emotion; we *do* have access to situations mentioned in the texts that *might* have evoked terror in those involved in the situation.

There is, alas, a further problem. *Very* few of the texts we will look at are explicit enough about the situation to sense whether it would have been a terror-evoking situation. This vagueness opens the door to differing, even opposing interpretations by contemporary interpreters. Much depends upon what the interpreter *expects* to see.

Another question seems obvious. Are there specific words used in the texts that might help us to tag situations that might evoke terror? This question also has an ambiguous answer. There is no specific Greek term used in the New Testament that *has* to be translated by "terror." Words for "fear" do exist, of course, *but only the context could lead a translator to use the term "terror."* The question of context returns us to the perspective of the interpreter. In order to make the point but not to get involved in the mass of detail, let me give a simple illustration.

In the NRSV the word "terror" occurs in its translation of the New Testament three times. In Mark 16:8 the translation reads, "For terror and amazement had seized them." There is actually only one verb in the Greek, φοβέομαι ("to fear," which can have a wide range of meanings, positive as well as negative), which the translators have altered into two nouns. The Greek is most simply translated: "For they were afraid" (RSV). The verb, φοβέω, occurs elsewhere ninety-four times in the New Testament, but in none of these did the NRSV translators decide "terror" an appropriate translation. It should be noted that in the Markan text the response is to (presumably) divine epiphany. In Acts 10:4, also in response to divine epiphany, Cornelius stares at the angel "in terror" (RSV, translating the adjective ἔμφοβος). This word appears four other times in the New Testament, "terror" not being chosen for any of the other instances by the NRSV translators.[8] Finally, the word "terror" appears in Romans 13:3, here referring to a possible reaction to political authorities, who are not a "terror" to people acting correctly. The Greek is the noun, φόβος (the most common word for "fear," again, as is the case with the correlate verb, used positively as well as negatively). This word appears forty-six other times in the New Testament, for none of which the NRSV translators think the translation "terror" is appropriate. This small window out onto the thicket of the problems of translation shows clearly how ambiguous our texts are, and how the dispositions of translators are inevitably involved in decisions made. If this is the case with textual experts, how careful must we be in our assessments of texts which might illustrate our theme! The conclusion is that a word study is not helpful for our purposes.[9]

What I will do, then, is to focus on texts that describe *situations* that might, from our perspective, evoke terror. I will then do a second thing of some importance. I will look to see how the situation is explained theologically. In what way is the imagined terror put into a theological context? Ultimately this may be the most important part of the study. Is there a way or ways in which Christian faith can help one in a situation of terror to withstand the threat of obliteration of the meaning structures of one's life?

Situations That Might Evoke Terror

I take it that the theme for the volume is to study the reaction to *human* threat. For the New Testament texts, however, this is a sharp narrowing of perspective. Indeed, perhaps the majority of texts at our disposal reflect "terror" before *God,* and God's eschatological judgment. For our modern sensibilities, this may come as a genuine surprise. Many of us do not believe in any life after death; if we do, we may so emphasize the God of love that we think there is no place for hell or punishments for sinful living (if there is even such a thing as sin). Thus we cannot really understand that texts such as that in Hebrews should be taken seriously: "For if we sin deliberately after receiving the knowledge of the truth, there no longer remains a sacrifice for sins, but a fearful prospect of judgment, and a fury of fire which will consume the adversaries. . . . It is a fearful thing to fall into the hands of the living God" (Heb. 10:26–27, 31 rsv). Could people really be in terror of God's eschatological judgment? The inclination is to take such warnings as crowd control—efforts simply to get people to obey. The idea is that the *writer* is surely too sophisticated to believe that the threat is real, but he or she hopes the reader is not.

I strongly suspect this is a facile contemporary evasion of the world in which Jews and Christians originally lived. We have to acknowledge that in that world the greatest terror might well have been evoked by images of God's judgment and punishment rather than by threats by humans. It is no accident that, in fact, the theological strategy in the texts I will inspect is often to put the threat by humans within the larger context of God's judgment, for that is the greater cause for anxiety. Since, however, the terror before God is not the subject of our volume, I will not further belabor this point. I hope, however, that the reader will always keep it in mind.

237

Paul and Jesus

It is perhaps amazing—or maybe not—that in Paul the trouble-maker we have an explicit, historical situation of possible terror so early in the life of the church. Paul acknowledges that he was punished or disciplined by both Jewish and Gentile authorities (2 Cor. 11:23–25); the most extreme situation, however, of which we have evidence is his incarceration on capital charges. He writes to the Philippians from prison and informs them that he may be executed—certainly an opportunity for an attack of terror.[10] The situation is obscure, but a few things seem reasonably clear. He is in a Roman prison somewhere awaiting trial on charges that could lead to execution. Since there is no reason to think that being a "Christian" (a term that in Paul's lifetime probably did not yet exist) was at that time a capital crime, he must have been arrested on other charges—although he suggests that the *real* reason that he was charged was religious, covered over by an explicit political charge.

Whatever the actual situation was, in prison awaiting a life-and-death trial is certainly possible cause for terror. It fits our working definition—a threat to life with no power to control the situation. *Yet we simply cannot know whether Paul felt terror.* He writes serenely, as if the outcome really doesn't matter. In fact, he claims that a death sentence would be preferable (Phil. 1:23). Does he mean what he says or is he whistling in the dark? On the basis of what he *says* one would conclude that he has so integrated the unknown future into his theology of apostleship and assurance of life with Christ after death that terror has been nullified or controlled. There is no real way of getting behind his words.

The other obvious place to look for a personal example is the passion narratives in the Gospels. Is Jesus ever allowed to show terror in this situation?[11] Given the church's common faith in the resurrection of Jesus, it is not surprising that any sense of terror has been replaced by a kind of stoic, temporary waiting: soon it will all be over. There is one scene, however, in which the theological facade seems to become fragile: that of Jesus in Gethsemane. Jesus prays that he may not have to face death. The Markan terms used to describe Jesus' emotions are stark: θαμβέω, ἀδημονέω, περίλυπος. The usual terms to translate are "greatly distressed and troubled" and "very sorrowful," respectively. Matthew follows Mark, though replacing θαμβέω with λυπέω. In Luke all emotion is denied Jesus; here it is the disciples who have λύπη (Luke 22:45). The Markan words suggest Jesus is experiencing more than just "sadness" (a bland translation of the forms of λύπη) as he faces death.[12] Is he in terror? Is it a panic attack?

While the Markan story is focused on narrative, there are exemplary elements, which may explain why this particular story shows strong feeling in Jesus, absent from all the remainder of the account. When Jesus returns the first time to the sleeping disciples, he admonishes them: "Watch and pray so that you will not fall into temptation. The spirit is willing, but the body is weak" (14:38). What is the temptation into which they should not enter? In the context, the temptation has to relate to what Jesus came close to but did not finally fall into: the temptation to escape the consequences of obeying God's will (such as might happen when the disciple is accused in some public confrontation). Jesus, on the one hand, openly exhibits the fear of the situation; on the other, he resists letting himself be overcome by the fear. Thus he is an example of how one may remain faithful despite a situation of terror.[13] At this one place—and perhaps only here—the story of Jesus becomes a paradigm for the faithful follower in the face of persecution.[14]

Threats to Communities

To turn to evidence that speaks of situations in the faith communities that might have provoked terror is to become engulfed in a sea of possibilities that threatens length and coherence. What follows is more an outline than a discussion. I save for the end of the section those documents in which the threat begins to become ominous. At the end of the section I will make some attempt to summarize and give perspective, but the direction of the summary can be suggested here: *there is ample evidence of situations of harrassment, but almost none that would suggest a persecution so serious that terror would have been almost inevitable.*[15]

Synoptics. I assume that pre-authorial material in the Synoptics most likely reflects a pre-seventies, Jewish rural social setting in which antagonists are mostly Jewish coreligionists. I assume that authorial material is certainly post-seventy, perhaps more urban, reflecting an increasing Gentile population, both in the churches and in the outside environment.[16]

Mark depicts a chilling scene in the apocalyptic material in 13:9–13 (a mixture of pre- and authorial material). Intra-Jewish discipline, confrontation in Gentile (perhaps even Roman) courts, and innerfamilial strife because of affiliation with the Jesus movement is "predicted" for believers. Clearly these are threatening situations; could they produce terror? Matthew uses this material, putting most of it in a section describing missionary activity, which indicates even more explicitly the harrassment of believers who were proclaiming the message of (or about) Jesus (cf. also Matt. 5:10–11, 44). Luke does not add significantly to the material.

The Pauline communities. In general, it seems fair to say that Paul does not address situations in his churches that he thinks are situations of terror. Only two situations call for specific mention.

239

Thessalonica. Here the dominant word used is θλῖξις ("affliction"—
1 Thess. 1:6, 3:3, 4 [verb]—in 3:7 it refers to Paul). Πάσχω ("to suffer")
appears in 1 Thessalonians 2:14, where the author draws a parallel between
the experiences of the Thessalonian believers and those of the churches in
Judaea. Does the story in Acts 17:1–9 illuminate Paul's language? Suffice
it to say here that neither in Acts nor in 1 Thessalonians is there sufficient
indication that that community was in a situation that would cause terror.

Philippi. The community is also experiencing some hostility from the
outside (1:27–30)—Paul calls them "opponents." The community is being
frightened, scared, *intimidated* by them. "Intimidated" is potentially a strong
word, but unfortunately one cannot know how strong to make it without
further information, and Paul does not supply it. There is no indication that
courts and governments are involved. Had there been, Paul's parallelism
between his present incarceration and their difficulty would have been
more pointed (1:30).

Deutero-Pauline communities. One might anticipate that, in the later communities of the Pauline traditions, reference to persecution and opposition
would be clearer on the general judgment that persecution began to occur
more frequently as the church spread and drew more attention to itself.
But in general, the letters in this tradition[17] show no interest in dealing
with outside opposition other than opposing Christian groups. Paul is honored as the prisoner, but others do not suffer with him. Second Thessalonians refers to the church as suffering, but the nature of this situation is
never explained. Second Timothy also shows some concern for the suffering of Paul, who exhorts Timothy to join in the witness that produces suffering (1:8). Also in this document is the most general maxim in the entire
New Testament relating Christianity and response to it from the outside:
"Indeed all who want to live a godly life in Christ Jesus will be persecuted"
(3:12 RSV).

Thus the entire Pauline literature, covering a period of perhaps sixty to
seventy years, manifests little communal suffering and only the barest hints
of situations that might cause terror.

The Threat Becomes Ominous

John (perhaps 90–100 C.E.). There is no need to rehearse the arguments
that locate the Johannine community as once mostly Jewish but now
excluded from the synagogue by the actions of synagogue leaders.[18] As
such, there seems to have been explicit rejection and hostility[19] (eventually this becomes a mutual stance) but not persecution in any physical way.
A remarkable passage, however, occurs in 16:1–2. After "predicting" that
the followers would be ejected from the synagogue, Jesus adds: "The hour

is coming when everyone who kills you will think to be making an offering to God" (my translation). The cultic language is startling, but the hard problem is to imagine who, if anybody, is doing the killing. Jews almost certainly did not have the *ius gladius* (a view shared by the Gospel itself 18:31), thus any execution would have involved Roman courts. It is possible that the Gospel is late enough to reflect Roman hardening of attitudes once it has become clear (in part signalled by the Jewish stance) that the Jesus followers are not Jews (any longer). If so, then the sequence—ejection from the synagogue, losing the protection accorded Judaism, execution—would make some sense. That might be a situation that would be cause for terror. It must be acknowledged, however, that there is no other hint in the Gospel (or the Johannine epistles) that this situation had been realized. Mob violence is also a possibility.

Hebrews. This treatise provides us with one of the rare descriptions of external opposition that seems specific—and yet even that hope dims under hard questioning. The document is notoriously difficult to delimit in terms of date, location, and audience; I judge that it was written in the latter part of the first century and to Gentiles. The believers were "second-generation Christians. . . . (who) had been Christians for some time."[20] In 10:32–34 the author reminds the readers of their past as a church.

> But recall the former days when, after you were enlightened, you endured a hard struggle with sufferings, sometimes being publicly exposed to abuse and affliction, and sometimes being partners with those so treated. For you had compassion on the prisoners, and you joyfully accepted the plundering of your property, since you knew that you yourselves had a better possession and an abiding one.

At some time in the past, the community had experienced a violent attack upon its members. Public humiliation, arrest, and seizure of property are the descriptions of the attack.[21] The researcher instinctively calls to mind Philo's description of the horrible attack on the Jewish community in Alexandria.[22] There public humiliation and seizure (and destruction) of property were acts of mob violence—although acquiesced to by the civil and Roman authorities. Such "private" mob violence could be the situation referred to in Hebrews, although the mention of prisoners makes it difficult to think no official involvement occurred. In the widespread scene of violence Philo narrates, a Jew would never know whether his life or that of his family was safe, let alone whether his house would be plundered or burned. One could easily imagine the terror aroused in community members. We are not necessarily at a point in time where official Roman persecution is involved, even of the sort evident in the Pliny correspondence. Mob mentality can be even more terrorizing than official accusations.

There is one final passage which may help locate the social situation that is reflected in the document. Throughout the treatise, the role of Christ has been argued to be effective in a way the Jewish sacrificial system is not. Why is this such an important argument for the author? In 13:10–14, he seems to refer to a situation in which the Christians have been hiding behind the protection that the synagogue offered Jews. Jews were given legal rights by the Romans to live their religion without hindrance either from the Romans themselves or from the local governments.[23] Even after the end of the rebellion against Rome (70–72 c.e.), the Jewish community maintained these rights. The earliest Jesus communities were either Jewish or (like Paul) assumed that Gentile members were part of the Israel of God. It is likely that it is only toward the end of the first century that the separation began to be obvious, in part because Jews seem to have become edgy about Gentile churches with their theology of Jesus as Lord. The situation in the Gospel of John may reflect that situation (cf. my comments on John 16:2 above).

The passage in Hebrews 13 exhorts the Christian community to "go to him [Jesus] outside the camp and bear the abuse he endured" (v. 13). That means, I believe, to give up any claim for the protection of the synagogue and accept the inevitable: that Christians are not Jews and thus cannot claim the protection afforded the synagogue. The author clearly sees that such a move means opening the community to "abuse." The word is ὀνειδισμός (the same word that has appeared in other "persecution passages," such as Heb. 10:33 itself—cf. also Matt. 5:11 and 1 Pet. 4:14). If that is the situation, then the treatise may date toward the end of the first century, putting it in the same period as the Gospel of John and, perhaps, 1 Peter. All three of these documents then reflect the increasing pressure brought on churches in various locales as it becomes apparent that Christians must stand on their own, independent of any protection from the synagogue.[24]

First Peter. If there is any New Testament text that would seem to point to a situation of terror, it is this late first-century letter to churches in provinces in what is now Asia Minor. Several passages hint at conflict between believers and the outside world (1:6; 2:19; 3:6; 3:14–16); in these passages nothing is said that would compel the judgment that the communities addressed by the author of 1 Peter were undergoing specific persecution. This seems to change in 4:12–19, a passage worth citing in its entirety.

> Beloved, do not be surprised at the fiery ordeal[25] which comes upon you to test you, as though something strange were happening to you. But rejoice in so far as you share Christ's sufferings, that you may also rejoice and be

glad when his glory is revealed. If you are reviled with the name of Christ blessed are you, for the spirit of glory and of God rests upon you. But let none of you suffer as a murderer, or a thief, or a wrongdoer, or a mischief-maker; but if one [suffers] as a Christian, let him not be ashamed [this word may hint at the meaning: "let him not recant"] but let him glorify God with this name [i.e. Christian]. For the time has come for judgment to begin with the household of God; and if it begins with us, what will be the end of those who do not obey the gospel of God? Therefore let those who suffer according to God's will do right and entrust their souls to a faithful Creator [mostly RSV, with my revisions].

For many earlier interpreters, this passage speaks of official persecution against believers simply because they are believers. Beare (1961) may serve as an example. "These verses [15–16] make it unmistakably clear that the writer is speaking of governmental action all through this passage; the profession of Christianity is being punished as a crime, like murder and theft."[26] Beare reads the situation out of Pliny's correspondence and dates 1 Peter accordingly.[27]

Achtemeier (1996), to the contrary, sees 1 Peter rather "more due to unofficial harassment than to official policy, more local than regional, and more at the initiation of the general populace as the result of a reaction against the lifestyle of the Christians than at the initiation of Roman officials because of some general policy of seeking out and punishing Christians."[28] In a related issue, one needs to note that in 5:8 the author identifies that what is happening to his addressees is also happening in "the world." Two interpretations are possible here: either "world" means the locus of outside, hostile society, or it indicates the spacial entirety of human society (i.e. the Greco-Roman world). The RSV translates: "throughout the world." If this is the correct reading, then whatever is happening to the churches addressed in Asia is also known to be occurring in the larger *oikomene*. Thus, *if* 1 Peter refers to serious, perhaps official persecution, then this persecution is said to be empire-wide. Since the tendency in recent scholarship is clearly to deny the existence of such a persecution, the conclusion is that what is known to be happening "throughout the world" is merely general harrassment.[29]

In my judgment, this points to something more than verbal abuse. The word "suffer" (4:13, 15, 16—implied) is, granted, such a general term that no decision can depend on this term in and of itself. Nevertheless, in verse 15 the suffering is attached to the charge of murder or theft, accusations that had legal consequences (granted there are two other terms in the list of a more general nature). In verse 16, the term "Christian" is added to the list of those who may suffer. Given the parallelism between murderer and thief on the one hand and Christian on the other, it is hard for me to doubt

243

that some legal action is at stake. That is, believers are being punished *because* they claim the name "Christian." The charge is serious, because believers may be tempted to deny the faith under this pressure;[30] they are instead charged to glorify God by accepting the name of Christian. That is, we have a situation in which a believer is charged with the name "Christian." He must confess or deny his allegiance with the movement. That the name "Christian" suddenly emerges in this persecution context lends credence to the suspicion that some dire legal confrontation is being described. It sounds to me very much like a matter of life or death.

The passage, 5:8–9, may not extend this situation to the larger, spacial world. The qualitative reading, "out there, in evil society," is a more natural translation and fits usages in other early Christian writers such as Paul and the author of the Gospel of John. If this is the case, as I believe it is, the verse makes no judgment about how widespread the persecution is thought to be.

This means that 1 Peter does not have to be yoked with *any* official persecution we know about, not empire-wide Roman attacks nor the time and situation of Pliny. It is hard to doubt that (just as with Hebrews) many attacks on believers occurred in various guises, from outside abuse and harrassment to local and Roman courts, at various times and at various locales. First Peter and Hebrews are, in my judgment, examples of sporadic, local— but *serious*—persecution that must have occurred in situations about which we have no external, supportive evidence. How many such events there may have been we just cannot know. Let us try to avoid the temptations of speculations!

The Book of Revelation. The reader might well think that once at this document, one has arrived at a secure place where persecution and terror abound. Indeed, terror does abound, but from the perspective of the author, the terror is caused by the horrifying agents of God's apocalyptic invasion of human history. Here, if ever in the New Testament, is my judgment at the beginning of this paper affirmed—that the most terror evoked in early Christianity is caused by fear of God's judgment, not human assault.

But what about the author's refrain of violent persecution of the pure believers, resulting in prison and death (2:10, 6:9–11, 7:14, 13:5, 20:4)? These seem to suggest a widespread official assault on the churches. Lack of any evidence of such a widespread persecution (even Pliny does not fit) has led some scholars to conclude that the persecution depicted is what the author thinks *should* happen if believers were genuinely faithful, but hasn't happened yet.[31] There is no evidence, in fact, that such widespread attacks ever did happen during the possible lifetime of the author.

The most specific anticipation concerns the church at Smyrna. "Do not fear what you are about to suffer. Beware, the devil is about to throw some of you into prison so that you may be tested, and for ten days you will have affliction. Be faithful unto death, and I will give you the crown of life" (2:10). Here the author tells the Smyrnans what is in store for them. Were they not aware of it? Why does the author have to tell them what they ought already to be fearing? This suggests that the upcoming persecution is not as obvious as it might be. But is it unjustified anticipation?

Who has, ultimately, the correct view—the author or the Smyrnans, who don't, somehow, "see" what the author sees? J. M. P. Sweet makes a provocative analogy. "A recent parallel might be the attempts of Bonhoeffer and others to alert the 'German Christians' of the 1930s to the true nature of Hitler's *Reich,* at a time when men were dazzled by his achievements and he was widely regarded as civilization's bulwark against Bolshevism."[32] Bonhoeffer's "predictions" became all too true in just a few years. The author of Revelation may have been shown to be similarly insightful by the time of the persecution during Pliny's proconsulship, perhaps only ten to twenty years in the future (even if this was a "local" persecution). For our purposes, however, we have to acknowledge that it is unlikely that his text describes events that had already occurred by the time of his writing.

Summary

We have no first-hand evidence of terror. We are limited to hints and allusions, rarely anything that qualifies as a description, of *situations* that might, *in our world,* cause a reaction of terror. So far, in effect, I have created a brief history of emerging persecution. What little we know enables us to hazard the following conclusions. "Christianity" began as a Jewish sect in Palestine and Christians were, to an extent we do not know, harrassed by other Jews. As missionaries like Paul helped communities in the larger Mediterranean world to emerge, some harrassment also emerged there, perhaps because the spread of Judaism to Gentiles was not smiled upon by cities suspicious of Jews to begin with. Paul is a good example of a missionary who took it from both sides—Jew and Gentile. But in this early, pre-seventy period, Rome does not seem to have become involved, except for the isolated pogrom instigated by Nero.

After the Jewish revolt against Rome (that is, after 70 C.E.), lines gradually solidified. Gradually it became clear that "Christians" were not Jews and had no legal standing in Roman judicial perspective. Gradually Jews began to communicate that they wanted to disassociate themselves from "Christians." The churches were now exposed and vulnerable to increasing Greek and Roman suspicion. At some point, probably in the nineties, sporadic, legal persecution began in Roman courts (probably local courts had already engaged in suppressive activity).[33] By the time of Pliny, the die is certainly cast.

The key word is "sporadic." Harrassment and ridicule had been there from the beginning—sporadically (both temporally and geographically). When legal persecution began, it was sporadic. What the believer knew is that "it" had happened elsewhere. Would "it" happen to her and her community? By the nineties, a Christian knew that the name he accepted was one of opprobrium. This did not quell the numbers flocking to the church (although persecution seems, not surprisingly, to have put at least a temporary damper on enrollment—cf. Pliny). It is hard to doubt that Christians knew it could happen to them. They had to live in some anxiety that their lives and property were not safe.

Would this more or less constant anxiety lead to a stance of terror? Certainly in those groups that *experienced* persecution, terror would be a "natural" response. Whether terror would infiltrate the psyches of those who were at the moment "safe" but who knew that "it" had happened in a neighboring town is a question I do not think I can answer. In our time, it would depend upon individual emotional strengths and commitment levels. I remind the reader that my definition of terror included the notion that it would likely, at least temporarily, displace the rational structures, the world into which the person had been educated. When that happened, what protection would Christian beliefs have been against extreme fear? This leads me to the final issue I want to discuss—the theological judgments that are placed in the texts that warn against attacks of persecution. Why are they there and how effective might they have been?

Theological Defenses

Why does persecution occur at all if Jesus is God's Messiah? Something has gone wrong, badly wrong. Not only is this probably an instinctive, kneejerk reaction to persecution and rejection; it has to be answered if adherents are to persevere in such a risky new movement. Theological rationales thus function in part as damage-control mechanisms. If a reaction of terror threatens to overwhelm the usual rational structures (in this case, faith), then reinforcement of these structures is an urgent task of such theological rationales. How much more so if this structure is a newly acquired one, as it would be to most Christians, particularly those of non-Jewish culture. Thus it is not surprising that most of the texts we have looked at indicate some reason for the dangerous situation of believers—although the theological warrants are brief and sometimes have the flavor of *ad hoc* thinking.

What is interesting to note is the kind of rationale *not* given. Of course we do not expect to find modern-type sociological or psychological reasons. But what is perhaps surprising is that "the *human* enemy is evil" attitude is also *almost* entirely missing. Yes, Revelation has an anti-Roman stance, but the specific passages that allude to persecution do not contain any specific reference to Romans. It is the Devil who lies behind the imprisonment of the Smyrnans (2:10), just as the synagogue, which may be involved in the expected trial, is a synagogue of Satan (2:9). Does this mean that the Romans and Jews are so evil they can be equated with Supreme Evil, or does it mean that the Romans and Jews are but tools of Supreme Evil? For our modern senses, this may seem a trivial distinction. For the ancient world, which lived in myth as *the* reality, the difference is crucial.

The same priority of spirit over flesh is found in 1 Peter 5:8–9: "Your adversary the devil prowls around like a roaring lion, seeking some one to devour. Resist him, firm in your faith, knowing that the same experience of suffering is required of your brotherhood throughout the world" (RSV). All-too-human attackers of the church are given the face of demonic, invisible Evil. In Ephesians 6:12 the human enemy disappears: the church's fight is against the invisible powers of darkness, not those of "flesh and blood."

We referred above to one sentence in the Gospel of John (16:2) that spoke of some form of capital punishment. While no rationale is listed here, elsewhere it is the Jews who are responsible for persecuting Jesus, and in a violent passage the Jews are said to have the Devil as father (8:44). The context is the rejection of Jesus, and in John this includes the rejection of the church. Hence also here Supreme Evil may lie behind human activity of rejection.

A decidedly anti-Jewish blame for persecution is found in 1 Thessalonians 2:14–16, introduced by a stated parallel between persecution of the Thessalonian church and that of Judean churches by the Jews. Then follows a list of evils stereotypically said to be characteristic of the Jews. Supreme Evil is absent from this scenario.[34]

Most of the other rationales are variations on the general eschatological framework of Jewish apocalypticism. By that I mean that faith lies in the assurance that history is unfolding according to a divine plan. In Gethsemane, Jesus submits to God's will. Paul in Philippians can't decide whether it is better for him to be with Christ or to remain to do God's work, a work which is related to the divine plan for human history. The apostle introduces his catalogue of apostolic misfortunes by saying it shows him to be a true servant of Christ (2 Cor. 11:23). Hebrews puts the persecution text (10:32–34) within the context of eschatological promise ("a better possession and an abiding one"). In chapter 13 the author justifies the exhortation to separate from Judaism (to leave the symbolic city of Jerusalem)

247

because of the eternal city which is to come (v. 14).[35] Eschatological reward is also the rationale in Matthew's beatitude (5:10).

The most remarkable eschatological rationale is found in 1 Peter 4:12–19. Here the persecution is understood as the beginning of the final judgment, a judgment that *begins* with the church but will extend to the entire world. Persecution is the judgment upon the church by God! It calls to the author's mind the biblical passage (Proverbs 11:31, LXX), "If the righteous man is scarcely saved, where will the impious and sinner appear?" Neither evil humans nor Supreme Evil are agents, yet this is the same author who speaks of the devil trying to devour believers!

In general, the brunt of these admonitions is to turn attention away from the local scene where the persecutors are humans, whether Jews, or Greeks, or Romans, and to show that what is crucial is the much larger panorama of God's eschatological drama. Terror is minimized and, hopefully, controlled by understanding any terrifying moment as one ultimately under God's control, one that will ensure the selfhood and safety of the believer. It is as if the author were saying, Do not fear what you *see*—what is done to you by ordinary humans who have no real control over the world. Put your trust in the ultimate Lord's control over human history, whose final act will unfold soon, ensuring your safety and eternal salvation. The present, earthly threat is put within the context of divine/satanic warfare. This means that *no* rationale has to be provided for the historical situation. It is allowed to remain, in effect, meaningless. To hope in God's ultimate meaningfulness and thus to be free to assess a *historical* situation as meaningless is the ultimate achievement of this kind of theological perspective.

Whether this was effective, who can say? But before we too easily dismiss this approach as another negative dimension of eschatological pie-in-the-sky, let us consider that unless there is meaning outside of the self, then all experiences are potentially self-defeating because they have no reference outside of the self—and therefore *no meaning.* Negative experiences such as persecution are then particularly likely to result in the dissolution of the self.[36] If one is to survive terror without permanent self-destruction, then one *must* have a meaning structure that transcends the self.

The writers of the New Testament chose not to let the drama of meaning play out in the human sphere. They affirmed by this that there is a larger structure of meaning than human hate and fear. In a moment of terror, to be able to put oneself into the larger perspective, in which God ultimately triumphs over world, could enable the believer to sustain himself with hope in a new world, despite threatening opposition. It might help him live whatever life was left without the canker of bitterness and hate which would otherwise consume the person, even if he survived the threat. Who is to say that that is not the best result possible? Maybe it would give us courage to make a similar stand against evil in our own day.

Terror Next Door: A Homily on Extreme Fear in Our Midst

Walter J. Burghardt, S.J.

Consider your own call, brothers and sisters: not many of you were wise by human standards, not many were powerful, not many were of noble birth. But God chose what is foolish in the world to shame the wise; God chose what is weak in the world to shame the strong; God chose what is low and despised in the world, things that are not, to reduce to nothing things that are, so that no one might boast in the presence of God. He is the source of your life in Christ Jesus, who became for us wisdom from God, and righteousness and sanctification and redemption, in order that, as it is written, "Let the one who boasts, boast in the Lord."

1 Corinthians 1:26–31

Brother will betray brother to death, and a father his child, and children will rise against parents and have them put to death.

Mark 13:12

Terror, *Webster's Unabridged* informed me four decades ago, is "a state or instance of extreme fear, fear that agitates body and mind." Being normally inquisitive, I am aware that the Internet search engine *Google* has found 616,000 entries for terrorism. Being reasonably intelligent, I am aware of terror on national and international levels: bombing of the federal building in Oklahoma City, bombing of the American embassies in Nairobi and Dar es Salaam; radical leftist organizations like the Japanese Red Army, Germany's Red Army Faction, Italy's Red Brigades; ethno-nationalist terrorist movements like the Abu Nidal organization, the IRA, the Basque separatist group ETA; the Holocaust; the World Trade Center. I am aware that some are motivated by a religious imperative, even appealing to their Scriptures to justify their actions—aptly called "holy terror."

As a tiny contribution to an extensive issue, I dare to suggest that terrorism, like charity, may well begin at home. I shall go on to suggest, as a Catholic Christian, what our Scriptures and our theologies have to say on this matter. I shall conclude with some personal observations and recommendations.

I

Without neglecting terror abroad, I shall stress terror at home. Not home as our national community as a whole. I mean home as the family, the neighbor next door, a judge, the local gang, uncaring politicians, the local constabulary, immigrants, our prison situation, child sexual abuse—whatever individual, group, or situation incites fear by its actions or its very presence—fear that agitates body and/or mind.

Family. To be young is to be confused and confusing. In the moving screenplay *The Forty Blows,* François Truffaut showed us thirteen-year-old Antoine Doinel at once terrified and rather proud of a mother who conceived him out of wedlock, wanted to abort him, doesn't really like him very much, and who is always bawling him out "for nothing . . . for little things." His father is "all right, I guess. But he's a bit of a coward because he knows my mother's unfaithful, but he says nothing so that there won't be any fights at home." He works out of one troublesome situation only to fall into another and is constantly ridden by anxiety. He runs away because he cannot face the anger at home and is sent to a center for juvenile delinquents because his father can no longer endure him. "Do whatever you want with him; take him away, put him in the country somewhere. We can't figure him out. He needs some real punishment."[1] Terrorism indeed.

Our neighbors. Example? "The Elephant Man" of stage and screen. When a compassionate surgeon, Frederick Treves, first saw him, John Merrick was twenty. He was terribly misshapen, "the most disgusting specimen of humanity" Treves had ever seen. Giant nodes extended his head like masses of dough; its circumference was no less than his waist. Another mass of bone protruded like a pink stump from his mouth, making of it only a slobbering aperture, turning speech into torture. From his back hung sack-like masses of flesh covered by a kind of loathsome cauliflower skin; from his chest, a bag of flesh "like a dewlap suspended from the neck of a lizard." A hip disease had left him permanently lame, unable to walk without a stick.

When Treves came upon him, Merrick was a circus freak, exploited for his ability to shock, to make people throw up; he had no other way to live. "He was shunned like a leper," Treves recalled, "housed like a wild beast, and got his only view of the world from a peephole in a showman's cart." Terrorism indeed.

Treves housed Merrick in the London Hospital, with his own bed-sitting room and a bathroom. Merrick, he discovered, was highly intelligent, acutely sensitive, romantically imaginative. The cruelty of his fellows had not embittered him. The transformation began when a young widow entered his room, wished him good morning, and shook his hand. Merrick sobbed uncontrollably; apart from his mother, she was the first woman who had ever smiled at him, ever touched his hand. From then on he lost his shyness, loved to see his door open and the world flock to him, from actress Madge Kendal to the Princess of Wales. He died at twenty-eight. He had told Treves, "I am happy every hour of the day."[2]

More frightening still "next door." A friend in Reading, Pennsylvania, tells me of a nauseating incident in that city. A man took from school the eight-year-old child of his former girlfriend—took her by telling the teacher that the mother had forgotten that the child had a doctor's appointment. He called the mother, told her he had the child, that she could have the child if she (the mother) would only talk to him. She agreed, but he fled. More than a week later the child was found in a shallow grave; she had been suffocated and/or drowned with a chain around her neck. Terror indeed.

Legal terror. In Texas it is not uncommon for a defendant to remain in jail for months before ever seeing a lawyer. "In recent years the Texas Court of Criminal Appeals has upheld death sentences in at least three cases in which the defense lawyers slept during trial. The trial judge in one case reasoned that while the Constitution requires that a defendant be represented by a lawyer, it 'doesn't say the lawyer has to be awake.'"[3] Terror indeed.

Gang violence. In my own backyard, Washington, D.C., in a single five-year period, 224 children were killed by gunfire. Some were deliberate targets, others just happened to be there, at least one lay in a cradle. In consequence, children in our nation's capital were planning their own funerals: how they wanted to look, how to be dressed, where to be waked. They simply did not believe they would be around very long. Little wonder that our children have been planning for the worst, as if their own murders are inevitable, as if their own dreams will surely be just as cruelly cut short.[4] Terror indeed. And it is but one aspect of child terror.

All American children are at risk from the proliferation of guns which threaten all of us everywhere; from the pollution of our air, water, earth, airwaves, and Internet with smut and toxic substances; from the breakdown of family not only from out-of-wedlock births but pervasive divorce and erosion of extended family supports; from epidemic substance abuse and from domestic violence that knows no race or income limits; and from the erosion of

251

civility evidenced by road rage, profane language, and the coarse public discourse which pervades our culture.[5]

Terror indeed.

Uncaring politicians. Among industrialized countries, the United States ranks first in military technology, first in military exports, first in Gross Domestic Product, first in the number of millionaires and billionaires, first in defense expenditures, but fourteenth in the proportion of children in poverty, sixteenth in efforts to lift children out of poverty, eighteenth in the gap between rich and poor children, twenty-second in infant mortality, last in protecting our children against gun violence.[6] Terror indeed.

The local constabulary. From Los Angeles to New York City, blacks and Hispanics walk in fear of the police who are sworn to protect them. An unarmed African-American is savagely beaten by police arresting him; unarmed Amadou Diallo is shot forty-one times by police who think he is going to shoot them.[7] Terror indeed.

Immigrants. A century ago we Americans were proud to proclaim the "world-wide welcome" inscribed on a tablet in the pedestal of the Statue of Liberty:

> Give me your tired, your poor,
> Your huddled masses yearning to breathe free,
> The wretched refuse of your teeming shore.
> Send these, the homeless, tempest-tost to me,
> I lift my lamp beside the golden door.

As I write not only are Americans resisting immigration for economic reasons, but within U.S. immigration policy detention of immigrants reveals horror stories. In 1999 there were 200,000 immigrants in varying lengths of detention; by the end of 2001, it is estimated, there will be over 302,000. For lack of bed space in facilities owned and operated by the U.S. Immigration and Naturalization Service, 60 percent of detainees are currently housed in city and county jails. Once there, they are routinely housed with inmates held on criminal charges or those with criminal histories. In remote areas contact with attorneys is difficult, language always a problem. In San Pedro, California, a husband and wife were held in separate units for sixteen months, never allowed to visit each other or write directly. While in custody they lost their home; their three children, the oldest fifteen, were left to fend for themselves in Los Angeles.

Listen to a Jesuit friend of mine, Thomas L. Sheridan, retired professor of theology, who helps the Jesuit Refugee Service at a detainee center in Elizabeth, New Jersey: "There are no windows; they never breathe fresh air or see the light of day except through one skylight. One woman has been there for almost three years. It would break your heart to see them. They have such a lost and hopeless look on their faces." Terror indeed.

Our prison situation. Two decades ago, Fr. Michael Bryant started as the District of Columbia jail's full-time minister. At that time he believed that the U.S. justice system was fair, impartial, and balanced. After listening to thousands of men and women in that jail, he now recognizes that "our system of criminal justice is not fair, is not impartial, and is not balanced."[8] Blacks make up only 13 percent of our national population, Hispanics 9 or 10 percent; yet 48 percent in prison are black, 18 percent Hispanic. What do they have in common with the whites? They are poor, addicted, under-educated, and jobless. Our sentencing is more and more punitive: no more parole on the federal level, "three strikes and you're out" in California, minimum sentencing legislation. Two thirds return to prison. Terror indeed.

Death row. Few of the informed deny that innocent persons have been executed; the only real question is how many. As far back as 1987 a study in the Stanford Law Review identified 350 cases in the twentieth century in which innocent people were wrongly convicted of crimes for which they could have received the death penalty. Of that number perhaps twenty-three were executed; New York led the list with eight.[9] Time and again I imagine with horror the terror on the faces of those men moments before a lethal injection. Terror indeed.

Child sexual abuse. I was startled to learn that 1.38 percent of girls and 2.16 percent of boys are sexually abused before the age of eighteen; that in 1994, 345,400 sexual-abuse incidents were reported to Child Protective Services in the United States; that 90 to 95 percent of such cases go unreported to police.[10] Terror indeed.

II

Given these examples of terror, how ought we react precisely as Christians? As a Catholic Christian and theologian, with a profound involvement in the Hebrew Testament and the New Testament, I find it important but inadequate to simply condemn all such terror as unjust on ethical and legal grounds. Important because without the efforts of ethical and legal justice to treat people as they deserve, life on earth would turn into a jungle, where might makes right, and the prize goes to the swift, the smart, and the strong. Inadequate because neither philosophy nor the law, neither human reason nor the U.S. Supreme Court can command a four-letter word that raises us above the beast. I mean love. No one can lay this burden on humans save the God who shaped us, the God whose very name is Justice, the God who gives a more profound meaning to justice than all our earthbound excogitations could ever conceive. This leads me to the heart of my message: biblical justice.

A splendid Scripture scholar has left us a fine working definition of biblical justice: "fidelity to the demands of a relationship." Behind this, he pointed out, lay a whole way of life.

> In contrast to modern individualism the Israelite is in a world where "to live" is to be united with others in a social context either by bonds of family or by covenant relationships. This web of relationships—king with people, judge with complainants, family with tribe and kinfolk, the community with the resident alien and suffering in their midst and all with the covenant God—constitutes the world in which life is played out.[11]

The operative word here is "relationships." All life, even and primarily the life of the triune God, is summed up in relationships. For us on earth, the relationships are basically three: to God, to people, to the earth. Love God above all else; love every human person as a child of God, as an image of God, as a brother or sister, like another self; touch "things," earth and sea and sky, whatever is not human, with reverence, with respect, as a gift of God.

My point? Terrorism is a reaction to relationships—perceived relationships, often a skewed, distorted, perverted perception. Examples? When the leadership in Iran perceives the United States as Satan, the Evil One. When a fair number of Protestants used to see in Revelation's "Babylon the great, mother of whores and of the earth's abominations" (Rev. 17:5) the pope of Rome or the Roman Catholic Church as a whole. When a serial killer strangles a number of prostitutes because they befoul his perception of woman. When the Nazis exterminated six million Jews as inferior humans, a peril to Aryan purity. When the U.S. Supreme Court declared that slaves were property.

Here indeed is terrorism. A perverted perception of proper relationships leads to injustice in action: unnumbered millions killed, wounded, or missing in World War II; the mistrust, suspicion, even hatred generated by centuries of religious misunderstanding and intolerance; totalitarianism and concentration camps.

On the other hand, even an accurate perception of right relationships raises its own problems and can lead to terror. To make relationships right, individuals, groups, and nations have risen up in protest, occasionally with violence. Assume, for the sake of argument, that a just war is possible—the American Revolution, World War II against Germany and Japan. How can you kill your enemy and still claim to love him? How can you bomb Dresden mercilessly, drop an atom bomb on Hiroshima that has left 202,000 dead of radiation,[12] and claim a right relationship with Germans and Japanese? And for all our good intentions in Vietnam, we could not prevent a massacre of innocent civilians at My Lai. My Lai itself is indefensible, and yet, ironically, to destroy terrorism, must we not at times terrorize? To restore right relationships, must we not at times redefine the love that lies at the basis of biblical justice?

On an individual level, justified anger can lead to undesirable relation ships. Take the reaction to poverty-stricken Limerick expressed in a memoir by Malachy McCourt: "I was a smiley little fella with a raging heart and murderous instincts. One day I would show THEM—yes, you rotten f—ing arsehole counter-jumping stuck-up whore's-melts nose-holding tuppence-ha'penny-looking-down-on-tuppence snobs. I'll go back to America where I was born and I'll fart in yer faces. And I did."[13]

Historically, right relationships often take time to develop. In America it remained for the Quakers of the seventeenth century to speak out against slavery as a moral wrong, an injustice, a serious flaw in relationships. It took radical abolitionists like John Brown to invade the South to free the slaves. Not until 1865, when the Thirteenth Amendment to the Constitution was adopted, were all slaves freed. Even then, it took the Supreme Court to the middle of the twentieth century to impose what the Sermon on the Mount had been unable to achieve: no racial discrimination in housing, education, public accommodations, and employment. The turning point: when a black lady, Rosa Parks, refused to give up her bus seat to a white passenger. The cutting edge: when Martin Luther King Jr. led 200,000 blacks and whites on a March on Washington, his dream of the day when all persons would be judged not by their color but by their character. Still we struggle.

The words "my sisters and my brothers" leap easily to our lips. The reality is all too frequently written in blood. Not unexpectedly, Jesus was right on target in a somewhat different context: "Brother will betray brother to death" (Mark 13:12).

III

Finally, what of us, privileged to proclaim God's justice from the pulpit? It is not our task to solve complex issues in a short sermon. It is our task to help form consciences, to lay out issues with clarity, to suggest or even at times declare where the gospel applies. We cannot be content with glittering generalities, abstract principles. We need the courage for concrete directives, not only on issues of faith but also with regard to sociopolitical action by Christians in the world. What can we do, what can we say, to help establish right relationships in situations that make for terror?

Start with one haunting symbol of the gulf that severs the haves and the have-nots, the gulf that provokes the extreme fear we call terror, the gulf that is a seedbed of violence and crime. I mean hunger. The president of Bread for the World has put the situation bluntly:

The world has already made progress against hunger. There are fewer under-nourished people in the developing world today than there were 25 years ago, despite the population explosion. But more than 800 million people around the world still suffer from chronic hunger, and hunger has increased in Africa. And among the industrialized countries, the United States is the only nation that still puts up with widespread hunger: 31 million people in the United States still struggle to put food on the table.[14]

What can we do? We don't need new programs. Since 1996, millions have lost government assistance, especially food stamps. "If just the Food Stamp Program were as strong now as it was in 1996, in today's economy we'd have half as many hungry people as we do."[15] Our task? To pressure government to provide greater access to nutritional food through domestic programs that already exist. Such pressure is effective. Churches in Birmingham, Alabama, worked so effectively on their representative in Congress, Spencer Bachus, that during a hearing of the House Banking Committee on debt relief this Southern Baptist held up an address by John Paul II and said: "I've never read much by Catholics before, but I don't know how any Christian could read this and not think we ought to write off these debts. If we don't reduce this debt, people in poor countries are going to be suffering for the rest of their lives. And I think we are going to be suffering a lot longer than that."[16]

This, we must tell our people, is not simply human compassion, admirable as such compassion is. This is the biblical justice, the justice of God that Jesus will stress at the Last Judgment with his shattering decla-ration to those on his left, "*I* was hungry and you gave me no food," for "whatever you did not do for one of the least of these, you did not do for me" (Matt. 25:42a, 45 NIV). Inadequate we indeed are as individuals to feed a hungry country; but as the Body of Christ, millions upon millions of com-mitted Christians graced with the good things of God's earth, we can feed every hungry Christ from Maine to California. That is why I dare say to all Christians what a sympathetic Protestant said to a Roman Catholic, "If you could get your act together, you'd be dangerous."

Take another example that makes for extreme fear, for terror: our penal system. We can add our voices to those who want to replace the retribu-tive model of justice, basically a model that punishes, with the restorative, based on biblical justice, with a view to healing. The restorative model, which brings the offender and the victim together with mediators and rep-resentatives of the court, has begun to show promise in New Zealand, was used in South Africa by the Truth and Reconciliation Commission, and can point to early stages in about six hundred U.S. jurisdictions. Relationships are reestablished, sorrow is expressed, even forgiveness is possible.[17]

So it is with each instance, each situation, of terror. Our task as preach-ers of biblical justice? Raise awareness. Persuade our people to live four precepts fashioned by theologian Bernard Lonergan. (1) *Be attentive.* Know the data, the facts. It is Jesus' insistence, "Pay attention to what you hear" (Mark 4:24). (2) *Be intelligent.* Rid yourself of prejudices, of myths, of "This is what everybody says." (3) *Be reasonable.* Marshal the evidence, examine the opinions, judge with wisdom. Here community cooperation must replace the Lone Ranger. (4) *Be responsible.* "Do something; act on the basis of prudent judgments and genuine values."[18]

How do Christian men and women of biblical justice get that way? They are in close union with Christ our Lord. How shall we change our world, its rugged individualism, its excessive consumerism, its growing violence, its deep-rooted racism—yes, the terrorism in our culture? *We* shall not do it; *God* will do it, or it will not happen. And still, God will normally do it through us, through men and women whose dynamism for change is not their own naked humanity but the power of God. God needs us, but only because God wants to need us, wants humanity to cooperate with divinity in the love that saves a child, a family, a community, the world God's Son loved unto crucifixion. But remember, even our cooperation is grace, is a gift. If you are embarrassingly aware of your very human weakness, listen to St. Paul as he addresses not only the Christians of Corinth but today's Christians as well (1 Cor. 1:26–31):

> Consider your own calling, brothers and sisters: not many of you were wise by human standards, not many were powerful, not many were of noble birth. But God chose what is foolish in the world to shame the wise; God chose what is weak in the world to shame the strong; God chose what is low and despised in the world, things that are not, to reduce to nothing things that are, so that no one might boast in the presence of God. He is the source of your life in Christ Jesus, who became for us wisdom from God, and righteousness and sanctification and redemption, in order that, as it is written, "Let the one who boasts, boast in the Lord."

And you might add to God's call Paul's awareness of a gift that accompanies each call: "I can do all things through him who strengthens me" (Phil. 4:13).

17

The Tortured Christ

Jürgen Moltmann

The writer Jean Améry was only able to write about it twenty-two years after the fact: in 1943 he was taken prisoner and tortured by the SS in Belgium. His hands were tied behind his back and pulled up until his shoulders were dislocated, then he was whipped unceasingly. Writing about this experience, he said: "Beyond this no one can see into a world ruled by the principle of hope." Several years later he committed suicide. He was right: in the hell called torture, which destroys bodies and souls and shatters human personality, there is no hope. For this reason Dante placed a sign above hell's gates that read "Abandon every hope, all you who enter here." This also holds for torture chambers: no one leaves them intact; no one returns from them unchanged—not the victims of torture and certainly not the torturers.

How do people come to torture other people?

Religious Motives

Formerly I thought only personal sadism, terrorism, or wars in which "the ends justify the means" led to torture. The more I investigated, however, the more I recognized with alarm that torture can have religious motives. During the Iranian revolution under Khomeini it was said that the revolutionary guards wanted to torture and destroy the bodies of their enemies, whom they held to be God's enemies, in order to save their souls. I recall a film in which an Australian prisoner of war who had stolen a chicken from the Japanese commander was punished by being nailed to a door. This was justified as a means of cleansing his sinful soul. Similarly, it says in the Bible: "Punish him with the rod and save his soul from death" (Prov. 23:14, NIV). "It is better for you to lose one of your members than for your whole body to be thrown into hell" (Matt. 5:29b). Paul wanted to hand over a member of the church in Corinth "to Satan for the destruction of the flesh, so that his spirit may be saved in the day of the Lord" (1 Cor. 5:5). If we go a step further we arrive at the concepts of hell and its agonies that were developed in Christianity and Islam—for "hell" is nothing less than a religious version of the torture chamber. Biblical dictionaries define "hell" as the place "where the devils and the condemned must suffer eternal agony" (torture). According to the church father Cyrill, "hell is the land of death, empty of life; a region of darkness, void of light; an abyss filled with the sighs of the damned, who find no merciful ear to hear them; a depth out of which they cry miserably, meeting none who would be moved; where they ask mercy of all, yet are heard by no one; where all are abandoned and find no comforter." According to Gottfried Büchner's *Hand Concordance*, "All senses are tortured there: sight through eternal darkness, hearing through howling and chattering teeth, smell through the stench of sulfur, taste through the bitterness of eternal death, touch through eternal torture."

Such torture is endless; its fire is inextinguishable. No one ever returns from this hell. Tertullian thought the cries of the damned in the fiery pit enhanced the joy of the believers in heaven, a thought also to be found in eighteenth-century theology. It reflects a Christian revenge fantasy: just as the heathens rejoiced when Christian martyrs died in agony in the arena, Christians in heaven would rejoice at the heathens being tortured in hell.

We can all picture the apocalyptic delight and excruciating detail with which the torture of nonbelievers in hell was rendered in medieval paintings. Earthly torture chambers are finite physical agonies that at some point are put to an end by death, but cruel apocalyptic fantasies know no limits: the torture is to last eternally. No death arrives to deliver the dammed; the fire of the hellish stake burns "inextinguishably." In the collective imagination the two have mutually strengthened each other: earthly torture served to anticipate and thus prevent the eternal torture of hell, and eternal torture in hell was used to justify earthly torture. The hellish agonies of torture reserved for nonbelievers and the godless, conceived of with apocalyptic delight, were certainly the model for all methods of turning other people's lives into "hell." What seems to me particularly infamous is when the body is not even tortured in order to "save" the victim's soul, but instead, the bodily agonies of those burning and the agonies of the soul at judgment are described in gleeful detail. In this scheme, enmity is put to an end apocalyptically through the annihilation of all enemies, not by overcoming hostility through love as in Jesus' Sermon on the Mount. Whoever is against torture and protests against the lives of others being made into hell must be able to free himself or herself from apocalyptic friend/enemy thought patterns. As long as our religion contemplates a "hell" for God's enemies and for our enemies, there will continue to be direct and indirect justifications for earthly torture chambers.

Legal Motives

On the next level we find the religious justification of torture in *penal atonement* and in *punishment as deterrence.* In penal atonement, a degree of suffering is inflicted on the perpetrator equivalent to the suffering he or she has caused, an eye for an eye and a tooth for a tooth. At the core of the matter is not the perpetrator him or herself, but rather the divine world order that has been damaged through the perpetrator's action and that now must be restored through atonement. Through the perpetrator's penalty something cosmically important takes place. The punishment involves what is dear to the perpetrator: in former times this was the body; in European modernity, personal freedom. This is why imprisonment has replaced physical torture. Whoever has suffered a long imprisonment knows how very much the loss of freedom can demolish a person psychologically and physically. Because it was formerly thought that atonement had cosmic dimensions affecting the restoration of a divinely instituted world order, punishment took place publicly. Originally it was not meant as a public festival but rather as a kind of open-air worship service of the people, directed toward appeasing the deity and putting heaven in a favorable mood.

Deterrence is always related to penal atonement and consisted in the public torture of a criminal. The public torture was meant to deter potential criminals, but also to oppress political and social rebellion on the part of subjugated peoples. It was a means of public terrorism directed against conquered peoples. The torture of the Roman cross, as a result of which Christ died in full public view, was the penalty for insurrection against the *"Pax Romana"* and for the rebellion on the part of slaves. After the Spartacus insurrection, seven thousand crosses hung with dying slaves lined the *Via Appia.* The public mass executions carried out by the German army of occupation during the Second World War, especially in Poland and Russia, also served to terrorize subjugated peoples. The same thing is happening today in the Balkans. Whoever opposes torture and its abolishment must also give up penal atonement and punishment as deterrence.

Profane Motives

Do the ends justify the means? This question also touches on the religious sphere, if only at its boundaries, as the German version of the saying illustrates: "Do the ends *sanctify* the means?" Is it allowable to torture prisoners of war in order to extract information? Is this merely a matter of whose interests prevail, or are there limits which never are to be violated under any circumstances? Is there an end that justifies the means of torture, or does the means of torture discredit every end so much that it can no longer be a human end? Many people, not only soldiers or police officers, point to exceptional situations they believe justify the use of torture in order to extract vital information. But can a government permit the violation of its ends through the means of torture without losing its self-esteem? Ends that "sanctify" the means of torture lose their sanctity, i.e., they become "profane" and are no longer ends for which it is worth living. Every government needs this self-respect because its legitimacy depends upon it. The Germany in whose name the Nazis committed gruesome tortures for twelve years lost all of its splendor in our eyes. A government that tortures cannot be a "Fatherland."

Governments whose splendor is their constitution, whose value is based on respect for human dignity and human rights, cannot permit torture, not even in exceptional situations. Even if it seems justified in a particular case, an absolute limit exists because the very basis of the democratic constitutional state is at stake. A soldier or police officer who tortures other persons in the name of the government destroys it rather than protects it.

Personal Motives

Among torturers and those who are willing to engage in torture, it is possible to find people whose motivations are perverse, people who enjoy raping and inflicting pain, who are carried away by the dizziness of power to the point of shattering other people's lives by imposing their will upon them. Apparently the chance to torture others attracts sadists, but many other forms of daily sadism also exist: not only officially sanctioned torturers are sadists. On the other hand, not all concentration camp guards in Nazi Germany who enjoyed torturing helpless prisoners were sadists. Even worse were those who seemed totally devoid of feeling, who were "only doing their duty," as they put it, who felt "bound to obey." The professional machinery of systematic torture and murder is perhaps even more terrifying than perversities of sadism because it can capture any of us once we begin to ignore our personal conscience or allow others to decide for us.

Whoever opposes torture and wants to abolish it must see to it that sadists do not get a chance to act and make sure that personal conscience prevails over so-called "emergency orders" or the "power of the circumstances," which are so often mentioned as justification for torture.

261

The Tortured Christ Is the Brother of All Victims of Torture

The story of a passion occupies the center of the Christian faith: the story of the betrayed, renounced, tortured, crucified Christ. No other religion has a tortured figure at its center. This has provoked the abhorrence of many aesthetes, from Cicero to Goethe, but it has also evoked the sympathy of empathetic people. The powerlessness and abandonment of the crucified Christ stirs our compassion, just as does the helpless child in the manger. What does the crucified Christ have to do with our topic? Does his torture justify the torture of Christians or the torture of Christianity's enemies here on earth or—particularly—in hell? Does the tortured Christ signify the end of all torture because he is the end of every religious or secular justification for torture?

Pilate "had Jesus flogged," as Matthew, Mark, and John tersely put it in their stories of the Passion. The commentaries remark: "Flogging was one of the most serious punishments among the Jews. The wrongdoer was bound naked to a pole and was beaten with a bent whip by a court servant exercising all his strength. The Jews never allowed the number of lashes to exceed thirty-nine; Romans set no limits." Why did they carry out such beatings before the execution? Apparently it was meant to break the victims' physical and mental resistance and perhaps also to weaken them in order to shorten their death agony.

The Gospels tell the story of Christ's Passion in great detail, but show neither masochistic delight in suffering nor strive to awaken pity. They tell the story as God's story: God with us, accompanying us in our suffering and in our torments; God for us, inasmuch as we are guilty. They speak of the solidarity of the incarnate God who is with us to the death, and tell also of God our representative, who takes our place.

Reading the story of Christ's Passion from this point of view, we discover his progressive self-emptying, which involves a loss of human and then also of divine relationships. His male disciples flee after his arrest by the Romans, one of them betrays him, another denies him, the rest distance themselves from him. All of this meant a loss of identity as master and teacher.

Jesus was crucified "outside the gates" of the holy city. The Romans crucified him as an enemy of the *Imperium Romanum* and therefore—according to their understanding—as an enemy of the human race (this was a pretext also used later to persecute Christians). This meant a loss of identity as a person. He died with the shout "My God, why have you forsaken me?"

The story of the Passion is the story of Christ emptying himself to the depths of misery. If this Christ is not just any person among many others, but rather the Messiah, Israel's liberator and the redeemer of the human race, then his story expresses first of all God's solidarity with all victims of violence and torture: Christ's cross stands among the countless crosses which line the ways of the powerful and the violent, from Spartacus to the concentration camps. His suffering does not rob dignity from the suffering of others. Rather, his suffering takes its place fraternally alongside theirs as a symbol of the fact that God participates in our suffering and bears our pain. Among the countless, anonymous victims of torture, the "suffering servant of God" is always to be found. They are his comrades in suffering because he became one of them in his suffering. The tortured Christ looks at us with the eyes of one who has suffered torture. This is what the fifty-nine-year-old Archbishop Oscar Arnulfo Romero of San Salvador discovered: "In the eyes of his tortured, oppressed people he saw the disfigured countenance of the crucified God."

The crucified Jesus became the brother of all crucified people. That is the way in which he is the Son of Man and the redeemer of humankind. He does not help us through miracles by virtue of his superior powers, but rather through his wounds on the strength of his very powerlessness: "Only the suffering God can help," wrote Dietrich Bonhoeffer in his Gestapo cell, recognizing Christ as his brother in his moment of need. The suffering God helps through his communion with the victims of torture: "If I make my bed in hell, behold, you are there." Certainly not every victim of torture feels this subjectively, not even Christians. Without any doubt, the "dark night of the soul" also descends on the torture chambers and on the solitary confinement cells. Sometimes all direction is lost in the darkness, all feeling dried up. But objectively, the tortured Christ is present in all victims of torture and the godforsaken Christ is present in those forsaken by God. This brings us back to the topic of hell. Formerly the Apostles' Creed read "he descended to hell, on the third day he rose from the dead. . . ." When and how did Christ experience hell? According to an ancient interpretation, he suffered hell after his death, when he descended to the underworld of the dead in order to preach the gospel of redemption to them. Luther thought that Christ experienced hell in dying, between Gethsemane and Golgotha, when he tasted the bitterness of abandonment by God.

Both explanations complement each other: the dying Christ, betrayed, abandoned, tortured, lonely, afraid, experienced in his own body and in his own soul that which we call "hell." The Christ who went to the dead and took salvation to them has been resurrected to eternal life. Therefore not only "death" has been swallowed up by victory: hell, too, has been robbed of its sting.

What we experience as "hell" has been transformed objectively since Christ's descent into hell. There is someone who brought hope into hell: Dante has been disproved. There is someone who has opened up hell's gates and led out the dead, as is illustrated by every Easter icon in the Ortho-dox churches. If "hell" is the place where God's abandonment is located, ever since Christ's descent into hell it has ceased to exist. If devilish tor-mentors once triumphed in hell over human beings, they have been robbed of their victory ever since the resurrection of the dead Christ. "I do believe in hell," said Berdyayev, "but I don't believe there is anyone in there." I say that because Christ was in hell, no one in hell can be without hope. In that case, "hell" can no longer mean for the Christian faith what it once was, namely, an everlasting religious torture chamber. Its gates are open, its walls are shattered, the trumpet blast of liberation is already resound-ing in it. Whoever clings to Christ neither fears "hell" nor threatens oth-ers with hell's torture. Believers will tell whoever still feels bound to speak of hell for biblical reasons: "Where, O hell is your victory?! Thanks be to God, who gives us the victory through our Lord Jesus Christ" (1 Cor. 15:57).

The Resurrected Christ Is the Judge of All Torturers

In former times, torture took place publicly and the corpses were left lying in the open air as a deterrent. Today, torture takes place secretly, behind closed doors, and the corpses "disappear"; they are buried or burned so that no one can find traces of them nor remember their names. The mur-derers want to avoid all possibility of future accusation and prosecution. This is why it has been so difficult to find traces of the disappeared in Argentina and Chile. Already at the end of the Second World War, Himm-ler had concentration camp victims dug up again and the corpses burned in order to obliterate their traces.

"Resurrection" also means that the dead return, those who lived in the past rise up, and the nameless are called by name. Judgment consists in this: the murderers will not triumph over their victims in the end and tor-turers will be called to account for their actions. Even people who no longer believe in a personal God have this longing for justice and understand that resurrection means that the dead will experience justice. For Christians, the resurrected Christ is the Firstborn in the resurrection of the dead, the leader, and therefore also the initiator of divine judgment on torturers and murderers. It is understandable that the victims and their descendants say, "After Auschwitz we can no longer speak of God." But the perpetrators and their descendants should rather say, "We must talk about God after Auschwitz because we stand under his judgment." To claim "God is dead" in such a situation is merely an attempt to avoid responsibility. God ensures justice for the victims of violence and God judges the perpetrators of vio-lence. Otherwise it would be impossible for a world of peace ever to become reality.

In his book *The Sunflower*, Simon Wiesenthal reports that as a prisoner in a concentration camp, he was called to the deathbed of a SS man who wanted to confess to him as a Jew that he had participated in mass shootings and burnings of Jews. Wiesenthal was unable to speak and left in silence, but the question stayed with him. His story has been published together with the answers of many European politicians, philosophers, and theologians. They make it clear that no one can forgive a guilty person in the name of his dead victims. It is furthermore clear that there can be no reparation for such a past. In order for someone to be able to live at all burdened by such guilt, atonement is necessary. Without forgiveness of guilt, those who acknowledge their guilt cannot live, for they lose their entire self-respect. There can be no forgiveness of guilt without atonement, yet atonement is not a human possibility. No human being could possibly atone for such injustice, but can God provide atonement?

The sacrifice for atonement was part of the old covenant. God provided a scapegoat so that the sins of the people could be transferred onto the animal and carried off into the desert, away from the people. In the Jerusalem temple there were equivalent rituals of atonement. The prophet Isaiah (chapter 53) had his vision of the suffering servant of God, who takes away the sins of the people. In these examples it is always God himself who has mercy on the sinners and carries their guilt away. God himself is the atonement for the people.

How does this occur? God transforms human guilt into divine suffering by "bearing" human guilt. This is what the new covenant in the blood of Jesus Christ is about. Through his Passion and his death on the cross, Christ becomes not only the brother of the victims but also the vicarious atonement for the perpetrators. "You who bear the sins of the world, have mercy upon us." This prayer joins us to all perpetrators and brings us into the sphere of divine mercy. Mercy is a kind of love that overcomes its own injuries, that bears the suffering produced by guilt, and that steadfastly holds on to the object of its love.

Victims of injustice have a long memory, for the traces of their suffering are deeply engraved. Perpetrators have short memories: they do not know and do not wish to know what they have done. They depend on the victims if they are to be converted from death into life. One cannot offer one's victims reconciliation, but one can cooperate in setting signs of atonement through service for peace, working toward recovering one's self-respect.

If Christ is the torturers' judge, they are confronted in him with a victim of torture. In the hour of truth, all masks fall and the torturers come to know themselves as they really are. Their judgment consists of this. If Christ is their judge, then they are faced with him "who bears the sins of the world." This is the hour of justice that creates new life. What can *we* do for torturers? To be honest, nothing at all. We can leave them alone in silence and relinquish them to God's wrath. We can make them aware of the fact that Christ, whom they have tortured and murdered in their victims, is their divine judge. We can include them in this prayer: "You who bear the sins of the world, have mercy upon us." To put it simply, we must leave them to God and should play "god" toward them neither for good nor for evil. To condemn them or to forgive them is not our task.

When injustice occurs massively, when no alternatives seem to be in sight, a sense of familiarity sets in, both in the minds of the victims and of the perpetrators. How can we recover from this apathetic state, which is one of our cultural ills? I remember how I always became painfully aware of the barbed wire in POW camp when a group of prisoners was allowed to return home. The breath of freedom that blew into camp on those occasions made us quite ill. When freedom is near, our chains begin to chafe. When hunger and thirst for righteousness are awakened in us, we no longer want to accept injustice but rather fight against it. Let us, therefore, strengthen our will to live our own lives and promote the lives of other people, the life of all of creation. In doing this we will find that our resistance against torture will grow. Let us hunger and thirst for righteousness and teach others to do so as well. Then injustice will be perceived as such, exposed and rejected.

18

Terror and the Children of God: A Meditation on Fear and Ministry with Inner City Youth

Harold Dean Trulear

On the evening of that first day of the week, when the disciples were together, with the doors locked for fear of the Jews, Jesus came and stood among them and said, "Peace be with you!" After he said this, he showed them his hands and side. The disciples were overjoyed when they saw the Lord.

Again Jesus said, "Peace be with you! As the Father has sent me, I am sending you." And with that he breathed on them and said, "Receive the Holy Spirit. If you forgive anyone his sins, they are forgiven; if you do not forgive them, they are not forgiven."

Now Thomas (called Didymus), one of the Twelve, was not with the disciples when Jesus came. So the other disciples told him, "We have seen the Lord!" But he said to them, "Unless I see the nail marks in his hands and put my finger where the nails were, and put my hand into his side, I will not believe it."

John 20:19–25 (NIV)

I don't know what they were doing there. I wish I knew. I wish knew what they were doing in that room, that room with the doors locked—doors locked "for fear of the Jews." I know that we know who they were. They were Jesus' disciples, maybe even former disciples at this point. Their leader had been captured, arrested, and executed. They figured they were next.

That tells us the "why" of why they were there. They were in fear. Fear of capture. Fear of arrest. Fear of execution. Fear of the Jews.

Not just any Jews, mind you. New Testament scholar and Payne Seminary president Obery M. Hendricks reminds us that the disciples were Jews themselves. Hendricks claims that John's use of the term "the Jews" was a clear indictment of religious and political power and its abuse by those in charge. It is the temple establishment that brings fear. It is the institutional pressure to maintain the prerogatives of power that brings fear. It is the all-too-human quest to routinize and reify the status quo on behalf of the reigning order that brings fear. It is the active pursuit of all dissent that threatens the existing order that brings fear. "The Jews," offers Hendricks, is a phrase John uses just as African-Americans have talked about "white folks," "The Man," and "Mister Charlie." These terms have much more to do with power and its oppressive abuse than it does with a person or a people.

So they locked themselves in a room out of fear. They had lived with a certain amount of fear for much of their adult lives. They knew about, and perhaps some of their families experienced, the attack on young Hebrew children after the birth of Jesus, how the establishment came after any "pretenders to the throne," killing in the name of the status quo. The Rachel who wept inconsolably after that first night of the "Holy Innocents" could have been their mother, their aunt, their grandmother, weeping like an inner-city mother lamenting the slaying of her son, whether by rival drug dealers controlling turf or uniformed representatives of the establishment. They knew something about fear.

John reminds us in the seventh chapter of his Gospel that the fear factor was a community phenomenon. After the Feast of Tabernacles, people gathered to secretly discuss the identity of Jesus, but "no one would speak openly about him for fear of the Jews" (v. 13). They knew something about fear. So here they are—locked in a room because of fear. I wish I knew what they were doing in that room. It would help me understand more about fear, about terror, about the ways in which we behave when the fear factor looms largest. It would help me make sense of the response of oppressed people when fear so grips them that they absent themselves from the fray and retreat to a place of some temporary safety. It would help me understand the response of some of my friends, your friends, and loved ones who are locked in their upper rooms of fear.

You may ask what this has to do with ministry with urban youth, city youth in general, and the work some of you do with high-risk kids in particular. You may strain to see the parallels between the fear of the disciples and the tough, hardened outlook of street kids. But there's no strain; you know the deal. Behind the tough exterior is an impressionable interior. Beneath the bravado of *gangsta* is the burden of grief. Behind the macho mask is a fragile face. Beneath the confrontational front is the *Imago Dei* stamped within the child, the children of God whose response to fear is to fight fire with fire, and who bring their own brand of fear.

That's why I want to know what the disciples were doing behind closed doors. That's why I want to know what was going on in that room with the doors locked. That's why I want to know the activities of those barricaded within a temporary sanctuary for fear of those who controlled "the real sanctuary." Were they plotting an escape? Were they trying to figure out a way to move on from Jerusalem without being picked up by "five–0"? Were they praying, turning to a higher power like so many rappers do when they get "paid" for a successful record or "pained" by a rival's bullet? Were they finger pointing, turning on each other like East Coast–West Coast rivals? Were they blaming one another for their plight, deriding Peter for false *machismo,* taunting Simon Zealots for not being revolutionary enough, "playa-hatin'" John for not doing something while he witnessed their boy go down on Calvary? Were they strengthening their bond of solidarity under these toughest of times, vowing to "go down together" if need be, rather than letting any one of them hang alone as they had Jesus? I want to know what they were doing in that room— that locked room.

I know what my kids do in those locked rooms. You know it, too. You may not have thought of them as the terrified occupants of barricaded space, but as you think about it, it's fairly easy to see. They, too, have known fear all of their lives. They were raised in neighborhoods where many are afraid to tread, except when they commute in to collect rent on an old property or pay tithes in their home church. They fear the future with its bleak promises. They fear success at school, for fear it will alienate them from friends in the 'hood. They fear the system and its offers of acceptance that seem duplicitous when held up to the scrutiny of how that system's representatives accept, don't accept, ignore, or even exploit them. They fear each other as they develop a bald sense of the tribalism that has come to characterize so much of this country in its reaction to growing diversity, and turn on each other in a display of internalized oppression. They fear streets and alleys, corridors in schools, and places where it's "not safe," all the while realizing that if they do have opportunity to move to other safe spaces, they will be regarded with suspicion and hostility. They are locked in rooms for fear of the powers, both as they exist outside of them and have become internalized within them. This is a real fear. Like the disciples, they learned it early. They are the children who attended the summer camp for "underprivileged children" in western Pennsylvania, who surprised their counselors when, after a stiff breeze blew through the oak tree above their cabin, dropped to the floor and rolled under tables and cots. When their counselors asked what happened, they were told that the youngsters had been trained in their households to "hit the floor" whenever they heard gun-

269

shots, and the rattling noises of the acorns falling on the roof brought about an immediate Pavlovian response to the sound of danger.

They lock themselves in rooms filled with a music whose bold declarations of self-affirmation through money and madness mirror an insecurity produced by hopelessness. To offer sexuality, whether promiscuous or prowess or both, as a manner of self-affirmation points to the warning Cornel West offered in *Prophetic Fragments* almost two decades ago.[1] West noted that popular African-American music had been steeped in a tradition of relationships. The lyrics, from the blues to R&B, posited the idea that relationships mattered—someone cares, whether a friend, lover, momma, or whomever. Even if you had "found love on a two way street and lost it on a lonely highway," it was evidence that relationships were possible, even more, something to be valued.

They lock themselves in bad relationships, seeking protection through gangs who promise to take care of them and their families. Their gang becomes a family that offers a livelihood and a life, bonding and brothering, safety and security. That's why I wonder if the disciples were working on solidarity issues: sometimes the response to fear is to group together, to come together, for safety and security. Gangs do that, and we've known that ever since Lewis Yablonsky's classic study of violent gangs some forty years ago when he first offered the notion that gangs are families. They offer the security for which we all long; it is a part of our humanness, our need for relationality that is part of the *Imago Dei* of a triune God.

I was reminded of this when visiting the ministry of an ex-gang leader in Detroit, Michigan. Alex Montaner had found God while in prison, and returned to his neighborhood on early release. Convinced that his release was an act of grace, he and his parish priest developed the GRACE program: Gang Retirement And Continuing Education and Employment. When Montaner went to negotiate space for his program among the rival gangs, he was met with skepticism. But the tension was not over the issue of "gang retirement," that is, getting youth out of gangs; rather it was over whether young people who left the gangs would receive the care they needed without the protection and relationships of the gangs. They asked Montaner if he and the GRACE program would be able to make sure that their recruits from among the local gang membership received the protection and provision that gangs give to those who feel helpless before the powers that be. The gang leaders told Montaner he had to provide three things for anyone who wanted to leave a gang and join his program. First, anyone entering GRACE who wanted to complete their education had to get their high school diploma or GED. Second, they had to be provided with a good job (no minimum wage dead-end position where the most difficult task might be asking, "Do you want fries with that?"). Third, the job offered would have to have a benefit package. When I asked Montaner where that last and surprising request came from, he offered that gang leaders knew that health care was an issue for the poor and they provided financial support for medical expenses for gang members. Who knew that OGs (original gangsters) knew anything about HMOs? The gang was a family; Montaner's ministry had to provide for its recruits like a family as well.

Here is the entrance for the emissary of Christ. Here is the opening for the ministry. Behold, here is the opportunity for the church to be the family for the fearful, the sanctuary for the scared, and the safe territory for the terrorized. Montaner comes into the room, moves behind the locked doors, and offers something. Montaner's agreement to provide education, jobs, and benefits is the key. It is the key because it involves the essential elements of Jesus' response to the fear of his disciples who sat locked behind the doors.

First, Jesus comes to them in the room. The doors are locked, but Jesus comes in anyway; miraculously and surprisingly, he appears. Miles Jones, professor of homiletics at Virginia Union University names it thus, "Jesus keeps showing up!" He is the Christ who "shows up." Storms on your boat? Look out on the water, Jesus shows up. Disease in your family? Look by the bedside, Jesus shows up. Sitting by the Bethesda pool waiting for the angel to trouble the waters? Look on the portico, Jesus shows up. Standing by an empty tomb wondering where they've taken the body belonging to your help from ages past? Look in the garden, Jesus shows up. Locked in a room because of fear? Through the barricades designed to keep out the powerful, Jesus shows up. Montaner showed up in the community. Jesus shows up in the community. Where the powerful cannot go with their dilapidated textbooks, failed social programs, and minimum wage jobs, Jesus shows up. He shows up every time you show up, not just on Sunday for a commuter's worship, but as a trust-building presence that offers again the same peace he offered prior to the crucifixion, a peace that cannot be taken away, legislated out of existence, ended by budget cuts, stopped by a change in administrations, thwarted by self-interested taxpayer revolts, dashed by the abandonment of historic institutions, or crushed by the exodus of a sanctuary-seeking middle class. It is a lasting peace, and if the disciples have forgotten its existence, Jesus shows up to remind them.

This offer of peace is the second key element to the Montaners and all who would go into those locked rooms in the name of the one who shows up. Peace, shalom, wholeness, healing, and the opportunity for the larger life that the Spirit gives is the offer Jesus puts on the table. They can't overcome fear without it, can't defeat the terror apart from it, can't confront the powerful unless it takes a hold of them and puts them on solid footing. The wholeness Montaner offers includes jobs, education, and benefits. That's important security for young people raised to hit the floor when acorns hit the roof. It demonstrates that this is not just another empty promise but a lasting commitment. The terrified need assurance that something and someone will be there for them with what they need in that very moment, for their safety and security. For young gang members, a relationship with Montaner and his "deliverables" of jobs, education, and benefits is the down payment on such security. For disciples in a locked room, the need is for peace.

GRACE's deliverables are peace-filled. But most important, they are rooted in the power of the only one who can guarantee peace and wholeness through victory over a death cheered on by the very power structure of which the disciples had been afraid. When we offer that peace to these young people, they are changed. When they get a hold of this peace that passes all human understanding, they are made new. When this peace gets a hold of them, they come out of that locked room and preach a gospel of peace, even in the face of powerful opposition.

I wish I knew what they had been doing in that locked room. But God be praised, I know what they did when they came out. They preached until thousands came to know the power they had been given. They looked at a lame man and said, "Silver and gold, have I none, but such as I have, give I unto you. In the name of Jesus, rise up and walk." They prayed in prisons until the dungeons shook. They overcame prejudice to take their message to the Gentiles. They walked through town with divine pharmacies in their shadows. They ministered to the poor and anointed the sick. They offered accounts of Jesus' life in word and deed. They endured hardships, opposition, and martyrdom, and the only locked rooms they faced now needed keys from the other side, and even that couldn't stop angels from ministering to them. They turned a world upside down because Jesus met their fear with peace. God grant that we might receive that same peace and move beyond the locked doors that threaten to imprison us all. May we watch the formerly fearful move in the power of God.

19

God Hears Their Cries; God Dries Their Tears

Jacqueline J. Lewis-Tillman

Thus says the Lord: I will return to Zion, and will dwell in the midst of Jerusalem; Jerusalem shall be called the faithful city, and the mountain of the Lord of hosts shall be called the holy mountain. Thus says the Lord of hosts: Old men and old women shall again sit in the streets of Jerusalem each with staff in hand because of their great age. And the streets of the city shall be full of boys and girls playing in its streets. Thus says the Lord of hosts: Even though it seems impossible to the remnant of this people in these days, should it also seem impossible to me, says the Lord of hosts? They shall be my people and I will be their God, in faithfulness and in righteousness.

Zechariah 8:3–6, 8b[1]

Then I saw a new heaven and a new earth; for the first heaven and the first earth had passed away, and the sea was no more. And I heard a loud voice from the throne saying, "See the home of God is among mortals. He will dwell with them as their God; they will be his peoples and God himself will be with them; he will wipe every tear from their eyes. Death will be no more; mourning and crying and pain will be no more, for the first things have passed away." And the one who was seated on the throne said, "See I am making all things new."

Revelation 21:1, 3–5[2]

Brianna didn't like it at the new house. It was crowded, and it made her feel afraid. So she curled up in a corner, all by herself, while the other children fought for space, food, and air in the cramped and dreary home. Mommy Charisse said that "they" gave her the wrong kids; they should have given her back the older ones. Even so, she said it was better for Brianna to be here than to be with the Spanish people at the foster home. Brianna cried. Mama and Poppy were fun at the other house. The tree was pretty and had a lot of lights. Brianna and her little sister shared a pink room. Sitting on Santa's lap, taking baths together, and story time seemed far away now. At this new house Mommy and the mean lady yelled and made Brianna's head hurt. Brianna cried, and they said, "Shut up, stupid. You're gettin' on my last nerves. Make somebody sick." And they punched her, and they put cold things around her wrists so she could not move.

Brianna cried, once again.

One day the mean lady wanted to comb Brianna's hair. It hurt, so Brianna kept moving around. "Be still before I hurt you. Stop crying before I give you something to cry about." The belt stung Brianna's butt, arms, and back. Then the blows came faster and harder. She screamed when the mean lady took her head and smashed it against the table.

Brianna stopped crying.

Brianna was twenty-three months old when she died. She was the eighth child born to Charisse, a woman with an IQ of fifty-eight, and herself a victim of childhood abuse. The "system" intervened and took Charisse's children. It failed when they were returned to her just before Christmas last year. The flow of Brianna's tears could not wash away all that is diseased and rotting about the child welfare system in cities like Washington, D.C., nor can they cleanse systems all over the world that oppress God's children.[3]

Children are hungry in New York and in New Delhi. They dodge bullets in Israel and in Sudan. They are homeless in Chiappas and in Chicago. They are abused in Washington and in Bosnia.

Children are crying.

Young people need better schools and cleaner air and water. They need better health and dental care. They need safe communities and warm homes. They are poor, hopeless, and heartbroken. They are afraid.

Hear them crying?

Little girls are abandoned outdoors in China and sold into slavery in Ghana. Children in the Dominican Republic have playgrounds that are streets in which raw sewage flows. Young Israeli and Palestinian boys are taught early a zealous hatred that causes them to lose limbs and even their lives.

Hear them crying? See their tears?

When babies cry, when children are hurting, it feels to me like time stands still. It's as though nothing should happen until the child is comforted and consoled.

On some middle class street, in a softly lit home, baby Jane cries, and mommy stirs to go care for her. She rubs her back or nurses her to sleep again. On some farm, little boy Jon cries, and daddy moves to comfort him. He is scooped off the ground, cradled in his arms, and rocked gently until

274

the pain is eased and his ego repaired. In some classroom, young Curtis is teased by his classmates. His teacher spots choked-back tears and keeps him after class to reassure him.

This is the kind of "good enough" care about which psychologist D. W. Winnicott writes.[4] We can't stop our children from experiencing hurt, but we show up to wipe tears, to bandage knees, to encourage self-esteem. Good enough care responds to the child's need for food, clothing, and shelter. Good enough care mirrors to the child that she or he is good and capable, and provides safety enough that engenders trust in the world and in the child's own abilities. Good enough care responds to cries. It dries tears and solves problems.

Some children cry, and it seems as though no one shows up. Who hears the cries of the world's poor children? Who dries the tears of the abandoned, hopeless, hungry, suffering children of our world? Who cares enough to give good enough care? It may at times seem impossible for us to save the world's poor and disenfranchised children. We hear them cry. We see their tears. It is all so daunting. It may seem a task too overwhelming, too unwieldy. Depressed by it all, we remain passive and uninvolved. "What can I do?" we wonder.

We cry the tears of the overwhelmed, the despondent, the helpless. We feel forsaken and abandoned ourselves as we seek to understand where God is in all of this. When and how will God come to save? Surely God sees, surely God hears. Surely God cares enough to come, to save, to heal. Does God see our tears? *Thus says the Lord of hosts: Even though it seems impossible to the remnant of this people in these days, should it also seem impossible to me, says the Lord of hosts?*

These are assuring words from Zechariah's prophesy. When Haggai and Zechariah were prophesying, Cyrus, the Persian king, had conquered Babylon and freed the captive Israelites there.[5] These two prophets encouraged the rebuilding of the temple, the purifying of worship, and the purifying of the community. They believed that when these things happened, God would usher in the wonderful Messianic age where God's people would be blessed with fruitfulness and prosperity, and Israel would be restored to its place of leadership among the nations. What seemed impossible to a despondent, captive people—away from their homeland and unable to worship their God—was indeed possible, declared Zechariah. Returning to God, purifying one's self and one's worship, would lead to God's return.[6] That meant restoration and wholeness for God's people. That meant God attending to the tears of God's people. Zechariah's prophesy spoke of safe places for the vulnerable in the community, the very old and the very young. *Thus says the Lord of hosts: Old men and old women shall again sit in the streets of Jerusalem, each with staff in hand because of their great age. And the streets of the city shall be full of boys and girls playing in its streets.*

What Zechariah wrote some five hundred years before the birth of Christ is echoed in John's vision of the second coming of the Messiah. He also wrote of the kingdom age as one of restoration and healing.[7]

See the home of God is among mortals. God will dwell with them, they will be his people and God himself will be with them. God will wipe every tear from their eyes. Death will be no more; mourning and crying and pain will be no more, for the first things have passed away.

Like Isaiah before him, John's vision described the kingdom age as bringing about the renewal of creation. A new heaven and a new earth meant for all of creation freedom from imperfections and transformation by the glory of God. God would no longer need to be worshiped in a tabernacle; God would dwell among God's people.[8] The nearness and intimacy of God's care includes wiping away every tear from the eyes of God's people. God cares enough to come close by, close enough to nurture, to comfort, to heal. That is good enough care.

Zechariah and John proclaim a quickly coming reign of God. No more death. No more mourning and crying and pain. No more tears. Old people will be sitting in the streets. City streets will be full of boys and girls playing.

God hears the cries of poor children. God sees their tears.

And God comes.

Comes as a baby himself. Eats. Sleeps. Laughs. Plays. Cries.

Grows, teaches, preaches, prays, plays. Rests, heals, weeps.

Dies, rises from the dead.

Lives. In you. In me.

Equipping. Restoring. Listening. Healing.

God hears the cries of poor children. God sees their tears. God comforts, heals, and dries their tears. When we return to God, God returns to us.

Here is something we can do, something very important, a critical work on behalf of our children: Return to God. The one who testifies to these things says, "Surely I am coming soon. Amen! Come Lord Jesus!" (Rev. 22:20). Amen!

Come Lord Jesus, soon. Even as we come to you.

Let us hasten to return to our God, who hears the cries of poor children and who dries their tears. Amen.

Self-Denial for Racists and Their Victims in Japan: A Homily

Andrew Sung Park

> Then Jesus told his disciples, "If any want to become my followers, let them deny themselves and take up their cross and follow me. For those who want to save their life will lose it, and those who lose their life for my sake will find it. For what will it profit them if they gain the whole world but forfeit their life? Or what will they give in return for their life?"
>
> Matthew 16:24–26

Introduction

We hear about racism in the U.S. and European countries, but are rarely informed about racism in Japan—more accurately speaking, ethnocentrism in Japan. Most permanent residents have suffered from discrimination against them. Ninety percent of the foreign residents are Koreans.[1] I will focus on Japanese ethnocentrism against ethnic peoples, particularly Koreans. The aim is to explore the reality of ethnocentrism and challenge Japan to rectify its biased practice in light of self-denial. In addition, by discussing Japanese ethnocentrism and suggesting its possible resolution, we may have an opportunity to reflect upon U.S. racism from a more detached perspective.

The Terror of Japanese Ethnocentrism

Japan has ethnic groups; among them the major groups are Ainu, an indigenous people concentrated in Hokkaido in northern Japan, and ethnic Koreans who were brought to Japan during its colonization of Korea. Japan annexed Ainu Moshiri in 1868 and renamed it "Hokkaido" in 1889. To assimilate the Ainu into Japanese society, the Hokkaido Former Aboriginal Protection Act was declared in 1899. Ainu language and culture were forbidden. The Ainu, however, have survived. Japan acknowledged to the United Nations in 1991 that the Ainu were indigenous to the land. Later, the Japanese government refused to acknowledge the Ainu as indigenous people, however, for an internal report in 1996 warned that if the Ainu were acknowledged as indigenous people, they would take the chance to reassert their sovereignty, claim land rights and the restoration of their resources, and call for recompense for the crimes of colonization.[2]

In 1910 Japan subjugated Korea. Japanese colonial policy against Korea was extremely cruel. They banned the usage of the Korean language, changed Korean names into Japanese, and appropriated and exported much of the Korean rice to Japan. Since 1939, many Koreans had been brought to Japan to serve as forced labor in Japanese mines and factories. By the end of World War II in 1945, there were an estimated 2,300,000 ethnic Koreans. With the war's end in August 1945, about 600,000 Koreans had little choice but to remain in Japan.

On April 28, 1952, with the San Francisco Peace Treaty, the Japanese government unilaterally deprived Korean residents of their Japanese nationality, stating that until their status was decided legally, they could remain residents in Japan without having obtained resident qualification, thus pushing their status into legal limbo.[3] This act is more evil than the Japanese-American internment in terms of pulling the rug out from under them, stripping people of their citizenship arbitrarily. Furthermore, the Alien Registration Law forced Korean residents to succumb to fingerprinting, a procedure required of criminals. Today the majority of young ethnic Koreans are second or third generation. Nevertheless, as a result of anti-foreign government policies, they have been treated as foreign residents. Many are not naturalized Japanese and have been denied the rights and status of full citizenship. An estimated one percent of the 120 million people in Japan are either North or South Korean nationals, or Japanese nationals of Korean descent.[4]

Counterterror

To change a racist or ethnocentric society, it is essential for us to focus on the asset of self-denial. In following Jesus, self-denial is stressed. Whoever wishes to keep one's life safe will lose it; whoever loses his or her life for Christ's sake will find it. Self-denial is the way to life. Can we raise this principle of self-denial to a social level? I believe that the rule of self-denial can be applied to races and nations, too. It is inescapable for races or nations to deny themselves if they desire to find their true selves. This is the reason why the past great cultural groups and civilizations declined and faded away. According to Arnold Toynbee, they declined because they failed to respond successfully to challenges—human and environmental. A challenge of history is a group self-denial.

In the U.S., Asian-Americans are working together to fight racism. In Asia, Asians are divided and discriminate against each other. Japan is the place where nationalism and ethnocentrism are conspicuous. If individuals are racists, it is rather easy to notice their racism. But if the whole nation is racist, it is very difficult to detect the spirit of racism from inside. This may be the reason why a race or a nation easily fails to meet the challenge of just history. It is sometimes necessary to wake a race or a nation from outside when it is submerged in racism.

Self-denial should be interpreted from two different perspectives: from the perspective of the sinners and from their victims. There are four levels of self-denial for both of them. To find their own lives, undergoing self-denial is unavoidable for both groups.

First, self-denial means acknowledging the reality of racism or ethnocentrism. To the victims of ethnocentrism, self-denial means to acknowledge that they are victimized. They must see how much they have been wronged and why they have been victimized. They need to acknowledge that they suffer discrimination not because of their shortcomings or their sins in the past but because of the aggressive ethnocentrism of Japan and its nationalistic jingoism. It is difficult for victims to acknowledge their victimhood, for such an acknowledgment reminds them of their vulnerability and pain in the past. It is rather easy for victims to forget or blame themselves; "I don't want to think about it," "All that is now just water under the bridge," "It is my fault to let it happen," "It is due to my weakness; if I were stronger, I could push back such an attack," or "Shame on me; I should have done this or that." Rather than blame themselves, they need to identify and confront the real culprits, not escape from reality. When they pin down the culprits and issues openly, a new hope for change and healing begins to dawn.

To wrongdoers, self-denial means to acknowledge their wrongs. Japan should acknowledge its past atrocities that were done on the basis of nationalism and ethnocentrism. In order not to repeat past mistakes, Japan has to teach its flawed history to its children. Covering up its past by revising the content of school textbooks does not help anybody. Japan needs to reexamine where and when it went astray and how to prevent such a mistake from happening again. It should courageously expose its buried stories to the world: its "comfort women" conscription,[5] its Nanjing massacre,[6] the massacre of ethnic Koreans during the Great Kanto Earthquake,[7] the

279

massacres of Koreans in Tinian Island and other locations,[8] the maltreatment against the Korean A-bomb victims,[9] and the job discrimination against ethnic Koreans and other ethnic peoples. Presently, Japan has denied many of its past criminal acts against humanity. Such a denial is not the self-denial that leads it to life, but is self-destruction in the long run. Its acknowledgment of past transgressions is the sheer courage to live in honesty and truthfulness—the courage that its posterity will learn, be proud of, and appreciate.

One bright note is that Japan has made serious efforts at an official level to grapple with these problems. In 1993, the prime minister, for the first time, described the war as aggressive and colonial, and in 1995, the Diet adapted a resolution expressing formal "regret" over it. The government has conceded its official involvement in establishing and managing "comfort houses" for Japanese soldiers and the inhumane conscription of the comfort women. A fund, supposedly private but with strong official patronage, was established to compensate surviving comfort women, and unambiguous letters of apology from the prime minister, accompanying solaria, were issued to the first of the former victims in 1996.[10]

These modest advances, however, provoked fierce opposition, prompting several infamous new organizations in the mid-1990s. Inside the National Diet, Liberal-Democratic Party (LDP) members who insisted on the justice of the war's cause strongly opposed any apology. Outside the Diet, under the leadership of a Tokyo University professor, Nobukatsu Fujioka, the Liberal View of History Study Group and the Society for the Making of New School Textbooks in History were established in 1995 and 1996. Their mission was to infuse a sense of pride in the history of Japan and to secure the deletion of all references to comfort women from school history textbooks. Fujioka and his group called the comfort women "professional prostitutes." This sort of view upheld by Fujioka and his colleagues is comparable with the Holocaust denial that was officially forbidden in France and Germany.[11]

If Japan denies the past evil, it can keep discriminating against Ainu, ethnic Koreans, and other ethnic groups. Only when it acknowledges its wrongs in the past can Japan clean up its act in the present and advance its history.

Second, self-denial for ethnic Koreans means to negate a negated self. Authentic self-denial helps the Koreans affirm their self-identity by denying the self projected by Japanese. Japanese have attempted to depict Koreans as an inferior and second-rate people. This projected image of Koreans is groundless. No evidence proves that Koreans are less intelligent than Japanese. To the contrary, Korean children excel in science and math competitions. In the Third International Mathematics and Science Study, Korean and Singapore eighth graders who were randomly selected won the competitions on the world level.[12] This fact does not prove that Koreans are smarter than Japanese. In the U.S., some Euro-Americans regard African-Americans as inferior to them in intelligence. This is not true. The data of large scale IQ testing have shown African-Americans in some northern states scoring higher than Euro-Americans in some southern states.[13] By and large, intelligence is influenced by social conditions and circumstances. Racism and ethnocentrism, based on people's intellectual performance, are morally and scientifically untenable.

One of the common misunderstandings concerning self-denial is the belief that it denotes self-debasement. It is absurd, however, for victims to deny their human dignity and worth. Japanese have denied ethnic Koreans before they deny themselves. Ethnic Koreans should never internalize the negative image of them. Negating the negated self is the true sense of self-denial for ethnic Koreans. This is the same with ethnic groups in the U.S. All victims of racism should deny the images of their denied selves. Such double denial means to locate their genuine selves and affirm their self-worth.

For the Japanese, self-denial means denouncing national pride and their abuse of power. It is an act of limiting the power of Japan to control others. However, self-denial for Japanese is not to abandon or amputate their national dignity and honor, but is to actualize them in the truest sense. Japan was defeated by the U.S. Its humiliated national ego is a denied self, not self-denial. Its national psyche is so repressed that it looks for an outlet of its deep frustration. The nation arose from ashes externally, but it has suffered humiliation and shame internally. As a defeated nation, it may have harbored its disappointment and resentment and can easily project them onto its neighbors, particularly onto vulnerable ethnic groups. Any prejudice and discrimination based on such defeatism are hazardous and self-defeating. Japan's task is to deny the denied self to restore its authentic national honor by restoring human dignity, justice, and sublimity. Rather than resign themselves to their false superiority complex, haughtiness, and abusive power, the Japanese must come to discover their true identity in self-denial.

Japan has badly treated its ethnic groups and its neighbors. It needs to stop denying their human rights and civil rights. It needs to remember how Japanese-Americans have been mistreated in the U.S., particularly during World War II. Recently Korea has mistreated its foreign workers. Korea should stop treating them badly by remembering how ethnic Koreans have been mistreated in Japan. Why is it that people wish that their own people be treated well in other countries while discriminating against other ethnic groups in their countries? These ironic situations should be used as teaching tools to correct our discrimination against other ethnic peoples.

Third, self-denial means being buried with Christ. Finding one's true self begins with the negation of the negated self and then moves into a solidarity with Christ. To be faithful to the call to self-denial, ethnic Koreans need to die and be buried with Christ. In actuality, the burial with Christ signifies plunging themselves into nothing. Once ethnic Koreans reduce themselves to nothing, they can start from nothing. Then any experience, including pain, is a gain for them. Only when they are willing to die with Christ can they live. This method of self-denial has worked for me. Its symbol is a death with Christ, purging myself every morning. Then, whatever I experience, even loss, is a gain. For Alfred North Whitehead, the aim of life is the intensity of experience. Thus, if I have a choice between nothing and pain, I will choose pain (Kierkegaard). When I begin with nothing, I can thank God for allowing me to experience something.

For Japanese, self-denial at this stage means to support the causes of the oppressed. It is a move beyond turning around and not oppressing them. It is an active involvement in social transformation. Those Japanese who are converted to social justice and equity should devote their energy to helping other ethnic groups restore their own dignity and rights and fulfill their dreams. This is the way to build up Japan. Leaving Japan where it is is to let it rot in injustice. When they truly love their nation, they build it upon the foundation of fairness, dignity, and honor, not upon prejudice, shame, and conceit. Further, they give their lives to the cause of equity and humanity. If Japanese Christians and their sympathizers can do this, Japan shall find its life.

One of the major religions in Japan is Buddhism. It emphasizes emptying as the way to arrive at enlightenment. Self-denial may be compared to self-emptying in Buddhism. Buddhism teaches that there are two selves: the small and the universal self. Emptying (Sunya) is to forget the small self and to let the universal self live. Emptying is not merely becoming devoid, but filling oneself with the greater or universal self.

By highlighting self-denial and self-emptying, Japanese Christians and Buddhists can cooperate in restoring social justice and integrity, eliminating collective prejudice and social discrimination against ethnic groups. This cooperation can be a contact point of interreligious dialogue in Japan.

A good example of self-denial is the Tibet experience of Sadhu Sundar Singh, an Indian Christian mystic. While crossing a range of the Himalayas in a heavy snowstorm, Sundar Singh found a Tibetan who feared traveling alone.

The cold was so intense that they had already begun to despair of reaching their destination alive, when they saw a man who had slipped down a slope of snow some thirty feet below the path, lying there unconscious. The Sadhu asked his companion to help him carry the man to the village. The Tibetan, telling him that he was a fool to try to help another when he could barely save himself, left him and hurried on ahead. The Sadhu went down the slope and just managed to get back on to the road again with the man on his shoulders and struggled slowly along. Some distance farther on he perceived his former companion sitting by the wayside. He called, but there was no answer—he was frozen dead. The Sadhu himself meanwhile had become thoroughly warmed by his exertions and, as result of this warmth and of the friction between their bodies, the man he carried also gradually became warmer and came to; and both reached the village alive and full of thankfulness.[14]

If anyone pursues his or her life alone, he or she will lose it; if anyone seeks to share his or her life with others, he or she will find it. If any nation tries to save its life alone, it will lose it. When it shares its life with others, it will find its life. Japan can grow great with its commitment to make its ethnic groups and neighbors grow great. When it shares its resources and gifts with its ethnic peoples and its neighbors, it will truly find its life.

Fourth, self-denial means resistance in the Spirit for ethnic Koreans. If ethnic Koreans partake in resistance while gnashing their teeth, they will not last long but will burn out quickly in their efforts to change the ethnocentric nation. Although social circumstances and pressure make it extremely difficult to stand firm against injustice, they need to resist discrimination, absurdity, and evil in Japan. Resistance is a form of care. If there is no care, people don't resist, but let it go. If people care, they resist social evil to create a fair community and make the community livable. Resisting evil with good seems impossible, but is only possible in the Spirit: "Do not repay anyone evil for evil, but take thought for what is noble in the sight of all" (Rom. 12:17). While they are crucified with Christ, such courage for resistance springs from the Spirit.

In other words, self-denial denotes filling the purged or empty hearts with the Spirit in their efforts to resist. The job of transforming Japanese society is a lifelong mission. Not by their own might, but by the strength of the Holy Spirit, they should work for the change of the nationalistic ethnocentrism. Letting the Spirit grasp them is to allow the repose and joy of the Holy Spirit to overflow through them in their spirit-filled life. Working for truth in the Spirit is the source of joy. Not only by believing in the final triumph of truth and justice but also by living their victory now, they never lose heart or despair, but live the profuse life of elation here and now. Not after passing through this stormy life but in the middle of it, they live the full-fledged life of salvation in the Spirit because they died with Christ. No more death, but only life in Christ! Subsequently, in the center of their resistance work, they taste the life of freedom, abundance, and healing that the Holy Spirit provides. That is, in the heart of a storm, they celebrate the grace, peace, and jubilation of Christ and take a nap with him.

For the Japanese, the last stage of self-denial is to bury the nationalistic Japan to inaugurate a new inclusive Japan. It is to let Japan participate in the self-emptying of Jesus so that it may rise with a new self. Let the dead bury the dead! Let a new Japan live! When the Japanese sympathizers work with ethnic Koreans and other ethnic groups in changing the national ethnocentrism, they need a new image of Japan in the Spirit prior to changing it. The new image will lure them to relentless participation in social transformation. In the Holy Spirit, they can envision such a just Japan and materialize the life of a new Japan. By denying the small Japan and by envisaging a large Japan, they can help Japan live its true life now.

Conclusion

Although I have focused on Japan, my intention has been to include the U.S. in this discussion. The principle of self-denial may be equally applied to the U.S., too.

Someday both Japanese and other ethnic groups in Japan will enjoy the equity of relationships with full understanding and mutual respect. When the Japanese understand the poignant history of their ethnic groups, they will rise above their prejudice and advocate the rights of their ethnic people. If Japan fails to do so, there will be only a bleak future in Japan. It will lose its life. The life of Japan depends upon this issue of justice. Whether Japan will experience a defeat in moral and spiritual realms or will live its full life hinges upon how it treats ethnic Koreans and other ethnic groups. In this sense, ethnic Koreans and other ethnic groups can be a great source of blessings for Japan in its journey toward its true self. Without changing its view of prejudice and its discriminatory behavior, Japan will never reach its authenticity in spite of prospering in wealth; it will only disappear into the dim shadows of history. Nationalism, ethnocentrism, and racism are just illusions. There is nothing in them. God and history will judge these illusions. It is a matter of time before truth prevails over untruth and falsehood. Therefore, when Japan accepts the challenge of its ethnic groups through self-denial and self-emptying, it will find its genuine life and shall live.

Part 5

Reflections on Christian Understandings of Terror

Small Actions against Terror: Jewish Reflections on a Christian Witness

Peter Ochs

Here is a painful, and painfully necessary, collection of essays by Christian theologians honoring a Christian theologian who is also a Christian victim of terror. The honoree, David Suh, offers a disarmingly matter-of-fact account of a Christian life of redemptive action in the face of terror. His account stimulates some colleagues to write comparable accounts of personal suffering and redemptive resistance. It stimulates others to compose Christian responses on behalf of people victimized by a variety of types of terror: Christians terrorized by Chinese, Japanese, North or South Korean totalitarian oppression; Christians terrorized by oppressive Christian regimes or institutions; Jews terrorized by Christians and Christians terrorized by Romans; fathers who terrorize their daughters; men who terrorize women; adults who terrorize children. There are social, theoretical, and theological responses as well: meetings of religious reasoning and witness, where hope and grace offer words and actions for responding to terror without hiding its darkness behind reasons. Behind all the accounts and responses lie, spoken or unspoken, narratives of the cross, of God incarnate, terrorized and broken in the body of Jesus of Nazareth and then risen as the resurrected Christ.

What is another Jew to say after reading this collection—in this case, a Jew of the age after *Shoah* ("Holocaust") who, in the months before and after writing this essay, finds himself also writing a study of "Judaism After *Shoah*"?

Well, what I did, for much more time than is my wont, was remain silent. Images of David Suh, then of Kosuke Koyama and the many others, replaced my own words for a while. There were many words I could say about a people's response to terror, since I was, after all, in the middle of writing a detailed theological response to my people's narratives of terror in the *Shoah*. But I felt as silent in the face of David Suh's narratives of suffering as I had for most of my life in the face of narratives about my relatives' relatives, and so many others, in the *Shoah*. When some words came, I did not know how to connect words about Judaism after *Shoah* to the words of Christian authors, re-experiencing their and others' sufferings through narratives of cross and resurrection. So, I decided to share with you the unresolved inner dialogue (within my own mind, that is) that remains my Jewish response to these Christian accounts and reflections on terror.

The dialogue begins with a brief reflection on the *Shoah*, then I consider a Christian narrative of terror, then a Christian narrative of response to terror, then a Jewish reflection on these responses, then what I imagine a Christian theological response to be, then a Jewish theological response, and so on. For different readers, different stages in the dialogue may hold more meaning than others.

If the Song of Songs Is a Dialogue of Lovers, Then Here Is a Dialogue of Lamenters

The Grandchildren and Great-Grandchildren of the Terrorized

I write this section during the week of *Yom Shoah*, "Holocaust Memorial Day," 2001 (5761). As Dale Irvin writes, the twentieth century was indeed the century of terror. My people became for many a prototype for all victims of terror. Every Jew in the world today can tell a similar story: that at least some part of his or her extended family or kin group failed to survive the Nazi Holocaust—approximately 7/16 of the entire people died—and the family memories are not just of death but of unimaginable degradation and limitless dehumanization. Terror. And not only the Nazi Holocaust, but millions more of this period murdered by Stalin's regime, preceded near the end of the previous century by the terrors and mass murders of the Russian pogroms. I belong to a people who ended more than one thousand years of Diaspora in Europe with memories primarily of sadness and confusion, often of death and terror.

For readers of this book, I need not, however, say more about what happened to my people in the *Shoah*. Most readers will already recognize the "Holocaust" as not only an historical event but by now a typological word, a trope for the "environment and condition for terror itself." Despite more

288

recent and very different images, many may hear the word "Jew" still as a lingering trope for "victim." If I do not write here of these aspects of what happened to the Jews in the past century, it is not, however, because I fear redundancy; there is no limit to how many times the stories collected in this book, like the stories of the *Shoah*, need to be heard. It is, rather, because I belong to a generation of Jews who wore memories of the *Shoah* as swaddling clothes, but for that very reason devoted much of their lives to "what comes next." Not to forget—to the contrary!—but to explore what must come next in our own families' lives and in the lives of our neighbors.

As the long-suffering authors of this volume's essays know too well, the psycho-spiritual consequences of terror live on not only in the lives of the victims, but also in the lives of their children and their children's children. When my mother-in-law double locks the doors of her comfortable suburban home, what she fears outside are not her well-employed, middle-class neighbors, but lingering apparitions of eleventh-century Crusaders, Chmielnicki's seventeenth-century henchmen, and twentieth-century storm troopers and informants. The memories of terror are not only locked deep within her family's subconscious but also enacted visibly in her parents' and her siblings' visceral habits: the ways they have learned to jump at the sound of a telephone (what bad news may be coming?), to be tentative with "strangers" in the home (what are they looking for?), to wonder—for no apparent reason at all—when it may be time to "move on" (when will they turn against us?), and even more subtly, the ways they have learned to breathe (not too deeply), to hold their children (too tightly), to talk, to eat, to worry.

For these reasons, I trust, Exodus speaks of God's "visiting the iniquity of the parents upon children and the children's children, to the third and fourth generation" (Exod. 34:7). The implied theme of divine *lex talionis* in no way applies to the victims of *Shoah*,[1] but the Exodus text understands very well the duration of terror. I have learned that the memory of terror is transmitted, generation to generation, not only in the lives of Jews I know—the memories of the flesh—but also in the texts and texture of Judaism itself. This is, in fact, the immediate subject matter of much—in unseen ways perhaps all— of the Jewish theology and philosophy written since the *Shoah* and perhaps for several generations to come. How and when will the terror of *Shoah* leave the bodies and unconscious of its grandchildren?

The Parents and Grandparents

David Suh writes,

My grandfather organized the Korean soldiers to fight against the invading Japanese. . . . He was arrested, and he died in prison. When my grandmother heard the rumors of [his] death, she decided to kill all the children and her-self (but she spared my father who was only three). . . .

My father was beaten up by the Japanese police. . . . The North Korean police often harassed [my father]. . . . We found his body on the bank of the Deadong River. . . .

I am a Korean, . . . neither Japanese nor Chinese. This meant that I was harassed and sometimes beaten by my classmates because I was a Korean. . . . Korea was liberated from Japanese colonialism at the defeat of the Japan-ese. . . . No sooner had we settled in the old home town, [than] we found out that the Red Army had marched into North Korea to start a pro-Communist government which would persecute Christians. Some of us teenage middle school kids tried to organize an anti-Communist student club. We were caught on the spot, interrogated, tortured and punished by the school authorities. (Then came the Chinese, then the South Korean government, then while pre-siding as Dean of the College of Liberal Arts and Science in Seoul, I was called out to be arrested by the military intelligence agents. . . .)

Three generations of Korean political and religious leaders were terror-ized by a succession of four totalitarian regimes. How will the terror live on in the bodies and unconscious of their children's children? One answer may come from asking what *else* the parents and grandparents bequeathed to their children along with the terror. Two possible answers come to mind, as responses to two further questions: Were the parents and grandparents immobilized by the terror or were they able to act in response to it and, if so, did they transmit their tendencies to action to their children? Were the parents and grandparents able to write about their experiences? We have David Suh's answer to both questions in the first chapter of this book: *he* wrote, and he wrote not only of suffering, but also of action, or of what I will call the "small actions" of response to terror.

Small Actions of Response

My grandfather was a heroic fighter for national independence, killing so many powerful Japanese invaders. . . .

My father was a Confucian Puritan. . . , both Confucian and Christian Puri-tan . . . [He] was a Christian nationalist, [who] refused to pay respect to the Japanese Shinto shrine. . . . He preached on Moses, Exodus and the liberation of the Hebrew people. . . . For that he had to go jail every so often. . . . [When we found his body,] he was strung together with five other preachers . . . .

Right in the middle of a faculty meeting . . . I was called out to be arrested by the military intelligence agents. . . . I walked out of that torture chamber in one piece. . . . I packed up my things from my university office and left. After one year of work at the Presbyterian Theological Seminary, I was ordained and called to Hyundai Presbyterian Church. . . . I was deeply involved in the parish ministry. . . . In the meantime, as a dismissed professor, with some 200 of us, I struggled for our reinstatement and joined the people's movement for human rights and democracy in South Korea.

This is indeed a family of action. If terror is violence whose victims are made ignoble, then, according to this narrative, the grandfather, father, and son did not, in some fashion, receive this terror *as* terror. Each of them *acted* in the fashion of human beings—leaders in fact—who did not lose their integrity *as* human beings, even *as* leaders. The portrait of the grandfather belongs to a narrative of just response to aggressive violence; that of the father is comparable to late Second Temple narratives of response to Greco-Roman oppression. The self-portrait of the son suggests something else. Terror is portrayed here, but also resistance as displayed through a series of "small actions": saying no here, protesting there, enduring here, organizing there. These are local actions guided by a norm or an ethic that has either escaped the demoralizing weight of terror, or—what? What sense can we make of the relation of small actions to terror? And, since the one who performed small actions is also the one who narrated his experience, will we learn anything by asking if one's tendencies to write are in any way related to one's tendencies to small actions? In search of a response, I return to the history of Jewish responses to terror, for it is, before anything else, a history of writing.

The Literature of Destruction

The history of Jewish responses to terror overlaps, unfortunately, with the entire *history* of Judaism. After the unspeakable horrors of the *Shoah* and of the twentieth century more broadly, it is hard for me to comprehend the fact that Israel has known the horrors of mass terror many times before. ("Israel" is what we often call ourselves, short for "the people Israel" or "children of Israel"; one might consider this the indigenous designation of the Jewish people.) I wish this fact were "merely" literary, but even the mass destructions portrayed in the biblical literature—the destruction of the Northern Kingdom of Israel in 721 B.C.E. and the Southern Kingdom of Judah in 586 B.C.E.—have left behind an ample archaeological as well as literary record. What we call "Judaism," in fact—meaning rabbinic Judaism rather than the religion of the ancient Israelites—may itself be labeled Israel's response to the *Chorban*, or Destruction of the Second Temple in 70 C.E. If we include the Roman destructions through 135 C.E., then this period of terror destroyed a greater percentage of Israel's bodies than the *Shoah*. It also destroyed all the most visible institutions of the Second Temple religion of Israel. I take time to mention this fact because it warrants our characterizing the foundational literatures of the Tannaitic sages— the Mishnah and Tosefta and the various midrash collections including the Passover Haggadah—"rabbinic Judaism's literary response to destruction."

More than this—and this "more" frightens me—we may also reread the Tannaitic literature as replaying the typological form of the Bible as an ordered series of literary responses to mass destruction. According to the *narrative*, this includes the destructions of "the Flood," of the "Bondage in Egypt," of the Assyrian invasion, and of the First *Chorban*. In each case, the narratives portray not only the mass destruction of human life but also of the defining sociopolitical and theological organization of the people.

The literary scholar David Roskies has collected a volume of Israel's responses to each of these destructions: *The Literature of Destruction.*[2] However horrible the individual lamentations contained in this collection, I am most upset by the table of contents itself, for it shows how the biblical typology is replayed not only in early rabbinic literature but also throughout the horribly predictable cycle of literature that marks every epoch of Jewish life through today. Here is a sampling.

In response to the first *Chorban:*

> Alas,
> Lonely sits the city
> Once great with people! . . .
> Judah has gone into exile
> Because of misery and harsh oppression . . .
>
> Lamentations 1:1, 3[3]

In response to the second *Chorban* and the following wars with Rome:

It is related that when Rabbi Akiva was taken out for execution, it was the hour for the recital of the *Shema*, and while they combed his flesh with iron combs, he directed his mind to accepting upon himself the kingship of heaven with love. His disciples said to him: "Our teacher, even to this point?" He said to them: "All my days I have been troubled by this verse, *"and thou shalt love the Lord this God with all this soul"* [which I interpret] "even if He takes thy soul." Now that I have the opportunity shall I not fulfill it? He prolonged the word *ehad* (one) until he expired while saying it.[4]

In response to the Exile from Spain in 1492:

> Gone my song, gone my joy when I bring to mind
> Seville: it is lost, it is utterly lost.
> Gone God's congregation and students of the Law . . .
> My soul shrinks away, is lost for the loss
> Of all my congregations—destroyed, destroyed.
>
> Judah ben David[5]

In response to the Russian pogroms in 1903 (which brought two of my own grandparents to the United States):

> Who cries *Revenge! Revenge!* accursed be he!
> Fit vengeance for the spilt blood of a child
> The devil has not yet compiled . . .
> No, let that blood pierce world's profundity.
> Through the great deep pursue its mordications,
> There eat its way in darkness, there undo,
> Undo the rotted earth's foundations!

Hayyim Nahman Bialik[6]

During the *Shoah* (in the Vilna Ghetto, 1941):

> Because of hunger
> Or because of great love—
> Your mother will bear witness—
> I wanted to swallow you, child,
> When I felt your tiny body
> Cool in my hands
> Like a glass
> Of warm tea. . . .
> I wanted to swallow you, child,
> To taste
> The future waiting for me.
> Maybe you will blossom again
> In my veins.
> I'm not worthy of you, though,
> I can't be your grace.
> I leave you to the summoning snow. . . .

Abraham Sutzkever[7]

From the perspective of this history of narratives, Judaism appears inseparable from a history of literary responses to terror. Whether or not the Jewish victims of these destructions engaged in small actions of response, we know that some of them *responded by writing*. From one historical period to the next, these written responses both varied in certain respects and remained the same in other respects. They remained the same in the way they returned to and reinterpreted biblical tropes; crafted language in both careful and innovative ways; and voiced the mundane misery and bleakness of terrorized life as they saw it, apparently avoiding other-worldly substitutes or explanations. The responses appear to vary in the way the authors blamed either themselves or God for their suffering. In this sampling, for example, Lamentations revisits a Deuteronomic theodicy of sin and punishment; the *Talmud* portrays its sages as martyrs and, therefore, Israel as Suffering Servant; the Eastern European and Yiddish poets report some change in the very being of creation and creator—where either one or both are essentially wounded or disrupted or in some way bound up by the events of destruction and exile. But what of mundane *actions* in response to or against the oppressors or authors of terror?

I would distinguish between two types of Jewish responses to terror. One is portrayed in the Jewish literature of resistance to oppressors: narratives of the ancient Israelite judges, of the Maccabees, of the resistance fighters in the Warsaw ghetto, or of Zionist fighters since the first Yishuv or settlements before the twentieth century. As in David Suh's portrayals of his father and grandfather, these are models of individuals or large collections of individuals who are able to identify and react against those they take to be the specific agents of oppression and terror. The other Jewish response to terror is less obviously portrayed in the literature, but it is the one most central to (and in some ways definitive of) the religion of Judaism. In this case, groups of individuals may be "agents" of terror and of resistance, if by "agent" we mean "instrument" or proximate cause. In this sense, Isaiah refers to "Ashur" as "rod of God's wrath." But the agent of terror—or "rod"—is the agent of an ultimate cause, *as is* the agent of response.

To observe the second kind of Jewish response is to discover divine agency as it is displayed in the Jewish literature. This discovery entails the process of *"midrash,"* or of "pulling"[8] a second level of meaning from out of the narrative. In fact, it is a level with as many sublevels of meaning as there are sublevels of agency in any action. If, for example, Jacob acts in some way toward Esau (say, sending out family members to greet him), his specific act displays some rules of action (some prudential, some ethical, and so on), and those rules of actions, themselves, display some aspect of the "rule of rules" or purpose that gives unity to the patriarchal narratives themselves. This purpose shares in the purpose of Israel's transhistorical relation to God, which in turn shares in the purpose of God's relation to humanity. Israel's literary responses to its times of destruction may be reread as responses to breaches in one or more of these sublevels of agency. If Esau were to strike Jacob, we might read this as a sign merely of something amiss in the relationship between Jacob and Esau. But if, God forbid, the people of Esau were to terrorize the people of Jacob, we might read this as a sign, minimally, of some breach in the rules of action that guide Esau's people or that guide the society that joins the two peoples. Depending upon the dimension of terror, we might read it, maximally, as a sign of some breach in the rules of patriarchal society—that is, of the patriarchal covenant—or of Israel's covenant (Lamentations, Judah ben

David), or even of God's very covenant with humanity or with creation (Bialik).

But where is the *action* in this second type of response? It must have to do with *repairing* one of these deeper levels of breach—the kind of repair that Jacob could not achieve simply by striking back at Esau. To say, with Isaiah, that "Ashur is rod of God's wrath" is to discover that there are much more frightening agents of terror than any one despot or even any one totalitarian leader. There is the civilization that engenders such leaders, the fundamental rules of action that inform that civilization, and whatever broken, breached, or malformed covenant that may engender such rules. But what action can possibly contribute to repairing this dimension of disruption?

Before examining other dimensions of the Jewish literature, I would like to return to the Christian literature of this collection and see if there are references to this dimension of repair.

Christian Literatures of Redemption

According to a midrash in the Babylonian Talmud, when the Israelites say to Moses *naaseh v'nishmah*, "[whatever the Torah says,] we will do and we will be obedient" (Exod. 24:7), they are teaching us that "action comes before understanding": the Word of God is displayed first in what we do and only secondarily in how we theorize about it (*Tractate Shabbat* 88a). Let us read David Suh's account of "small actions" in the face of terror as narratives of God's Word in action! Then we may read his colleagues' writings in this volume as the enacted word come to understanding, that is, as Christian reflections on the deeper meanings of small actions. I am drawn to several features of these reflections—or more precisely, to several features of the way I reread them through Jewish eyes.

To act in response to terror is to act as someone other than this victim of terror.

Victoria Erickson's analysis of terror shows that the subject of this book is not merely the terror caused by that person there who is torturing me, but the much deeper and more sinister evil in which that person must participate: "Terror is its own *being*; perhaps it is Satan or evil in its most complete manifestation." In this view, the victim of terror cannot be simply "I" as this body here, but only as sign and representative of something larger than I. "Terror's method is to degrade the other, erasing the human face of its target, so that it is free to destroy the target. . . . Terror seeks to destroy God's creation." It is therefore "the lived experience of a kind of chaos that disrupts, fragments, and scatters the ongoing interactions that produce human life." It is the degradation of a people as well as given individuals and, thereby, of the human as image of God. To respond to terror is therefore to act, in this sense as my body and as myself, but to act at the same time by way of the transcendence of this particular body and self: it is a self-assertion that is at the same time self-transcendence. For Andrew Park, this is a kenotic self-denial that affirms the self by denying the self that was negated: participating, at once, in the immediate acknowledgement and confession of the oppressor-self as oppressor and the victim-self as victim *while also* denying both—affirming this future self as nonoppressor and this future self as nonvictim.

To act as someone other than oneself is to act in relation to the memory of some-one else's actions. For the Christian, this is to act, ultimately, in "remembrance of me." Small actions are made in remembrance of Christ.

"Thus says the Lord of hosts: even though it seems impossible to the remnant of this people in these days, should it also seem impossible to me?" For Jacqueline Lewis-Tillman, to act in the face of terror is to act counter-factually. In Michelle Lim Jones's terms, this is to act "in the hope of trans-formation," which is the final message of the Christian gospel. This is, in Jürgen Moltmann's words, to act in relation to the life of Christ, for "the tortured Christ is the brother of all victims of torture," and "his story expresses . . . God's solidarity with all victims of violence and torture." To act now in the face of this terror is possible when "Jesus comes to [the oppressors and victims] in the room," to receive "the emissary of Christ," and to find that "Jesus keeps showing up" (Trulear). In sum, "for Chris-tians, faithful remembrance of the past is a spiritual exercise freighted with eucharistic overtones ('do this in remembrance of me'). The 'real presence' of Christ in history is found in such acts of remembrance" (Irvin).

To act in remembrance of Christ is to act in remembrance of the victim of terror who died and was resurrected. This is to act in relation to future redemption rather than to present terror alone. To act this way is to act AS resurrected.

"Torture and death had been overcome in the resurrection, which is a sign of God's ultimate intentions for human history" (Irvin). "Grace's deliv-erables are peace-filled. But most importantly, they are rooted in the power of the only one who can guarantee peace and wholeness through victory over a death cheered on by the very power structure of whom the disci-ples had been afraid" (Trulear). "The gospel story of the life, death, and resurrection of Jesus Christ must serve as the substantive *fons et origo* of hope in the context of the persistent struggle for justice, peace, wholeness, and redemption" (Akinade). "Persecution is [to be] understood as the begin-ning of the final judgment," (Scroggs) as indicated in 1 Peter 4: "If any of you suffers as a Christian, do not consider it a disgrace, but glorify God because you bear this name. For the time has come for judgment to begin with the household of God; if it begins with us, what will be the end for those who do not obey the gospel of God?" "In general the brunt of these admonitions is to turn attention away from the [merely?] local scene, where the persecutors are human . . . and to show that what is crucial is the much larger panorama of God's eschatological drama" (Scroggs). "The cross itself, a powerful symbol of Roman political terror, became a symbol of divine activity and redemption in history for Christians" (Irvin).

To act in remembrance of Christ is to act in relation to a community of Christians, rather than as oneself alone.

It is to act, at once, in pursuit "of the truth of the Bible" *and* by taking part "in social action" (Kajiwara). For Walter Burghardt, the "operative word" in such action is "relationships": "terrorism is a reaction to perceived relationships," and the response to terrorism must be to reorder relationships. Small actions are thus actions in community, which means within *some particular community* and some particular church. Israel remains the type of such a community and such a church, and a prime example is the African church of Akintunde Akinade that "rises from the ashes," with a renewed, christological hope. Jesus "is active in the struggles of millions of Lazaruses in Africa," and this action is realized through the African ideal of "community and interrelationships," the African "communitarian ethos."

This must be, at once, the resurrected community of the future AND the suffering community of the present, in other words the community both of God and of the human.

To act in the face of terror is possible only if one suffers here the evil of terror *and* if one, at the same time, is somehow graced with participation in that future community in which one can act, again, not as victim but as agent of the suffering and redeeming God. Luis Rivera-Pagan offers one striking illustration in the grace that allows Father Bernard Boyl and Bartholome de Las Casasa to live *in* and then speak prophetically *against* Spanish Catholic oppression of Native Americans—Boyle in the company of Columbus and Las Casas as critical historian of the colonial establishment of Hispaniola. James Cone speaks, comparably, of the *prophetic* character of Martin Luther King Jr.'s responses to oppression: "King took the American democratic tradition of freedom and combined it with the biblical tradition of liberation and justice as found in the Exodus and the prophets." King's suffering belongs to the here and now, his nonviolence to the future community—not an other-worldly future "that often characterized white evangelical Protestantism," but the future that is about to come "soon" through the agency of our actions for justice. Donald Shriver gives voice to the malaise of modern western society most generally. Timothy Light writes of and out of what he takes to be the conditions of this malaise, for example the oppressive presence of modern Western imperialism and foundationalism. And Kosuke Koyama writes of and out of what is perhaps the emblematic context of twentieth-century terror: "In all civilizations rulers use the absolute to authenticate their rule and bolster their power. The absolute, by definition untamable, is then tamed. It is this moment that generates violence. One may adore the absolute. . . . One

297

must not equate oneself with the absolute." To tame the absolute is thus to commit the sin of our age, "fabricated transcendence." "The crucified Christ" is a "scandalous symbol" of the sin of this "false transcendence," and Koyuma writes within the present-futurity of that symbol.

To act with respect to the resurrected community is to act with respect to ITS rules of action—its rules of economic, social, political, and sacramental activity, that is to say its rules of justice, relationship, charity, love, peace, and holiness. To act this way is to engage in small actions that are small—local and concrete and immediate— because they are of our humanity in this world, and that are also infinitely large, because they are of God's redeeming action in the world to come. To act this way is therefore to participate in the transformation of a wounded and dying community into a resurrected community.

Small actions are achieved by acting here in light of what is there and will be here: "finding common ground with others, materializing memories, seeking to understand wholeness" (Erickson). This is to affirm myself as other, that is, myself as it will be in the future community, and this is self-affirmation as self-transcendence. Small actions are therefore concrete social actions—caring for neighbors, responding to uncaring politicians and unjust prisons (Burghardt). For Katherine Moon, the agency of such actions is not merely the individual, but also the group, the community, even the nation or people as a whole—Korean women acting against their marginalization, weaker nations acting against their marginalization by the stronger nations. Small actions are offered "to heal and mend brokenness in the world," "sounding the alarm against injustice and oppression" (Han). These are actions now for social justice (Cone), now against genocide (Shriver), now against the oppression of women, children, strangers. In all these ways, to engage in small actions is to re-read catastrophes as, in Tony Carnes's words, "intrusions" into fixed worlds of "custom and habit" that must now be changed for the better.

For the Christian to engage in small actions in response to terror is therefore to act as another, through the grace of a future resurrection that God has somehow made present.

Jewish Literatures of Redemption

By now, you may begin to sense what I have discovered for myself in the process of writing this essay: that what may be most scandalous to Jews and Christians about each other's faith narratives may, in fact, be signs of what, on deeper levels of interpretation, we most share. For the Christian authors in this collection, the Christian victim's capacity to act in response to terror belongs to the grace of his or her participation in the suffering, death, and resurrection of Christ, which is the grace of participating in the prototypical narrative of being-victim-of-terror-who-becomes-agent-of-response-to-terror, which is the grace of living now in the future of the redeemed and redeeming community. We have so far seen the literature of Israel's suffering-and-death under terror, but the literature also narrates Israel's resurrection from this terror: the resurrection of a *community and people in covenant with God,* which resurrection has a biblical type but shockingly a series of antitypes in post-biblical history. For the Jew facing terror, in other words, the capacity to act nonetheless appears to lie in the grace of his or her participation in the suffering, death, and resurrection of Israel, which is the grace of participating in Judaism's prototypical narrative of being-victim-of-terror-who-becomes-agent-of-response-to-terror, which is the grace of living now in the future of the redeemed and redeeming community. Here are some textual illustrations.

Redemption from Egyptian bondage

> The Lord continued, "I have marked well the plight of My people in Egypt and have heeded their outcry because of their taskmasters." . . . "I have come down to rescue them. . . . I will send you." Moses said, "Who am I that I should go?" . . . He said, "*ehyeh imach,* I will be with you." . . . "Thus shall you say to the Israelites, '*ehyeh* sent me to you'" (Exod. 3:7–14).[9]

The partriarchal/matriarchal religion of Abraham died in Egypt, but it was reborn as the Mosaic religion of the One whose Name is with Israel in its suffering, and of the people of Israel that is united under the legislative force of Torah.

Chorban: First Destruction

> But you, Israel, My servant, Jacob, whom I have chosen, Seed of Abraham my friend—You whom I drew from the ends of the earth. . . . To whom I said: You are My servant. . . . Fear not, for I am with you . . .
> This is My servant, whom I uphold, My chosen one, in whom I delight. I have put My spirit in him, He shall teach the true way to the nations. . . . Who formed you, O Israel: Fear not, for I will redeem you. . . . You are Mine (Isa. 41:8–10; 42:1; 43:1).[10]

The religion of the dialectic of monarchy and prophet died in the First Destruction. In the very place of exile, however, in Babylon, the religion of Israel was reborn as the religion of Second Isaiah, Ezekiel, and Ezra: a religion of scribal priests who would redact and reteach the Torah as well as maintain it, and whose reteaching would gradually become the legislative voice of Torah within the Second Commonwealth.

Chorban: Second Destruction

> All Israel has a place in the world to come, as it is written, "Your people shall all be righteous, they shall possess the land forever; there are a shoot of My planting, the work of My hands in whom I shall be glorified" (Isa. 60).

> Moses received Torah from Sinai and transmitted it to Joshua, and Joshua to the elders, the elders to the prophets, the prophets to the members of the Great Assembly. . . . Simeon the Just was one of the last members of the Great Assembly. He used to teach: The world rests on three things: on Torah, on service to God, and on acts of lovingkindness (*Pirke Avot* 1).

> Rabbi Tarfon used to teach: You are not obligated to finish the task, neither are you free to neglect it (*Pirke Avot* 2).

The religion of biblical Israel died in the Second Destruction: the religion maintained by temple service, as defined by the literal word of the written Torah, and as lived by Israel only on its holy soil. In its place, directly out of the fires of *Chorban,* the religion of rabbinic Judaism was reborn: a religion that inherited the Torah teachings of the scribal priests and the central beliefs of their Pharisaic defenders. These are belief in the ressurection of the dead, in life in the world to come (*olam haba*) as well as in this world, and belief that, on Sinai, God gave Moses two torot, not one: the written Torah *(torah she b'chtav)* and the the oral Torah *(torah she b'al peh),* carried through a chain of transmission to the rabbinic sages.

Galut in Muslim Afro-Asia and Christian Europe, with its refrain of pogrom, forced conversions, and displacements:

> God both creates and destroys; indeed, he destroys by creating and he creates by destroying. . . . Consider the comment attributed to R. Abbahu on the verse, "There was evening and there was morning, the first day" (Gen. 1) "From here [we learn that] the Holy One, blessed be He, created worlds and destroyed them, until He created these. He said: These give me pleasure, but those did not give me pleasure" (*Genesis Rabbah* 3:7). . . . The full implications of these ideas are drawn out in the medieval kabbalistic sources. According to a bold idea expressed in the *Zohar* and further developed in the Lurianic material of the sixteenth century, the first act of divine creativity involves the elimination of the forces of impurity from the Godhead. This act of catharsis of evil is related to the attribute of judgment or divine limitation, which is referred to in the Lurianic kabbalah by the technical term *tsimtsum* (withdrawal). . . . From this perspective, we can speak of divine suffering at the very core of existence. If God did not suffer his own death as the infinite, there would be no existence outside of the infinite God" (Elliot Wolfson).[11]

The self-sufficiency of rabbinic Judaism died during Israel's medieval and modern exile. This means that the public framework of rabbinic piety was more or less maintained, but only as supported by the emergence of new elite and esoteric discourses among its religious and intellectual leadership. As Wolfson indicates, the *kabbalah* intensified rabbinic tendencies to transform the negativity of destruction into an attribute of God and, thus, paradoxically, into a vehicle of redemption. God not only suffers with us; he also suffers in himself. In fact, our suffering is but a reflection of divine suffering. Our redemption comes only through God's own, and our prayers are no longer our only means for eliciting divine help; they are also our means of returning divine assistance to God himself. "Torah, divine service, and acts of lovingkindness" uphold the world because they contribute to the restoration of the creator's own name: the name through which the world is created and through whose repair the world will be repaired.

Shoah and Modernity

And now, after the destructions of the twentieth century? The Jewish people live now, I trust, in the early days of the next resurrection. They inherit the narratives and religious transformations of previous resurrections: biblical, rabbinic, kabbalistic. But there must be another one unfolding now, or else my many colleagues in Jewish scholarship, thought, and theology could not be so active as they now are. We do not yet know the shape—the transformed rules—that will guide this resurrection of Judaism, except to expect that it will, indeed, bring biblical, rabbinic, and kabbalistic Judaisms into an innovative relation to something additional. Will that addition include some form of academic inquiry, some form of theological dialogue with Christianity and Islam, some form of cooperative sociopolitical action in the name of a future community and relation to the ongoing terrors of Western civilization?

Small Actions in the Resurrection of Broken Worlds, Terrorized Worlds

Still in the middle of an inner dialogue, I arrive no further than these last comments—for now—on what I have learned from this painful but painfully necessary book.

I learn that, for Christians, to live and act after terror is perhaps to live and act by way of the resurrection of Jesus Christ; and I suggest now that, for Jews, to live and act after the terror of *Shoah* is to live and act by way of the periodic suffering-unto-death and resurrection of Israel. I use these words with some trepidation. By Israel's "suffering unto death," I refer, on a plain sense level of reading, to the flesh-and-blood suffering and death

301

of most of the flesh-and-blood Jews who resided in Central and Eastern and Southern Europe from 1939–1945. But I also refer, on another level of reading, to the collective death of an historically specific culture of the people Israel and epoch of Judaism. I know that Christians speak of Jesus Christ as having died and been resurrected once and for all in the first century; I do not know if they would speak of this on another level as well, and, if so, if they would speak of his suffering this death and resurrection again and again. Although I in *no* way like or want this to be the case or to be the basis for a Jewish theology, I cannot avoid the inductive observation that, in Israel's case, it appears not as a once and for all, but as a *gilgul* (repeated cycle) of death and resurrection. The resurrection is of the body of Israel, and that is visible primarily as a linguistic body: the body of Israel's collective language-in-use, *which means its ways of acting in the world.*

Israel calls its "way of acting in the world" its Torah. The rabbinic sages refer to the behavioral rules within Torah as the *halacha:* literally "the way," but often, and sometimes misleadingly, translated as "Jewish law." It is misleading for those unfamiliar with how this "law" works: for example, how it includes intention or spirit as well as act, and how it is centered in what the medieval pietist Bahya ibn Paquda called "duties of the heart" as well as, and beyond, the "duties of the limbs." Some Jewish practitioners themselves may be unfamiliar with the historical evidence for how this law changes over time. There is change and adjustment within each epoch of Jewish life, but I believe Israel's periods of terrible destruction tend also to mark periods of qualitative change in its overall systems of religious practice. This means that each resurrection of Israel corresponds to a reaffirmation and transformation of its practice of Torah. This is a reaffirmation of the written Torah and of the oral Torot that mark *each* previous resurrection, and it is a transformation of the *lived and interpreted meanings* of the written Torah and of the written texts of the previous oral Torot. All previous interpretations are retained and all are subject to reinterpretation. For these periods of resurrection, the reinterpretation is not merely *ad hoc* and individual, but also discloses new overall patterns of interpretation. New patterns of interpretation entail new patterns of action, as well as new patterns of communal leadership, of institutional organization, and of relations to and with the environing world—the created world and the non-Jewish social world. These changes all operate on the levels of both fundamental theology (or religious social theory) *and* specific everyday action. But this, to repeat, does not mean that everything changes on these levels: the fundaments of theology remain as do the most elemental, everyday rules of action. Of these rules, the most enduring are often displayed in the smallest or recurrent of actions, such as loving and caring for, in the various and different ways one loves and cares for spouse, children, parents, teachers, students, neighbors, coreligionists, strangers, the poor, the weak, the distressed, the foreign, the irritating and offensive and abusive, the other.

This long and detailed summary of the change and resurrection of Torah and Israel therefore ends on a very simple note. Resurrection brings with it the renewed life of the everyday actions of Torah, especially the smallest actions. This implies that Israel's periods of death may bring interruptions in Israel's everyday Torah, which is the possibility that individual members of the people may, in the terror of destruction, lose confidence in—or even knowledge of—the people's habitual rules for tending to the small, everyday needs and values and obligations of self and other. *To live, however, in the heart of terror and death and not to lose one's capacity for such "small actions" is to live already in the grace of the life that will come after this death.* This is to live already in the life of resurrected Israel. In times of peace— even in times of threat and violence that have not yet wounded an epoch of Israel's religion—we *expect* each member of our people to perform the small acts that Torah requires. Such acts are *required,* not merely applauded or hoped for. In times, however, of terror and death, an epoch of Israel's religion may itself be wounded, and we should therefore *not expect each individual to perform what is normally required.* We may, instead, be grateful for such acts *as signs and expressions of grace,* or, in different terms, as signs and expressions of the prevenient capacity to act already in terms of the peace that is yet to come. However one must act, God forbid, in the time and place of the death camps, is a matter between the individual and God alone, God the Creator or, by grace, God the Redeemer.

I believe these small acts are our ultimate signs of the resurrection. This book's Christian authors and readers may hear that word as a sign of the resurrection of Christ; some Jewish readers may hear the word, as I do, as a sign of the resurrection of Israel. Both sets of readers might join me in hearing it, as well, as a sign of the grace, the hope, and the redemptive action that can possibly—but need not—appear in times of terror, or of suffering unto death. I must add "but need not," because I want to respect the test that Irving Greenberg asks us to make of any theological claim or theodicy after the *Shoah.* Citing Elie Wiesel's testimony—"Never shall I forget the little faces of the children, whose bodies I saw turned into wreaths of smoke beneath a silent blue sky"[12]—Greenberg asks that we test any claim about the *Shoah* by asking, "can we utter it, God forbid, in the face of the burning children?"[13] In respect for his request and the suffering it recollects, I cannot presume the presence of the redeeming God in every time of terror; I can only make note of the possibility and then await the testimonies of what actually happens in this historical moment or that. The alternative is to adopt a theological posture as if it were a system of propositions—generally or always true if they are not false—rather than the propositional or verbal expression of an intimate relationship with the God whose personality precludes my anticipating its every action! And if I refer to "grace, hope, and redemptive action," I also cannot presume that it applies only to us on earth. I do not know whether or not God's suffering can be so great as to preclude the enactment of God's will in relation to this or that historical occasion. My judgments belong, after all, to the life of the people Israel, who live still in the trauma of a previous time of terror. I cannot therefore presume that my judgments belong to the life that is yet to come for this people, rather than to the life that died in that terror, or to some place between death and life in which grace remains as much a memory of something past as an anticipation of what might (and might not) be touched in the present. And if I remain in a terrible past, then I cannot yet know that our suffering or God's suffering is interrupted by new life. Only Job's sorry comforters would presume to offer propositional doctrines as substitutes for the touch of grace *(chen v'chesed)*.

Contributors

Akintunde Akinada is an ordained minister in the Anglican Church of Nigeria. He is assistant professor of religion at High Point University in North Carolina. Akinada coedited *The Agitated Mind of God: The Theology of Kosuke Koyama* with Dale T. Irvin. He is a frequent lecturer and consultant on Islamic and indigenous African religious traditions.

Walter J. Burghardt, S.J. is a senior fellow at the Woodstock Theological Center, Georgetown University, and the founder and director of the Center's project Preaching the Just Word. He is a much appreciated and illuminating editor in the Christian academes. The founding editor of *The Living Pulpit*, Burghardt previously served as editor and editor-in-chief of *Theological Studies*, a journal that thrived under his editorship for forty-four years. Burghardt is the author of eighteen books, including *Long Have I Loved You: A Theologian Reflects on His Church* (Orbis, 2000).

Tony Carnes directs the Seminar on Contents and Methods of the Social Sciences, Columbia University, the International Research Institute on Values Changes, and the Research Institute for New Americans. Among many other citations, he was given the Best News Reporting Award by the Evangelical Press Association in 1998. His most recent book, *New York Glory: Religions in New York City* (NYU, 2001), was edited with Anna Karpathakis.

James H. Cone is Charles A. Briggs Distinguished Professor of Systematic Theology at Union Theological Seminary in New York City. He is an ordained minister in the African Methodist Episcopal Church. He is the author of eleven books and over fifty articles and has lectured at more than eight hundred universities and community organizations throughout the United States, Europe, Africa, Asia, Latin America, and the Caribbean. He is best known for his ground-breaking works, *Black Theology & Black Power* (1969), *A Black Theology of Liberation* (1970), *God of the Oppressed* (1975), and *Martin & Malcolm & America: A Dream or a Nightmare?* (1991). His most recent publication is *Risks of Faith* (1999).

Victoria Lee Erickson is an ordained minister in the United Church of Christ and chaplain and associate professor of the sociology of religion at Drew University; she is the author of *Where Silence Speaks: Feminism, Social Theory and Religion* (Fortress Press, 1993).

Jin Hee Han is professor of biblical studies at New York Theological Seminary. He is an ordained Presbyterian minister. In 2000–2001 he served as president of the Mid-Atlantic Region of the Society of Biblical Literature. His work also includes service as assistant editor of *Jesus' Jewishness: Exploring the Place of Jesus Within Early Judaism*, edited by James H. Charlesworth (Philadelphia: American Interfaith Institute; New York: Crossroad, 1991); contributor to the *Anchor Bible Dictionary* (New York: Doubleday, 1992); and consultant for the Korean transla-

305

tion of the Rule of the Community (1QS) in its international edition for the Dead Sea Scrolls Project, Princeton Theological Seminary.

Hisashi Kajiwara is professor of religion at Nagoya Gakuin University, Aichi, Japan. He is an ordained minister of the United Church of Christ in Japan. He has done much to make black theology accessible in Japan. He has also been an activist in citizens' movements. He is the author of *Toward the Promised Land: Martin Luther King, Jr. and the Civil Rights Movement* (Shinkyo Shuppansha, 1989); *Martin L. King* (Shimizu Shoin, 1991); *A Theology of Liberation* (Shimizu Shoin, 1997); and *Following in His Steps: The Faith of Martin Luther King* (Shinkyo Shuppansha, 2000). He has also translated many books of liberation theology into Japanese. They include James H. Cone, *A Black Theology of Liberation; God of the Oppressed; Martin & Malcolm & America: A Dream or a Nightmare;* and others.

Dale T. Irvin is an ordained American Baptist Minister and professor of world Christianity at New York Theological Seminary. He is the author of *Christian Histories, Christian Traditioning* (Orbis, 1998) and co-coordinator with Scott Sunquist of the History of the World Christian Movement Consultation that will publish a History of the World Christian Movement Vol.1: Earliest Christianity to 1453 (2001) and Vol. 2 (forthcoming in 2002, Orbis). He is executive publisher of *The Living Pulpit*.

Michelle Lim Jones is currently a doctoral student at Drew University. She is writing a dissertation on immigrant Korean women's Christology. She is a favored teaching assistant among theological school students and a longtime supporter of women's causes and the development of an Asian women's feminist agenda.

Kosuke Koyama is professor emeritus of ecumenical studies at Union Theological Seminary, New York. Previously he was a lecturer at Thailand Theological Seminary, dean at South East Asia Graduate School of Theology, senior lecturer in religion at University of Otago, New Zealand, and professor of ecumenics and world Christianity atUnion Theological Seminary. In 1996 he retired to Minneapolis.

Jacqueline J. Lewis-Tillman is an ordained minister in the Presbyterian Church (USA). She was the organizing pastor of the Imani Community Church, a new church development in Trenton, N.J. Lewis-Tillman is a doctoral candidate in psychology and religion at Drew University ; she is also the Director of the Foundation for Exceptional Children, Washington, D.C.

Timothy Light is professor of comparative religion and Chinese at Western Michigan University. Previously, he taught at the Chinese University of Hong Kong, the University of Arizona, Ohio State University, and Kalamazoo College, combining various administrative duties with teaching English and then Chinese language and linguistics. His current research is on religions in contact and religious syncretism. He is an active Episcopal layperson.

Jürgen Moltmann is the retired professor of systematic theology on the Protestant Faculty of the University of Tübingen, Germany. One of the most respected and revered theologians alive today, Moltmann is the author of many books, including *The Spirit of Life: A Universal Affirmation* (Fortress, 1992) and *Jesus Christ for Today's World* (1994).

Katharine H. S. Moon is associate professor of political science at Wellesley college, teaching and researching in international relations and East Asian politics. Her areas of focus include gender and women in international politics, militarization, and social movements in East Asia. She is the author of *Sex Among Allies: Military Prostitution in U.S.-Korea Relations* (Columbia University, 1997) and is currently working on a book that examines anti-Americanism in Korea-U.S. relations. She is also researching the role of culture and gender in diplomacy and negotiation. She serves on the editorial board of several international relations journals and as consultant to nongovernmental organizations in the U.S. and Korea.

Peter Ochs is Edgar Bronfman Professor of Modern Judaic Studies at the University of Virginia. He coauthored DABRU EMET, A Jewish Statement on Christianity, and the book version of this statement, *Christianity in Jewish Terms* (Westview, 2000). He cofounded the Society for Textual Reasoning and The Society for Scriptural Reasoning dedicated to the hermeneutics of peace that binds Muslims, Jews, and Christians. Among other works are *Peirce, Pragmatism and the Logic of Scripture* (Cambridge, 1998), *Reviewing the Covenant: Eugene Borowitz and the Postmodern Renewal of Theology* (SUNY, 2000), and *Reasoning after Revelation: Dialogues in Postmodern Jewish Philosophy* (with Robert Gibbs and Steven Kepnes, Westview Press, 1998).

Andrew Sung Park is professor of theology at United Theological Seminary, Dayton, Ohio. He is an ordained minister in the United Methodist Church and a widely respected expert on the healing of the deep wounds of a victim. His publications include *The Wounded Heart of God: The Asian Concept of Han and the Christian Concept of Sin* (Abingdon Press, 1993) and *Racial Conflict and Healing* (Orbis Books, 1996). *Racial Conflict and Healing* received a Gustavus Myers Award as an outstanding book on the subject of human rights in North America in 1997.

Luis N. Rivera-Pagán is professor of humanities at the University of Puerto Rico and 1999–2000 John A. Mackay Visiting Professor at Princeton Theological Seminary. He is author of several books, among them, *A Violent Evangelism: The Political and Religious Conquest of the Americas* (Westminster/John Knox Press, 1992) and *Mito, exilio y demonios: literatura y teologíía en Améérica Latina [Myth, Exile, and Demons: Literature and Theology in Latin America]* (Publicaciones Puertorriqueññas, 1996).

Robin Scroggs is Edward Robinson Professor of Biblical Theology, emeritus, at Union Theological Seminary in New York. Over the years he has focused on Paul's theology and the sociological backgrounds of early Christian texts. Among other titles, he is the author of *Paul for a New Day, The New Testament and Homosexuality,* and *The Text and the Times.* He now lives in Pompton Plains, N.J., where his wife pastors a Presbyterian church.

Donald W. Shriver is emeritus president of the faculty and William E. Dodge Professor of Applied Christianity at Union Theological Seminary in New York, where he served from 1975–1996. An ordained Presbyterian minister, Shriver holds six honorary degrees and is a fellow of the new American Academy in Berlin. His twelve books include *An Ethic for Enemies: Forgiveness in Politics* (Oxford 1995, 1997).

David Kwang-sun Suh is emeritus professor of theology at Ewha Woman's University in Seoul, Korea, where he served as dean of the college, dean of the graduate school, and dean of the chapel. Suh is an ordained Presbyterian minister, commissioned member of the World Council of Churches, member of EATWOT, executive member of the Asia Alliance of YMCAs, and the former president of the World Alliance of YMCAs. A leader in the *minjung* theologians movement, Suh is the author of many related books and articles including *Korean Minjung in Christ* (CCA, 1990).

Harold Dean Trulear is vice president and director of Faith Based Initiatives at Public/Private Ventures, an action-based research firm specializing in social programs and policies affecting poor youth, their families, and communities. A former missionary with Youth for Christ in Paterson, N.J., Trulear has been a part-time member of the faculty at the Center for Urban Theological Studies in Philadelphia since 1987 and was named a Faculty Fellow in the Institute for the Advanced Study of Religion at Yale Divinity School, where he is a lecturer in church and society.

Notes

Introduction

1. Emmanuel Lévinas, *Alterity and Transcendence* (London: Athlone Press, 1999).

2. M. M. Bakhtin, *Toward A Philosophy of the Act*, trans. Vadim Liapunov, eds. Vadim Liapunov and Michael Holquist (Austin: University of Texas Press, 1990).

3. E. V. Walter, "Violence and the Process of Terror." *American Sociological Review* 29, no.2 (April 1964): 248–257.

4. David C. Rapoport, "Fear and Trembling: Terrorism in Three Religious Traditions." *The American Political Science Review* 78, no.3 (1984): 658–677.

5. James A. Leith, *The Terror: Adding the Cultural Dimension.* Canadian Journal of History 32, no.3 (1997): 315–337.

6. David Kwang-sun Suh, *The Korean Minjung in Christ* (Hong Kong: The Christian Conference of Asia, 1991).

7. Ethnomethodology refers to the study of the people's method of accomplishing everyday life.

8. Tony Ingle, "Terror at 0.0 Feet." *The Symposium* 2, no.1 (1999): 7–8.

Chapter 2

1. The Annexation Treaty was signed on August 22, 1910. On August 29 the Imperial Rescript on the Annexation and the Treaty that was signed on August 22 were made public. The 1965 Japan-Korea Treaty reads: ". . . it also confirms that all treaties or agreements concluded between Japan and Korea on or before 22 August 1910, the date of the annexation of Korea to Japan, are already null and void" (Article 2).

2. Among Korean people, the year 1905 is perceived as the beginning of the Japanese rule since the Japanese control had began already in that year by two Resident Governors, Hirobumi Ito (1905–09) and Arasuke Sone (1909–10). Ito (1841–1909) was a central figure in the creation of the Meiji Constitution which laid the foundation for the imperial system: "Article 3. The person of the emperor is sacred and inviolable." In 1909 Ito was assassinated in Harbin by An Chung-gun, a member of the Korean independence movement. Saito and Ugaki were appointed twice. Saito was a navy admiral. The rest of the governors were all army generals. Koiso and Minami were tried by the Far Eastern War Criminal Tribunal in Tokyo and condemned to life imprisonment. They died in 1950 and in 1956, respectively.

3. Institute of Asian Cultural Studies, International Christian University, Tokyo, 1984, p. 136.

4. *Topography of Terror, Gestapo, SS and Reichssicherheitshauptamt on the "Prinz-Albrecht-Terrain," A Documentation*, Eds. Reinhard Rurup, Verlags Willmuth Arenhovel, 1989.

5. "Idolatry is the elevation of a preliminary concern to ultimacy. Something essentially conditioned is taken as unconditional, something essentially partial is boosted into universality, and something essentially finite is given infinite significance" (Paul Tillich, *Systematic Theology,* 1:16).

6. "Mount Fuji, Mount Baekdu, and Mount Sinai: The Echos of the Mountains" in *The Agitated Mind of God, The Theology of Kosuke Koyama,* eds. D. T. Irvin and A. E. Akinade (Maryknoll, N.Y.: Orbis Books), p. 116f.

7. Iwanami Shinsho (Iwanami Newbook Series), *Shukyo Danatsu o Kataru (Suppression of Religions Narrated)*, eds. Kenji Koike et al., (1978), p. 179.

Interrogator: Is it true that your scripture holds that all human beings are sinners?

Rev. Sugano of the Holiness Church: Yes.

Interrogator: Then is the emperor a sinner?

Rev. Sugano: As long as the emperor is a human being, he cannot be but a sinner.

Interrogator: Does this mean that the emperor needs redemption by Christ?

Rev. Sugano: As long as the emperor is a human being, in order to be saved, he needs redemption.

Other books of the Iwanami Newbook Series used for this article are *Nikkan Heigo Shoshi (A Short History of the Annexation of Korea to Japan)*, 1966, *Nihon Tojika no Chosen (Korea under the Rule of Japan)* by Kentaro Yamabe, 1971, and *Tenno no Saiki (The Imperial Ritual)* by Shigeyoshi Murakami, 1977.

8. *Ohmotokyo* (Nao Deguchi, founderess, 1837–1918) is, like *Tenrikyo, Konkonkyo, Maruyamakyo*, one of the people's religions that originated in the nineteenth century. *Omotokyo* teaches eschatological renewal of all things by the restoration of social justice in the world.

Chapter 3

1. Mircea Eliade, *The Myth of the Eternal Return or, Cosmos and History*, Willard R. Trask, trans. (Princeton: Princeton University Press, 1954), pp. 150–151.

2. Walter Benjamin, *Illuminations*, Hannah Arendt, ed. (New York: Schocken Books, 1968), p. 257.

3. R. Scott Appleby, *The Ambivalence of the Sacred: Religion, Violence, and Reconciliation* (Lanham, Md.: Rowman & Littlefield Publishers, 2000), p. 19.

4. See Rudolf Otto, *The Idea of the Holy*, John W. Harvey, trans. (New York: Oxford University Press, 1958), pp. 11–40.

5. Appleby, *The Ambivalence of the Sacred*, pp. 28–29.

6. Ibid, pp. 27, 29.

7. Ibid, p. 31.

8. "We heard him say, 'I will destroy this temple that is made with hands, and in three days I will build another, not made with hands,'" (Mark 14:58). See also Mark 15:29; Matt. 26:61 and 27:40; and John 2:19.

9. The literature on martyrdom is extensive, but among the best introductions are Peter Brown, *The Cult of the Saints* (Chicago: University of Chicago Press, 1981); and W. H. C. Frend, *Martyrdom and Persecution in the Early Church* (Oxford: Blackwell Press, 1965).

10. On the inversion of ecclesiastical order found in the vision of the martyr Saturus in *The Passion of Perpetua and Felícitas*, see Zaida Maldonado Pérez, "Death and the 'Hour of Triumph': Subversion within the Visions of Saturus and Polycarp," in *Theology: Expanding the Borders*, María Pilar Aquino and Roberto S. Goizueta, eds. (Mystic, Conn.: Twenty-Third Publications, 1998), pp. 126–131.

11. On the transformation of the fire of a public execution into a pillow on which he could lay his head in the vision of Polycarp prior to his arrest, see Maldonado Pérez, "Death and the 'Hour of Triumph,'" pp. 133–137.

12. Rodney Stark, *The Rise of Christianity: A Sociologist Reconsiders History* (Princeton: Princeton University Press, 1996), p. 177, has pointed out the importance this had in helping to reduce the "free-riders" in Christian communities and thereby increase the level of commitment among members overall.

13. Enrique Dussel, *A History of the Church in Latin America: Colonialism to Liberation (1492–1979)*, Alan Neely, trans. (Grand Rapids: Eerdmans, 1981), p. 308, noted that with his words on the cross, "Father forgive them, for they know not what they do" in Luke 23:34, "Jesus introduced us to the critique of ideology."

14. Maureen A. Tilley, trans., *Donatist Martyr Stories: The Church in Conflict in Roman North Africa* (Liverpool: Liverpool University Press, 1996), xiii.

15. The fourth-century church historian Eusebius reports that shortly after the Council of Nicaea in 325, Constantine sent a letter to Shapur II, the Shah of Shahs of Persia (*Life of Constantine* 4.9–13). In the letter the Roman emperor asked his Persian counterpart to extend his protection to the Christians under the latter's dominion. Constantine had heard that the districts of Persia were filling with Christians, and encouraged Shapur to recognize the religion. As another early Christian historian named

Sozomen noted, "the emperor extended his watchful care over all the Christians of every region, whether Roman or foreign" (*Ecclesiastical History* 2.15). Within two decades Shapur II launched one of the most ferocious periods of persecution Christians had yet faced. Estimates of martyrdoms run in the tens of thousands in the Persian empire during this period.

16. Sidney H. Griffith, "Christians, Muslims, and Neo-Martyrs: Saints' Lives and Holy Land History," *Sharing the Sacred: Religious Contacts and Conflicts in the Holy Land, First-Fifteenth Centuries CE* (Jerusalem: Yad Izhak Ben Zvi, 1998), pp. 163–207 examines a number of the martyrdom narratives from the seventh through tenth century under Islamic rule in the East, and the conditions under which these occurred.

17. The manner in which violence has been sacralized has been explored by a number of theorists, among them René Girard and Victoria L. Erickson. See René Girard, *Violence and the Sacred* (Baltimore: Johns Hopkins University Press, 1977); idem, *The Scapegoat* (Baltimore: Johns Hopkins University Press, 1986); and Victoria L. Erickson, *Where Silence Speaks: Feminism, Social Theory, and Religion* (Minneapolis: Fortress Press, 1993).

18. For a brief introduction to various theories, see James Turner Johnson, "Just War," in *The Westminster Dictionary of Christian Ethics*, James F. Childress and John Macquarrie, eds. (Philadelphia: Westminster Press, 1968), s.v.; and more recently, Lisa Sowle Cahill, *Love Your Enemies: Discipleship, Pacifism, and Just War Theory* (Minneapolis: Fortress Press, 1994).

19. Toby Foshay, "Resentment and Apophasis: The Trace of the Other in Levinas, Derrida and Gans," in *Shadow of Spirit: Postmodernism and Religion*, Philippa Berry and Andrew Wernick, eds. (London and New York: Routledge, 1992), p. 88.

20. Reinhold Niebuhr, in *The Irony of American History* (New York: Charles Scribner's Sons, 1962), writes on p. 155: "Yet the Christian faith tends to make the ironic view of human evil in history the normative one. Its conception of redemption from evil carries it beyond the limits of irony, but its interpretation of the nature of evil in human history is consistently ironic." Cornel West, "Subversive Joy and Revolutionary Patience in Black Christianity," in *Prophetic Fragments* (Grand Rapids: Eerdmans / Trenton: Africa World Press, 1988), writes on p. 162: "The black interpretation of the Christian gospel accented the tragedy in the struggle for freedom and the freedom in a tragic predicament."

21. Ibid.

22. See Dale T. Irvin, *Christian Histories, Christian Traditioning: Rendering Accounts* (Maryknoll, N.Y.: Orbis Books, 1998).

Chapter 4

1. Cornel West, *Prophetic Fragments* (Grand Rapids: Eerdmans /Trenton: Africa World Press, 1988), p. 162.

2. See James Traub, "The Worst Place on Earth," *New York Review of Books*, Vol. XLVII, Number II, June 29, 2000.

3. See *The Economist*, May 13–19, 2000.

4. Desmond Tutu, "Africa's Dilemma: Conflicts, Challenges and Possibilities," *Tamtam*, 11 (1996/1): 6.

5. The "African Report" in K. C. Abraham, ed., *Third World Theologies: Commonalities and Divergences* (Maryknoll, N.Y.: Orbis Books, 1990), p. 47.

6. Orlando Patterson, *Slavery and Social Death: A Comparative Study* (Cambridge: Harvard University Press, 1982).

7. Thabo Mbeki, "Africa Needs Her Own Renaissance," *Tamtam* December 1998–February 1999, p. 38.

8. K. C. Abraham, *Third World Theologies*, p. 28.

9. The New Delhi Report quoted in Philip Potter, "Doing Theology in a Divided World" in *Doing Theology in a Divided World*, Virginia Fabella and Sergio Torres, eds. (Maryknoll, N.Y.: Orbis Books, 1985), pp. 16–17.

10. Jürgen Moltmann, "Towards a Political Hermeneutics of the Gospel," *Union Seminary Quarterly Review* XXIII, no. 4 (Summer 1968): 313–314.

11. See Paul Lehmann, *Ethics in a Christian Context* (New York: Harper & Row, 1963), p. 104.

12. Musimbi Kanyoro, "A Life of Endless Struggle or Stubborn Hope: An African Feminine Perspective on Jubilee," *The Ecumenical Review* 49, no. 4 (October 1997): 401.

13. Walter Brueggemann, *Living Toward a Vision: Biblical Reflections on Shalom* (New York: United Church Press, 1982), p. 15.

14. Musimbi Kanyoro, "A Life of Endless Struggle or Stubborn Hope: An African Femi-

nine Perspective on Jubilee" *The Ecumenical Review* 49, no. 4 (October 1997): 402.

15. Kwesi Dickson, *Theology in Africa* (Maryknoll, N.Y.: Orbis Books, 1984), p. 62.

16. Robert N. Bellah et al., *Habits of the Heart* (New York: Harper and Row, 1985), p. 153.

17. Mercy Amba Oduyoye, "The Values of African Religious Beliefs and Practices for Christian Theology" in *African Theology en Route*, Kofi Appiah-Kubi and Sergio Torres, eds. (Maryknoll, N.Y.: Orbis Books, 1979), pp. 110–111.

18. See Ada Maria Isasi-Diaz, "Solidarity: Love of Neighbor in the 21st Century" in *Lift Every Voice: Constructing Christian Theologies from the Underside*, Susan Brooks Thistlethwaite and Mary Potter Engel, eds. (Maryknoll, N.Y.: Orbis Books, 1998), p. 32.

19. Ibid.

20. Gustavo Gutiérrez, *A Theology of Liberation* (Maryknoll, N.Y.: Orbis Books, 1986), p. 175.

21. Quoted in Yap Kim Hao, *Doing Theology in a Pluralistic World* (Singapore: The Methodist Centre, 1990), p. 175.

22. See Gustavo Gutiérrez, *The Power of the Poor in History* (Maryknoll, N.Y.: Orbis Books, 1984), p. 140.

Chapter 5

1. Genesis 1:1–2:3, which has been invoked to support causes that range from ecology to eschatology, was a text for survival for the people in the Babylonian exile, to whom the Genesis text declared that Elohim created the heavens and the earth, though the Babylonians claimed Marduk did. Elohim rests on Sabbath, in which the people of Israel, who lost the temple of Jerusalem, found "a sanctuary of time" (see Abraham J. Heschel, *Sabbath: Its Meaning for Modern Man* [New York: Ferrar, Straus and Young, 1951], p. 29.).

2. Gil Bailie (*Violence Unveiled: Humanity at the Crossroads* [New York: Crossroad, 1995], p. 133) gives expression to the prominent tone of violence in the biblical corpus, when he says, "The Bible I have before me has 1679 pages. On page 8 the first violence occurs. It results in the first death."

3. See Genesis 37:27.

4. Cf. In the secondary literature in biblical studies, the phrases "holy history" or "history of salvation" appears as the English translation of *heilsgeschichte*, a word cited in J. C. K. von Hofmann of the nineteenth century.

5. W. Gunther Plaut, ed., *The Torah: A Modern Commentary* (New York: Union of American Hebrew Congregations, 1981), p. 486.

6. Second Kings 24:14 creates an impression that the Babylonian exile left the land of Canaan empty: "[King Nebuchadnezzar of Babylon] carried away all Jerusalem, all the officials, all the warriors, ten thousand captives, all the artisans and the smiths; no one remained, except the poorest people of the land." The book of Lamentations seems to confirm that assumption, as it begins, "How lonely sits the city that once was full of people!" (1:1). "The roads to Zion mourn, for no one comes to the festivals" (1:4). However, Jeremiah, who records a much smaller number of exiles in 52:28–30 than 2 Kings does, makes references to the life after the destruction in Judah, where he remained in spite of the offer of comfort Nebuzaradan the Babylonian captain of the guard promised him in Babylon. Archaeological finds confirm that the life outside Jerusalem continued with the people of the land after the destruction.

7. Jeremiah 6:25; 20:3, 10; 46:5; 49:29. Cf. Psalm 31:13.

8. R. P. Carroll, *Jeremiah* (London: S.C.M. Press, 1986), p. 203.

9. William L. Holladay, "The Covenant with the Patriarchs Overturned: Jeremiah's Intention in 'Terror on Every Side'" in *JBL* 91:305–20.

10. Later in the book Jeremiah portrays the deep impact of terror upon Egypt (46:5) and by Babylon (49:29), using the same words.

11. See S. D. Snyman's "Violence in Amos 3, 10 and 6, 3" in *CBQ* 71:44–45 for a summary of various proposals about this expression.

12. The camp of peasant revolt does not change the precarious course of the settlement, as it portrays it as an internal conflict, not as an external invasion. Destruction and mayhem continue to feature in the picture, while it is no longer Israelites killing Canaanites, but Canaanites killing one another.

13. Cf. 1 Kings 11:16 reports that Joab "had eliminated every male *(kl-zkr)* in Edom." The Talmud (Baba Bathra 21a-b) preserves a tradition that Joab killed only the males, because his teacher taught him to read in Deuteronomy 25:19, "You shall blot out the male *(zekor)* of Amalek." David corrects him to read the sen-

tence as "You shall blot out the remembrance *(zeker)* of Amalek."

14. Hans J. Jensen, "Desire, Rivalry and Collective Violence in the 'Succession Narrative'" in *JSOT* 55:39–59

15. Susan Niditch, *War in the Hebrew Bible: A Study in the Ethics of Violence* (New York: Oxford University Press, 1993), p. 134.

16. While the term "state" runs the risk of anachronism, it is used here so that it may facilitate comparison with state-sponsored terror in other social contexts including the contemporary situations. Effective communication is certainly hampered by semantic confusion, but absolute purism in language can turn a discourse into something of impossibility.

17. Itumeleng Mosala, "Violence and the Prophets" in *Theology and Violence: The South African Debate,* Charles Villa-Vicencio, ed. (Grand Rapids: Eerdmans, 1987), p. 103.

18. After Nathan, no prophet is mentioned until 1 Kings 11:29, in which the prophet Ahijah the Shilonite declares that Jeroboam will be king over the ten tribes after the secession of the northern kingdom.

19. See Bustenay Oded's *War, Peace, and Empire: Justifications for War in Assyrian Royal Inscriptions* (Wiesbaden: Dr. Ludwig Reichert Verlag, 1992) for a discussion of war as a major concern with which the Assyrians were preoccupied.

20. A. T. Olmstead, "The Calculated Frightfulness of Ashur Nasir Apal" in *JAOS* 38:290–263.

21. Lori L. Rowlett, *Joshua and the Rhetoric of Violence: A New Historicist Approach* (Sheffield: Sheffield Academic Press, 1996).

22. Rowlett, *Joshua*, p. 12.

23. Ibid.

24. Ibid., p. 183.

25. Klaus Koch, *The Prophets*, 2 vol. (Philadelphia: Fortress Press, 1982).

26. Ibid., 1:5.

27. Phyllis Trible, *Texts of Terror: Literary-Feminist Readings of Biblical Narratives* (Philadelphia: Fortress Press, 1984).

28. Ibid., p. 28.

29. Irmgard Fischer, "'Go and Suffer Oppression!' Said God's Messenger to Hagar: Repression of Women in Biblical Texts" in *Violence Against Women*, Elisabeth Schüssler Fiorenza and M. Schawn Copeland, eds. (London: S.C.M. Press; Maryknoll, N.Y.: Orbis, 1994), p. 81.

30. See Robert Good's "The Just War in Ancient Israel" in *JBL* 104:385–400 for a discussion on the jural meaning of war in the Old Testament.

31. See Isaiah 13:6, 9; Jeremiah 46:10; Ezekiel 30:3; Joel 1:15, 2:1–2, 2:11, 31, 3:14–15; Amos 5:18–20; Obadiah 1:15; Zephaniah 1:14–18.

32. Albert Curry Winn, *Ain't Gonna Study War No More: Biblical Ambiguity and the Abolition of War* (Louisville: Westminister/John Knox, 1993), p. 55.

33. Raymund Schwager, *Must There Be Scapegoats? Violence and Redemption in the Bible,* Maria L. Assad, trans. (San Francisco: Harper & Row, 1987), p. 55.

34. Winn, *Ain't Gonna*, p. 55.

35. John Yoder, "'To Your Tents, O Israel': The Legacy of Israel's Experience with Holy War" in *SR* 18:351.

36. Carol P. Christ, "Feminist Liberation Theology and Yahweh as Holy Warrior: An Analysis of Symbol" in *Women's Spirit Bonding,* Janet Kalven and Mary I. Buckley, eds. (New York: Pilgrim Press, 1984), p. 205.

37. The formula of "Fear not" as an introduction of theophany (Genesis 15:1; 21:17; 26:24; 28:13; 46:3; Lamentations 3:57) was common in the ancient Near East. The king of Hamath offered a prayer while he was under seige: "And Baal-shamaym answered me, and Baal-shamayn [spoke] to me through seers. . . , 'Fear not, for it was I who made you king and [I shall stand] with you; and I shall deliver you from all [these kings] who have forced a siege upon you'" (J. C. L. Gibson, *Textbook of Syrian Semitic Inscriptions,* vol. 2: *Aramaic Inscriptions* [Oxford: Clarendon, 1975], pp. 9–11). The phrase also appears in a non-theophanic context as words of encouragement in the holy war that called for absolute faith (see Gerhard von Rad, *Holy War in Ancient Israel,* Marva J. Dawn and John Howard Yoder, trans. and ed. [Grand Rapids: Eerdmans, 1991]) or in actual battle situations (see Edgar W. Conrad, *Fear Not Warrior: A Study of "'al tîra'" Pericopes in the Hebrew Scriptures,* Brown Judaic Studies 75 [Chico: Scholars Press, 1985]). See Exodus 14:13; Deuteronomy 20:3; Joshua 8:1; 10:8, 25; 11:6; Judges 7:3; 1 Samuel 23:16.

38. Joachim Begrich, "Das priesterliche Heilsorakel" in *ZAW* 11:81–92.

39. Hyacinthe M. Dion, "The Patriarchal Traditions and the Literary Form of the Oracle of Salvation" in *CBQ* 29:205.

40. See Genesis 32:30; Exodus 3:6, 33:20; Judges 6:22–23, 13:22–23; Isaiah 6:5, etc. In these accounts virtually everyone survives the divine encounter. On the one hand, that has to do with the nature of the report, which would not have been made if the person had been killed by the incident. On the other hand, the survival of the divine encounter functions as a conventional motif of vindication, for that only would mean God has found the person worthy to live.

41. In his classical work on God's involvement in human situation as attested in the prophets, Heschel (*The Prophets* [New York: Harper & Row, 1962], 2: 4) declares, "God does not stand outside the range of human suffering and sorrow. He is personally involved in, even stirred by, the conduct and fate of man."

42. René Girard, *Job: The Victim of His People,* Yvonne Freccero, trans. (Stanford: Stanford University Press, 1987), p. 157.

43. It is only in the Christian triumphalism that the fang of terror is broken. The process of struggle to overcome the grip of terror continues both in the First and Second Testaments. At any rate, the debate on which of the two brings out Girard's point better than the other could bring back the Girardian conflict of mimetic doubles.

44. René Girard, *The Scapegoat,* Yvonne Freccero, trans. (Baltimore: Johns Hopkins University Press, 1986), p. 39.

45. Bailie, *Violence Unveiled,* p. 33.

46. René Girard, *Violence and the Sacred* (Baltimore: Johns Hopkins University Press, 1977), p. 55.

47. This perspective approaches the biblical accounts of God's violence "as human projections" (see Raymund Schwager, "The Theology of the Wrath of God" in *Violence and Truth: On the Work of René Girard,* Paul Dumouchel, ed. [Stanford: Stanford University Press, 1988], p. 44).

48. Note that the text identifies Abel as his brother again and again (Genesis 4:2, 8, 9).

49. Cf. The Priestly tradition that ascribes it to the breach of trust on the part of Moses and Aaron (Numbers 20:12; cf. Deuteronomy 32:50–52; Psalm 106:32–33).

50. Robert North, "Violence and the Bible: The Girard Connection" in *CBQ* 47:13 refers to Girard's comment on the passage, which "succeeds better than the New Testament in interpreting properly the death of Christ."

51. U. Milo Kaufmann, "Expostulation with the Divine: A Note on Contrasting Attitudes in Greek and Hebrew Pity" in *Twentieth Century Interpretations of the Book of Job,* Paul S. Sanders, ed. (Englewood Cliffs, N.J.: Prentice-Hall, 1968), p. 66.

52. Alicia Winters, "The Subversive Memory of a Woman: 2 Samuel 21:1–14" in *Subversive Scriptures: Revolutionary Readings of the Christian Bible in Latin America,* Leif E. Vaage, ed. (Valley Forge: Trinity Press International, 1997), pp. 142–154.

53. Winters, "Subversive Memory," p. 153.

54. Walter Brueggemann, *The Prophetic Imagination* (Philadelphia, Fortress Press, 1978), pp. 49–51.

55. T. R. Hobbs, *A Time for War: A Study of Warfare in the Old Testament* (Wilmington: Michael Glazier, 1989), p. 197.

56. Jon L. Berquist, *Judaism in Persia's Shadow* (Minneapolis: Augsburg Fortress, 1995), p. 178.

57. René Girard (see note 42 above) finds Job as innocent as Jesus, but less subversive than Jesus, for "by revealing how the world functions, [Jesus] threatens its foundations more seriously than Job." While Jesus of Nazareth may function as a more forceful example of the Girardian system of sacred violence than any other figure, Job's pungent words are unparalleled, as they subvert the fundamental credibility of God's governance, arguing that God, the stifling watcher of humanity (Job 7:20) seems either unable or unwilling to run the world with any discernible standard.

58. James M. Kennedy, "Peasants in Revolt: Political Allegory in Genesis 2–3" in *JSOT* 47:3–14.

59. Kennedy, "Peasants in Revolt," p. 7.

60. North, "Violence and the Bible," p. 15.

61. Herbert Danby, trans., *The Mishnah* (Oxford: Oxford University Press, 1933), p. 166.

62. Danby, *Mishnah,* p. 170.

63. Niditch, *War,* p. 129.

64. Ibid.

65. Robert W. E. Forrest, "Paradise Lost Again: Violence and Obedience in the Flood Narrative" in *JSOT* 62:17.

66. José Miguez Bonino, "A Covenant Life: A Meditation on Genesis 9:1–17" in *Ecumenical Review* 33:344. In a related scene in *Enuma Elish,* Marduk places his bow in the heavens after his victory over Tiamat.

67. See Bernard F. Batto, "The Covenant of Peace: A Neglected Ancient Near Eastern Motif" in *CBQ* 49:201–10 for the mythological background of the motif of planting peace as a signal of the coming paradise. Batto finds its vestiges in the Hebrew Bible in Exodus 34:25–29; Leviticus 26:3–6; Ezekiel 34:25–30; Hosea 2:18–25; Zechariah 8:12.

68. Midrash ha-Gadol 11:9, cited in Plaut, *Torah,* p. 85.

Chapter 6

1. Richard Konetzke, *Colección de documentos para la historia de la formación social de Hispanoamérica* (Madrid: Consejo Superior de Investigaciones Científicas, 1953–1958),1:1.

2. Johannes Meier, "La presencia de las órdenes religiosas en el Caribe durante la dominación española," *Missionalia hispánica* 43, Núm. 124 (1986): 363–372.

3. Diego Alvarez de Chanca "Carta al ayuntamiento de Sevilla," en *Revista de la Universidad de La Habana* 196–197 (1972): 280–299.

4. Konetzke, *Colección de documentos,* 1: 38–57; Rafael Altamira y Crevea, "El texto de las leyes de Burgos de 1512", *Revista de historia de América,* Vol. 4, diciembre 1938, México, pp. 5–79; and Lesley Byrd Simpson, *The Laws of Burgos, 1512–1513* (San Francisco: J. Howell Books, 1960).

5. Kirkpatrick Sale, *The Conquest of Paradise: Christopher Columbus and the Columbian Legacy* (New York: Alfred A. Knopf, 1990), pp. 152–183; and Felipe Fernández Armesto, *Columbus* (Oxford: Oxford University Press, 1991), pp. 133–152.

6. *Testamento y codicilio de Isabel la Católica* (Madrid: Dirección General de Relaciones Culturales del Ministerio de Relaciones Exteriores, 1956), pp. 66–67.

7. Lewis Ulysses Hanke *La lucha española por la justicia en la conquista de América* (Madrid: Aguilar, 1967), p. 54.

8. Konetzke, *Colección de documentos,* Vol. I, pp. 89–96.

9. Ibid., pp. 471–478; Joaquín F. Pacheco, Francisco de Cárdenas y Luis Torres de Mendoza, eds., *Colección de documentos inéditos relativos al descubrimiento, conquista y organización de las antiguas posesiones españolas de América y Oceanía, sacados de los Archivos del Reino y muy especialmente del de Indias* (Madrid: Lmp. De Quiros, 1864–1884), Vol. 8, pp. 489–495.

10. Ibid.

11. Cf. Luis N. Rivera-Pagán, *A Violent Evangelism: The Political and Religious Conquest of the Americas* (Lousville: Westminster/John Knox Press, 1992), pp. 42–62.

12. Justo L. González, *Y hasta lo último de la tierra: historia ilustrada del cristianismo, Vol. 7: La era de los conquistadores* (Miami: Editorial Caribe, 1980).

13. Juan Ginés de Sepúlveda, *Demócrates segundo o de las justas causas de la guerra contra los indios* (edición crítica bilingüe, traducción castellana, introducción, notas e índices por Angel Losada) (Madrid: Consejo Superior de Investigaciones Científicas, 1951).

14. Lewis Ulysses Hanke, *Aristotle and the American Indians: A Study in Race Prejudice in the Modern World* (Chicago: Henry Regnery Co., 1959; Bloomington: Indiana University Press, 1970); Bartolomé de las Casas, "Disputa y controversia contra Juan Ginés de Sepúlveda," en *Tratados* (2 vols.) (México, D. F.: Fondo de Cultura Económica, 1965), Vol. I, pp. 217–459.

15. Bartolomé de las Casas, "Brevísima relación de la destruición de las Indias," *Tratados,* Vol. I, 5–23; Mendieta, Jerónimo de, O. F. M. *Historia eclesiástica indiana* (1596) (tercera edición facsimilar) (México, D. F.: Editorial Porrúa, 1980), pp. 68–71.

16. On the issue of the Spanish conquest of America and genocide, cf. Rivera-Pagán, *A Violent Evangelism,* pp. 169–179.

17. *De procuranda Indorum salute. Educación y evangelización* (Madrid: Consejo Superior de Investigaciones Científicas, 1987).

18. Bartolomé de las Casas, *Del único modo de atraer a todos los pueblos a la verdadera religión* (México, D. F.: Fondo de Cultura Económica, 1942).

19. Hernán Cortés, *Cartas de relación* (México, D.F.: Editorial Porrúa, 1985), p. 11.

20. Hernán Cortés, *Documentos cortesianos, 1518–1528* (ed. José Luis Martínez) (México, D. F.: Universidad Nacional Autónoma de México—Fondo de Cultura Económica, 1990), p. 165.

21. Bartolomé de las Casas, "Algunos principios . . . ," *Tratados,* Vol. II, pp. 1235–1273.

22. "Carta al Papa Alejandro VI (febrero 1502)" in Cristobal Colón, *Textos y documentos completos: Relaciones de viajes, cartas y memoriales* (Consuelo Varela, ed.) (Madrid: Alianza Editorial, 1982), pp. 285–288.

23. Cf. Ramón Iglesia *El hombre Colón y otros ensayos* (México, D. F.: Fondo de Cultura Económica, 1986).

24. Text in Vicente Murga Sanz, *Historia documental puertorriqueña, Vol. III, Cedulario puertorriqueño, tomo I (1505–1517)* (Río Piedras: Editorial de la Universidad de Puerto Rico, 1961), pp.123–127; critique in Bartolomé de las Casas, *Historia de las Indias* (3 vols.) (México, D. F.: Fondo de Cultura Económica, 1951), l. 3, c. 2, t. 2, pp. 435–438 (henceforth *H. I.*).

25. James A. Brundage, *Medieval Canon Law and the Crusader* (Madison: University of Wisconsin Press, 1969).

26. Christian Duverger, *La conversión de los indios de la Nueva España. Con el texto de los "Coloquios de los Doce" de Bernardino de Sahagún* (Quito: Ediciones Abya Yala, 1990).

27. Américo Castro, *La realidad histórica de España* (8ᵛᵃ· ed. renovada) (México, D. F. Editorial Porrúa, 1982).

28. *Textos,* pp. 15–16.

29. Fernando de los Rios, *Religión y estado en la España del siglo XVI* (México, D. F.: Fondo de Cultura Económica, 1957), p. 37.

30. Bernal Díaz del Castillo, *Historia verdadera de la conquista de la Nueva España* (México, D. F.: Editorial Porrúa, 1986).

31. Pedro de Leturia, *Relaciones entre la Santa Sede e Hispanoamérica, 1493–1835* (3 vols.) (Caracas: Sociedad Bolivariana de Venezuela; Roma: Universidad Gregoriana, 1959), Vol. I, p. 10.

32. Bartolomé de las Casas, *Los primeros memoriales* (La Habana: Universidad de La Habana, 1972), p. 76.

33. Cf. Richard Greenleaf, *The Mexican Inquisition of the Sixteenth Century* (Albuquerque: University of New Mexico Press, 1969).

34. *Historia eclesiástica indiana,* pp. 15–18, 174–177. Mendieta, however, errs with respect to Luther's birthdate. The German reformer was born in 1483, not 1485.

35. Fray Toribio de Benavente (Motolinia), *Historia de los indios de la Nueva España: Relación de los ritos antiguos, idolatrías y sacrificios de los indios de la Nueva España, y de la maravillosa conversión que Dios en ella ha obrado* (ed. Edmundo O'Gorman) (México, D. F.: Porrúa, 1984).

36. *Recopilación de las Leyes de los Reinos de las Indias.* Mandadas a imprimir y publicar por la Magestad Católica del Rey Don Carlos II, Nuestro Señor (4 tomos) (quinta edición) (Madrid: Boix, Editor, 1841), libro 1, título 1, ley 1, t. 1, p. 1

37. Cf. Beatriz Pastor, *Discurso narrativo de la conquista de América* (Premio de ensayo de Casa de las Américas, 1983) (La Habana: Casa de las Américas, 1984), pp. 42–46.

38. *Textos,* p. 253.

39. Hernando Colón, *Vida del almirante don Cristobal Colón, escrita por su hijo Hernando Colón* (edición y notas de Ramón Iglesia) (México, D. F.: Fondo de Cultura Económica, 1984), pp. 122–123; *Textos,* pp. 291–305.

40. Ibid., pp. 297–298.

41. *Cartas de relación,* p. 38.

42. In Silvio A Zavala, *Las instituciones jurídicas en la conquista de América* (segunda edición revisada y ampliada) (México, D. F.: Porrúa, 1971), p. 349.

43. Fidel de Lejarza, "Franciscanismo de Cortés y cortesianismo de los franciscanos," *Missionalia hispánica* 5 (1948): 43–136.

44. *Cartas de relación,* pp. 203–204.

45. Ibid., p. 280.

46. Ibid., p. 282.

47. Rivera-Pagán, *A Violent Evangelism,* pp. 93–98.

48. *La lucha española por la justicia, passim.*

49. Cf. the excellent essay by Justo L. González, "The Christ of Colonialism," *Church & Society* 82, no. 3 (January/February 1992): 5–36.

50. Antonio Ybot León, "Juntas de teólogos asesoras del estado para Indias 1512–1550," *Anuario de estudios americanos* 5 (1948): 397–438.

51. Robert Streit, O. M. I. "Zur Vorgeschichte de I. Junta von Burgos, 1512," *Zeitschrift für Missionswissenschaft,* Vol. 12, pp. 165–175.

52. *Columbus,* p. 67.

53. To distinguish it from the also clear, unequivocal, and loud voices from the Native Americans, such as Guarionex, Hatuey, and Aguebaná, whose direct testimonies, however, we are deprived of. The European monopoly of the written word unfortunately distorts every historiographical attempt to reconstruct the voice of the oppressed.

54. *H. I.*, l. 3, cs. 3–7, t. 2, pp. 438–455.

55. Ibid., pp. 441–442.

56. *Colección de documentos inéditos*, Vol. 32, pp. 377–378; Diego Venancio Carro, *La teología y los teólogos españoles ante la conquista de América* (2 vols.) (Madrid: Escuela de Estudios Hispanoamericanos de Sevilla, 1944), Vol. I, pp. 58–61.

57. Ibid., p. 62–63.

58. Gustavo Gutiérrez, "En busca de los pobres de Jesucristo: evangelización y teología en el siglo xvi," in Pablo Richard (ed.), *Materiales para una historia de la teología en América Latina* (VIII Encuentro Latinoamerica-no de CEHILA, Lima 1980) (San José, Costa Rica: CEHILA DEI, 1981), pp. 137–163.

59. The Las Casas bibliography is immense. As scholarly companions are indispensable two books by the Spanish Dominican historian Isacio Pérez Fenández, *Inventario documentado de los escritos de Fray Bartolomé de las Casas* (Bayamón, Puerto Rico: CEDOC, 1981); and, *Cronología documentada de los viajes, estancias y actuaciones de Fray Bartolomé de las Casas* (Bayamón, Puerto Rico: CEDOC, 1984).

60. David Henige, *In Search of Columbus: The Sources for the First Voyage* (Tucson: University of Arizona Press, 1991).

61. Lewis Hanke, "Bartolomé de las Casas, historiador," in Las Casas, *H. I.*, pp. ix–lxxxviii.

62. Juan Friede, *Bartolomé de Las Casas: Precursor del anticolonialismo* (México, D. F.: Siglo XXI, 1976).

63. Reproduced as appendix in Bartolomé de las Casas, *De regia potestate o derecho de autodeterminación* (ed. por Luciano Pereña, et al.) (*Corpus Hispanorum de Pace*, Vol. VIII) (Madrid: Consejo Superior de Investigaciones Científicas, 1969), pp. 282–283.

64. In Agustín Yañez, ed., *Fray Bartolomé de Las Casas: Doctrina* (México, D. F.: Universidad Nacional Autónoma, 1941), pp. 161–163.

65. Marcel Bataillon, *Estudios sobre Bartolomé de las Casas* (Barcelona: Península, 1976).

66. José Martí, "El padre Las Casas," in *La edad de oro* (La Habana: Editorial Gente Nueva, 1981), pp. 160–170.

67. Simón Bolívar, "Carta de Jamaica (6 de septiembre de 1815)," *Escritos fundamentales* (ed. Germán Carrera Damas) (Caracas: Monte Avila Editores, 1982), p. 46.

68. Manuel Giménez Fernández, *Bartolomé de las Casas, Vol. I: Delegado de Cisneros para la reformación de las Indias (1516–1517)* (Sevilla: Escuela de Estudios Hispanoamericanos, 1953; reimpr. Madrid: Consejo Superior de Investigaciones Científicas, Escuela de Estudios Hispanoamericanos, 1984); *Bartolomé de las Casas, Vol. II: Capellán de Carlos I, poblador de Cumaná (1517–1523)* (Sevilla: Escuela de Estudios Hispanoamericanos, 1960; reimpr. Madrid: Consejo Superior de Investigaciones Científicas, Escuela de Estudios Hispanoamericanos, 1984).

69. Ramón Menéndez Pidal, *El padre Las Casas, su doble personalidad* (Madrid: Espasa Calpe, 1963).

70. *The Revised English Bible, with the Apocrypha* (Oxford University Press and Cambridge University Press, 1989), section of the Apocrypha, p. 122.

71. Las Casas quotes this Latin text in two slightly diferent ways in *H. I.*, l. 1, c. 24, t. 1, p. 130, and *H. I.*, l. 3, c. 79, 7. 3, p. 92.

72. Edwin Edward Sylvest Jr., *Motifs in Franciscan Mission Theory in Sixteenth Century New Spain Province of the Holy Gospel* (Washington, D. C.: Academy of American Franciscan History, 1975).

Chapter 7

1. The first two quotations by Heschel are from a Peace Movement Poster of the late 1960s, unreferenced. The third is from Heschel's *The Prophets*, Part II (New York: Harper and Row, 1962), p. 64.

2. This is the calculation of Jonathan Glover, *Humanity: A Moral History of the Twentieth Century* (New Haven: Yale University Press, 2000), p. 47, based on the 1989 edition of Ruth Leger Sivard, *World Military Expenditures*. These 87,000,000 estimated deaths in war, 1914-1989, however, do not include the mass murders of their own citizens by various governments. The "engineered" death total has to be well above one hundred million and may even approach two hundred million. The real total will never be

known, for the perpetrators have succeeded in erasing the remnants and the memory of untold numbers of their victims. Were I to recommend two books for reading more deeply into the subject of this essay, one would be Glover's. The other would be Gil Baillie, *Violence Unveiled*, quoted here at the end. Cf. note 20. Others estimate the total at 175,000,000 or 200 per hour.

3. Glover, p. 414.

4. Robert Jay Lifton, *The Nazi Doctors: Medical Killing and the Psychology of Genocide* (New York: Basic Books, 1986), p. 503. Nazis believed that Jews and other undesirables would fatally infect the master race if allowed to live.

5. Cf. Christopher Browning, *Ordinary Men: Reserve Police Battalion 101 and the Final Solution in Poland* (New York: Harper Collins, 1992), especially pp. 55–70.

6. Cf. Browning, pp. 159–189. On p. 170 he discounts the claim that German soldiers were forced by threats of severe punishment to perform these duties. In over forty-five years "no defense attorney or defendant in any of the hundreds of postwar trials has been able to document a single case in which refusal to obey an order to kill unarmed civilians resulted in the allegedly inevitable dire punishment." He also discounts at length the famous theory of Daniel Goldhagen that Germans as a nation were swept up collectively in "eliminationist anti-semitism." This form of social determinism not only obscures the role of individual decision but ignores distinctions between a multitude of levels of collaboration and resistance among Germans in the Nazi era.

7. Mark Osiel, *Ever Again: Legal Remembrance and Administrative Massacre*, Pennsylvania Law Review 144 (1995).

8. James M. McPherson, *Battle Cry of Freedom: The Civil War Era* (New York: Ballantine Books, 1989), p. 572.

9. A minister friend of mine served in the Korean War in 1952. Later, in his Presbyterian church, he debated capital punishment with a parishioner who stoutly defended it. "Have you ever killed a man?" my friend inquired. "No" came the answer. "*Well I have*, and you never forget it." A head guard in the Texas prison which conducts executions commented recently that "if jurors had to draw straws to see who was going to pull the switch or start the lethal injec-

tion, there wouldn't be as many executions." (*New York Times*, 17 December 2000, p. 44.)

10. Lifton, p. 504. The Eiseley quote comes from his unpublished essay, "Man, the Lethal Factor."

11. Interview with Gus Niebuhr of the *New York Times* at the University of Louisville, April 2000, broadcast by PBS-Channel 15 on January 14, 2000.

12. James W. Loewen, *Lies My Teacher Told Me: Everything Your American History Textbook Got Wrong* (New York: Simon and Schuster, 1995), p. 167.

13. Antjie Krog, *Country in My Skull: Guilt, Sorrow, and the Limits of Forgiveness in the New South Africa* (Times Books; New York: Random House, 1999), p. 159.

14. Kenneth Patchen, *The Journal of Albion Moonlight* (New York: New Directions Paperback, 1961), p. 10.

15. W. H. Auden, *For the Time Being: A Christmas Oratorio*, in *Religious Drama/1* (Living Age Books; New York: Meridian Books, 1957), p. 60.

16. Ibid., p. 16.

17. These quotations come from Glover, pp. 220, 212, and 222–223.

18. This display of some sixty photographs was collected by James Allen of Atlanta from postcards sent by witnesses to their friends, now published in book form, *Without Sanctuary* (Santa Fe: Twin Palms Publishers, 2000). Cf. also Orlando Patterson, *Rituals of Blood: Consequences in Two American Centuries* and R. Scott Appleby, *The Ambivalence of the Sacred: Religion, Violence, and Reconciliation* (New York: Rowman and Littlefield, 2000).

19. I can only assume that those who chose this name for an American submarine did so in honor of the Texas city by that name, without much attention to the meaning of the Latin. The choice was a major affront to any honest attempt to relate Christian theology to national defense.

20. Gil Baillie, *Violence Unveiled: Humanity at the Crossroads* (New York: Crossroad, 1995), p. 209.

21. Ibid., pp. 267–270.

22. As reported by the *New York Times*, 23 November 1997.

23. Baillie, p. 270.

Chapter 8

1. The data used in this paper about catastrophe and terror in the postcommunist world are from the *Fears in Post-Communist Society Project led by Vladimir Shlapentokh, Samuel Kliger*, Tony Carnes, and others, which was funded by the National Foundation of Euro-Asian and East-European Studies. A random stratified survey of Russians was conducted in 1996 (1350 respondents), 1998 (350 respondents), and 1999 (1000 respondents). Additionally, the project used the results of a seminar on fears conducted in Moscow in 1997 and content analysis of about 1000 articles, which appeared in the Russian media in 1996–1997.

A five item scale contained these alternatives: "I don't feel any uncertainty in this sense," "Some concern," "Strong alarm," "Constant fear," and "I don't know, didn't think about it." In this chapter "strong alarm" is equated to fear and "constant fear" to "terror." Qualitative interviews generally confirm this equation.

2. Vladimir Shlapentokh, "Russian Patience: Reasonable Behavior and a Social Strategy" in *Archives European Journal of Sociology* 26, 2: 247–280. In 1994 62% of Russians considered patience their second most important trait. In the same survey Russians did not cite patience as a national virtue of any other people such as the British, Uzbeks, and Jews. Yuri Levada, "Trevogi i ozhidania," *Moskovskie Novosti*, January 15, 1995: 141–142.

3. Tony Carnes and Samuel Kliger, "Religion and Moral Values in Russia: Transition to the Post-Communist Era" in Anson Shupe and Bronislaw Misztal, *Religion, Mobilization, and Social Action* (Westport: Praeger), pp. 128–159.

4. Cf. Meredith Kline, *Image of the Spirit* (Grand Rapids: Baker Book House, 1980); J. Luzarraga, *Las Traditiones de la Nube en la Biblia y el Judaismo Primitivo* (Rome: Biblical Institute Press, 1973); T. W. Mann, *Divine Presence and Guidance in Israelite Traditions* (Baltimore: The Johns Hopkins University Press, 1977); Patrick D. Miller, *The Divine Warrior in Early Israel* (Cambridge: Harvard University Press, 1973); A. L. Oppenheim, "Akkadian pul(u)h(t)u and melammu," *Journal of the American Oriental Society* 63: 31–34.

5. Mark Juergensmeyer, *Terror in the Mind of God* (Berkeley: University of California, 1999). Also see Mark Juergensmeyer, ed., *Violence and*

the Sacred in the Modern World (London: Frank Cass and Co. Ltd., 1992).

6. Ernest Lee Tuveson, *Redeemer Nation* (Chicago: University of Chicago Press, 1968), appendix. Also see David G. Rowley, "Redeemer Empire: Russian Millenarianism," *The American Historical Review* 105: 1.

7. Robert Conquest, *The Great Terror* (New York: Macmillan, 1968); *The Great Terror: A Reassesment* (Oxford: Oxford University Press, 1990); *Harvest of Sorrow* (Oxford: Oxford University Press, 1986).

8. Leonid Gozman and Alexander Etkind, *The Psychology of Post-Totalitarianism in Russia* (London: Centre for Research into Communist Economics, 1992), p. 76.

9. For a recent version of this argument, see N. Biryukov and V. Sergeyev, *Russia's Road to Democracy: Parliament, Communism and Traditional Culture* (Aldershot: Edward Algar, 1993). For a long time, Russian political culture has had some liberal democratic actors. See Jeffrey W. Hahn, "Continuity and Change in Russian Political Culture," *British Journal of Political Science* 21: 393–421. Walicki Andrzej, *Legal Philosophies of Russian Liberalism* (Oxford: Clarendon Press, 1987).

10. However, there are some antimodern aspects of Leninism, like its value on obedience to the collective and hostility to democratic capitalist individualism. Cf. John Gray, *Totalitarianism, Reform and Civil Society* (London: Routledge, 1993), p. 158.

11. See the works of Andrei Platonov, Vasili Grossman, and Alexander Solzhenitsyn who have described the significance of fear in Soviet society. On fear in German totalitarianism, see, for example, Hans Fallada, *Jeder stirbt fuer sich allein* (Reinbeck: Rowohlt, 1964); and Anna Seghers, *Das Seibte Dreuz* (Darmstadt: Luchterhand, 1988).

12. The terrorist incidents were manipulated by the government to consolidate the public standing of Vladimir Putin. On August 9, 1999, Yeltsin appointed his security chief Putin as his fifth prime minister and heir apparent. Public support of the new prime minister however, was very low. According to an August survey conducted by the Fund of Public Opinion, only 2% of Russians supported Putin as a presidential candidate. After the explosions, however, Putin's support for the presidency climbed to

22%, surpassing that of all other politicians in the country, according to a October Fund for Public Opinion survey. This led to accusations by General Alexander Lebed and others that maybe the government was using terror bombings to push people its way. Andrei Piontkovsky, a respected political analyst in Moscow, made parallels between the explosions in Moscow and the way the Nazis used the burning of the German Reichstag in 1933 to justify totalitarian rule. In fact, about a third of Russians believed that their leaders were involved in the explosions, according to various opinion polls.

13. Richard Pipes, *Russia Under the Bolshevik Regime* (New York: Alfred A. Knopf, 1993), pp. 337–368.

14. See Czeslan Milosz's poignant *The Captive Mind* (New York: Vintage Books, 1951).

15. "What we are fighting for?" in Paul Avrich, *Kronstadt 1921* (Princeton: Princeton University Press, 1970), p. 241. Cp. Arthur Koestler, *Darkness at Noon* (New York: Bantam Books, 1968).

16. Alexander Solzhenitsyn, "The Smatterers" in Alexander Solzhenitsyn et al., *From Under the Rubble* (London: Fontana/Collins, 1976), p. 274.

17. Cf. David B. Pillemer, *Momentous Events, Vivid Memories* (Cambridge: Harvard University Press, 1998). Eviatar Zerubavel, *Social Mindscapes: An Invitation to Cognitive Sociology* (Cambridge: Harvard University Press, 1997), pp. 81–84, 87–93, 95–97, 100–101. Sigmund Freud, *Moses and Monotheism* (New York: Vantage, 1967/1939), pp. 119–121.

18. Cf. Vladimir Shlapentokh, *Fear in the Post-Communist World*. Paper presented to the conference on "Fears and Hopes in Post-Communist Society Entering the Twenty-first Century" April 13, 2000, p. 29.

19. Vladimir Shlapentokh, "Fear of the Future in the Modern World: A Russian Case in *International Journal of Comparative Sociology* (1998) 9: 161–176; and ibid., "Catastrophism on the Eve of 2000: Apocalyptic Ideology between Russia's Past and Future in *Demokratizatsia,* Winter (1997): 5.

20. See the Burkean critique of the application to Soviet society of utopian liberal economic laws and abstract democratic rights in Peter Murrell, "Conservative Political Philosophy and the Strategy of Economic Transition" in John H. Moore, ed., *Legacies of the Collapse of Communism, and Traditional Culture* (George Mason University Press, 1994), pp. 165–179.

21. Cf. Grigory Vainshtein, "Totalitarian Public Consciousness in a Post-totalitarian Society" in *Communist and Post-Communist Studies* 27 (3): 247–259.

22. Ibid, p. 248.

23. Nikolai Biryukov and Victor Sergeyev, *Russia's Road to Democracy: Parliament, Communism, and Traditional Culture* (Aldershot, Eng.: E. Elgar, 1993). Some like Victor Aksiuchits located the source of today's troubles in the cultural and spiritual traditions started in the distant past. Some say that the roots lie in the schism between the followers of Avvakum's traditionalists (the Old Believers) and the reformers in the seventeenth century. Aksiuchits locates the roots in a fifteenth century opposition between the "non-possessor" school of Nil Sorsky, which stressed traditional Russian spirituality, "inner activity," and concentration on spiritual self-perfection and the "Possessor" school of Joseph of Volokolamsk, which stressed subordination, discipline, and the acquisition of material wealth in close relation to the State.

24. See the debates about the ecological issues in Surgey Kurginian and Valentin Koptivg, *Zavtra;* and Vladlen Loginov, "Novoie srednevekovie" in *Nezavisimaia gazeta,* November 22, 1994, p. 3.

25. Cf. Leslie Holmes, "Normalization and Legitimation in Post-Communist Russia" in *Development in Russian and Post-Soviet Politics,* Stephen White et al., eds. (New York: Macmillan, 1998), pp. 309–330.

26. See *Literaturnaia Gazeta,* May 9, 1995.

27. Vladimir Shlapentokh, *Soviet Intellectuals and Political Power* (Princeton: Princeton University Press, 1990). In comparing the mentality of Russian intellectuals in the 1970s and 1980s with their ancestors in late Czarist Russia, Alexander Shpagin notes that the latter generation lack the apocalyptic presentiment and apprehensiveness of the earlier generation that "tore the personality into parts and broke the world around." Alexander Shpagin, "Rekviem v stile rok" in *Literaturnia Gazeta,* August 31, 1994, p. 7.

28. See VTSCIOM 5 (1994); 6 (1994); 2 (1995). In a survey conducted in August of 1994, Russians described the situation in the country

as "critical" (40%), "alarming" (20%), or "catastrophic" (22%). See *Nezavisimaia Gazeta*, August 17, 1994, p. 6. At the end of 1994, only 16% of Russians, according to VTSCIOM, strongly believed in an improvement in the country. According to VTSCIOM, 25% thought that in 1995 "the country will continue to slide into an abyss," and 12% expected "anarchy." See *Moskovskie Novosti*, January 15, 1995, p. 3. Also, see Yuri Levada, ed., *Est Mvenie* (Moscow: Progress Publishers, 1991); and Ibid., *Sovietskii Proskei Chelovers* (Moscow: Progress Publishers, 1993).

29. Vladimir Yadov, "About Some Characteristics of the Russian Alarming Mind." Paper given to the annual meeting of the American Association for the Advancement of Slavic Studies (AAASS).

30. One of the coresearchers on the catastrophe project suggested that the fears were artificial and imposed on the Russian masses by the media (Boris Grushin, "The image of impending catastrophe as a weapon in political struggle." Paper presented to the annual meeting of American Association for the Advancement of Slavic Studies (AAASS). For example, he denigrated the fears of civil war. But in fact, Russia in the post-Communist period moved to the brink of civil war several times; for example, in September-October of 1993, there was a confrontation between the president and the parliament. According to Grushin's own data cited in his paper, in November of 1993 only 11% of Russians considered fear of civil war as "strong" or "very strong." In the wake of the shelling of parliament by Yeltsin, this figure jumped to 24%.

31. Twenty-seven percent attributed their sense of fear and terror to the media and 5% to talks with friends, relatives, and colleagues.

32. Ted Gurr's "relative deprivation" theory says that deterioration of living conditions coupled with a gap between people's real lives and their expectations is a sufficient cause for "riots and disorder." Ted Gurr, *Why Men Rebel* (Princeton: Princeton University Press, 1974). Resource mobilization theories stress the possibility of organizing for improving living conditions. The Russian case has met the requirements of Charles Tilly and other resource mobilization advocates but the situation hasn't in fact generated a major mass protest movement. See Charles Tilly, *From Mobilization to Revolution*

(Reading, Mass.: Addison-Wesley, 1978); William A. Gamson, *The Strategy of Social Protest* (Homewood, Ill.: Dorsey Press, 1979); Doug McCarthy and Zald Mayer, "Resource Mobilization and Social Movements: A Partial Theory" in *American Journal of Sociology* 82, 5: 1212–1241; and Anthony Oberschall, *Social Conflict and Social Movements* (Englewood Cliffs: Prentice-Hall, 1973).

33. VTSIOM, pp. 1, 28.

34. Goskomstat, p. 156.

35. *Argumenty I Fakty*, 1994, p. 50.

36. F. J. Teggart, *Theory and Processes of History* (Berkeley: University of California Press, 1941); Ibid., "The Humanistic Study of Change in Time" in *Journal of Philosophy*, June 19, 1926: XXIII; Ibid., "The Argument of Hesiod's *Works and Days*" in *The Journal of the History of Ideas*; Stanford M. Lyman, "The Science of History and the Theory of Social Change" in *Max Weber's Political Sociology: A Pessimistic Vision of a Rationalized World*, Ronald M. Glassman and Vatro Murvar, eds. (Wesport: Greenwood Press, 1984); Ibid., "The Acceptance, Rejection, and Reconstruction of Histories: On Some Controversies in the Study of Social and Cultural Change" in *Structure, Consciousness, and History*, Richard Harvey Brown and Stanford M. Lyman, eds. (Cambridge: Cambridge University Press, 1978); Robert Nisbet, *Social Change and History* (New York: Oxford University Press, 1969); Tony Carnes, "Frederick J. Teggart on 'Entering California': Self-Reflections on Migrations, Religion, and the Humanistic Sciences" in *Surviving the Twentieth Century: Social Philosophy from the Frankfurt School to the Columbia University Seminars*, Judith T. Marcus, ed. (New Brunswick: Transaction Publishers, 1999). Cf. Erich Auerbach, *Mimesis* (Toronto: Doubleday, 1952); and Thorlief Boman, *Hebrew Thought Compared to Greek* (New York: W. W. Norton Co., 1960).

37. A tension between Marxist and Leninist thought was a practical difference in the interpretation of economic crises and revolution. One reading of Marx's *Capital* would emphasize that the crises of capitalism and revolution are not causal factors themselves because they are the inevitable outworking of economic structural contradictions. Of course Lenin, who had some actual practice at revolution, focused much more on the opportunities and mechanics of catastrophe, terrors, and their rationalizations.

38. Cf. Walter Laqueur, " The Causes of Failure" in *A World of Secrets* (New York: Basic Books, 1985), pp. 255–292.

39. Ironically, Grushin, a founding member of our catastrophe survey group, is also the source for one of the most vehement denunciations of "fear mongers." He has elaborated a theory of "non-grass roots" causes of the catastrophic mindset of the people in Russia. He describes "the main characters generating and mulling the images of the impending disasters" as the chief officers of the executive branch, both central and regional, top politicians belonging to the opposition, mass media, "especially those which focus an all-out criticism of the country's leadership, the double-tongued friends of the people including traditional Russian hysterical women and 'God's tools' from the ranks of intelligentsia and lower-intelligentsia." See his paper "The image of impeding catastrophe as a weapon in political struggle" presented at the annual meeting of American Association for the Advancement of Slavic Studies (AAASS) (November 1995). On the eve of the financial and economic catastrophe of August 17, 1999, Daniil Dondurei accused the Russian media of fomenting fears (*Izvestia*, August 5, 1998). On "concocted catstrophism," see the article by Yeltsin's former press secretary, Viacheslav Kostikov: "Rekviem dlia rodiny" in *Nezavisimaia Gazeta* (February 2, 1999), p. 12.

40. Vladimir Shlapentokh, "Fear of the future in the modern world: a Russian case," in *International Journal of Comparative Sociology* 2:161–176; Ibid., "Catastrophism on the eve of 2000: apocalyptic ideology between Russia's past and future," in *Demokratizatsia*, Winter 5:1–20; Vladimir Shlapentokh, Vladimir Shubkin, and Vladimir Yadov, eds., *Katastrofichseskoie Soznanie v sovremennom mire (The catastrophic mind in the contemporary world)* (Moscow: Rossiiskaia assotsiatsia Nauchnykh Fondov, 1999); Emil Mitev, Veroniak Ivanova, and Vladimir Shubkin, "Katastroficheskoie Soznanie v Bulgarii i Rossis" (the catastrophic mind in Russia and Bulgaria) in *Sotsiologiuchekie isseldovania* 10; Vladimir Shubkin and Veronika Ivanova, "Strakhi v post Sovietskom Prostrantsve" (Fears in the spot soviet space), *Monitoring Obshchetvennogo* 3; Vladimir Iadov, "Strakhi v Rossii" (Fears in Russia), *Sotsiologicheskii Journal* 3; Vladimir Shubkin, "Strakh kak faktor sotsialnogo povedenia". *Sot-*

siologicheskii Journal 3:15–30; Ibid., "Ekologicheskia katastrofa strashnee revolutisii" (The ecological fears are more scary than revolution), *Delovoi Mir* 2; Ibid., "Struktura strakhov i trevog v sovremnennoi Rossii" (The structure of fears and anxieties in contemporary Russia), *Mir Rossii* 2; Vladas Gaidys, "The economic attitudes that make a difference," *Baltic Review (Tallinn)* 13:45–46; Ibid., "Attitudes towards the economic system in the Baltic states," in *Cultural Encounters in East Central Europe Report* 11:61–73; Ibid., "Political activity and passivity in Lithuania," in *Pilsoniska Apsina. Riga: Filozofijas un sociologijas instituts* 2:191–202; Ibid., "Political values: stability vs. lability," in *Values in the time of changes*, A. Mitrikas, ed. (Vilnius: Institute of Philosophy and Sociology, 1999), pp. 74–88; L. Kesselman and M. Matskevich, "Individual optimism/pessimism in the contemporary Russian transformation," *Sociology: theory, methods, marketing* 1–2:164–175.

41. Pitirim Aleksandrovich Sorokin, *Man and Society in Calamity: The Effects of War, Revolution, Famine, Pestilence upon Human Mind, Behavior, Social Organization, and Cultural Life* (New York: Greenwood Press, 1968).

42. See Robert Bailey III, *Sociology Faces Pessimism* (The Hague: Martinus Nijhof, 1958); Charles Fritz, "Disaster" in *Social Problems*, Robert Merton and Robert Nisbet, eds. (New York: Harcourt Brace and World, 1961); Gary Kreps, "Disaster and the Social Order" in *Sociological Theory* 3:49–65; Ibid., "Classical Themes, Structural Sociology, and Disaster Research" in *Sociology of Disasters: Contribution of Sociology to Disaster Research*, Russell Dynes, Bruna De Marchi, and Carlo Pelanda, eds. (Milan: Franco Angeli, 1987), pp. 357–402; Samuel Prince, *Catastrophe and Social Change, Based upon a Sociological Study of the Halifax Disaster* (New York: Columbia University Press, 1920); E. L. Quarantelli, "The Nature and Conditions of Panic" in *American Journal of Sociology* 60:267–75; Ibid., *Panic Behavior in Fire Situations: Findings and a Model from the English Language Literature* (Newark: Disaster Research Center, University of Delaware, 1981); Marta Wolfenstein, *Disaster: A Psychological Essay* (Glenocoe: Free Press, 1957); Albert H. Cantril, *Hopes and Fears of the American People* (New York: Universe Books, 1971).

43. See Nicholas Demerath and Anthony Wallace, "Human Adaptation to Disaster" in *Human Organization* 16:1–2; Russell Dynes, "Dis-

aster as a Social Science Field" in *National Review of Social Sciences* 13:75–84; Ibid., *Organized Behavior in Disaster* (Lexington, Mass.: D.C. Heath, 1970); Russell Dynes, E. L. Quarantelli, and Gary Kreps, *A Perspective on Disaster Planning*, Report series no. 11. (Newark: University of Delaware, Disaster Research Center, 1972); Gary Kreps, "The Organization of Disaster Response: Some Fundamental Theoretical Issues" in *Disasters: Theory and Research*, E. L. Quarantelli, ed. (London: Sage, 1978); Gary Kreps, "The Organization of Disaster Response: Core Concepts and Processes" in *International Journal of Mass Emergencies and Disasters* 1:439–467; Irving Janis and Leon Mann, "Emergency Decision Making: A Theoretical Analysis of Responses to Disaster Warnings" in *Journal of Human Stress* 3:35–48; Dennis Mileti, Thomas Drabek, and J. Eugene Haas in *Human Systems and Extreme Environments* (Boulder: Institute for Behavioral Science, University of Colorado, 1975); Ronald Perry, *Comprehensive Emergency Management: Evacuating Threatened Populations* (Greenwich: JAI Press, 1985); Jerry Rose, *Outbreaks: The Sociology of Collective Behavior* (New York: Free Press, 1982); E. L. Quarantelli, *Disasters: Theory and Research* (London: Sage, 1978); Ibid., *Evacuation Behavior and Problems* (Newark: Disaster Research Center, University of Delaware, 1980); James Wright and Peter Rossi, *Social Science and Natural Hazard* (Cambridge: Abt Books, 1981); A. Mozgovaia, *Sotsialnyie Problemy Ekologii* (Moscow: Institute of Sociology, 1994); Peter E. Hodgkinson and Michael Stewart, *Coping with Catastrophe: A Handbook of Disaster Management* (London; New York: Routledge, 1991).

44. See Bonnie Green, "Conceptual and Methodological Issues in Assessing the Psychological Impact of Disaster" in *Disasters and Mental Health: Selected Contemporary Perspectives*, Barbara Sowder, ed. (Rockville, Md: National Institutes of Health, 1985); J. Eugene Haas and Thomas Drabek, "Community Disaster and System Stress: A Sociological Perspective" in *Social and Psychological Factors in Stress*, Joseph McGrath, ed. (New York: Holt, Rinehart and Winston, 1970); Thomas Kurian, *The New Book of World Rankings* (New York: Facts on File, 1991); Eli Marks and Charles Fritz, "The NORC Studies in Human Behavior in Disaster" in *Journal of Social Issues* 10:26–41; Ronald Perry and Michael Lindell, "The Psychological Consequence of Natural Disaster: A Review of Research on American Communities" in *Mass Emergencies* 3:105–15; E. L. Quarantelli, "What Is Disaster? The Need for Clarification in Definition and Conceptualization in Research" in *Disasters and Mental Health: Selected Contemporary Perspectives*, Barbara Sowder, ed. (Rockville, Md.: National Institutes of Health, 1985); Daniel Slottje, ed., *Measuring the Quality of Life across Countries: A Multidimensional Analysis*, (Boulder: Westview Press, 1991); Stuart Walker and Rachel Rosser, eds., *Quality of Life Assessment: The Key Issues in the 1990s* (Dordrecht: Kluver, 1993); Mike Davis, *Ecology of Fear* (New York: Holt, 1998); Rafael López-Pedraza, *Anselm Kiefer: The Psychology of "After the Catastrophe"* (New York: George Braziller, 1996); David R. Marples, *Belarus: From Soviet Rule to Nuclear Catastrophe* (New York: St. Martin's Press, 1996).

45. Angus Campbell, *The Sense of Well-Being in America* (New York: McGraw, 1971); Angus Campbell, P. Converse, and W. Rogers, *The Quality of American Life: Perceptions, Evaluations, and Satisfactions* (New York: Russell Sage Foundation, 1976); Frank Andrews, ed., *Research of the Quality of Life* (Ann Arbor: The University of Michigan, 1–2, 1986); E. Allard, *A Frame of Reference for Selecting Social Indicators* (Helsinki: Comentationes Scientarum Socialism, 1972); Rose Schumacher, G. Stevens, T. O'Donell, L. Torrence, and K. Carney, *World Quality Of Life Indicators* (Santa Barbara: ABC-CLIO, 1989); Robert Lauer, *Social Problems and the Quality of Life* (Dubuque: Brown, 1982).

46. See Amos Tversky, *Decision Making: Descriptive, Normative and Prescriptive* (Cambridge: Cambridge University Press, 1982); George Von Furstenberg, *Acting Under Uncertainty* (Boston: Kluver, 1990); Niklas Luhmann, *Risk: A Sociological Theory* (New York: Gruyter, 1993).

47. Barry Glassner, *The Culture of Fear: Why Americans Are Afraid of the Wrong Things* (New York: Basis Books, 1999).

48. Samuel Prince, *Catastrophe and Social Change, Based upon a Sociological Study of the Halifax Disaster* (New York: Columbia University Press, 1920).

49. Magnus Ranstorp traces the rise of terrorism to intrusions and events under the general rubric of "chaos." See his 1996 "Terrorism in the Name of Religion" in *Journal of International Affairs* 56 (1): 41–62. Sonia L. Alianak asso-

ciates the occurence of messianic assassins with "shocks," "The Mentality of Messianic Assassins" in *Orbis* 44 (2): 283–94.

50. (Chicago: University of Chicago, 1997), p. 69.

51. Erich Goode and Nachman Ben-Yehuda, *Moral Panics* (Oxford: Blackwell, 1994).

52. David C. Rapoport and Yonah Alexander, eds., *The Morality of Terrorism* (New York: Columbia University Press, 1989).

53. See "the hierarchy of Russian traditional values" for 1990–1999 in Elena Bashkirova, *Value Change and the Survival of Democracy in Russia (1995–2000)* (Moscow: ROMIR, 1999).

54. VTSCIOM 12:5.

55. This thesis was developed by Vladimir Yadov in various presentations in 1995.

56. VTSCIOM 3:36–37.

57. Vladimir Shlapentokh, *Public and Private Life of the Soviet People* (Oxford: Oxford University Press, 1989).

58. Cf. Richard Rose, "Distrust as an obstacle to the Civil Society" in *Studies in Public Policy about Eastern Europe Between State and Market* (Strathclyde: Center for the Study of Public Policy, 1998), p. 226.

59. Tony Carnes, "New Russian Entrepreneurs." Paper presented to Eastern Sociological Society (Boston), Spring 1996, p. 28.

60. Cf. Ernest Gellner, *Conditions and Liberty: Civil Society and Its Rivals* (London: Hamish Hamilton, 1994).

61. Christopher Smith, author of *American Evangelicalism,* found that the "Nons" whom he interviewed were made up of two groups. "One group is not very well-educated and not very engaged with society including religion," he observes. "The other group is well-educated with a higher proportion of people with a master's [degree]. They are successful secularist-type of people. The non-religious are more likely to be single and divorced, younger. They could be life-cycle groups: their relations are either not formed or are disrupted." Smith also suggests that "non-religious" "means in between churches. They still do such religious things as pray." Could the Russian non-religious be in between Communism and something else? Personal communication, November 3, 1998.

62. Between 1992 and 1995 we followed a panel of 220 new Russian entrepreneurs. They were much less likely to identify with any religion in comparison to the general population. Mostly, new Russian entrepreneurs focused on work to the exclusion of religious interests. However, among those expressing a religious identification, the proportion of Protestants was much greater than for the general population. New Russian entrepreneurs were also more likely than the general population to esteem the Bible, which seems to them more concrete than religious ceremonies.

Chapter 9

1. Although it may not be recognizable, I want to thank the Columbia University Seminar on Contents Methods in the Social Sciences for hearing the first public draft of this paper in October of 2000.

2. Everett Fox, *The Five Books of Moses* (New York: Schocken Books, 1965).

3. Hannah Arendt, "On Violence" as excerpted by Manfred Steger and Nancy Lind, eds. *Violence and Its Alternatives* (Hampshire, Eng.: Palgrave Publishers, 1965).

4. Georg Simmel, *On Women, Sexuality, and Love* (New Haven: Yale University, 1984), p. 157.

5. Ibid, pp. 191–192.

6. Georg Simmel, *Conflict and the Web of Group Affiliations* (Glencoe: Free Press, 1955).

7. Jeffrey Bloechl, *Liturgy of the Neighbor: Emmanuel Levinas and the Religion of Responsibility* (Pittsburgh: Duquesne University Press, 1966).

8. Emmanuel Lévinas, "The Face," UNESCO 92:67.

9. Emmanuel Lévinas, *Outside the Subject* (Stanford: Stanford University Press, 1994).

10. Emmanuel Lévinas, *Of God Who Comes to Mind* (Stanford: Stanford University Press, 1986). See also Adriaan T. Peperzak, *Ethics as First Philosophy* (New York: Routledge, 1995).

11. Emmanuel Lévinas, *Nine Talmudic Readings.* Trans. Anne Aronowicz (Bloomington: Indiana University Press, 1990).

12. Ibid., p. xxiii.

13. Georg Simmel, *On Individuality and Social Forms* (Chicago: University of Chicago Press, 1971). Ibid., *The Sociology of Georg Simmel.* Translated, edited, and with an introduction by Kurt H. Wolff (Glencoe: Free Press, 1950).

14. Simmel, *On Individuality,* p. 123.

15. Howard Becker, *Systematic Sociology, on the Basis of the Beziehungslehre and Gebildelehre of*

Leopold von Wiese und Kaiserswaldau (New York: J. Wiley & Sons; London, Chapman & Hall, 1932).

16. Theodore Caplow, "A Theory of Coalitions in the Triad" in *American Sociological Review* 21 (4): 489–93.

17. Theodore M. Mills, "Power Relations in Three-Person Groups" in *American Sociological Review* 18 (4): 351–357.

18. Henry Frank Guggenheim, http://www.hfg.org/ and http://www.hfg.org/html.pages/mag4/toc.htm in "Teaching About Violence," *HFG Review* 4 (1): 43

19. Portions of the following argument appear in "Religion Class at Sing Sing Prison," T. Carnes and Anna Karpathakis, eds. in *New York Glory: Religions in the City* (New York University Press, 2001); and in "Sacred Text and Social Theory in Sing Sing Prison," Thomas O'Connor, ed., forthcoming *Journal of Offender Rehabilitation* Spring 2002.

20. Harold Garfinkel, "Conditions of Successful Degradation Ceremonies" in *The American Journal of Sociology* LXI, no. 5 (March 1956): 420–424.

21. Erving Goffman, *The Presentation of Self in Everyday Life* (New York: Doubleday Anchor Books, 1959); Ibid., *Stigma: Notes on the Management of a Spoiled Identity* (Englewood Cliffs, N.J.: Prentice-Hall, 1963); Charles Horton Cooley, *Social Organization: A Study of the Larger Mind* (New Brunswick, N.J.: Transaction Press, 1993).

22. Garfinkel, "Conditions," p. 420.

23. Robert Gephardt Jr., "Status Degradation and Organizational Succession: An Ethnomethodological Approach" in *Administrative Science Quarterly* 23: 553–581.

24. Whole degradation ceremonies are characterized by their minute details. For an interesting biblical example, see R. N. Whybray, *The Succession Narrative: A Study of I Kings 1 and 2* (London: S.C.M. Press, 1968).

25. Susan Baker, "The Principles and Practices of Ecofeminism: A Review" in *Journal of Gender Studies* 2 (1): 4–26.

26. David Knights and Hugh Willmott, "Power and Subjectivity at Work: From Degradation to Subjugation in Social Relations" in *Sociology* 23 (4): 535–558.

27. Gloria Cowan and Kerri F. Dunn, "What Themes in Pornography Lead to Perceptions of the Degradation of Women?" in *Journal of Sex Research* 31 (1): 11–21.

28. Jean Francois Lae, "Work Incapacity in the Mass Transportation System in Paris, from Protection to Sanction" in *Societes Contemporaines* 8: 107–125.

29. Sarah C. Neitzel, "Priests and Proletarians: the Catholic Gesellenverein, 1847–65" in *Fides et Historia* 16 (1): 35–44.

30. John Walton, "Marx for the Late Twentieth Century: Transnational Capital and Disenfranchised Labor" in *Social Science Quarterly* 64 (4): 786–809. For a discussion of Foucault on subjectivity as fetished in identity see: David Knights and Hugh Willmott, "Power and Subjectivity at Work: From Degradation to Subjugation in Social Relations" in *Sociology* 23 (4): 535–558.

31. Harrison Trice, "Rites and Ceremonials in Organizational Cultures" in *Research in the Sociology of Organizations* V (4): 221–270.

32. See also a French study outlining methods for resisting degradation: Serge Paugam, "The Status of Assisted Poverty" in *Revue francaise de Sociologie* 32 (1): 75–101.

33. Per Mathiesen, "Bureaucratic Categories and Ethnic Ascriptions: An Analysis of a Norwegian Housing Program in a Sami Region" in *Ethnos* 13 (3–4): 236–245.

34. Rai S. Gandhi, "The Extremes of Ethnic Violence: Some Explanations of Upper Castes-Scheduled Castes Conflicts in India" in *Humbolt Journal of Social Relations* 19 (2): 359–389.

35. A. DeVos George, "Ethnic Adaptation and Minority Status" in *Journal of Cross Cultural Psychology* 11 (1): 101–124.

36. Joseph Gabel, "Racism and Alienation" in *Praxis International* 2 (4): 421–437; and Orlando Patterson, *Slavery and Social Death* (Cambridge: Harvard University Press, 1982).

37. Heinz Ulrich, "Between Adaptation and Autonomy: East German Studies on the Collapse of Values. Several Selected Results from the Studies STUDENT 89 and STUDENT 90" in *Kultursoziologie* 1 (3): 45–57.

38. Ernst Porterfield, "Black-American Intermarriage in the United States" in *Marriage and Family Review* 5(1):17–24.

39. Jack Corzani and Lionel Dubois, "West Indian Mythology and Its Literary Illustrations" in *Research in African Literatures* 25 (2): 131–139.

40. Gloria Cowan and Kerri F. Dunn, "What Themes in Pornography Lead to Perceptions of the Degradation of Women?" in *Journal of Sex Research* 31 (1): 11–21.

41. John Stoltenberg, *Refusing to be a Man* (New York: New American Library, 1990).

42. Michael G. Dalecki and Jammie Price, "Dimensions of Pornography" in *Sociological Spectrum* 14 (3): 205–219.

43. Robert W. Dumond, "The Sexual Assault of Male Inmates in Incarcerated Settings" in *International Journal of the Sociology of Law* 20 (2): 135–157.

44. Carole J. Sheffield, "The Invisible Intruder: Women's Experiences of Obscene Phone Calls" in *Gender and Society* 3 (4): 438–488.

45. Judith Kiellberg Bell, "Women, Environment and Urbanization: A Guide to the Literature" in *Environment and Urbanization* 3 (2): 92–103.

46. Brindavan C. Moses, "So-Called Development, Environmental Degradation and People's Struggle Against Them" in *Religion and Society* (Bangalore) 37 (11): 79–84.

47. Jeffrey E. Nash and Anne Sutherland, "The Moral Elevation of Animals: The Case of Gorillas in the Mist" in *International Journal of Politics, Culture and Society* 5 (1): 111–126.

48. Lynne A. Foster, Christina Mann-Veale, and Catherine Ingram-Fogel, "Factors Present when Battered Women Kill" in *Issues in Mental Health Nursing* 10 (3–4): 273–284.

49. Miroslay Zivkovic, "Roots, Constitution and Heritages of Gerontology," in *Socioloski-Preqled* 7 (1): 5–26.

50. Robert A. Pearlman, Kevin C. Cain, Donald L. Patrick, Helene E. Starks, Nancy S. Jecker, and Richard F. Uhlmann, "Insights Pertaining to Patient Assessments of States Worse than Death" in *Journal of Clinical Ethics* 4 (1): 33–41.

51. George A. DeVos, "Ethnic Adaptation and Minority Status" in *Journal of Cross Cultural Psychology* 11 (1): 101–124.

52. Evelyn Kallen and Lawrence Lam, "Target for Hate: The Impact of the Zundel and Keegestra Trials on a Jewish-Canadian Audience" in *Canadian Ethics Studies* 25 (1): 9–24.

53. See also Kenneth A. Strike, "Humanizing Education: Subjective and Objective Aspects" in *Studies in Philosophy and Education* 11 (1): 17–30.

54. On the notion of erotic invisibility, see Diane Tong, "Photographing Gypsies" in *Journal of Mediterranean Studies* 2 (1): 98–100.

55. Bruce A. Jacobs, "Getting Narced: Neutralization of Undercover Identity Discreditation" in *Deviant Behavior* 14 (3): 187–208.

56. Paul Creelan, "The Degradation of the Sacred: Approaches of Cooley and Goffman" in *Symbolic Interaction* 10 (1): 29–56. See p. 33.

57. Ibid., p. 36.

58. Ibid., p. 38, 39.

59. Ibid., pp. 40–41.

60. Orlando Patterson, *Slavery, Social Death or Communal Victory: A Critical Appraisal of Slavery and Social Death* (Port of Spain, Trinidad: Economics and Business Research, 1996).

61. Ibid., p. 42.

62. Gay Becker, *Disrupted Lives: How People Create Meaning in a Chaotic World* (Berkeley: University of California Press, 1999).

Chapter 10

1. Keith Howard, ed., *True Stories of the Korean Comfort Women*, Young Joo Lee, trans. (London: Cassell, 1995), p. 45.

2. The Rainbow Center is a shelter and advocacy center for Korean spouses and girlfriends of U.S. servicemen, based in the New York City area.

3. Christine B. N. Chin, *In Service and Servitude: Foreign Female Domestic Workers and the Malaysian "Modernity" Project* (New York: Columbia University Press, 1998).

4. G. Cameron Hurst III, "URI NARA-ISM": Cultural Nationalism in Contemporary Korea," *Universities Field Staff International (UFSI) Reports*, 33 (1985): 1.

5. Katharine H. S. Moon, "South Korea Movements against Militarized Sexual Labor," *Asian Survey* 39, no. 2 (March/April, 1999).

6. Bert Klandermans, "The Social Construction of Protest and Multiorganizational Fields" in *Frontiers in Social Movement Theory*, eds. Aldon Morris and Carol Mueller (New Haven: Yale University Press, 1992), p. 80. For "frame alignment," see David Snow, E. Burke Rochford Jr., et al., "Frame Alignment Processes, Micro-Mobilization and Movement Participation," *American Sociological Review* 51, no. 4 (August, 1986): 464–481.

7. Author interview, Seoul, winter, 1992.

8. *Kijich'on* means military camptown.

9. See Katharine H. S. Moon, *Sex Among Allies: Military Prostitution in U.S.-Korea Relations* (New York: Columbia University Press, 1997).

10. Laura C. Nelson, *Measured Excess: Status, Gender, and Consumer Nationalism in South Korea* (New York: Columbia University Press, 2000), p. 144.

11. Ibid., pp. 134–136.

12. Author conversations with Sea-Ling Cheng, spring and winter, 1999. Cheng is a graduate student of Anthropology at Oxford University and has focused her field research on foreign nationals, primarily Filipinas, living and working in the Korean *kijich'on* areas.

13. *Chosun Ilbo* (Daily News), May 4, 1971 (eighth U. S. Army translation).

14. Katharine H. S. Moon, *Sex Among Allies*, p. 147. See pp. 146–147 for more details on the boycott and protest. From the perspective of African-American airmen who had led the boycott, the campaign was itself a protest against the local Koreans' discrimination against black soldiers.

15. *Newsweek*, U.S. Edition, April 10, 2000.

16. *Los Angeles Times*, August 22, 1992.

17. Hagen Koo, "Strong State and Contentious Society" in *State and Society in Contemporary Korea* (Ithaca: Cornell University Press, 1993).

18. Katharine H. S. Moon, "Migrant Workers' Movements in Japan and South Korea" in *Social Movements in the Age of Globalization*, ed. Craig N. Murphy (London: Macmillan, forthcoming).

19. Joint Committee for Migrant Workers in Korea, http://kpd.sing.kr.org/jcmk/situation/situation_engl.html.

20. Moon, "Migrant Workers' Movements in Japan and South Korea."

21. Author conversations with Kim Yonja, February, 1997.

22. *Newsweek*, U.S. Edition, April 10, 2000.

23. Chung Chang Kwon, "The People We Met in Vietnam," *People to People* (Seoul, Korea: Korea House for International Solidarity, 2000), pp. 16–20 (in Korean).

24. Kim Ra, "'Song for Bungtau': Preparing for the Cultural Festival for Peace," *People to People* (June/July, 2000), pp. 83–87 (in Korean).

Chapter 11

1. *The Works of Francis J. Grimke*, ed. C. G. Woodson (Washington D.C.: Associated Publishers, 1942), 1: 354.

2. Cited in Albert J. Raboteau, "'The Blood of the Martyrs is the Seed of Faith': Suffering in the Christianity of American Slaves" in *The Courage to Hope: From Black Suffering To Human Redemption*, eds. Quinton H. Dixie and Cornel West (Boston: Beacon Press, 1999), p. 31.

3. James Baldwin, *The Fire Next Time* (New York: Dell, 1964), p. 46.

4. Martin Luther King Jr., "Letter From Birmingham Jail" in his *Why We Can't Wait* (New York: Harper, 1963), pp. 90–91.

5. *A Testament of Hope: The Essential Writings of Martin Luther King Jr.*, ed. James M. Washington (San Francisco: Harper & Row, 1986), p. 233.

6. Ibid., p. 286.

7. Martin Luther King Jr., "Thou Fool," Sermon, Mount Pisgah Baptist Church, Chicago, Ill., August 27, 1967.

8. *The Autobiography of Malcolm X*, with the assistance of Alex Haley (New York: Grove Press, 1965), p. 222.

9. Martin Luther King Jr., "Religion's Answer to the Problem of Evil" in *The Papers of Martin Luther King, Jr., Volume I*, Claybone Carson, Senior Editor (Berkley: University of California Press, 1992), p. 432.

10. W. E. B. Du Bois, *The Souls of Black Folk* (Greenwich: Fawcett, 1961), p. 23.

Chapter 12

1. James H. Cone, *A Black Theology of Liberation* 3d ed. (Maryknoll, N.Y.: Orbis, 1986); and James H. Cone and Gayraud S. Wilmore, *Black Theology: A Documentary History* (Maryknoll, N.Y.: Orbis, 1993).

2. Diana L. Eck, *Encountering God* (Boston: Beacon Press, 1998); and *Darsan: Seeing the Divine Image in India* 3d ed. (New York: Columbia University Press, 1998).

3. Francis L. Gross Jr., *Days with Uncle God-Momma: A Man's Retreat Diary* (New York: Crossroad, 1995).

4. Gustavo Gutierrez, *We Drink from Our Own Wells*, Matthew O'Connell, trans. (Maryknoll: Orbis, 1984); and *Gustavo Gutierrez: Essential Writings*, James B. Nickoloff, ed. (Maryknoll, N.Y.: Orbis, 1996).

5. Ralph Harper, *On Presence: Variations and Reflections* (Philadelphia: Trinity International Press, 1991).

6. John Hick, *God Has Many Names* (Philadelphia: Westminster Press, 1980); and *Disputed Questions in Theology and the Philosophy of Religion* (New Haven: Yale University Press, 1993).

7. Kosuke Koyama, *Mount Fuji and Mount Sinai: A Pilgrimage in Theology* (London: SCM Press, 1984); and *Waterbuffalo Theology* (London: SCM Press, 1974).

8. Margaret R. Miles, *Desire and Delight: A New Reading of Augustine's Confessions* (New York: Crossroad, 1992); *Reading for Life: Beauty, Pluralism, and Responsibility* (New York: Continuum, 1997); and *Plotinus on Body and Beauty* (Oxford: Blackwell, 1999).

9. Sallie McFague, *Models of God and Theology for an Ecological, Nuclear Age* (Philadelphia: Fortress Press, 1987).

10. Kathleen Norris, *Dakota: A Spiritual Geography* (New York: Ticknor and Fields, 1993); and *The Closter Walk* (New York: Putnam, 1996).

11. C. S. Song, *The Tears of Lady Meng* (Geneva: World Council of Churches, 1981); and *Jesus and the Reign of God* (Minneapolis: Fortress Press, 1993).

12. David Kwang-sun Suh, *Theology, Ideology, and Culture* (Hong Kong: World Student Christian Federation, 1983); and *The Korean Minjung in Christ* (Hong Kong: The Christian Conference of Asia, 1991).

13. Virginia Fabella, Peter K. H. Lee, and David Kwang-sun Suh, eds., *Asian Christian Spirituality: Reclaiming Traditions* (Maryknoll, N.Y.: Orbis, 1992).

14. R. S. Sugirtharajah, ed., *Asian Faces of Jesus* (Maryknoll, N.Y.: Orbis, 1993); and *Frontiers in Asian Christian Theology: Emerging Trends* (Maryknoll, N.Y.: Orbis, 1994).

15. Robert Schreiter, *Constructing Local Theologies* (Maryknoll, N.Y.: Orbis, 1985).

16. Paul Tillich, *Systematic Theology* (Chicago: University of Chicago Press, 1951); *Theology of Culture* (New York: Oxford University Press, 1959); and *Christianity and the Encounter of World Religions* (Minneapolis: Fortress Press, 1994).

17. Thomas Merton, *The Way of Chuang Tzu* (New York: New Directions, 1965); and *Contemplative Prayer* (New York: Doubleday/Image Books, 1989).

18. Daniel Dennett, *Kinds of Minds: Towards an Understanding of Consciousness* (New York: Basic Books, 1996); and *Brainchildren: Essays on Designing Minds* (Cambridge: MIT Press, 1998).

19. Howard Gardner, *The Mind's New Science: A History of the Cognitive Revolution* (New York: Basic Books).

20. Steven Pinker, *How the Mind Works* (New York: W. W. Norton & Co., 1997).

21. E. Thomas Lawson and Robert McCawley, *Rethinking Religion* (Cambridge: Cambridge University Press, 1993).

22. Harvey Whitehouse, *Arguments and Icons: Divergent Modes of Religiosity* (New York: Oxford University Press, 2000).

23. Carol Gilligan, *In a Different Voice: Psychological Theory and Women's Development* (Cambridge: Harvard University Press, 1982).

24. Susanne K. Langer, *Philosophy in a New Key: A Study in the Symbolism of Reason, Rite, and Art* (Cambridge: Harvard University Press, 1957).

25. Bryan Magee, *Confessions of a Philosopher: A Personal Journey through Western Philosophy from Plato to Popper* (New York: Random House, 1997).

26. Thomas Kuhn, *The Structure of Scientific Revolutions* (Chicago: University of Chicago Press, 1962).

27. Paul Feyeraband, *Against Method* 3d ed. (New York: Verso, 1993).

28. George Steiner, *Real Presences* (Chicago: University of Chicago Press, 1989).

29. M. Basil Pennington, *Centering Prayer* (New York: Doubleday/Image Books, 1980).

30. Gary Dorrien, *The Word as True Myth: Interpreting Modern Theology* (Louisville: Westminster/John Knox Press, 1997); and *The Remaking of Evangelical Theology* (Louisville: Westminster/John Knox Press, 1998).

31. (Maryknoll: Orbis, 1978).

32. (Leavenworth: Forest of Peace Publications, 1989).

33. (New York: Doubleday, 1995).

34. (New York: HarperCollins, 1994).

35. p. 101.

Chapter 13

1. (Tokyo: Shinkyo Publishing Company, 2000).

2. Quoted in James H. Cone, *Martin & Malcolm & America: A Dream or a Nightmare* (Maryknoll, N.Y.: Orbis Books, 1991), p. 315.

3. (New York: Harper & Row, 1958).

4. (Philadelphia & New York: J. B. Lippincott company, 1970).

5. (New York: The Seabury Press, 1975).

6. (New York: The Seabury, 1972).

7. (Nashville: Abingdon, 1982).

8. (New York: Maryknoll, 1991).

9. James H. Cone, *My Soul Looks Back* (Maryknoll: Orbis Books, 1986), p. 36.

10. Ibid., p. 37.

11. Ibid., p. 39.

12. The Mainichi Newspaper, June 13, 1970.

13. Martin Luther King Jr., *Where Do We Go From Here: Chaos or Community?* (Boston: Beacon Press, 1967), p. 167.

14. Cone, *God of the Oppressed*, op. cit. p. 104.

15. Toshiro Suzuki et al., eds., *The Complete Works of Knzo Uchimura* (Tokyo: Iwanami Shoten, 1894–96), 26: 4.

16. C. S. Song, *Jesus, The Crucified People* (New York: Crossroad, 1990), p. 12.

17. Ibid., p. 217.

18. Martin Luther King Jr.'s speech "I Have A Dream" at March on Washington for Jobs and Freedom, August 28, 1968. Also see the "Eulogy for the Martyred Children," delivered on September 22, 1963 at Sixteenth Street Baptist Church, Birmingham, Alabama.

19. See Edwin O. Reischauer, *The Japanese Today: Change and Continuity* (Tokyo: Charles E. Tuttle Company, 1988), p. 128.

Chapter 14

1. I cannot reveal her real name in this article. I consulted with her while I was working as Interim Director for the Korean American Women's Battered Center in New York City.

2. *Gwon-sa-nim* is the Korean word which refers to a woman "elder" or "presbyter" in Korean/Korean-American churches.

3. *Ban-chan* are the Korean traditional side dishes, such as *kimchi*, dried anchovies, vegetables, and so on.

4. Ephesians 5:22–23: "Wives, be subject to your husbands as you are to the Lord. For the husband is the head of the wife just as Christ is the head of the church, the body of which he is the Savior" (NRSV).

5. The Rev. Sook Ja Chung, "The Prayer of the Battered Women (1)," in *Hanbandoaes_o Dasi Salahnanun Yeosungsipyun* (*Women Psalms live again on the Korean Peninsula*), (Seoul, Korea:

Korean Association of Women Theologians, 2000), pp. 125–126.

6. Confucius. *The Analects*. Translated with an Introduction By D. C.Lau. (New York: Penguin Books, 1979), Introduction.

7. Bae Yong Lee, *Yukyomoonhwaui Gajokyunriwa Yeosungui Jeeeui—Chosunsidaelul Joongsimeuro* —(The Family Ethical codes of Confucius Culture and the status of women—during Yi Dynasty period—in *Hankuk Yeosungsa* (The Studies of Korean women) (Seoul, Korea: The Institute of Korea Women's Studies at Ehwa Women's University, 1995), p. 3. This excerpt translation was done by Michelle Lim Jones.

8. Kyung Il Kim, *Kongjaga Jukeuoya Naraga Sanda* [*Confucius must die in order for Country to live*] (Seoul, Korea: Bada Press, 1999), p. 7. This excerpt translation was done by Michelle Lim Jones.

9. Ibid., p. 5.

10. One famous scholar of later Confucianism, Yi Lee wrote that "the intelligent man erects the castle, while the intelligent wife demolishes the castle" (Kyung Il Kim, *Kongjaga Jukeuoya Naraga Sanda*, p. 5). When I was a schoolgirl, I used to hear the following maxims describing intelligent women: "A plate will break when three women get together; women and dried cod fish should be beaten every three days."

11. Members of the "1.5" generation are children of immigrants who came to America with their parents, who have had some schooling in both the motherland and in America, who have significant exposure to "Korean culture," and can speak both languages.

12. David Kwang-sun Suh, "*Hankunyeosungkwa Jongkyo* (Korean Women and Religion)," in *Yeosunghak (Korean Women's Studies)* (Seoul, Korea: Ehwa Women's University Press, 1998), p. 276. This excerpt translation was done by Michelle Lim Jones.

13. Ibid., p. 277. Excerpts translated by Michelle Lim Jones.

14. David Kelsey, *The Uses of Scripture in Recent Theology* (Philadelphia: Fortress Press, 1975), p. 18.

15. *Yeosunghak* (Korean Women's Studies), p. 282.

16. Elisabeth Schussler Fiorenza, *Bread Not Stone: The Challenge of Feminist Biblical Interpretation* (Boston: Beacon Press, 1984), x.

17. Elisabeth Schussler Fiorenza, "Breaking the Silence—Becoming Visible" in *Concilium*. December, 1985, pp. 3–16.

18. The Korea Gospel Weekly, December 31, 2000.

19. Rita Nakashima Brock, "Dusting the Bible on the Floor : A Hermeneutics of Wisdom" in *Searching The Scripture: A Feminist Introduction*, ed. Elisabeth Schussler Fiorenza (New York: Cross Road, 1993), p. 69.

20. Brock, p. 73.

21. Eun Sun Lee, "The Prayer of the Battered Women (2)," in *Hanbandoaeseo Dasie Salahnanun Yeosungsipyun (Women's Psalms live again on the Korean Peninsula)*, (Seoul, Korea: Korean Association of Women Theologians, 2000), pp. 125–126.

Chapter 15

1. The high priests would not have had any authority in Damascus, making impossible any imprisoning, much less bringing people to Jerusalem. The most likely "persecution" by Paul and others like him would be convincing local synagogues that they should discipline some of their members, probably for deviance from accepted obedience to the Torah. What this discipline consisted of would, in its greatest physical severity, have been the thirty-nine lashes (granted, a horrible assault on the body), which Paul himself received five times (2 Cor. 11:24).

2. Cf. Claudia J. Setzer, *Jewish Responses to Early Christians* (Minneapolis: Fortress, 1994) for an overview of the evidence, too complex for me to discuss here.

3. Usually dated at 250, under Decius.

4. The Christians are, however, appropriately vilified: Tacitus, *Annales*, xv.44; Suetonius, *Vita Neronis*, xvi.

5. Pliny, *Epp.* X.xcvi–xcvii.

6. It is significant that the word "Christian" appears prominently in this correspondence. It appears in the New Testament only three times (Acts 11:26, 26:28; 1 Peter 4:16) and the word "Christianity" never. Paul does not know the term. That Suetonius and Tacitus apply the term to Nero's violence *does not mean that that term was used by Nero himself*. It is unlikely that the term had been coined by then. Most scholars think the term was first derisively applied to believers by outsiders, probably by the late first century.

There was initially some confusion in the minds of outsiders as to the distinction between Jewish groups and those who believed in Jesus. There was a certain political advantage to claiming Jewish status, which may have encouraged believers in Jesus to continue to think they are Jewish. Awareness by the larger world that followers of Jesus were *not* Jews was probably not awakened until the end of the first century, perhaps sparked by Jewish denial that "Christianity" is a sister faith. About the same time indications of persecutions against Christians begin to emerge. Clearly by the time of Pliny, "Christian" is a common term of opprobrium.

Once the term becomes *the* one to point to believers in Jesus, I suspect that it becomes pivotal in the trials of believers. Pliny asks the accused if they are Christians. In the Martyrdom of Polycarp (xii.1), the judge has his herald proclaim three times: "Polycarp has confessed that he is a Christian." The passage in 1 Peter 4:12–16 reads the same way.

7. This implies a change of the way certain New Testament texts have been read, notably 1 Peter. I will discuss this document below.

8. The other instances are Luke 24:5, 37; Acts 24:25, and Revelation 11:13. All except Acts 24:25 are responses to divine epiphany.

9. For words which in certain context *might* point to terror, or situations of terror, see the helpful collection in Johannes P. Louw and Eugene Nida, *Greek-English Lexicon of the New Testament Based on Semantic Domains* (New York: United Bible Societies, 1989). Under their "Table of Domains," one might look at sections 20, 21, 22, 25, and 39.

10. Cf. the commentaries for detailed discussion of the issues. I go into the political possibilities in some detail in my brief commentary in *Asceticism and the New Testament*, Leif E. Vaage and Vincent L. Wimbush, eds. (New York: Routledge, 1999), pp. 187–207.

11. I work here from the view that what we have in the Gospel stories are primarily stories which reflect the views of the church and are not primarily historical reporting.

12. Cf. the struggles of Taylor (and others he cites) to come to terms with the strength of the saying (Vincent Taylor, *The Gospel According to St. Mark* [London: MacMillan, 1957], p. 554).

13. One could also reflect on the function of Jesus's cry: "My God, my God, why have you

forsaken me?" There are, in addition, passages which point to Jesus as the exemplar, or cause, for negative reaction by the outside to the church. See John 15:18–21; Matthew 10:24–25.

14. There are a few other known believers mentioned as being killed presumably because they were believers, although none of these deaths can be said to be due to a general law that a Christian is to be punished by death: Stephen (Acts 7:54–8:1), James, the brother of John (Acts 12:2), James, the brother of Jesus, as well as others (presumably believers in Jesus) in an execution masterminded by a high priest, during an interval between procurators, in 62 c.e. (Josephus *Ant.* xx.200), and Antipas (Rev. 2:13). Thus we *know* four people killed because of their faith over a period of roughly thirty years. There were probably others (e.g. Josephus' "some others"), but in general, this record does not support the notion of widespread persecutions leading to serious results during this early period.

15. The reader may be startled to see that I do not include material from the Book of Acts. Assessment of this material is difficult from a historian's point of view. I agree with the many scholars who think that the author is more interested in making political points at this time of writing (end of the first century) than in reproducing the history of the early church. The stories he tells are vivid and show much local resistance to the early communities, but it seems to me impossible to know how to evaluate historically these stories. In one respect his scenario is surprising, because the author was writing at a time when the Gospel of John, Hebrews, 1 Peter, and Revelation show evidence of emerging conflict between the church and the outside Greco-Roman world. It seems to me that the author of Acts wants to play down any suspicion of *Roman* displeasure with the church, perhaps precisely because in his day that displeasure is beginning to manifest itself.

16. I am painfully aware that disputes over what is pre-authorial, and even whether such a layer can be demonstrated, rage unabated in scholarly circles. My judgments should imply where I stand on these issues.

17. Colossians, Ephesians, the Pastorals, and probably 2 Thessalonians.

18. Cf. J. Louis Martyn, *History & Theology in the Fourth Gospel* (Nashville: Abingdon, 1979);

Raymond E. Brown, *The Community of the Beloved Disciple* (New York: Paulist Press, 1979).

19. For ejection, cf. 9:22, 12:42, 16:2; for rejection, cf. 15:18–21.

20. H. Attridge, *The Epistle to the Hebrews* (Philadelphia: Fortress Press, 1989), p. 12.

21. But death, either by mob violence or official execution, had not happened, assuming this is the meaning of the vague expression in 12:4.

22. Vividly described in *The Embassy to Gaius.*

23. The issue is immensely complex and cannot be detailed here. For an introductory guide to the sources and a historical reconstruction, cf. E. Mary Smallwood, *The Jews under Roman Rule* (Leiden: E. J. Brill, 1981).

24. The "former days" of the persecution mentioned in Hebrews 10:32 then might have had nothing to do with the increasing danger due to separation of church and synagogue. Otherwise, the "former days" would be relatively recent in relation to the time of writing.

25. Πύρωσις—literally "burning" or "exposure to the action of fire," hence an ordeal of being burned, although the notion of "ordeal" may read a bit into the word. Even if it is appropriate, it does not necessarily mean a legal process.

26. Frances Wright Beare, *The First Epistle of Peter* (Oxford: Blackwell, 1961), p. 166.

27. This is typical of the circular reasoning that plagues scholars in their dating of this document. They try to find external situations that fit their reading of the letter. Then they date the letter accordingly. But it is *their* reading of the data that determines how the document is supposed to fit with the external situation. Thus reading 1 Peter 4:12–19 as reflecting Pliny dates the letter at 110 or so. Achtemeier, on the other hand, reading the same passage as an example of pre-"Plinian," dates the document earlier, perhaps close to 80 c.e. (Paul J. Achtemeier, *1 Peter* [Minneapolis: Fortress, 1996], pp. 36, 49–50).

28. 1 Peter, 35–36. He is typical of recent interpreters such as J. N. D. Kelly, *A Commentary on the Epistles of Peter and of Jude* (New York: Harper, 1969), p. 10; and John H. Elliott, *A Home for the Homeless* (Philadelphia: Fortress, 1981), p. 80.

29. This change in scholarly direction is probably part of a more general tendency to turn early Christianity into a "middle-class," bourgeois group of communities, away from the

older, "lower-class," oppressed communities of people, once popularly depicted. This change is associated with names such as Robert Grant, Abraham Malherbe, and Wayne Meeks, and is probably now the dominant perspective on social location. It was well on its way to prominence by the late seventies, cf. R. Scroggs, "The Sociological Interpretation of the New Testament: The Present State of Research," in R. Scroggs, *The Text and the Times* (Minneapolis: Fortress Press, 1993), pp. 51–56. In my judgment, this perspective has moved too far away from the evidence towards turning the early communities into safe, comfortable, non-threatening groups, but this larger issue cannot be discussed here.

30. Ἀισχύνω, "to act shamefully," may imply an act of denial of the faith here, as it seems also to have in Philippians 1:20. Ἐπαισχύνω clearly has this meaning in Mark 8:38.

31. So Adela Yarbro Collins, *Crisis and Catharsis: The Power of the Apocalypse* (Philadelphia: Westminster, 1984); Leonard L. Thompson, *The Book of Revelation: Apocalypse and Empire* (New York: Oxford, 1990); a mediating position seems to be taken by M. Eugene Boring, *Revelation* (Louisville: John Knox, 1989).

32. J. M. P. Sweet, *Revelation* "Westminster Pelican Commentaries" (Philadelphia: Westminster, 1979), p. 34.

33. The scenes in Acts may well suggest the kinds of actions taken by local courts, at least by the time of the writing of Acts.

34. I, and a number of other scholars, consider this passage a post-Pauline gloss. Even if so, the gloss lies well within the time-frame of the New Testament writings.

35. Hebrews also uses the notion of God's discipline as what a father does to sons—to accept discipline (i.e. persecution) is to know one is a true son (Heb. 12:7–11).

36. Bruno Bettelheim, reflecting on his own experiences and his memories of fellow prisoners in German concentration camps, makes the following observations about the terror of entering such camps. "It seems that most, if not all, prisoners reacted against the initial shock of arrest by trying to muster forces which might prove helpful in supporting their badly shaken self-esteem. Those groups which found in their past life some basis for the erection of such a buttress to their endangered egos seemed to suc-

ceed." In other words, the rational structures of their self-understanding were helpful in their retention of "self-esteem." Cf. Bruno Bettelheim, "Individual and Mass Behavior in Extreme Situations," in *Surviving and Other Essays* (New York: Knopf, 1979), p. 59. I thank Dr. Mestancik for bringing my attention to this essay.

Chapter 16

1. See *The Adventures of Antoine Doinel: Four Screenplays by Francois Truffaut* (New York: Simon and Schuster, 1971).

2. Quotations from Ashley Montagu, *The Elephant Man: A Study in Human Dignity* (New York: Dutton), pp. 14–16, 18, 22, 29, 34, 63–64, 77.

3. Bob Herbert, "Criminal Justice," *New York Times* OP-ED, June 24, 1999, A31. The paragraph is actually a quotation from Stephen Bright, director of the Southern Center for Human Rights.

4. See the editorial "Children Too Ready to Die Young," *Washington Post*, November 3, 1993, A26.

5. Children's Defense Fund, *The State of America's Children Yearbook 2000* (Washington, D.C.: Children's Defense Fund, 2000), pp. xiv–xv.

6. Ibid., p. xv.

7. From various newspaper accounts.

8. "The U. S. Penal System: Restorative and/or Retributive Justice?" a panel discussion coordinated by Raymond B. Kemp, *Woodstock Report*, no. 61 (March 2000) pp. 3–10, at 4; see also p. 5.

9. See Robert M. Morgenthau's OP-Ed article, "What Prosecutors Won't Tell You," *New York Times*, February 7, 1995.

10. Sources at my disposal do not go beyond 1994, but suffice for my purposes in this sermon.

11. John R. Donahue, S. J., "Biblical Perspectives on Justice," in *The Faith That Does Justice: Examining the Christian Sources for Social Change*, ed. John C. Haughey, S.J. (Woodstock Studies 2; New York: Paulist Press, 1977), pp. 68–112, at 69. More recently, Donahue has stated that his "earlier reflections should be supplemented by the reflections of J. P. M. Walsh" in the latter's *The Mighty from Their Thrones: Power in the Biblical Tradition* (Philadelphia: Fortress Press, 1987). See Donahue, *What Does the Lord Require? A Bibliographical Essay on the Bible and Social Justice* (Studies in the Spirituality of Jesuits

25/2: March 1993; St. Louis: Seminar on Jesuit Spirituality, 1993), pp. 20–21; see also the revised and expanded edition of the latter work (Saint Louis: Institute of Jesuit Sources, 2000), pp. 24–25.

12. Estimates as of 1990 in the Japanese section of the Library of Congress, Washington, D.C.

13. Malachy McCourt, *A Monk Swimming: A Memoir* (New York: Hyperion, 1998), p. 2.

14. David Beckmann, "Let's Cut Hunger in Half," *U.S. Catholic* 66, no. 1 (January 2001): 24–27, at 24.

15. Ibid.

16. Quoted ibid., p. 26.

17. See the November 15, 2000, Statement of the Catholic Bishops of the United States, *Responsibility, Rehabilitation, and Restoration: A Catholic Perspective on Crime and Criminal Justice* (Washington, D.C.: United States Catholic Conference, 2000).

18. See Bernard J. F. Lonergan, S.J., *Method in Theology* (New York: Herder and Herder, 1974), esp. pp. 14–15, 55, 238–42, 357, 363.

Chapter 18

1. Cornel West, *Prophetic Fragments* (Grand Rapids: Eerdmans/Trenton: Africa World Press, 1988).

Chapter 19

1. Bruce M. Metzger and Roland E. Murphy, eds., *The New Oxford Annotated Bible, New Revised Standard Version* (New York: Oxford University Press, 1991). Scriptures are from this version of the Bible.

2. Ibid.

3. Scott Higham and Sari Horowitz, "Brianna: Buried in System's Mistakes," *Washington Post*, December 16, 2000, Section A.

4. Donald W. Winnicott, *Playing and Reality* (London and New York: Routledge, 1971). Winnicott's discussion of good enough mothering and on good enough environments inform my thinking on good enough care.

5. Carol L. Meyers and Eric M. Meyers, *Anchor Bible*: Haggai; Zechariah 1–8 (Garden City: Doubleday, 1987).

6. Elizabeth Achtemeir, *Nahum-Malachi: Interpretation: A Bible Commentary for Teaching and Preaching* (Louisville: John Knox Press, 1986).

7. Charles H. Talbert, *The Apocalypse: A Reading of the Revelation of John* (Louisville: Westminster/John Knox Press, 1994).

8. M. Eugene Boring, *Revelation: Interpretation, A Bible Commentary for Teaching and Preaching* (Louisville: John Knox Press, 1989).

Chapter 20

1. In Ha Yi, *Theology of Sojourners* (in Korean) (Seoul: The Christian Literature Society of Korea, 1998), p. 151.

2. Zohl de Ishtar, "Japan's indigenous people claim their rights" in Encyclopaedia Britannica (1999–2000). The Ainu formerly lived on all four major Japanese islands but were pushed northward over the centuries by the Japanese. Intermarriage with and cultural assimilation by the Japanese have made the traditional Ainu virtually extinct. Of the approximately 24,000 persons on Hokkaido who are still considered Ainu, hardly any are purebloods and very few maintain the language and religion. Most of them now resemble the Japanese in physique. "Ainu," in Encyclopaedia Britannica (1999–2000).

3. Yasunori Fukuoka, "Ethnic Koreans: Past and Present" in *Saitama University Review*, 31 (1996): 3.

4. Ibid.

5. Historians say up to 200,000 women from Korea (80%), China, Taiwan, and the Philippines were forced into sexual slavery by the Japanese military and sent to military brothels known as comfort stations. They were recruited by force, abduction, and deception and were sent to where Japanese soldiers were: Japan, Thailand, Malaysia, Papua New Guinea, and Myanmar (Burma). Associated Press, "Victims of WWII Sexual Slavery Sue" in *AsianWeek* (29 September–5 October 2000) www.asianweek .com/200_09_28/news3_ww2aftermath.html.

6. It is referring to the Japanese army's massacre of as many as 300,000 civilians during the 1937–38 occupation of the Chinese city now known as Nanjing. Ginny Parker, "Japanese Accused of Whitewashing WWII History," in *AsianWeek* (29 September–5 October 2000) www.asianweek.com/200_09_28/news3_ ww2aftermath.html.

7. Japanese authorities and private citizens massacred thousands of Koreans at the time of the Great Kanto Earthquake (1923) on groundless rumors that Koreans had poisoned wells.

The citizens used bamboo spears to slaughter the Koreans.

8. Tinian is one of the Mariana Islands, part of the U. S. Commonwealth of the Northern Mariana Islands in the western Pacific Ocean. It lies 100 miles (160 km) north of Guam. Tinian was administered by Japan before World War II. After its capture by U. S. forces in 1944, the island was equipped with what were then the world's longest runways; from these were launched the planes that dropped atomic bombs on the Japanese cities of Hiroshima and Nagasaki in August of 1945 ("Titian," in Encyclopaedia Britannica). Recently, they found five thousand Koreans buried together. Chong In Park, "A Tree looking like a reincarnated Korean at the site of cremation" in *Chosun Daily*, Korean (22 March 1996):11.

9. There were as many as 70,000 Korean atomic bomb victims in Hiroshima (50,000) and Nagasaki (20,000). Forty thousand victims were killed and thirty thousand victims were injured. Twenty-three thousand people returned to Korea and they received no medical care for their A-bomb disease. Only seven thousand remained in Japan. Out of these seven thousand victims, five thousand could not receive the governmental medical care, because they had the wrong kinds of visas. They have suffered incredible subhuman ordeals. Nam Dong Suh, "The Power of Death that Threatens Humankind," (Korean) in *Thought of Christianity* (June 1983): 61.

10. Gavan McCormack, "Japan's Uncomfortable Past" in *History Today* 48 (May 1998): 6.

11. Ibid.

12. More than 100,000 children were picked randomly from each nation's eighth-graders or the national equivalent and were tested in the primary language of instruction. From National Public Radio News, December 4, 2000.

13. A. Newby, *Challenge to the Court* (Louisiana: Louisiana State University, 1967).

14. B. H. Streeter and A. J. Appasamy, *The Sadhu: A Study in Mysticism and Practical Religion* (London: MacMillan & Co., 1921), pp. 87–88.

Chapter 21

1. As the Talmudist and Auschwitz survivor David Halivni has recently and forcefully written, the conditions of the Jews before the *Shoah* did not meet the Bible's conditions for divine punishment.

2. (Philadelphia: Jewish Publication Society, 1988)

3. *Tanakh, The Holy Scriptures* (Philadelphia: Jewish Publication Society, 1985).

4. *Babylonian Talmud, Berakhot* 61b, trans. Maurice Simon (London: Soncino Press, 1958).

5. Judah ben David, "Know Judah and Israel," trans. David S. Segal in *Al naharot Sefarad* (By the Rivers of Spain), ed. S. Bernfeld (Tel Aviv: Mahbarot Lesifrut, 1956), pp. 206–209.

6. Hayyim Nahman Bialik, "In the City of Slaughter," trans. A. M. Klein in *Selected Poems of Hayyim Nahman Bialik* (New York: Bloch Pub., 1965), pp. 112–113.

7. Abraham Sutzkever, "To My Child," trans. C. K. Williams in *Poetische Verk I* (Tel Aviv, 1963).

8. From *l'drosh*, to dig or draw out.

9. *Tanakh.*

10. Ibid.

11. Elliot Wolfson, "Listening to Speak, A Response to Dialogues in Postmodern Jewish Philosophy" in S. Kepnes, et al., *Reasoning after Revelation* (Boulder: Westview, 1998).

12. Elie Wiesel, *Night* (New York: Hill and Wang, 1960), p. 43.

13. I am paraphrasing passages from Irving Greenberg, "Cloud of Smoke, Pillar of Fire: Judaism, Christianity, and Modernity after the Holocaust," in Eva Fleischner, ed. *Auschwitz: Beginning of a New Era?* (New York: KTAV Publishing House, 1977), pp. 7–55.